ALSO BY MARK CALDWELL

A Short History of Rudeness:
Manners, Morals, and Misbehavior in Modern America

The Last Crusade: The War on Consumption, 1862–1954

NEW YORK NIGHT

THE MYSTIQUE AND ITS HISTORY

MARK CALDWELL

SCRIBNER

New York · London · Toronto · Sydney

SCRIBNER
1230 Avenue of the Americas
New York, NY 10020

SCRIBNER and design are trademarks of
Macmillan Library Reference USA, Inc., used under license
by Simon & Schuster, the publisher of this work.

For information about special discounts for bulk purchases,
please contact Simon & Schuster Special Sales:
1-800-456-6798 or business@simonandschuster.com

DESIGNED BY LAUREN SIMONETTI
Text set in Adobe Garamond

Manufactured in the United States of America

1   3   5   7   9   10   8   6   4   2

Library of Congress Cataloging-in-Publication Data
Caldwell, Mark.
New York night : the mystique and its history / Mark Caldwell.
p. cm.
Includes bibliographical references.
Contents: New Amsterdam noir : the dark nights of Dutch Manhattan—Rattle watch nights
: city streets after sundown, from Peter Stuyvesant to the early republic—Hearthside and
rushlight : old New York at home—Broadway after dark : pleasures and hours of federal New
York—Bowery gals will come out to-night? : nighttime on the Bowery before the Civil
War—Under the rain of gaslights : from the Civil War to the gilded and gruesome 1870s—
Electric costumes and brass knuckles : glamour, crime, sports, and the commercialization of
night in the 1890s—Mr. Dieter vanishes, November 1923 : the Volstead Act, jazz, and *Earl
Carroll's Vanities*—From poorhouse to penthouse and back : at home, homeless, and on the
town in mid-1930s—When the lights went out : World War II, the 1950s and the suburban-
ization of night—Full moon over the Stonewall : the gay epiphany, discomania, and the surfacing of hidden night.
1. New York (N.Y.)—Social life and customs. 2. New York (N.Y.)—Social conditions. 3.
Night—Social aspects—New York (State)—New York—History. 4. Street life—New York
(State)—New York—History. 5. City and town life—New York (State)—New York—History. 6. New York (N.Y.)—Biography. I. Title.
F128.3.C35 2005
974.7'1—dc22
2005049039

ISBN-13: 978-0-7432-4276-9
ISBN-10: 0-7432-4276-9

Contents

CHAPTER FOUR

Broadway After Dark
Pleasures and Horrors of Federal New York 79

CHAPTER FIVE

"Bowery Gals Will You Come Out To-night?"
Nighttime on the Bowery Before the Civil War 112

CHAPTER SIX

"Under the Rain of Gaslights"
From the Civil War to the Gilded and Gruesome 1870s 148

New York Night

PROLOGUE

NIGHT, IN ITS PERPETUAL journey around the earth, speeds over the East River and reaches the foot of 42nd Street at 73 degrees, 58 minutes, and 4 seconds west longitude. It then pursues the sunset across midtown—and the 74th meridian—to where 42nd meets the Hudson, at 74 degrees, 7 seconds. On the evening of March 31, 2005, night dropped on the FDR Drive shortly after pedestrians' cell phone clocks blinked 5:19 p.m. Then it hurtled across the island roughly one and a half times faster than the speed of sound—just over 1,100 miles an hour—taking about eight seconds, swallowing one east-west block every half second.

Collaborating with land, water, and buildings, this astronomic nightfall, every day different and striking no other place on earth at just the same angle, dictates the look and feel of the oncoming dark hours. New York daylight is cold and hard-edged; at sunset it disappears almost without warning into fluid shadow. Office buildings empty. Fluorescent cubicles blaze on, and in the early darkness of late fall and winter afternoons the towers become geometric clouds of imprisoned light, winking off as the hours pass, as if lonely for their occupants, gone home to their apartments, suburbs, and exurbs.

Such is the classic evening rush hour scenario, still enacted in New York as it has been since the beginning of the 20th century and before. Yet it's no longer a universal rite, if it ever was: the city's nightfall harmonies are and always have been rich, with notes of day suspended into evening. Office hours flow into nightshifts; arriving crowds whirlpool into outbound multitudes as reverse commuters return from the suburbs to Penn and Grand Central Stations. Many of New York's largest industries—theater, restaurants, newspapers, and broadcasting—begin a crescendo of activity with each dusk. Seen through their vast windows, lofts may bask in expensive residential lighting or cringe beneath the harsh bluish tubes of a sweatshop. The lamp in an apartment building window may be illuminating an architect on charette or a writer on a deadline. The silky forms laughing and chattering behind the tinted glass of a club or restaurant are probably cutthroats engaged in the first skirmishes of the evening, when a hundred thousand gang wars for love and success are waged at their fiercest.

Stores close, the smaller ones with a crash of steel security gates, and the quieter stretches of commercial avenues turn into rows of illuminated grillwork. Behind the red crosses that mark the hospitals and the green globes of the police stations, shifts change. Radio traffic reports and local TV news arc into frenzy. The acrid fumes of diesel combustion, the flash of wheel sparks, and the chemical-industrial reek of brakes follow the commuter trains out into the suburbs. The later the hour the swanker the passengers: the loud workers peak at four or five, to be followed by the sweet-voiced bourgeois at six, seven, and eight.

Workdays repeat themselves; night reinvents itself with every sunset. After the commute, and as full darkness is accomplished, first restaurants come to life, then theaters, bars, and clubs, then after-hours dives—all of them venues for drama, rewritten every second it plays. Glamour, lust, license, and crime emerge from the shadows and parade under the lights, high life and low life, polished veneer and sweaty beastliness. Toward dawn, as if released at the rasp of iron hinges, succubae and incubi fly out: nightmare thoughts, in check during the day, point with skeletal fingers to remorse, death, and vanity, their victims everywhere—tossing alone in bed, staring at the ceiling beside a snoring stranger, or plodding home after the bartender jerks on the lights and watches the deflated customers file out.

Approached at night by air, road, or water, Manhattan is a spectacle, fireworks that rocketed up and froze in place. Towers rise in black masonry or glass and metal against the sooty satinness of the New York sky, an effect immortalized in the black-and-white prints favored by urban photographers of the 1940s and 1950s. As you walk or ride, the towers seem to change places, dipping and gliding in a formal dance, moving before and behind each other. As they rise they dissolve, columns of windows stacked in thousands, bursting aloft against the black East and Hudson Rivers—a liquid, invisibly mobile frame to countless pinpoints of light.

Empty side streets give way to avenues where crowds sweep like squalls, then blow away into nothingness. Yet Manhattan's dominant north-south axis makes even random movement seem purposeful. No other city is so polar, with uptown and downtown its lodestars, apparently fixed yet always shifting according to where you are, and eclectic in connotations as diverse as the city's demographics. "Downtown" somehow captures the clashing atmospheres of Wall Street and Greenwich Village, while Harlem and Carnegie Hill, mutually skittish neighbors, nonetheless share a distinctive uptown building style and sense of street space.

All the world's celebrated night cities have their own ways of rearing up from earth to illuminate the sky. Chicago's skyline is as vertical as New York's, architecturally stronger, and seen from aloft even more dramatic. But its character is entirely different—a jagged knife edge of light bolting up between the black vacancy of Lake Michigan and the level panorama of road lights stretching away into the Midwest. Paris, first to hang lanterns above its streets on moonless nights, first to set off fireworks for public display, remains unique in the warm brilliance flowing along its boulevards at night, bathing its public buildings and bridges, and shimmering along the Seine. In London, the Thames at night urges itself on, a cold void in the city's midst; light ranges from garish Piccadilly Circus and Leicester Square to serene neighborhoods of knitted, sibilant greenery and thick-curtained windows.

But New York's verticality exerts power everywhere. Even a stranger senses the interplay of levels: subways below the street, audible and smellable through their ventilation grids, more subways and conduits below the subways, communications racing invisibly through cables and between antennae and cell towers making spidery appearances on rooftops. A New Yorker, self-conscious about not looking upward, nonetheless feels the vertical pull almost as instinct. Aviation and photography have together created an archive of skyline images that, absorbed into consciousness, project the grandeur of an aerial view onto every corner and street, burnishing even the most desolate neighborhoods into ebullience.

A percussive clash between light and dark is what Henry James might have called the "note" of the contemporary New York night (though he lived to see Manhattan's earliest skyscrapers and detested them). In Manhattan, darkness rests at eye level, refreshed by the downglow from illuminated signs ten to 100 feet above the sidewalk. Streetlights, from stanchions that range from stark masts to neo-retro filigreed posts, discharge blasts of pink, blue, and yellow. Windows pile up to skyscraper crowns, some brooding, others floodlit and alive with fantastic traceries of mercantile Gothic exuberance. Whether clear or overcast, the Manhattan night sky behind them looks preoccupied, physically near the rooftops and pinnacles, yet also infinitely remote. Romantic moonlight is a rural thing. The city moon is aloof, hung far away in self-contemplation.

From a plane at 30,000 feet, passing on the way to somewhere else, New York looks like an organism too huge to survive, a Portuguese man-o'-war with tentacles and a tangle of semitransparent organs seeming to cost more in hugeness than they deliver in function. But we survive in spite of our gigantism thanks to the technology of connection: tunnels, cables, and tubes carry water, information, people, electric current, voices, steam, gas, sewage, images, shutting down only for repair, spelled by back-ups that usually somehow hold us together even though no human fully controls them. Policing, garbage collection, entertainment, medical emergencies, even lawbreaking: all demand transit, from trains and subways to police cruisers, trucks, fire engines, ambulances, and getaway cars. No one escapes: through wire, pipe, and wave, the city, the nation, and the world snake in and entangle everyone.

In the uncannily perfect fall weather of early September 2001, New York balanced on a pinnacle never so tall, rich, or cosmopolitan, so domineering as a global talisman. The city's euphoria, like the investment boom that stoked it, was a product both of substance and fantasy. The World Trade Center had dominated the sky over New York for almost exactly a generation, just long enough that a million or so New Yorkers had never known our skyline without the twin towers. When the planes struck and they toppled, gouging out chasms in both the earth of lower Manhattan and the consciousness of the city, they left us, at first, at a loss to cope. When they collapsed they diminished—for the first time in more than three centuries—a skyline forced relentlessly upward since 1697, when Trinity Church raised its first steeple above Wall Street. It was a hammer blow against a keystone of the city's pride. But in the 21st century any town that wants to make a statement can throw up a record-breaking tower; and the catastrophe presents an opportunity to reevaluate the urban texture.

And indeed new possibilities suggest themselves if one traces the urban spine backward through time. Strangely, as each new year slides offstage, revealing the city of the year before, and postwar skyscrapers disappear, the skyline seems to soar higher and higher in appearance. The twin towers, no matter how sobering their loss, were uninspiring boxes, popping up as if from a gigantic industrial extruder in the basement. They looked best at night, when they seemed to dematerialize, leaving two columnar stacks of light. And as one goes back, few towers, however remarkable in themselves, diminish Manhattan's urgent verticality as they vanish one by one, restoring the skyline to the appearance of its past. The bulky Worldwide Plaza evaporates from its bastion on Eighth Avenue in 1989, the refrigerator-like shoulders of the Morgan Bank Building sink back among the 17th-century artifacts still buried under Wall Street in 1988, and the Chippendale AT&T (now Sony) building on Madison Avenue is gone by 1983. Accelerating backward, the Pan Am (now MetLife) tower flips below ground in 1963, and then the skyline loses the Chase Manhattan headquarters on the Battery (1960), followed by Mies van der Rohe's fabled Seagram Building (1958), Lever House (1952), and the UN Secretariat (1947).

Yet what's left in the 1940s, with the products of a postwar building frenzy gone, looks startlingly leaner, bolder, stronger, and taller than ever afterward. In a mid-1940s night photo taken from the Municipal Building on Centre Street (just after the World War II dimout had been lifted), lower Manhattan is breathtaking—a bold, stark, and brave exertion of force against the sky. Three brutally handsome towers, all still standing today, dominated the skyscape: the slim Cities Services (now AIG) Tower at 70 Pine Street, spinning upward to a floodlit spire; then the massive Bank of the Manhattan Company at 40 Wall Street, with its huge pyramidal crown; lastly, the Farmers Trust Tower at 20 Exchange Place, a powerful square column with beveled corners and topped by three arches and a stepped pediment.

Together, surrounded by lesser but similar structures, they make the night city of the 1940s look boundless, their eccentric forms assured, inevitable, rocketing upward beyond the columns and church spires that once defined urban tallness. The walls are stone, the windows carved into their facades. In 1940 their lights would have been warm, incandescent rather than cold, gaseous fluorescent. As one circled the Battery by water, the towers in the foreground stood up, aloof, threatening, then seemed to deflate and sink into their streets as they receded. They posed a bold backdrop against the postwar crowds packed further north into the Stork Club, El Morocco, and their rivals, and to the wide-flung skyscrapers of midtown: the Metropolitan Life tower at 23rd Street, with its Light That

Never Fails, the Empire State at 34th, Chrysler at 42nd, General Electric at 51st, the RCA Building at Rockefeller Center. Nearer the street elevated railways, soon to vanish, still grated north and southward along Second, Third, Sixth, and Ninth Avenues. By day they cast deep shadows on the streets below. At night their tracks, stanchions, and stairways, visible embodiments of the darkness passing over the city, raised a roof of black noise over loiterers and revelers. Crowds streamed on and off the trains and down to the sidewalks. It was no accident that the ground-floor storefronts along Third Avenue became a favored site for gay bars; the Sixth and Ninth Avenue lines, passing just to the east and west of Times Square, disgorged and reabsorbed the crowds that thronged it.

And the Times Square of the early 1940s and late 1930s, despite lingering depression and the shadow of war, looked more alive and quicker-pulsed than the doggedly restored, upbeat spectacle of the present. This "old" Times Square gloried in its circus savor, its pasteboard, hand lettering, poster-cluttered theater entrances, its daubed-on paint, the popping electric bulbs of its frenetic, herky-jerky animated signs. During the World War II dimout unlit signs appeared, made of quarter-sized sequins stitched onto painted block letters (these made their debut and survived into the 1980s, reaching their tawdry best when the sequins began falling off). Even the paper and cardboard litter of the wartime and early postwar square was more pleasing than today's Styrofoam and wind-dizzied plastic bags.

Even back in the mortal poverty of the 1930s, a reaction against despair generated glorious extravagances like the Rainbow Room atop Rockefeller Center, Radio City Music Hall, and the vast, scintillating Art Deco International Casino north of Times Square. But during the 1920s, nighttime New York was at its zenith, more various and unpredictable than ever before or since. Prohibition-ridden New Yorkers were mad to squander at night the money they were raking in by day, and they parted with it in thousands of speakeasies, nightclubs, supper clubs, movie palaces, and legitimate theaters that offered an array of plays and musicals never equaled since. It was a cityscape without the RCA, Empire State, or Chrysler Buildings, yet New York still seemed towering and crowded, muscular and aspiring.

Past World War I, the city begins to resemble often sentimentalized Old New York, year by year shedding height, phones, radios, electric light, subways, railways, and streetcars. Movies drop away first, then nightclubs and restaurants catering to evening and late-night diners, leaving the theater as the 19th-century linchpin of respectable after-dark entertainment. Before 1900 there were proto-skyscrapers, many still standing now, but not nearly so high. The 30-story Park Row Building with its twin cupolas, and its 309-foot-high neighbor, the Pulitzer World Building (1890), modest-looking in photographs, nonetheless dwarfed the 284-foot steeple of Trinity Church, completed in 1846.

By 1880 the skyscrapers have sunk below the Trinity steeple, to ten or twelve stories, with windows lit by gas. In 1875 the Western Union headquarters at the corner of Broadway and Dey Streets was Trinity's nearest competitor, and was the tallest commercial structure in New York, boldly engineered to showcase the company's prestige and its place in the vanguard of technology. It was massive, and with an intricate, even frilly gray granite and red brick exterior and a great 23-foot-high hall on the seventh floor where 290 operators pattered out messages by the million 24 hours every day. A clocktower, slapped offhandedly on top, seems to have been intended as a respectful echo of the nearby St. Paul's and Trinity steeples.

Toward the Civil War, New York lowers its spine yet further and begins a two-century-long southward retreat from Inwood Hill, at the northern tip of Manhattan, to Harlem. By 1800 the developed area has shrunk back to Greenwich Village, then to present-day City Hall by the Revolution. Theaters are gone by 1730, leaving coffeehouses and a few public assembly rooms for exhibitions and dances. By 1695 all three successive Trinity Church buildings and their steeples are nowhere to be found, and by the 1660s the developed town has withdrawn downtown to Wall Street.

Below it, the settlers' Manhattan of the 1640s and 50s stretched for about 1,700 feet to the tip of the island, in a Dutch-looking village of perhaps 500 settlers, windmills, and gable-roofed houses. Yet the rivers were already beginning to thrum with shipping and trade, ferries plying back and forth from Brooklyn. A market drew shoppers and tradespeople to the open space at the foot of today's Broadway, outside the gates of Fort Amsterdam. Nobly named, the Fort was in truth a crumbling pile of dirt and wood. Nonetheless, it was the biggest structure in the new town, its flagpole the tallest thing in view, flying the orange, white, and blue colors of the Dutch West India Company. The sole nighttime gathering places were taverns, but they were numerous and filled with people socializing, exchanging news, and cutting deals.

Heat came from a hearth, light from a candle, a lamp, or sometimes a burning rush soaked in grease. Water had to be hauled up from a well as, a few yards away, excrement trickled and plopped into an earthen pit so close by it would have angered our current, yet-to-be-imagined department of health. For sweet water, untainted by the buildup of household waste, one walked north to the Fresh Water pond, fed by springs bubbling up out of Manhattan's angular bedrock and draining itself in two streams, one emptying into the Hudson and the other into the East River. In New Amsterdam and early New York it was pristine, a favorite source for drinking water, and fed the Tea Water Pump, which survived into the 1800s (the pump is long gone, but the pond is still there, buried under the Criminal Courts complex on Centre Street, its waters seeping ignominiously through the municipal sewers). Indeed 17th-century town life, not just in New York but in all save the very greatest European cities, was little more than rural life agglomerated. Trees for firewood stood within view of the front door. Cattle spent the night in town, and every morning a drover led them along the East River out to pasture near today's City Hall. Their return home each evening was one of the rituals, along with the ringing of the bell in Fort Amsterdam, that marked the onset of night.

A European ship passenger approaching Manhattan from Lower New York Bay in the 1600s at first saw little sign of human occupation. The earliest landmark to appear was the Navesink Highlands, rising helmetlike over the water. As the ship rounded it, Sandy Hook appeared, jutting into the bay from the west. But even here Manhattan still lay seventeen miles north, invisible, with no bridges or towers to herald it. Eleven miles past Sandy Hook, you came upon the Narrows, and found yourself nowhere in particular among a confusion of waterways, islets, and headlands. An occasional group of curious Indians might set out in a canoe to visit the ship and down a bumper of brandy with the crew, but nothing appeared that would strike a European as townlike. Six miles beyond the Narrows, you reached Manhattan; Brooklyn Heights rose up, not yet obscured by elevated roads or tall buildings and thus still meriting its name. Manhattan was a rocky headland, rising into a few undulating hills.

A late 17th-century Dutch visitor, Jasper Danckaerts, remarked that "as soon as you begin to approach the land, you see not only woods, hills, dales, green fields and plantations, but also the houses and dwellings of the inhabitants, which afford a cheerful and sweet prospect after having been so long upon the sea." He marveled at "how this bay swarms with fish, both large and small, whales, tunnies and porpoises, whole schools of innumerable other fish, which the eagles and other birds of prey swiftly seize in their talons when the fish come up to the surface, and hauling them out of the water, fly with them to the nearest woods or beach."

By the 1640s, the houses shrink and the taverns become darker and smaller, until they're few and humble—like the Wooden Horse, a minute barroom built in 1641 next to the Fort. No wall or city gate, closed and locked, guarded the village after dark. By 1624 the Fort and settlers are gone, leaving a wilderness of bay, river, tree, rock, and swamp. But not a vacant wilderness at all, and not in truth a wilderness; rather, a different kind of town. Manhattan was well populated before it was New York or New Amsterdam, a forest city, home to perhaps 15,000 Indians, all branches of the Algonquin tribe, whose ancestors had roamed the area for millennia. The Lenape were the most numerous (though not the only) group, and they weren't nomads, but moved seasonally among regular encampments as food supplies increased or waned.

Thus their settlement had all the essential social features of a city, lacking only the products of the fateful European belief that land could be owned and that owners should be planted on it. At night they kept fire and light, in Quonset-hut-shaped longhouses framed by bent saplings, covered with bark and ventilated by smokeholes. Trees grew everywhere, of course, as they do in present-day Manhattan. But the species were more various— the black locusts and sycamores New Yorkers began planting in the 1700s eventually took over and still dominate the streets today. And trees were the beginning of the city night. Pines still clustered thickly in the soil and rocks of lower Manhattan when the Dutch arrived. Their wood burned with a hot and bright (though smoky) light. Pine pitch, a highly flammable resin, made a peerless fuel for torches (probably the earliest human refinement of fire into a technology for artificial light, and thus perhaps the beginning of a night fit for activity rather than forced hibernation).

Long before Manhattan was Manhattan, long before it had a name at all, its trees made social life possible after dark, just as its land and water supplied food. An old Lenape legend of the origin of the world (first recorded by Europeans in the late 1600s) invokes these primal features in relation to the millennia of humans who would live on the island. In the beginning, the legend says, was only water, from horizon to horizon. A turtle rose from this sea. Its domed back, drying in the sun, became the earth. A tree grew in the midst. The first man sprang up from its roots; then the treetop bent toward the ground, and the first woman sprouted from its crest as the treetop touched the earth.

It's difficult to see in the Manhattan of today any trace of that primeval island. But not impossible. Perhaps the place to start is with a pair of trees: two gaunt pines growing close together, just west of Broadway, in the south graveyard of Trinity Church. Almost hidden in the corner between the walls of the church and the sacristy, they're nearly always in shadow. But at the right time, seen from the right vantage point, they make it possible to imagine the island of the Lenape and the earliest Dutch, surviving spectrally amidst four centuries of development.

Stand at the corner of Broadway and Rector Street on a clear late winter afternoon, and these pines loom starkly against the brown stones of the church. The steeple rises above, and above that an expanse of sky. When darkness falls, the pines sink gradually into the shadows between the church and attached chapel, the spire and the buttresses in sharp relief behind. Ignore the skyscrapers (easily done from here) and you see something like what would have been there in 1700. In darkness the brownstone church loses its shape; imagine it gone (the original church opened in 1697), multiply the pines in your imagination, and you see it as it was even in 1650—a graveyard, among the earliest in New Amsterdam.

Then, back still further, to the spring of 1643, the graves are empty, and the land is a garden belonging to the Dutch West India Company, bordering Broadway's ancestor, the Heerewegh, a dirt road whose name meant "Highway" in Dutch. The garden, once a community resource, was gradually being carved up, and part of it was in the process of falling into the grip of an obscure, ambitious, and none-too-scrupulous Dutch immigrant, Jan Jansen Damen. He would, by the mid-1640s, own all the land behind you, from Broadway to the East River. We will soon hear more of him.

Daylight in the New Amsterdam of the 1640s, when his story begins, was recognizably what it is now—allowing only for the cycling seasonal angles of the sun, the changing composition and density of whatever hung suspended in the air, and the buildings that carve New York's unsparing northern New World sunlight into angles of cold shadow and frigid glare. Daylight differed back then only insofar as it fell not on development but on an expanse of woods, hills, rock outcroppings, and moving water. But night light was very different, and the feel of it is probably beyond recovery. The fixed stars, now mostly invisible in the ambient glow of artificial light, have shifted their positions. First gas, then electric light, powered by alien machines throbbing all night in grim bastions at the city's edge and beyond, cut deep into night and transformed it.

Geophysically the night of the planet—sunset, darkness, circling moon, and more slowly turning stars—is much the same now as it was in the 17th century, or as it was a hundred or a thousand years before that. But the complex of thoughts, feelings, and sensations aroused by it has changed. When the sun set in the early spring of 1643, lights flickered up behind locked doors and shuttered windows. Taverns uncorked their wines and tapped their kegs. Customers began straggling in, taking down and packing their clay pipes, and settling in for a social or solitary evening.

Men, like Damen, were probably wearing the standard Dutch costume of the period: a coat, and beneath it a waistcoat and baggy, button-studded knee breeches, closing over stockings usually made of the same cloth and held up by garters. Details of styling varied, but the breeches and waistcoat were usually of one color (officials wore black, but otherwise tints varied). Shirts, often linen, had elaborate collars, ruffs, and cuffs; shoes and boots usually rose on high heels of layered black or brown leather. But the footfalls these boots sounded in the unlit and unpaved streets of New Amsterdam weren't those of the contented, plodding burghers with big paunches and small imaginations so comfortably dreamed up by Washington Irving. Some of them were setting out for places and experiences we can barely imagine, even in a newborn century that's supposedly seen everything.

Among these was Damen. Sometime after dusk fell on the evening of Monday, April 6, 1643, he could be seen sitting near Fort Amsterdam in the Wooden Horse tavern, probably smoking a pipe, and certainly drinking. He was brooding over a dark secret. It hadn't yet become a public sensation, but his fellow citizens were already whispering rumors of its full horror among themselves. As the hours ticked on, Damen's mood grew first grim, then sulfurous, and finally dangerous. It would, as the evening ripened, trigger an explosion that struck all the notes of urban night myth: pleasure and violence, intrigue, the furtive meeting of rock-solid burgher with roaming exile, and—in the upshot—the bursting out of horrific secrets concealed by the sun. The New York night was underway.

CHAPTER ONE

NEW AMSTERDAM NOIR
The Dark Nights of Dutch Manhattan

FOUR HUNDRED YEARS AGO the sun, sinking into the water meadows west of the Hudson, left Manhattan a dark outpost in the wilderness, lit only by candle and lamp flames, here and there feebly visible through shutters clapped to at dusk. Stranded and lonely New Amsterdam was, 3,000 miles from grandmother Europe and mother Amsterdam, and preternaturally silent it often was. But calm, peaceful, sunk in torpid sleep—never. Early Manhattan's nights were from the beginning a drama of outsized characters. Insider bearded outsider, neighbor crossed paths with neighbor, and meetings might end in farce, melodrama, love, tragedy, or all at once. The triangle of narrowing island was tiny, but its life immense, striking the spark that has illuminated the New York night ever since—bringing, as day often forbids, stranger into the company of stranger and transforming, into love or hatred, the relations between friend and friend.

In 17th-century New Amsterdam the European settlers strove to dominate a borderless territory whose scale they didn't realize and wouldn't have been able to comprehend if they were aware of it. Outside their makeshift village, the Indians—the rightful occupants by any fair measure—still gathered in seasonal encampments in the woods and along the shores, surrounding the presumptuous little Dutch fort with its straggle of houses. European and native had, in the colony's earliest decades, locked into an expedient but also distrustful interdependence. They daily needed, sometimes loved, often resented, fought, or murdered, and almost always misunderstood each other.

But during the winter and early spring of 1643 their relations spilled across the brink of catastrophe. Everyone was feeling the strain—particularly the two men who, late on the evening of Monday, April 6, 1643, sat in the pocket-sized Wooden Horse tavern, a warm beacon in an ocean of darkness. The muddy village lanes were unlit, and would remain so for half a century more, when feeble candle lanterns appeared, by city ordinance, to be hung from every seventh house on moonless nights. There would be no formally designated Town Hall until 1653, ten years in the future. Apart from the Schout Fischal—part sheriff, part prosecutor—and his minions, often as riotous as the drunks and thieves they hounded, no organized force patrolled the streets overnight until the first official night watch went on duty in 1658. There were no hospitals until 1660.

It was well past ten o'clock, the town's widely flouted bar closing hour. But alcohol was New Amsterdam's fuel, the volatile elixir that alternately glued it together and blew it apart. It was the colony's steadiest source of income, and trade in it was so profitable that it had early on become a nuisance: a 1648 ordinance complained that "one full fourth of the City of New Amsterdam has been turned into taverns for the sale of brandy, tobacco and beer." Any night, all night, even if the bars were shut, you could buy bootleg liquor from boats that quietly plied the rivers, selling to settlers and Indians alike: a 1656 law decried the rampant trade in alcohol along the riverbanks by "yachts, barks, scows, ships and canoes, going up and down."

Philip Geraerdy, the tavernkeeper, looked on uneasily as Jan Jansen Damen got drunker and drunker. The Wooden Horse, set in its own small yard, was eighteen feet by 25, with a single door, one window, and a thatched roof. Probably, like most Dutch taverns of the era, it had a locking cabinet for the drinks, and a rack of the clay pipes that were constant companions, both in business and pleasure.* By the 1640s the Wooden Horse had established itself as a rendezvous for soldiers from the garrison, but also attracted officials of the Dutch West India Company and prosperous landholders who owned the bouweries, or farms (perhaps Damen favored the place because his wife, Adrienne Cuville, was, like Geraerdy, French by birth).

Modest though his establishment was, Geraerdy was a forefather of New York nightlife. Born Philippe Gérard in France, he had come to the

---

* Clay pipes were the smoke of choice in New Amsterdam, among men, women, and small children (the puffing toddlers were a consequence of a 17th-century Dutch belief in the medicinal value of tobacco). Cigars were common in the Caribbean, but didn't become standard in New York until the 1840s.

colony with his wife, Marie, sometime before 1639. In 1641 he built his tavern on the northeast corner of today's Stone and Whitehall Streets. The name seems to have been a wry joke: as a soldier with the garrison Geraerdy had been sentenced to ride the wooden horse—a painful punishment in which the victim straddled two boards nailed together to form a sharp wedge that rested on four legs. A wooden horse's head adorned the front, and a tail the rear. Geraerdy rode with a pitcher in one hand and a sword in the other, probably to signify that he'd been shirking military duty by running a bar as a sideline.

Geraerdy's customer, Jan Jansen Damen, was 38 years old. Born in 1605, he'd emigrated from Holland to Albany around 1631, then resettled in New Amsterdam, where he quickly ingratiated himself with the colony's mercurial governor, Willem Kieft. By the late 1630s Damen was wheeling and dealing to combine several parcels of land just north of today's Wall Street into a farmstead that eventually stretched from the Hudson to the East River and included the ground on which Trinity Church now stands. Damen appears often in town records as a precipitator of both business deals and brawls, a quarrelsome and forbidding personage, respected for his business acumen (or at least his money) but held at arm's length because of his bad temper, drunkenness, and occasional violence.

In one imbroglio over money at his house he once struck his stepdaughter, Christina, threw her outdoors, whipped out a knife, raked it down her skirt, tore off her cap, and began pummeling her with his fists. Her husband, Dirck Holgerson, threw a pewter can at Damen's head to defend her. Damen lunged at him with the knife, and Holgerson prevailed over this berserk father-in-law only by stunning him with a blow on the head from a post picked up in the yard.

Such was the not-to-be-trifled-with figure who now sat in the Wooden Horse. He had stayed on long past closing time and drunk hard before he rose to leave. By then Geraerdy was alarmed enough to quietly slip his customer's sword out of its scabbard, and—sometime between midnight and one o'clock in the early morning of Tuesday, April 7, 1643—to escort him home. The neighborhood was, as always, awash in the sound of Manhattan's two great rivers, restlessly sweeping and eddying with their tides and currents. The Heerewegh was the main thoroughfare, up which Damen and Geraerdy were about to take perhaps the first midnight walk recorded in the history of the street later renamed Broadway by the English. In 1643 it was unpaved but began near where it does today, in a wide space before the Fort—roughly today's Bowling Green. In the 1640s, before a long-running series of landfill projects shouldered the rivers back, there was no Battery; the East River was 600 feet and the Hudson 1,200 feet closer to today's Bowling Green. Nothing in New Amsterdam could compete with the night sky or the water ceaselessly lapping at the land. Within a few hundred feet north of the Fort buildings began to thin, giving way to a cemetery along the Hudson, then gardens and vacant land, then another cemetery. The countryside, dotted with swamps and a refuge for hostile Indians, was beautiful by day but frightening at night.

Once Geraerdy and Damen had left the tavern, they probably walked toward the Fort—a wooden paling protected by a much trodden and deteriorating earthen berm, which the town was only now beginning to face with stone. Inside, along with the flagpole, there was a new stone church, just visible over the battlements. Then they turned right on today's Whitehall Street, heading north; the West India Company's windmill came into view, standing motionless at night, alongside the Hudson and just beyond the northwest bastion of the Fort. Taking a second right onto the Heerewegh, they now passed two more taverns on the left, the soldier-friendly establishments of Peter Cock and Martin Crugier. Then houses—mere cottages, most of them, at this hour, shuttered, dark, dead to the world, and surrounded by sizable gardens, even small orchards.

Damen lived just a quarter mile's up-island walk from the White Horse, but at night the muddy Heerewegh was frightening, haunted by drunks, the occasional insomniac pig, and Indians, whom Damen had good and very personal reasons to fear. The town was quiet, but not without hints of threat, even before the current tension between the Dutch and the Indians. Whoring sailors were not supposed to be abroad, but a 1638 law ordering them to return to their ships by sundown had been widely ignored. Town dwellers, seeking firewood or building materials, were known to steal out after nightfall to tear down the wooden fences that guarded outlying pastures and farm plots.

Damen and Geraerdy passed the West India Company's gardens, today the south graveyard of Trinity Church. Just beyond Wall Street—not yet laid out and still without the wall it was named for—they came to Damen's farm. At today's Pine Street, where the ground rose slightly, they turned right down a dirt lane. On their right was Damen's house* with its orchard and kitchen gardens. The land was still leased and much of it remained uncultivated, but Damen would own it outright the following year. Retracing their steps today, from the Transit Authority office building, 2 Broadway (whose saturnine bulk hunkers over any remaining buried traces of the Wooden Horse), the walk takes only fifteen minutes.

Then as now the after hours were, as Geraerdy seems to have sensed, the time for passions to flare out. As they approached Damen's house, they found it dark, locked, silent. Prolonged pounding, however, finally roused Dirck, Damen's servant (the records aren't clear as to whether this was the same man as his son-in-law), who suddenly jerked open the door and, pistol in hand, announced that he meant to kill Damen on the spot. A scuffle ensued, with Dirck brandishing the gun and the soused Damen lunging at him with his empty scabbard. Geraerdy held Dirck off with Damen's sword, while the enraged burgher stormed inside and emerged with a knife, which—in the pitch darkness—he sliced by mistake down Geraerdy's back, carving a gash underneath his right shoulder blade.

WHAT HAPPENED AT MIDNIGHT: FEBRUARY 25, 1643

Geraerdy survived (though his wound required attention from Dr. Hans Kierstede, New Amsterdam's leading surgeon). Geraerdy insisted he bore Damen no grudge. But this goodwill put him in a minority: Damen had become a pariah, one of the most hated men in the colony, and Dirck's sudden assault on his master was not anomalous. For all New Amsterdam was on edge in the aftermath of a far more harrowing night a few weeks earlier, in which Damen had been deeply involved. Now neighbor was snarling at neighbor, and the leading clergyman, Dominie (i.e., pastor) Everardus Bogardus, was denouncing Kieft, the increasingly hated governor. The tension broke out everywhere: by day in the restrained but still

---

* I have been able to find no definitive record as to where Damen was living in the spring of 1643. He had leased the tract near present-day Pine Street in 1638. While he didn't own it outright until 1644, Dutch land tenure practice encouraged a leaseholder to build. The owner was obligated to compensate the renter for any improvements made to the property, and such improvements often gave the lessee de facto ownership of the tract. Damen built a large new manor house on this land in 1648, but it's probable that he had earlier put up at least a small temporary dwelling soon after renting it. This would also account for his enmity with and apparent fear of Indians as described later.

palpable agitation of the colony's official records, and by night in tavern brawls.

New York's reputation both for lawlessness, and for its clash of races, ethnicities, languages, and classes, is often traced back to the 1800s. But the colony had been contentious from the beginning, founded by the Dutch West India Company not as a utopian experiment but as pure business, unsoftened by sentiment. The settlers were as polyglot and combative as the New Yorkers of later eras: Governor Kieft told the Jesuit missionary Isaac Jogues, visiting in 1643, that among them they spoke eighteen different languages. The company was authoritarian in spirit, but the three months' arduous sail across the Atlantic put it out of touch with day-to-day events. Also, while the fur trade was still in its infancy, the company had kept New Amsterdam afloat by selling wine, beer, and distilled liquor, and the colony acquired a reputation for dissoluteness: one agent wrote back to Amsterdam in September 1626 complaining that the inhabitants, from Peter Minuit down to the farmers and laborers, "draw their rations and pay in return for doing almost nothing, without examining their conscience or considering their bounden duty and what they promised to do upon their engagement."

But the darkest episodes of these early years rose not from tensions within the immigrant populace, but from the tense bond, half dependence and half suspicion, that had formed between the settlers and the much larger native population of Indians—a primordial instance of the uneasy dance of insider and outsider that would give the city night its rhythm. The tension could be rich and productive, but in Dutch Manhattan, it exploded in one of the most violent and macabre nights in New York history. Damen, up to his neck in the catastrophe, tried to dissociate himself from it but fooled no one.

Wednesday evening, February 25, 1643, began with a seemingly innocent supper party hosted by Kieft at his mansion in the Fort. As described by a later visitor, its large wood-paneled hall was decorated by 300 polished blunderbusses. In the study a collection of books vied with still more weaponry: "pistolls set in Rondellos, . . . also sundry Indian weapons, an Indian Stone hatchette, an ax, a Buckler, a poleax," and "some Scimitars very pretty to behold."* Among Kieft's guests in these

---

* This description dates from 1697. The mansion had been rebuilt in the 1670s, but at least some of its 1643 furnishings and its general character may have survived the overhaul.

gloomy chambers, two were worth remarking. One was Adrienne Cuville, Damen's wife (New Amsterdam women often kept their maiden names). The other was David de Vries, the governor's advisor, who, despite misgivings about his employer, seems not to have known what was afoot. Perhaps it was some sinister edge in Kieft's or Cuville's manner that unsettled him. "I remained that night at the Governor's sitting up," de Vries later remembered.

> I went and sat by the kitchen fire, when about midnight I heard a great shrieking, and I ran to the ramparts of the fort, and looked over to Pavonia [across the Hudson in New Jersey]. Saw nothing but firing, and heard the shrieks of the savages murdered in their sleep. I returned again to the house by the fire. Having sat there awhile, there came an Indian with his squaw, whom I knew well, and who lived about an hour's walk from my house, and told me that they two had fled in a small skiff, which they had taken from the shore at Pavonia; that the Indians from Fort Orange had surprised them; and that they had come to conceal themselves in the fort. I told them that they must go away immediately; that this was no time for them to come to the fort to conceal themselves; that they who had killed their people at Pavonia were not Indians, but the Swannekens, as they call the Dutch, had done it.

Indeed it was a night of atrocities, far worse than de Vries probably imagined at the time because it was no impulsive outburst but a cold-blooded plot, first laid in January or February, when Kieft and his co-conspirators had secretly authorized a massacre of Wiechquaesgeck and Tappan Indians. By the time the butchery was over, about 120 Indian men, women, and children had been slaughtered, about 40 at Corlaer's Hook (two miles beyond Damen's house), and 80 at Pavonia, across the Hudson in New Jersey. After midnight, the raiders began returning to the Fort flaunting their trophies: wounded, sometimes atrociously mutilated captives and a cargo of severed heads. De Vries may have been struck to the quick by this spectacle. But Adrienne Cuville was delighted—as became clear when, after the seven years it took for news of the slaughter to reach Amsterdam and be acted on, the Dutch West India Company dispatched a sternly worded interrogatory to Cuville, insisting that she respond under oath. Was it true, the dispatch demanded, that "when the heads of certain slain Indians were brought to the Manhattans," Cuville rushed out to "exult over the circumstance, and with her feet kick the heads which were brought in?"

Other records differ as to whether she kicked just one head or many, but even hers was not the direst of the night's atrocities. "Infants," de Vries reported, "were torn from their mother's breasts, and hacked to pieces in the presence of the parents, and the pieces were thrown into the fire and in the water, and other sucklings, being bound to small boards were cut, stuck, and pierced and miserably massacred in a manner to move a heart of stone." The next morning "some came to our people in the country with their hands, some with their legs cut off and some holding their entrails in their arms, and others had such horrible cuts and gashes that worse than they were could never happen."

Many if not most of the settlers had no inkling of the Kieft conspiracy and were appalled by the next morning's grisly news. Kieft took the brunt of their anger: people began remembering his mysterious behavior in the weeks leading up to the incident. De Vries noted that on Tuesday, February 24, the day before the massacre, "the Governor . . . began to state his intentions, that he had a mind to *wipe the mouths of the savages.*" But, as Adrienne Cuville's behavior at the Fort hints, Damen too was part of the conspiracy. So were several other owners of outlying farms, notably including Cornelis Van Tienhoven, who was both Damen's neighbor to the northeast and a relative: Van Tienhoven's wife, Rachel, was Adrienne Cuville's daughter by an earlier marriage.

Kieft had been spoiling for an attack, and apparently found a ready ear in landholders, like Damen and Van Tienhoven, who felt particularly vulnerable to Indian raids. This is suggested by another pointed question among the Dutch West India Company's written interrogatories, this one directed to Van Tienhoven, and asking about an entertainment given at Damen's house shortly before the February massacre. "Was not a mysterious toast dr[u]nk at an entertainment at the house of Jan Damen, by some few, though not by all then present, without the major part having been aware what it meant? . . . What was this mysterious toast and what was its purport?" Kieft proposed the toast, and while its exact words have been lost it seems to have been a coded permission to proceed to those in the know—including Damen and Van Tienhoven. The company further demanded, "what relationship exists between him, [Van] Tienhoven, and Jan Damen?" Evidently, this and follow-up questions imply Damen and several other plotters, having heard the toast, had then asked Van Tienhoven to draw up a petition to Kieft, seeking his permission to attack the Indians.

Nobody else at the gathering was to know exactly what was afoot until the early morning hours of Thursday, February 26, and when the plotters began hauling trunks and heads and body parts into the Fort. Outrage was the common response. The Eight Men, an elected board of advisors to Kieft, had included Damen. But his seven fellow councilors were so outraged by his involvement in the massacre that they refused to sit with him at a meeting (he protested that he'd signed the petition only at Kieft's urging). Enmities festered for years, rupturing friendships and alliances, flashing out in violent brawls. When the servant Dirck attacked Damen a few weeks after the massacre, it was surely a spillover from the general reservoir of poison still brimming, and mild under the circumstances.

Damen was a hated man, Adrienne Cuville a despised woman, and her daughter Rachel not much better thought of than her mother and stepfather. In 1641 she'd been publicly called "a woman in or about the fort" (a prostitute, in other words) "who pays money to boot"—apparently so ravenous for sex that if a prospect turned her down, she'd offer cash just for the pleasure of the tumble. This didn't, however, raise any impediment to Cornelis Van Tienhoven, who married her and in whom she more than met her match. As described by contemporaries, he was repellent: pale-haired and obese, with a bloated red face and a wen bulbing out from the side of one cheek. One complaint about him to the Dutch government called him "shrewd, false, deceitful and given to lying, promising every one, and when it comes to perform, at home to no one." He was a troublemaker, an adulterer, a drunkard, prone "to come out of the Tavern so full that he cannot walk."

Van Tienhoven was a scoundrel—loathed even more cordially than Damen. Though he was among the most dogged instigators of the massacre, he courted the Indians; when among them, he often waddled about clad only in a loincloth, "from lust after the prostitutes to whom he has always been mightily inclined" (to the Dutch, Indian women were synonymous with whores). But he was impervious to shame or to detraction; he and an abundance of similarly ungovernable men kept the passions of 1643 alive and boiling for months, even years; aftershocks of trouble kept breaking out. Drink was the usual trigger, and it tripped most readily at night.

One such incident happened in 1644 at the Stadts Herbergh, or City

Tavern. Built in 1642 on the bank of the East River, it was much bigger than the Wooden Horse and made of solid stone (the brick-marked outlines of its foundation can be seen today in the Goldman Sachs plaza, near the corner of Pearl and Broad Streets). Like the city-run hostelry in Amsterdam on which it was modeled, the Stadts Herbergh offered reliable accommodations to travelers and entertainment to citizens. It also served both as a shelter for refugees from Indian raids and intermittently as a jail.

Philip Gerritsen was the Stadts Herbergh's innkeeper, and on the evening of March 15, 1644, he and his wife threw a party for friends in one of the tavern's private parlors. The six guests at first might seem a solid but unremarkable collection of influential citizens: Everardus Bogardus, dominie of the church in the Fort, St. Nicholas, Dr. Hans Kierstede (the surgeon who had treated Geraerdy when Damen sliced him in 1643), and Gysbert Op Dyck, an associate of Kieft. All three had brought their wives, and the evening progressed congenially until a formidable trio materialized outside the door, which fronted Pearl Street and the East River.

They were all very drunk, but not drunks to treat lightly, and must have thrown an immediate chill on the party inside. The leader was Captain John Underhill (1597–1672), an English soldier and another crony of Kieft, Damen, and Van Tienhoven. He had been making trouble in New Amsterdam for years, mainly as a ruthless and violent Indian fighter (though he was also a Puritan who had served in the army of William of Orange and the author of a florid 1638 booklet, *Newes from America,* full of praise for the natural allure of New Amsterdam). Accompanied by two friends, Underhill clambered up the front steps, burst inside, and demanded to join the party. Gerritsen managed to decoy him into another room for a while. But after a brief parley, Underhill sent out a provocation: a request that Op Dyck come out of the parlor and join him.

When Op Dyck declined, Underhill and his henchmen went suddenly berserk, sweeping crockery off the shelves with their swords, then battering the door of the Gerritsens' parlor in an effort to rip it off its hinges. Mrs. Gerritsen kept them at bay with a lead bolt, and Gerritsen threw himself against the door, but the intruders overpowered him and burst in, Underhill bellowing, "Clear out of here for I shall strike at random." Somebody summoned Cornelis Van der Huygens, the Schout Fischal, from the Fort (a five-minute walk down Pearl Street). When he and a guard threatened to haul the rioters before Kieft, Underhill announced he'd happily talk to the governor—a sensible man, Underhill sneered—rather than the group now assembled at the Stadts Herbergh. In the upshot, the Gerritsens and their guests fled, leaving the tavern to the victorious rioters.

Underhill's drunkenness may have precipitated this incident, but its cast of characters suggests that post-massacre enmities lay behind it, because the party brought a fierce Kieft crony face-to-face with the governor's most vocal detractor. Dominie Bogardus, whose church stood beside Kieft's mansion inside the Fort, had become an uncompromising critic of the policies that led to the 1643 massacre. By 1644 Bogardus was roaring denunciations of Kieft from the pulpit of St. Nicholas, and Kieft ordering his soldiers to pound their drums and bellow outside the church windows in the hope of drowning out Bogardus's diatribes. Kierstede, whatever his political affinities, had just wed Bogardus's stepdaughter Sara Roelofs, and thus the party in Gerritsen's parlor bore an anti-Kieft tinge, and this may well be what riled Underhill. Since Op Dyck seems not to have been strongly identified with either the Kieft or anti-Kieft factions, Underhill's invitation may have been a pointed effort to make him declare his true allegiance. And Van der Huygens, the Schout Fischal, was an ally of Van Tienhoven; the two had sat with Kieft in a secretive meeting that may have plotted the 1643 massacre.

From the very beginning, New York was a city built on business, whether in fur, liquor, or real estate; and business depends both on the convivial exchange of favors and information and on murderous competition. Both governed the city's earliest days, and flamed out during its nights, as they always would, but with a raw nakedness not often repeated in later history. Night here has really never been a time of stolid rest after labor, but a release of energy too powerful for full play during the daylight. New Amsterdam was also, like New York after it, a city of strangers, of natives and aliens, veering between fascination and hostility—even more the bedrock truth beneath the later history of nightlife.

Next to the relative homogeneousness and imposed sobriety of Massachusetts Bay Colony, New Amsterdam had a multinational character that tended to render it tolerant, even uninhibited. In 1638 two visitors just arrived from Massachusetts went to Claes Corneliszen's house for a party and encountered a trio highly untypical of Governor Winthrop's colony: Maryn Adriaensen (another irascible Damen crony), Thomas Beeche, and Beeche's wife, Nanne. Once the wine had circulated, Nanne started in on the men, and "notwithstanding her husband's presence, fumbled at the front of the breeches of most all of those who were present." Beeche tried to stop her, but succeeded only in provoking a brawl, in which the participants began cutting off and rummaging through each others' purses (both men and women used them in the 1600s). It ended with Nanne Beeche fetching Maryn Adriaensen, a formidable figure in the colony at large, a smart slap in the face.

Women generally seem to have benefited by Dutch law, which granted them considerably more status than its English counterpart. They seem also to have inhaled the air of personal liberty that permeated New Amsterdam. When Kieft became governor in 1637, the colony already had a public prostitute, Griet Reyners, and when he tried to shut her enterprise down, she moved her headquarters to Brooklyn's Gravesend and thumbed her nose at him. In 1658, a woman, the wife of Christiaen Anthony, showed up at Hilletje Jans's house in a painted-on beard, wearing men's clothes, and demanding a pint of beer. Mrs. Hendrick Janzen Sluyter got into a 1659 dispute over money with a group of people who haled her into court because, they said, she had "hoisted her petticoats up to her back and showed them her arse" in the heat of the moment (she countered that she'd actually shown it only to her husband).

Misbehavior of this sort was most often taken in stride; there were few New Amsterdam Hester Prynnes. Dutch legal custom put settling disputes and resolving troublesome situations above meting out punishments, and even during its precarious early years the colony, despite its ferocity with the Indians, maintained a rough but real forbearance in handling citizens and a distaste for moralistic witch hunts—a trait still potent 300 years later when New York thumbed its nose at Prohibition. As the massacre attests, the city could turn murderous, but in this era disturbances were driven by personality rather than ideas, whether moral or political.

When rivalries ended, they tended to do so in the fatal casualties that typified the Renaissance drama of human ambition rearing against a hostile nature. Jan Damen died on June 21, 1651, on shipboard, returning from a trip to the Netherlands, leaving Adrienne Cuville a widow. Sea deaths—or rather a single sea death—also awaited Kieft, his Schout Fischal, and Dominie Everardus Bogardus, their sworn enemy. All three were aboard the *Princess Amelia* in 1647 when, on its way to Amsterdam, where Kieft and Bogardus were scheduled for a showdown before the authorities, the ship struck a reef in the Bristol Channel and sank. Some passengers survived, but Kieft, his Schout Fischal Cornelis Van der Huygens, and Bogardus all drowned together.

Van Tienhoven clung to public office for years. He became Schout Fischal of the colony in 1652, turning instantly into a sanctimonious scourge of the vices of others. On the evening of Sunday, October 18, 1654, he stormed into court, denouncing a tavernkeeper for permitting "drinking clubs, . . . with dancing and jumping and entertainment." He hauled one of the customers, apparently a prostitute, off to jail in a cart, and piously pronounced the whole thing "a most scandalous affair." Only in 1656 did the Dutch West India Company finally catch up with him, when he was dismissed as Schout Fischal. Then he vanished. He seems to have drowned himself: late that fall, on the morning of November 19, his hat and cane were found floating in the river—though a rumor circulated that this was a ruse, and that he and his brother had lit out into the bush, perhaps to the fur-trading lands up the Hudson.

Gysbert Op Dyck filled a few low-profile civic offices, and in 1656 secured permission to open a bar of his own in his house, next door to the Stadts Herbergh (which in 1653 had been turned into the Stadts Huis, or town hall). He served too as a messenger for the city court, witnessing an agreement for a transfer of lands to the colony from Indians living along the Delaware River. Ultimately, he secured a patent for Coney Island—a substantial grant. Hans Kierstede, the surgeon who patched up Philip Geraerdy after Damen's attack and attended the Bogardus party, evolved into a sharp critic of the Dutch West India Company's rule: in 1664 he signed the protest that helped precipitate the changeover to British control. He died in 1666, having invented a secret-formula ointment that was, as late as the 1890s, still on sale in his great-great-grandson's Broadway drugstore.

Geraerdy became a much respected figure. He was one of the few tavernkeepers who in 1648 appeared before the town council and swore to uphold the otherwise universally flouted tavern regulations. In 1653, after Peter Stuyvesant had replaced Kieft, the council named Geraerdy as among the town's "principal citizens and inhabitants," to be assessed for the honor of paying for the wooden and stone fortification about to be built on the north side of (and ultimately to give its name to) Wall Street.

Indoors, New Amsterdam's nightlife was still confined entirely to taverns or private homes. There were no ballrooms. There would be no theaters in New York until around 1732, no museums or formal exhibition spaces until nearly a century after that. Restaurants, at least in the form of establishments chiefly dedicated to the serving of food, didn't exist. The day's main meal was served in the afternoon, and in any case there seem to have been few full-fledged eating establishments as we know them: archaeological excavations at the site of the Stadts Herbergh have unearthed plenty of pipes and drinking vessels but few dining utensils (though it must have offered food, if only to the inmates sometimes jailed there).

Outdoors, under the sky, commercial sex was available, as frequent though often fragmentary court records show: the open ground outside the Fort's main gate, near today's Bowling Green, was a known gathering place for prostitutes, a reputation it was to keep for generations. And besides sex, the New Amsterdam night offered a natural atmosphere surely richer, vaster, and more fragrant than ever after—brilliant and serene when the moon was full, black and dusted with stars when it was gone. The town's whispering artificial light came from reddish or greenish or liverish flames of candles, oil lamps, and rushlights. Sound and aroma came from the two great waterways moving restlessly around it (both the East and Hudson Rivers flow sometimes south, sometimes north, depending on the tides). The woods and open country, though dark and quiet, were alive with animal and human life, Indians and settlers coexisting uneasily on their outlying camps and farms. The creation of a night world as we know it, with businesses, pleasures, and terrors uniquely its own, lay in the future, a product of economic growth, more people, more business, and new technologies that made life in the dark easier to lead.

FROM STADTS HUIS TO CITY HALL:
THE DUTCH NIGHT ENGLISHED

On December 12, 1658, as the nine o'clock evening bell began clanging atop St. Nicholas Church, Lodowyck Pos waited in front of the Stadts Huis—atop the same steps up which John Underhill had drunkenly charged fourteen years before, when it was still the Stadts Herbergh. Tonight Pos was taking up duty as, in effect, New York's first chief of police. Peter Stuyvesant, Kieft's successor, had been planning a night watch for years. But the first attempt to gather applicants failed in 1654, because nobody showed up at an enlistment meeting held by the town council, whose members waited glumly for a while in the deserted hall, then adjourned.

Now, four years later, Pos and eight subordinates had finally been hired. As per orders, they gathered a few minutes before the bell, just as the taverns were pretending to close, then fanned out on patrols until day-break. Every night, in rotation, four of the eight watchmen served, each receiving a payment of a little over a guilder for the night's work. Over the ensuing decades their numbers and appearance varied, but they were never less than conspicuous, wearing orange and blue uniforms, each bur-dened with a sword, musket, pistol, and lantern.

Each man also carried a rattlestick, the noise alarm that gave the force its name, the Rattle Watch. The rattlestick was a cucumber-sized hard-wood contraption consisting of a handle, a cogwheel, and a clapper. Flail-ing the handle spun the cogs against the clapper, producing a noise like a playing card against bicycle spokes or a New-Year's-Eve rattle. The Watch's cumbersome freight of weapons, uniforms, and equipment anticipated the guns, nightsticks, walkie-talkies, and cell phones New York cops still haul about with them today; like their successors, the Watch plodded their beats, swinging the rattlestick to summon help in an emergency, from nine at night until the Fort Amsterdam drum sounded the arrival of morning.

At first, they worked alone, but eventually—as much because of their own erratic behavior as the challenges of the job—they patrolled in pairs, changing partners every two weeks. On clear nights, they were supposed to venture up the island as far north as Thomas Hal's farm, near the present-day City Hall Park. In bad weather they turned back south at Maiden Lane, near the farm where Jan Jansen Damen's widow, Adrienne, still dwelt. They cried out the hours at every corner (not as monotonous a duty as it might seem, especially when divided among four men: there were only about a dozen street intersections in the New Amsterdam of 1658). They were also required to arrest anybody making noise or caught fight-ing, and to keep the detainees under control until morning, when the court opened.

Easy in principle, this seems to have been hard in practice: the Rattle Watch was the butt of constant complaints while it was operating, and it stumbled in and out of existence for most of the next century and a half. Sometimes the watchmen were paid, sometimes they were volunteers; on occasion they were, like juries, coerced into service. At least in the early 1700s, women were included on the draft rolls, as evidenced by a 1734 court case in which a woman named Deborah Careful claimed she'd been assessed an exorbitant sum to hire a substitute when her name came up for duty. But whatever their composition, the patrols had a reputation for

outdoing the criminals they stalked in lawlessness. Over the years people
reviled the watchmen for noise, drunkenness, peeing on the steps of City
Hall, sleeping in the streets, failing to call out the hours, mischievously
bellowing "Rise up from bed!" long before the morning drum, or deliberately shunning neighborhoods, like Pearl Street, where fed-up residents
had refused to pay their Watch tax.

When the Rattle Watch resumed in 1661 after a lapse, Pos reapplied
for his old post as captain, and the council reluctantly reengaged him,
noting that his previous service had provoked rampant complaint. But the
service stubbornly resisted improvement, and its dubious repute endured
for generations. In a 1757 letter to the *New-York Gazette* a reader vented a
widely shared opinion of the Rattle Watch and its various successors as a
"parcel of idle, drinking, vigilant Snorers, who never quell'd any nocturnal
tumult in their Lives; (Nor as we can learn, were ever the Discoverers of a
Fire breaking out,) but would, perhaps, be as ready to join in a Burglary as
any Thief in Christendom. A happy Set indeed, to defend the rich and
populous City against the Terrors of the Night." When the outcry got
loud enough, or in times of emergency, military or citizen guards replaced
the Watch. In 1663 a new Indian war broke out upriver, and a large contingent of soldiers from the Fort left the city to fight up the Hudson near
Kingston. Nervous about security, the council disbanded the Rattle
Watch and replaced it with a military guard of armed citizens. The watch
was divided into three companies of burghers, called "trainbands," but
still under the command of the unsinkable Pos. Four of the old Rattle
Watch men joined this new militia. Four others quit.

By the time the 17th century drew to a close, New York had taken on
its permanent name from James Stuart, the Duke of York, who took possession of it in the name of the king. The frontier ambience of the 1640s
had begun to dissipate, and the colony began a slow metamorphosis from
a Dutch to an English style of town life. Yet an apprehension of danger
and calls for public order continued. Frustration over nighttime policing
endured from the first night watch in 1658 through the 19th century and
into the present. But colonial New York seems to have been better policed
than either Boston, Philadelphia, or Charleston, South Carolina, its early
American rivals for the title of New World metropolis. As a matter of fact,
no city in the West, not even London or Paris, had a well-organized police
system much before 1800. Crime was beginning to become a popular bo-
geyman, though in America, at least judged by later standards, much of it

was little more than village rowdiness. The fabled long, dark alleys and back tenements of the 1800s still lay in the future.

1679:
JASPER DANCKAERTS'S NEW YORK

In early New York, life after dark didn't change rapidly at first, centering itself in the taverns, as it had since the founding of the colony. As yet music and drama had no formal existence; commercial sex remained an ad hoc business carried on mainly outside the Fort (now renamed Fort James) or in disorderly taverns. Yet despite early inklings of the big city's later fear of street crime, the combination of growth and a more peaceful climate of relations between Indians and colonists made nighttime activity less dangerous, and made for a more harmonious interchange between the city and the countryside.

Visitors now began to report not only the still new town's frontier rigors but the civilized pleasures of both it and its environs. Even Jasper Danckaerts, who arrived in 1679 on a mission to save New World souls, putting aside some of his suspicion of pleasure and its snares, confessed himself charmed in the diary he kept during his stay. His first impressions, naturally enough, came by daylight. Just past noon on Thursday, September 21, standing on the deck of the ship *Charles,* Danckaerts could see nothing: Manhattan and the headlands defending it from the Atlantic lay invisible, shrouded in a dense fog. But the ship's cat, frantic after its three-month voyage from the Netherlands, had scented the land before anybody else, scrambled high up into the rigging, and was sniffing eagerly in the direction of the shore.

Once the fog lifted, the *Charles* commenced its two days' sail up the bay, dropping anchor in the East River, at three o'clock Saturday afternoon, just off the foot of Broad Street. After a prayer of thanksgiving for safe arrival, Danckaerts and his companions disembarked. New York had taken on bulk since the days of Kieft, Damen, and Van Tienhoven; it was well on its way from outpost to self-important colonial town. The few dozen settlers who huddled in crude wooden houses near the fort back in 1624 had multiplied into thousands and dwelt in settlements that reached as far up the island as Wall Street. Despite its fifteen years in British hands, even in 1679 New York still looked and sounded like home to a visitor from the Netherlands, from the buildings and streets, to the people and customs, to the Dutch heard everywhere.

Danckaerts took lodgings at the house of Jacob Helleker and his wife, slept soundly, and, when he woke Sunday morning, perhaps because the townscape felt homey, Danckaerts showed less interest in buildings or thoroughfares than in Manhattan's natural gifts. He gloried in the city's "fine, pure morning air, along the margin of the clear running water of the sea, which is driven up this river at every side." In the late summer orchards and farmsteads, he praised the extraordinary size and quality of the peaches, pears, and mulberries abounding in this harvest month.

Sunday church services brought a less refreshing impression, however, in the sermon preached at St. Nicholas in Fort James by Dominie Nieuwenhuysen, fat, red-faced, and liable, in the heat of a tirade, to launch gobs of spit into the pews. The fastidious Danckaerts, disgusted, mopped himself up and embarked on his first evening out. He found the town roomy yet compact (less than 1,500 feet from the Fort to Wall Street), yet the possibilities were limited. Brothels were to be an 18th-century specialty, and if he saw them the fastidious Danckaerts never acknowledged the whores on parade outside the Fort: in any case he was, as a missionary, not the man to seek them out.

Rather he followed local custom and did what everyone with free time did for entertainment on Sunday evenings after the service: he headed for one of the taverns, still the universal resort of both sexes and everybody from clergy and civic leaders to the dregs, and still often open all night in defiance of ordinances. Some, though, offered more elaborate fare than the old Wooden Horse; a few had in effect become conference centers for business and government affairs, places to entertain guests, stopovers for travelers upstate or ferry passengers crossing between Manhattan and Brooklyn. They were also halls for the impromptu entertainments that hadn't yet found homes of their own: games, dancing, music, playacting, gambling, prostitution, and recreational rat-killing contests. Practically every nocturnal pursuit not conducted at home or in the bushes took place within the view of a bartender.

Early New Yorkers navigated by a mental compass different from ours: to them, the East River ran along the southern shore of Manhattan, the Hudson along the north; the Battery marked the western tip of the island, and what we now call uptown lay to the east (this made some sense: the axis of Manhattan in fact runs from southwest to northeast, and even now if you stand at the corner of Broad and Pearl Streets and look toward Brooklyn, you're looking almost due south, not east). Danckaerts's evening stroll led him north by modern reckoning. Most likely he took the same route Damen had in 1643, up Broadway to Wall Street; Damen's large farm, still owned by his heirs, had once seemed like an isolated frontier, but now it was part of a suburb that extended from Wall Street all the way to the Common (today's City Hall Park). There Danckaerts walked down a gentle bluff, then headed northward along a dirt road that led him up to the Fresh Water,* in 1679 still a bracing sight, a further illustration of Manhattan's still surviving rural character.

From the pond Danckaerts probably followed today's Bowery until he reached Adrian and Rebecca Corneliszen's tavern and brewery, about two miles outside town, at the corner of what's now Fourth Avenue and Astor Place, and hard by the farm Peter Stuyvesant had established for himself in 1651. Rebecca was the daughter of Jacob Helleker, with whom Danckaerts was boarding, and the establishment, though new, was already becoming a general resort. Danckaerts found the walk diverting and the tavern's setting "delightful." But he was disappointed by his first taste of the Corneliszens' New Netherland beer, which he found insipid; the company, which he thought dull (though it was headed by a placid old brewer, the first European born in New Amsterdam); and the tavern itself, "resorted to on Sundays by all sorts of revelers, . . . a low pot house." But Rebecca Corneliszen, ever amiable, took them out into her orchard and showed them a mulberry tree with leaves big as dinner plates, then the fist-sized pears she'd grown over the summer. They ambled the countryside in the dark until a cloudburst drove them back to the tavern. Then they headed downtown, teetering over a log thrown as a makeshift bridge across a salt marsh; there were a few night constables manning the Rattle Watch, and Danckaerts probably encountered them on his way back from the Fresh Water. Safe at the Hellekers' house, Danckaerts treated Rebecca's mother to a blunt lecture about the sinfulness of her daughter's way of life.

Over the remainder of September and October, he visited the longhouses of the Indians who had first greeted the *Charles* in the Narrows,

---

* Until it disappeared under landfill in the early 1800s, the Fresh Water was also known as Collect Pond ("kolk" is the Dutch word for "pond").

the squatter settlement of freed slaves and poor whites along Broadway in the low-lying land west of the Fresh Water, and across the East River to the house of Simon De Hart, near the Gowanus Creek where it empties into the Upper Bay (today it's the site of the Bush terminal). They sat before De Hart's roaring fire and devoured foot-long oysters, fished out of the creek, which today flows gloomily and sluggishly between the walls of abandoned factories.

On November 14, voicing no particular regret, Danckaerts left the city on a continuation of his missionary tour to New Jersey, Delaware, and Maryland. In 1679 it had been sixty-five years since the first ship of the Dutch West India Company arrived with its contingent of thirty settler families. Though economic conditions were shaky, relations between the Indians and the colonists, once so tense and violent, had eased.

New York was sailing a calm stretch in its turbulent history, and to people living there it must have seemed as if life after dark would forever be lived in the bar and taproom or by the domestic hearth. The town was full of life at night: as they do today, shelved, hidden, or forgotten selves took a deep breath and foraged out, in flight from or pursuit of whatever drove them. But there was no nightlife in the later sense. No transit system speeded one away from a family member's or neighbor's eye peering between the shutters, no sprawl of neighborhoods offered the lure of anonymity and a variety of diversions. There were no newspapers to list upcoming evening events and declare last night's mysteries and sensations; there were, mostly, no events to list and no halls to accommodate them. One chose between a quiet hearth at home or the company of a tavern.

Night would, in the 18th century, begin a long evolution from the mere twelve lightless hours of the circadian cycle into a world of its own, a dark mirror that obscured what daytime spotlighted and showed monsters and miracles to which morning and afternoon were blind. By the turn of the 19th century, an upstart economy of night began to take shape, a market of wide-open and hidden activities that echoed, parodied, and subverted day the way the alleys and carnival attractions of an amusement park imitate and distort the streets and stores of a city. But colonial 17th-century Manhattanites, Dutch, Anglo-Dutch, and English, still noticed the moon when they looked up; saw treetops closing in where the moon's luminescence ended; and above all they heard, felt, and scented the all-powerful bay and estuaries into which their island still jutted as an isolated promontory, sinking back into their embrace every night when darkness fell.

CHAPTER TWO

RATTLE WATCH NIGHTS
City Streets After Sundown,
from Peter Stuyvesant to the Early Republic

B Y THE DAWN OF the 18th century, a generation after Jasper Danckaerts left Manhattan, the brand-new, unmistakably English-looking Anglican Trinity Church dominated the horizon with its 180-foot steeple, just across Broadway from Jan Jansen Damen's old Dutch farmhouse. One could still walk from the site of the old Wooden Horse tavern to the outer limits of urban settlement in a half hour or less. But construction had raced past Wall Street, and now reached north as far as present-day City Hall: the population had risen to nearly 5,000 by 1700. The new century was to be an era of change, in which distinct neighborhoods began to shape themselves, gradually acquiring characters and reputations—for wealth or poverty, virtue or vice, business or pleasure, for followers of a particular trade or adherents of a particular religion.

As the town grew, rich professionals and businessmen clustered together in a teardrop-shaped district, its globe surrounding the Fort and tapering upward east by northeast—along the East River but well back from the wharves. Hanover Square and the Fort became neighborhood hubs for a critical mass of people with money, leisure, and transatlantic connections. Knowledgeable about the latest diversions enlivening the evenings of the great European capitals, they would soon begin importing pleasure gardens, coffeehouses, concerts, new plays, traveling exhibitions, restaurants, even night schools. Carriages with teams of purebred horses began appearing in an evening parade of showy equipages up Broadway, out into the country lanes, and back again.

Yet as wealth and its sparkle grew, so did poverty and its miseries, industry and its raw-boned ugliness. The citizenry was more sharply divided by class than had been true under the Dutch. Artisans and tradesmen, who lived and worked north and west of Hanover Square, formed a buffer zone around the merchants, but further northeast a manufacturing area had grown up between the Fresh Water and the East River. In whatever was left over—the far outskirts of the settled area, for example, and the East River docks and wharves—slums appeared. The swelling population and crowded harbors meant more trade and therefore more money, but also more strangers in the taverns, more sailors loose and drunk in the streets.

Public anxiety about crime mounted, and decades before the vogue of mystery novels and lurid tales of death in the alleyways, a new perception of night as nightmare began to exert a hold on the popular imagination. Drinking, gambling, and commercial sex thrived, expanding from freelance vice and lawbreaking into what citizens began to think of not as random nuisance but an underworld, brazenly commanding the streets and menacing anyone who didn't avert his or her eyes. The Rattle Watch, still the city's shaky first line of defense against mayhem, was little better than the erratic presence it had been when the Dogberry-like Lodowyck Pos led it in the 1650s.

And so, even as early as 1712, decades before the onset of Revolutionary jitters, it took little to jar New Yorkers into fright, and into the belief that alien others were prowling among them after sunset with murder in their hearts. In 1643 it had been the Indians. Now it was the Africans.*

John Crooke's Orchard and John Hughson's Tavern: Race and Violence in Pre-Revolutionary New York

Black men and women had been a significant part of the population since New Amsterdam days. By the turn of the 18th century nearly twelve percent of New York's population was African in origin, and included the largest cohort of slaves outside the South. Nor did their lot improve under the English, who were hard masters. New Amsterdam had hardly amounted to utopia: black slaves and freedmen often suffered from bad relations with white settlers and Dutch colonial officialdom. But under Dutch law whites and blacks (whether free or enslaved) stood equal in the

---

* Almost any term of racial identification applied to blacks in early New York is unsatisfactory. The common modern usage, African-American, doesn't reflect the life of an 18th-century city that had yet to acquire a fully American identity. Whether free or enslaved, most blacks in early Dutch New York were Africans in culture as well as race, as suggested by the midnight funeral customs described below. Thus, while "African" feels archaic to a modern reader, I'm using it here, along with "black," as most appropriate to the social context of this particular period.

eyes of the courts. Records show that even slaves were, particularly compared with the ferocity exercised against them in other colonies, treated humanely. They could, significantly, own property and make wills, leaving possessions to family and friends.

Well into the 1700s one was legally deemed a slave only if one's mother carried slave blood. This meant that in New Amsterdam and early New York there were white-skinned slaves living alongside black-skinned men and women who were free. In this inherently delicate atmosphere, the ascent of English law and custom, both harsher on matters of race than their Dutch predecessors, spelled trouble. A full year before Trinity Church held its first Anglican service in 1698, its officials had forbidden Negro burials in the churchyard, and later granted them the now-famed African Burial Ground—a damp, low-lying plot of unused terrain east of Broadway along the bank of the Fresh Water, between present-day Duane and Reade Streets. This location was an insult and meant to be: by now the Fresh Water had come to bear its name only as a mockery. Polluted by the area's new industries, notably tanneries, it was no longer the scenic rest stop Jasper Danckaerts passed on his 1679 walk to Corneliszen's tavern. The land around it had turned into a site for executions and a storage dump for weaponry and gunpowder.

While no detailed accounts survive of New York's early black funerals, they seem to have resembled rituals imported from Africa (all the graves thus far excavated in the African Burial Ground, for example, lie along the east-west axis common in Africa and in the American South). Mourners gathered near midnight, and carried the wood coffin of the deceased by torchlight to the grave, in a procession accompanied by music and the distraught wailing of the grief-stricken. In New York the late hour, the flaming torches, the strange music, and the ululation unnerved the nearby white population—to the point that in 1722 they enacted a law commanding that all slave burials be carried out by daylight and attended by no more than a dozen mourners.

Fear and superstition no doubt made white citizens read a subtext of rebellion into African funerals, and perhaps they weren't wholly mistaken. Blacks, more oppressed and deprived the more numerous they became and the more their labor augmented white wealth while adding nothing to their own, had become increasingly resentful. They'd been subjected to ever harsher laws and more savage punishments, banned from the city's chief Christian cemetery, scorned for their paganism yet often denied religious instruction, even when they wanted it. Elias Neau, a Huguenot refugee who saw it as his mission to convert the slaves to Christianity and teach them how to read and write, had set up a night school for them in 1703. This quickly stirred white ire, however, because it gave blacks a reason to be abroad after dark, and that reaction surely infuriated Africans for whom this was an only chance to master the language and adopt the dominant religion of the colony.

Shortly after midnight on Sunday, April 6, 1712, the pent-up resentments of the African population exploded. One by one, somewhere between 25 and 30 Africans (along with a few Indians), slipped into the moonlit orchard of John Crooke, armed with guns, swords, knives, and hatchets. Crooke's property was inconspicuous, lying almost in the middle of the town, off Maiden Lane in a neighborhood of law-abiding coopers. The conspirators waited until two o'clock, when the moon set, steeping the streets in darkness. Two of the Africans, John and Cuffee, then made their way to Peter Vantilbourough's house, near the East River quays in a community of well-off merchants and shipmasters. The raiders set Vantilbourough's outhouse on fire and waited until the commotion roused the neighbors, whom the rebels attacked as they showed up to help quench the blaze.

Robin, a slave, allegedly stuck a dagger into the back of his merchant master, Adrian Hoghlandt. Other whites fell from gunshots, an ax in the neck, a knife in the breast. There were a few survivors, but in the end eight whites lay dead. Hearing guns, the governor, Robert Hunter, ordered a cannon fired in the Fort, which woke the rest of the town. The conspirators fled north into the woods, pursued by militia. Six, knowing what surely lay ahead for them, committed suicide as the soldiers closed in. By the next day all the surviving plotters had been arrested.

Hunter tried to keep the city calm, but the rebels' aim seems to have been to kill as many whites as they could, then—in the resulting panic—to seize the governorship. This news provoked a fury against both actual and suspected conspirators: 21 were executed. Most died by hanging. Several were burned to death. But by far the most barbarous punishments fell upon those who either confessed to murder, or who were, whether truly or falsely, accused of it. Tom, who had shot Adrian Beekman in the chest with a handgun, was condemned to burn "with a slow fire that he may Continue in Torment for eight or Ten hours & continue burning in the said fire until he be dead and Consumed to Ashes."

Robin met with the worst cruelty, probably because he had killed his own master. He was hung up in chains near the African Burial Ground, and left to starve, staring helplessly out over the bleak landscape for three days and nights—the graves, the execution field, Catiemuts Hill, which rose above the Fresh Water, the flat scrub-covered pastureland that covered the site of the present-day City Hall, and the rutted High Road to Boston. When, toward the end, the Reverend John Sharpe of Trinity Church came on a pastoral visit and, as the clergyman later recalled, "exhorted him to confession," Robin—near death and with no reason to lie—protested his innocence. "He said he knew of the Conspiracy but was not guilty of any bloodshed in that tumult." Governor Hunter, stricken by such carefully pondered atrocities, wrote back to England that the cruelty of the punishments carried out against the slaves seemed disgustingly proportionate to friendship between their masters and the sentencing judges. Hunter's remonstrations to London, of course, were of little effect in dampening white vengefulness: the city began clamping down on slaves, and a new law forbade Negroes to appear in the streets after sundown unless they were carrying a lit lantern.

In 1712 New York had as yet no newspapers to spread either truth or falsehood, fact or rumor: the earliest reports of the rebellion appeared in the April 14 issue of the *Boston News-Letter*. Even without the goading of an aroused press, however, New Yorkers and country dwellers had begun to nurse a race-tinged picture of the city night as a coverer of anarchy and violence. And yet, despite persistent tension and small-scale eruptions, no further major outbreak of racial hatred happened for almost thirty years, until the winter of 1740 and 1741—one of the century's harshest. The Hudson froze solid. Six-foot snowdrifts clogged the streets; the normally arduous task of hauling fuel into the city for warmth became backbreaking. Thus in John Hughson's tavern, overlooking the arctic icescape on the Hudson, life was even harder than usual. Hughson and his sixteen-year-old indentured maid, Mary Burton, donning boots and men's work clothes, drove a sleigh up Broadway to gather firewood on the Commons, near the icebound Fresh Water.

It was almost their last taste of normalcy before a fateful disruption that began quietly, on the afternoon of Thursday, February 26, 1741. Down at the corner of Broad Street and Jews' Alley (near present-day South William), Rebecca Hogg was on duty in the shop and boardinghouse she ran with her husband, Robert. The store was respectable, but Jews' Alley—

named for a synagogue built toward the end of the 1600s—harbored several low sailors' dives. According to Rebecca Hogg's later recollection, just as she was readying herself to shut up shop for the day, a seventeen- or eighteen-year-old ship's boy named Wilson walked in, accompanied by a fellow sailor from the man-o'-war *Flamborough,* at present in port.

They said they needed checkered linen, and paid in Spanish coin for a bolt she showed them. But as she made change Hogg saw Wilson peer intently at the pieces of eight cramming her open till. She knew him already—he was friendly with a pair of servants attached to her boarders. What most aroused her suspicion, however, was Wilson's link with people whom a city official later called "some Negroes of very suspicious characters." Later, she named three in particular: Caesar, Prince, and Cuffee.* A few years earlier they'd broken into a tavern at night and stolen a supply of gin, which they then sold off, defiantly dubbing themselves "The Geneva Club." They remained uncowed even when lashed for their crime at the public whipping post.

Hogg smelled a looming robbery plot; hoping to ward it off, she made a show of sending the drawerful of coin off to a neighbor for weighing. The next two days passed without incident, but on the night of Saturday, February 28, someone broke into the shop through a loosely bolted side door that opened into Jews' Alley and made off with £60 worth of silver and dry goods. Suspicion, spurred by Mrs. Hogg's dislike of Wilson, quickly settled on Caesar, Prince, and Cuffee. That led the town's flared nostrils up to John Hughson's tavern, on the banks of the Hudson near Trinity Church.

Hughson had been keeping a low profile, living quietly with his wife, Sarah, his daughter (also Sarah), and Mary Burton. The Hughsons had also recently taken in a lodger. Her real name remains a mystery, though she was variously known as Newfoundland Peggy, or Margaret Carey, or Kerry, or Salingburgh, or Sorubiero. About 21 years old, Irish, beautiful, and apparently a recent immigrant from Newfoundland, she made her living by sex. Her room at the Hughsons' had a window through which clients and lovers climbed in for assignations and out when they were over.

Her string of aliases alone suggests a hard life, but Daniel Horsmanden, who became the city's prosecutorial voice in the bloodbath soon to

---

* Not the same man as the participant in the 1712 uprising. Cuffee was a common name for blacks at the time, probably an allusion to the color of a newly popular beverage: coffee.

occur, and who was more inquisitive about vice than suffering, branded her as "a person of infamous character, a notorious prostitute," and, more loathsome still, "the worst sort, a prostitute to Negroes." Hughson's tavern, like several others in town, catered to slaves; that alone made it a target for suspicion. And in fact Peggy and Caesar were lovers: he was a frequent visitor, paid her rent, and according to rumor had fathered her mixed-race baby, born around Christmas in 1740. In the days immediately following the robbery, rumors flew. Some of the stolen goods were found stashed in a crawl space beneath the floor of John Vaarck's bakery near the Fort—suggestive, because Caesar belonged to Vaarck, and though the cache couldn't be reached from within Vaarck's house, it was easily accessible from the yard of his next-door neighbor John Romme—a shoemaker, tavernkeeper, and suspected fence, whose bar was also a known haunt for slaves.

Next Tuesday Mary Burton showed up at the shop of James Kannady, constable and candle-seller. Along with measuring her out a pound of candles, Kannady's busybody wife, Ann, knowing Burton lived at the Hughsons', instantly set to work, proffering what Horsmanden called "motherly good advice" and a promise to get Burton freed from her indenture to Hughson if she talked. Kannady succeeded in prying a statement out of her, and dragged her before the mayor the next day to confirm it. At two o'clock in the morning on the night of the theft, Burton testified, John Gwin (an alias sometimes used by Caesar), appeared at Peggy's window, climbed in, and then spent the rest of the night with her. When Burton entered their room the next morning she noticed, apart from Peggy and Caesar, a quantity of silver and new speckled linen. They gave her two pieces of the silver and an apron-sized length of the cloth. Shortly afterward Caesar ordered two mugs of punch and bought a pair of white stockings, paying with yet another piece of silver.

Burton's deposition sent the constables straight to the Hughsons: did they know anything about the robbery? They swore they didn't. But the talkative Burton later said that as soon as the constables left, Mrs. Hughson hid the new linen first in the attic, then thought better of this and stashed it under the stairs. Finally, Burton added, on Tuesday morning, just before her candle-buying errand, Hughson's fellow tavernkeeper John Romme had shown up. Burton had, she said, accidentally overheard this exchange between Romme and her master:

"If you will be true to me, I will be true to you," Romme said.

"I will," Hughson replied, "and will never betray you."

This, to the suspicious, suggested that the Hogg robbery had been plotted by Caesar, carried out by the all-black Geneva Club, and abetted by two tavernkeepers long suspected of dealing in stolen goods and offering illegal havens to Africans.

For several weeks the investigation percolated. Then—at first an apparently unrelated event—a fire broke out in the Fort. John Peter Zenger's *New-York Weekly Journal* (which had been appearing since 1733) reported that on Wednesday, March 23,

> about one of the Clock, after noon, a Plumber being at work, in stopping a leak in one of the Gutters, in Fort George, the Roof of the House took fire, and the wind blowing very fresh at South East the Governors House, the Barracks, and Secretaryes Office, were in less than two Hours consumed.

Fire was not the obsession it was to become later, in early 19th-century mercantile New York. So this particular incident, clearly attributable to the roof repairer's soldering kit, produced only shock at the loss of a few important buildings. But then, over the next two weeks, five more unexplained blazes erupted at houses and businesses in odd corners of the city. None were serious, but in a town without running water and only primitive firefighting equipment, worry began to mount, nag, and revert to predictable obsessions. Soon the city was in full cry about gatherings of blacks in the dark of night at houses like Romme's and Hughson's.

In the upshot public opinion writhed itself into the lethal weapon everybody had been hungering for. Caesar, Prince, and Cuffee, whisperers sibilated, were the vanguard of a ring of slaves, whipped up by Hughson and Romme and bent on vengeance against the city: a massacre of citizens to be followed by a coup d'état. The mayor, John Cruger, fell under the influence of Horsmanden, the most aroused city council member, who hammered away without a thought for scruples. Newfoundland Peggy was arrested and thrown into the filthy prison occupying the basement of the new City Hall at Broad and Wall Streets. Authorities bribed a fellow inmate, Arthur Price, to spy on her, but this proved a dead end: he managed to extract from her only a passionate affirmation that Caesar, Prince, and Cuffee "were all truehearted fellows," and a hissed warning to Price himself: "For your life and soul of you, you son of a bitch, don't speak a word of what I have told you."

But other witnesses were falling all over themselves to talk. Young Sarah Hughson rushed in panic to a fortune-teller, who assured her that her father would escape execution and suffer only banishment for his role in the plot. This evidently induced her to gush forth a flood of damning testimony. The suspected, the accused, and the threatened now turned on one another, and Peggy eventually admitted that an insurrection had in fact begun in the fall of 1740 at Romme's, where she often dropped in to drink, sing, play dice, and linger till two or three in the morning. Around Christmas, she said, Romme had advised a group of ten or eleven Africans, gathered at his tavern, to incinerate the houses of the rich, murder the occupants, and make off with their money. She named those who seemed willing to pursue the conspiracy: Cuffee, Caesar, Cato, and Curaçao Dick. Mary Burton added that the intriguers continued to meet over the following weeks at Hughson's, and that they'd decided that once the rebellion had been mounted, Caesar would be declared governor and Hughson anointed as king.

Historians still disagree as to whether the events of 1741 were a true black rebellion or merely a white witch hunt. Threats and promises made to witnesses weaken confidence in their testimony. Supposedly the plot called for fires to be set at night, but they'd all happened in broad daylight. A few slaves confessed to setting particular fires, but these seemed random outbursts of discontent rather than parts of a blueprint for a coup. All the evidence was thin, and much of it contradictory. Nevertheless, an accusatory mania seized the town, playing out into a denouement even crueler and bloodier than the horrors of 1712. By the summer of 1741, 29 blacks, including Caesar, had been hanged or burned alive, and more than twice that number deported. Four whites were executed as well. One was a Catholic priest, John Ury, an innocent sucked into the maelstrom when racism merged easily with New York's already pronounced anti-Catholic bent.

The other white victims were John Hughson, his wife, Sarah, and Peggy, all brought together on June 12 to the execution ground near the Fresh Water, within view of Caesar's rotting corpse, displayed on a nearby platform. According to Horsmanden, John Hughson, believing that a band of angels would waft him off the scaffold, lifted one hand high, finger pointing heavenward, as if to identify himself to celestial rescuers. Sarah Hughson, Horsmanden reported, "stood like a lifeless trunk, with the rope about her neck; . . . she said not a word, and had scarce any visible motion." Peggy seemed determined to speak, until Sarah, according to some observers, reached over and gave her a sharp push. In the end New-foundland Peggy died silent, and the child she'd borne with Caesar passed into the care of young Sarah Hughson.

BEFORE THE REVOLUTION:
EVENINGS WITH THE YANKEE ARISTOCRACY

After 1741, New York's murderous fear of its slaves ebbed, overshadowed by the colonial wars, the Revolution, and the British military occupation of New York—though it no doubt added to the accumulating sense of threat that was now part of the urban night. Of course as the city grew, and began to immerse itself in the current of world events, it developed not only a secret nightlife but a public, purposefully civilized one meant to rise above the tensions and broils of the streets. Taverns quickly adapted to this new demand for sophistication, with a few proprietors lifting their establishments above the beer, wine, and grog of the common pothouse.

Nonetheless social drinking retained its prominence in mid-18th-century New York. Dr. Alexander Hamilton,* a Baltimorean who visited during the summer of 1744, wrote, "I was tired of nothing here but their excessive drinking," and this was a common sentiment among tourists and newcomers. There were nearly 1,100 taverns by 1800, but they'd begun to diversify. Hamilton boarded with Robert and Rebecca Hogg, who were still keeping shop at the corner of Broad Street and Jews' Alley. Hamilton liked Rebecca, who served the breakfast and tea, but branded Robert a lout: once, within his wife's hearing, Hogg had announced to the table that the best cure for female hysteria was "a good mowing." So, in search of better company, Hamilton took a short walk down Broad Street toward the river, and went to Robert Todd's tavern.

Todd's had become a favorite among the well-off and well-spoken. It served as the departure point for the Boston mail, which drew merchants and men of affairs, who made it the headquarters of a nightly gathering called the Hungarian Club, which convened a little after six and broke up around eleven, with Todd, a garrulous Scot, intermittently dropping in to deliver an impromptu lecture. The evening Hamilton attended, his topic was cooking. "Praised be God," Todd began, "as to cuikery, I defaa ony

* No relation to the founding father, who arrived on the scene almost thirty years later.

French cuik to ding [i.e., outdo] me, bot a haggis is a dish I wadna tak the trouble to mak." He was later heard upstairs, bellowing at a maid, "Dam ye bitch, wharefor winna ye bring a canle?"

Evening tavern clubs had become common, opening with a mock-solemn ceremony, followed by a discussion and a string of toasts. In theory it was to be a civilized forum, convivial but serious, for men of linked interests and sensibilities. Hamilton said, though, that for the Hungarian Club drinking was the featured event: "two or three toapers . . . seemed to be of opinion that a man could not have a more social quality or endue-ment than to be able to pour down seas of liquor and remain uncon-quered while others sunk under the table." He left the gathering at ten o'clock, and walked back up to the Hoggs' "pritty well flushed with my three bumpers."

But Todd's was more than a forum for genteel souse parties: it also sponsored formal evening concerts. Hamilton heard a flute and violin per-formance there on June 19 and remarked favorably on its quality. Eight years before, in January 1736, both the *Gazette* and the *Journal* advertised a concert at Todd's, which may have been New York's first public musical program, and it featured Charles Pachelbel (the son of Johann, composer of the inescapable "Canon"), in a concert that started at 6 p.m. on Janu-ary 21; tickets were four shillings, and could be bought in advance either at Todd's or next door at the Coffee House. Pachelbel played the harpsi-chord, and in that sense the program was professional, though the an-nouncements said the vocals, as well as the violin and flute parts, would be performed by "private Hands"—probably local amateurs, perhaps Pachelbel's students.

This wasn't the Academy of Music, or Carnegie Hall, but New York was beginning to assemble the necessary entrepreneurs, customers, ven-ues, and advertising media that helped to plant the idea of an evening out in the public mind. As new pastimes appeared, long-established busi-nesses retooled to accommodate them. Night schools like Neau's became common, widely attended by apprentices and indentured servants done with the day's work. Adrian and Rebecca Corneliszens' tavern, so unpre-possessing to Jasper Danckaerts in 1679, had been taken over by John Clapp in the 1690s. Because the place had become a stopover for travelers headed north, Clapp added a hackney coach depot and thus inaugurated New York's first true cab service. He founded the John Club, which met annually on June 24, the feast of John the Baptist. Clapp advertised the event in the almanac he published (New York's first), inviting every man in the city named John.

Clapp's, like the Corneliszens', was a magnet for country walks and rides: Benjamin Bullivant, a physician who visited in June 1697, stopped there on a midsummer Saturday evening drive with the governor of the colony, Colonel Benjamin Fletcher. Bullivant described it as "a kind of pleasure garden," praising its cider and mead (made, probably, from the apples and honey in Rebecca Corneliszen's orchards). Bullivant and Fletcher came back the next afternoon for one of Clapp's famous dinners: "an excellent Soupe—a dish of Beanes and bacon—a dish of roasted Lamb and Sallad—a dish of young peas—a dish of roasted chickens a Dish of tarts—a Dish of curds & Creame—a dish of Cherries, a dish of mulberries & Currants." Clapp had expanded the tavern into an early approximation of a modern city restaurant—a destination rather than just a stop, mixing the pleasures of atmosphere and food.

London and Paris were the metropolises New Yorkers looked to for innovations, and London's theaters and coffeehouses—both of which had evolved from taverns and inns—were among the earliest transatlantic imports, with coffeehouses the first to arrive. Europeans had tasted their first coffee in the 1600s, and it rapidly became a ritual both soothing and enlivening, ideal for conversation because it stimulated without clouding the mind. Coffeehouses appeared in London in the early 17th century; Procope, the pioneer Paris establishment, opened in 1686 (it remains in business today). New York's earliest imitation, the King's Arms, began as a tavern on the west side of Broadway in 1696.* Later it began serving coffee—along with food and drink—in green-curtained booths in the barroom. Having ordered, patrons could sit at leisure, browsing in an ample supply of newspapers and journals, in the 1700s still mostly dominated by commercial and shipping news.

Ideal places to discuss the papers, hear the gossip of trade, and make deals, the coffeehouses quickly evolved into male bastions—clubs for the city's well-connected merchants and officials. At the King's Arms one could reserve private meeting rooms upstairs; there was even a roof garden overlooking the Hudson. Both the King's Arms and the succession of coffee-

---

* Lord Cornbury, the governor from 1702 to 1708—best known for his public appearances in an elaborate 18th-century drag, possibly designed to remind the citizens of his blood relationship to Queen Anne—also apparently once rode his horse into the King's Arms bar and demanded a drink.

houses that followed it (most famously the Tontine, opened at the corner of Wall and Water Streets in 1793), were ideal places to do business, quickly became, in effect, New York's earliest commodities markets, and were a major step in the formation of the clubby, often informal syndicates of influential men that have been running much of the city's life ever since.

Coffeehouses were also, like the better taverns, a natural venue for entertainment. Dancing was common at both, and gradually became popular enough to be institutionalized. Dance assemblies, usually scheduled for Thursday nights, became a recurring feature of the New York season. One cycle began in the 1750s in the New York Arms on Broadway: each ball began at eight, went on till midnight, and charged a steep 8 shillings for admission. Another series, held in the Long Room of Burns's King's Head Tavern near the Battery, began Thursday, October 30, 1766, and recurred every two weeks.

George Washington remarked, during his residence in the city, on the pleasantness of an evening walk along the Battery, and even before that entrepreneurs had seen opportunities in alfresco nighttime entertainment. Encouraged by the success of country taverns like Clapp's, two pleasure gardens, Vauxhall and Ranelagh (both named after London models), were in business by mid-century. Ranelagh, opened by John Jones in 1765, lay along Broadway, near the present-day City Hall. It was just west of the Fresh Water and the African Burial Ground, but carefully fenced off to seem of another world entirely. Vauxhall, its chief rival in the 1760s, was further northwest, near the Hudson River between present-day Warren and Chambers Streets (P.S. 234 now stands near its site). When its owner, Samuel Fraunces (also the proprietor of Fraunces Tavern, still operating today), put Vauxhall up for sale in 1773, his advertisement described two sizable gardens, a house with four rooms on each floor and twelve fireplaces, plus a 26-by-56-foot banqueting hall with a kitchen underneath.

Pleasure gardens have largely vanished from the American landscape, though their atmosphere resembled perhaps their only 20th-century descendant: the revival of Bryant Park in the 1990s, with its restaurants, fast-food kiosks, and changing exhibits, summer-night movies, and performances— lively but reassuringly sedate. The pleasure gardens also prefigured the wholesome frivolity of modern corporate amusement and theme parks. Vauxhall, for instance, specialized in outdoor waxworks: in the summer of 1768 it showed off a Madame Tussaud's–style rendering of the life of Publius Scipio, the Roman conqueror of Carthage. The *pièce de résistance* was in a separate pavilion on the grounds—a montage of the general "standing by his tent pitched in a grove of trees." It showed until ten at night.

Ranelagh featured music, food, a candlelit dance pavilion, and private drawing rooms sequestered in the greenery. A band played Monday and Thursday evenings, and the gardens could handle large-scale dinners. But fireworks were its standout draw. Back in the 1600s, these had been reserved for major events like the arrival of a new governor, and seem to have been fairly simple in concept and execution. But by the mid-1760s they'd become standard during outdoor concert intermissions, and boasted clever and imaginative effects. A show at Ranelagh on May 14, 1767, included, according to the *Journal*, "Six Rockets, one Pigeon on a cord, which will communicate Fire to an illuminated Pedestal, which will change to China Fire and Italian Candles, after to an Egyptian Pyramid, changing to different Colours, then will communicate Fire to a Tornant,* and then to a Piece representing a Cistern of Water, going out and coming in several Times, after will communicate Fire to a Tornant of two Sorts of Brilliant Fire, which will communicate Fire to a Piece representing the Sun; the whole to conclude with a flight of Rockets and Hand Grenades."

Vauxhall, Ranelagh, and their ilk, like many earlier and later night resorts, kept closing, changing hands, moving, and reopening, but they became a perennial feature of the entertainment scene until the 20th century. Niblo's Garden, a long-lived attraction, debuted in 1829 and remained enduringly popular until it closed in 1895. German immigrants imported beer gardens to the city in the 1880s. And as late as World War I, theaters and nightclubs built roof gardens to draw summer business before the advent of air-conditioning. The original Ranelagh had vanished before 1800, but Vauxhall enjoyed a long if itinerant existence, around 1798 relocating to Broome Street between Broadway and the Bowery. In 1805 it decamped again, to a site bordered by present-day Astor Place, 4th Street, Broadway, and the Bowery—roughly the same location as Corneliszens' and Clapp's. This last Vauxhall featured, at various times, an equestrian statue of George Washington, a theater, and a labyrinth of groves, gravel walks, summer pavilions, and tables under the trees. A rectangle of private boxes, not unlike those in a theater, opened on to the garden and walled it off from the street.

---

* A Tornant seems to have been a sort of fuse, designed to transfer fire from one device to another in order to produce a continuous display of effects.

Newspapers, new to the 1700s, were an essential catalyst to the invention of nightlife, advertising the attractions at places like Vauxhall and Ranelagh, and reporting (haphazardly at first) what had been going on in the streets while the citizens slept. Like William Bradford's *New-York Gazette,* founded in 1725, most were four-page weeklies. None had the predatory 24-hour reporting staff that was to become common in the next century; at first they were mostly digests of commercial fact and political opinion. But eventually they became sounding boards that captured and amplified the leisure life of the town after dark: by the last third of the 1700s, they were running theater advertisements, reviews already full of the scoffs and sneers inseparable from the genre, and announcements of all kinds of intriguing exhibits and strange shows.

These were becoming numerous. Touring displays—animals, waxworks, magic lantern presentations, demonstrations of and lectures about scientific novelties like electricity—were more or less weekly events every fall and winter. Among the more remarkable, judging from the attention newspapers gave it, was Henry Bridges's Microcosm. It arrived from Philadelphia in 1756, and went on view every Monday, Wednesday, and Friday night in the Assembly Room of the New Exchange at the foot of Broad Street. Built by Bridges at Waltham Abbey in England in 1718, the Microcosm survived a transatlantic crossing to North America as well as the rough journeys from Philadelphia to New York and Boston.

It was—and is, since it still exists—in essence a mechanical clock, but with remarkably intricate works. An advertisement in the *New-York Mercury* called it "a most beautiful Composition of Architecture, Sculpture, and Painting," which "plays with great Exactness several pieces of Music, and exhibits, by an amazing variety of Moving Figures, Scenes diversified with Natural Beauties, Operations of Art, of Human Employments and Diversions of passing as in real life." Against slowly unfurling painted landscapes, the machinery executed a ballet of whirling stars and planets, a concert by the nine muses, a scene in a carpenter's yard. The show ended with a reveal, in which the audience saw all 1,200 wheels and pinions of the apparatus cranking, pumping, and spinning in synchrony. After its American tour the Microcosm went back to England; it now belongs to the British Museum.*

* Richard Altick's *Shows of London* (1978), pp. 60–62, features an engraving of Bridges's Microcosm in which it appears considerably larger than suggested by accounts in the New York newspapers.

INTO THE DARK:
THE GREAT FIRE OF 1776 AND THE URBAN UNDERWORLD

Night, despite incursions of civilization, never lost the frisson of terror that accounts for at least half its mythology. Cities are as much defenses against nightfall as platforms for daytime business—lit to ward darkness off even beyond the walls of home, populated to relieve isolation, and for much of history fortified and gated to exclude predators or invaders. And by the early 1770s, with tensions thickening as the Revolution approached, night fears, never quelled, mingled with the new diversions, and the press started to display a new alertness to the mysteries and anomalies of night as well as its amusements.

Newspapers had begun to cover occasional nightmares bolting out from the complacency if not the sleep of 18th-century rationalism—harbingers of the noirish atmosphere so essential to the romance of the 20th-century night. On January 3, 1771, for example, the *New-York Journal* reported the grim and bafflingly peculiar death of Hannah "Man-o'-War Nance" Bradshaw (the nickname reflected her heroic frame, capacity for drink, and hospitality to sailors). A visiting friend left her at seven o'clock in her one-room lodging at a house on Division Street on New Year's Eve, a little drunk but otherwise well.

Next morning, however, she failed to answer early knocks at her door. Shortly after 11 a.m. a woman who worked for her, increasingly worried, finally broke a window and saw what the *Journal* called "the most shocking spectacle imaginable." A charred four-foot-wide hole had opened up in the middle of the wood floor, and some of Bradshaw's skeleton had plunged about a foot into the dirt of the crawl space beneath. Surrounding the pit were a leg fragment still clad in its stocking and the remainder of her bones (some blackened, some burned to a light ash). Her flesh had been entirely consumed, except for intestines and some bits of head, shoulder, and leg. A bloodcurdling sludge, like lampblack, coated the ceiling, walls, and windows. Apparently, Man-o'-War Nance had spontaneously combusted.

So bizarre and memorable was the incident that 50 years later William Dunlap (1766–1839), who would become a mainstay of the post-Revolutionary New York cultural milieu, recalled it and insisted that it was no hoax. To this day no one knows whether or not spontaneous human combustion really happens (it has never been witnessed by an observer who could satisfy skeptics). The earliest purportedly factual description had been published in Paris in 1763, and the details of Nance's death are suggestively similar, as if, like more familiar ideas current in the early American republic, a fascination with spontaneous combustion were an import from France, even then in the avant-garde when it came to night. Whatever really happened to Hannah Bradshaw on New Year's 1772, her death heralds a new perception of night as a realm of mystery so potent that imagination often supplied material where the facts failed. This was, after all, also the dawning era of the Gothic novel, with its parade of uncanny nocturnal predators and creepy mysteries.

But it was only a premonitory shiver and a jolt to the imagination; as the 1770s progressed New York was increasingly preoccupied with shocks administered by hard reality: the city suffered severely in the earliest days of the Revolution. In August 1776, with war underway in earnest, Sir William Howe had already driven Washington and his forces from Brooklyn Heights. Then, on September 14, the Americans abandoned lower Manhattan, leaving confusion and panic behind. By September 15 citizens were fleeing the city as a flood of cheering Loyalists surged in and the British army patrolled the streets, sometimes trying to restore order, sometimes rubbing in their triumph or extracting vengeance.

Before the city could even begin to adjust, it was struck by another disaster on the scale of the 1643 massacre. The agent of destruction now was fire. Shortly after midnight on the morning of September 21, 1776, a blaze erupted in a small wooden house on or near Dock Street, hard by the slip at the foot of Whitehall. The source of the fire may have been the Fighting Cocks tavern (which had, according to one witness, become a dive for "men and women of a bad character").

A hard wind had set in from the southeast, barreling down the slopes of Brooklyn Heights and slamming into the Manhattan wharves. The weather had been dry, and the cedar shingles that zigzagged up and down the gables of the city (having replaced the old, fireproof ceramic Dutch roofing tiles) made an abundance of tinder. The flames jumped into them near where Broad Street ended at the East River. With all the lanes and alleys dark and empty, thanks both to the wind and fear of British troops, fire began a propulsive danse macabre to the north and west. Flames gobbled their way up Broad Street, rising ever higher as they reached the blocks between Broad and the Fort. They swept across Bridge Street, then across Stone Street, engulfing the site of Geraerdy's old Wooden Horse.

Following the route Jan Damen and Philip Geraerdy had taken in their 1643 midnight walk, it tumbled over Marketfield and Beaver Streets. It passed just north of the Fort's main gate, and eerily illuminated an empty pedestal: a leaden statue of George III on a horse that had stood behind a fence near the present-day Bowling Green, had been dragged down by a mob on July 10. Then the flames jumped across Broadway and devoured the mansion in which General Howe had set up his headquarters. There was no proper alarm: the Americans had taken away the city's fire bells when they decamped.

In any case the conflagration had reached a scale that mocked 18th-century firefighting techniques: now it made a right turn and began to grind up the west side of Broadway like a steamroller, smashing everything in its path. Block by block, fire began to tear away the darkness; flames, like serpentine floodlights, closed in on and soon began to illuminate the steeple of Trinity Church, at 180 feet the tallest structure in the city (in fact in North America), rising from its hill on Broadway, across from the site of Jan Damen's old manor house, demolished back in 1673.

Trinity wasn't to be spared. The fire snapped it up in the night's culminating and most horrific spectacle. Flames pounded the sanctuary and nave, then slapped at the tower, roaring up to the wooden pinnacle, which, according to the *New-York Mercury*, was now an inferno, "a vast Pyramid of Fire, . . . a most grand and awful Spectacle." In the darkness the burning tower was visible for miles west into New Jersey and miles east on Long Island. Washington's troops gazed on it awestruck from their encampment on Harlem Heights. The flames spiraled upward, consuming the stout wood beams into a frail skeleton tracery of ash, and the tower collapsed on itself as if vacuumed into the earth by a huge intake of breath.

This was almost 225 years to the day before the attacks on the World Trade Center.

With this final display the fire seems to have exhausted itself; it was out between ten and eleven the next morning. Recriminations were instant. The English blamed the Americans, saying that after the first outbreak other fires had been set at other locations by cabals of rebels determined to sour the British victory. The Americans denied this accusation, though without much conviction, because the fire had in fact spoiled the triumph of the occupiers. A full quarter of their newly conquered prize now lay in ruins.

Unlike Trinity, St. Paul's Chapel at Vesey Street survived. But much of the surrounding neighborhood had been charred—including the "Holy Ground," a tract so dubbed not only because much of it belonged to St. Paul's, but also ironically, because it had become notorious for its resident prostitutes. Vice, however, wasn't to be scoured out by fire, and the city's herd of black sheep quickly recovered from the setback. New Amsterdam's cradle, Philip Geraerdy's old neighborhood by the Fort, also wrecked, had been quickly reborn as a shameless sinkhole of license and lust whose sins outdid the well-groomed, pre-Revolutionary tartiness of the Holy Ground.

Few spoke in public about this new dockside Sodom. Canvas Town, or (its alternate name) Topsail Town, rose as a chaos of shanties almost overnight from the smoking wreckage. The most complete surviving description is in the memoirs of the man who never forgot Nance Bradshaw: William Dunlap—later a painter, writer, playwright, and theater impresario. In 1776 he was a child of ten, but, as he recalled just before his death in 1839, "over the ruins of this fire I have wandered, when a boy, in every direction." Many of the burned blocks had returned to a semblance of normalcy, but "the ruins on the south-east side of the town," he recalled, "were converted into dwelling places by using the chimneys and parts of walls which were firm, and adding pieces of spars, with old canvass from ships, forming hovels—part hut and part tent. This was called 'Canvass-Town;' and was the receptacle and resort of the vilest dregs brought by the army and navy of Britain, with the filthiest of those who fled to them for refuge."

Strangely, this neighborhood provoked little comment from others. George Washington, for whom the Battery was a favorite evening walk, never noted the tattered sailcloth-patched slum clearly visible from its eastern rampart (nor, for that matter, did he ever comment on the streetwalkers plying the Battery itself). Canvas Town began barely 50 feet from Fraunces Tavern, spared by the fire, Washington's favorite resort, and the site of his farewell to his officers in 1783. By 1785 the federal government began renting rooms in it to serve as offices.

Yet everybody seems either to have ignored or shrugged off without comment the squalor just outside Samuel Fraunces's windows, and Canvas Town continued to elude the beady eye of inquiry until 1784, when Mayor James Duane ordered a grand jury to investigate (said a report in the August 17 *Gazetteer*) "the riot and disorder which prevailed in the

South ward of this city." The jurors "went to each house and made a minute inquiry into the number of inhabitants, the manner in which they got their livelihood, and such other circumstances as occurred from the appearance of the place." In the upshot the jury decided to "suppress the numerous receptacles for the vicious and abandoned, in that part of the ward which passes under the denomination of—Canvas town." Bridewell, the city's first large prison (it had gone up near today's City Hall in 1775), was to receive most of those caught up in the subsequent sweep: it was, the *Gazetteer* sneered, "fitting up as a school for the reformation of manners!"

On September 30, the sheriff did indeed invade and demolish several shacks, but that seems barely to have dented trade; reputable citizens simply carried on their business in spite of it. On February 1, 1790, for instance, the first session of the United States Supreme Court met in the New Exchange building, on Broad Street near Water, and thus smack in the middle of Canvas Town's riot and revelry, which seems to have occasioned no particular comment. In early post-Revolutionary New York, the classes rubbed elbows intimately. It was not until the next century that the town had grown large enough for the poor and the rich to live out of each other's sight.

Though even Dunlap seemed unwilling to describe Canvas Town in detail, it's not difficult to guess what it was like: a modern South American urban shantytown, full of vice, certainly, but also desperation, its codependent twin. And though the canvas roofs were novel, the life beneath them wasn't. From the moment it was first built, in the 1730s, the Battery drew the prostitutes who had always haunted the vicinity of the Fort. As Dr. Alexander Hamilton described it in 1744, it was "a great half moon or semicircular rampart bluff upon the water, being turf upon a stone foundation about 100 paces in length, the platform of which is laid in some places with plank, in others with flag stone. Upon it there are 56 great iron guns, well mounted, most of them being 32 pounders."

And it was a streetwalkers' marketplace. "Mr. J[effrey]s told me," Hamilton continued, "that to walk out after dusk upon this platform was a good way for a stranger to fit himself with a courtezan, for that place was the generall rendezvous of the fair sex of that profession after sun set. He told me there was a good choice of pritty lasses among them, both Dutch and English." Prostitution, as the Holy Ground also attested, had plainly become a more elaborate affair than down-and-out women furtively soliciting drunken soldiers and sailors, or Newfoundland Peggy, living in a rented room in an obscure, out-of-the-way tavern like Hugh-son's.

Bought sex was beginning to condense into particular neighborhoods, and records from the era reflect an undercurrent of worry about "disorderly houses." The term dated back to Dutch times: Cornelis Van Tienhoven claimed to have closed one down in 1654. By the 1700s court records and newspapers were reporting them but usually without dwelling on detail, so it's rarely clear how they operated or who the clients were. Bawdy houses showed a predictable preference for marginal neighborhoods, with the Fresh Water a common location: Catherine O'Neil, alias Catherine Tregaw, kept one in the area and had gotten in trouble for it as early as 1767, when she faced a grand jury charge that she

> did keep and maintain a certain Common and illgoverned and disorderly house; and . . . there for her own lucre and gain unlawfully and willfully did Cause and procure certain evil and ill-disposed persons as well men as women of evil Name & fame and of dishonest Conversation to frequent & Come together in the said house; . . . and then and the said Other days and times, there unlawfully and willfully did permit and yet doth permit, the said men and women at unlawful times, as well in the night as in the day, to be and remain in the house . . . drinking, tipling, quarrelling, fighting, Whoring and misbehaving themselves to the great damage and Common Nuisance of all.

A disorderly house was not necessarily a full-fledged brothel of the kind that would proliferate early in the next century, permanently staffed and selling both sex and trimmings like food and drink. Rather, O'Neil's appears to have resembled Hughson's: a hybrid house of assignation and bar that catered to customers unwelcome elsewhere. The mention of "as well men as women of evil Name & fame" may suggest to the eagle eye of the 21st century a possible homosexual clientele as well. Whatever went on in her house, the court found O'Neil guilty. Her sentence isn't known, but the phenomenon didn't fade: two other women indicted for keeping disorderly houses in 1799 spent three months in prison, accompanied by hard labor in one case and a $100 fine in the other. Such comparatively light punishments suggest that disorderly houses were tolerated unless they became obtrusive enough to upset neighbors, and according to the historian Douglas Greenberg, keepers of disorderly houses in the period yielded the lowest conviction rate of any major crime, including crimes by officials, a well-protected group.

John Street Overture: Theater in the Later 1700s

Formal, socially countenanced entertainment kept pace, more or less, with demimonde entrepreneurship like Catherine O'Neil's. Theater became a dependable commodity in New York in the 1730s and 40s, with professional dramatic performances given on makeshift tavern or warehouse stages, along the lines of the early concerts at Todd's. Williamsburg, Virginia had opened a purpose-built playhouse in 1716, but New York seems to have lagged behind until 1732, when Manhattan could finally boast one or possibly two theater buildings, one on Broadway, near present-day Exchange Place, the other closer to the East River on either Pearl or Nassau Street. Two more appeared in 1758 and 1761.

But 1767 marked the first indelible breakthrough, with the opening of the John Street Theatre, just east of Broadway on the north side of the street. Unlike earlier houses it endured for a generation, spanning the Revolution, the occupation, and the early republic. It also left a well-documented history behind after it finally went dark in 1798. Its opening nights became much-commented-on social occasions, and prompted reviews by hatchet-wielding press critics. Actors became local celebrities, their triumphs, feuds, and debacles a constant topic of gossip. The city's elite, swanning from the boxes in the latest fashions from Europe, were the most dazzling of the audience, but everybody went there.

Both the inherently unpredictable nature of the theater business and the onset of the Revolution guaranteed the John Street Theatre an eventful history. In October 1774, the Continental Congress urged that all places of amusement be shut down, and John Street seems to have complied by the summer of 1775. Its leading actors, the British-born Hallams (New York's first true acting dynasty in the later Booth and Barrymore mold), sailed away to Jamaica and didn't return to New York for a decade. Nonetheless, the 1776 fire spared the theater building (though the flames passed within yards of it), and the occupying British army officers, whiling their spare time away on amateur theater, filled the gap left by the Hallams. On January 25, 1777, they reopened the John Street with

Henry Fielding's farce *The Tragedy of Tragedies; or, the Life and Death of Tom Thumb the Great*. Soon they gave the house a new finger-in-your-eye name, the Theatre-Royal. Navy and army officers acted all the parts; Major John André, better known to history as a spy and Benedict Arnold's co-conspirator, painted scenery for a hobby. Profits were supposed to go into a fund for the dependents of fallen soldiers (by 1778, however, the company had spent £3,169 on production expenses, leaving only £140 for the widows and orphans).

Once the Revolution was over and the John Street back in civilian hands, it began to find a voice of its own as a definitively American institution, gradually venturing beyond the 17th- and 18th-century English plays that had dominated its repertory both before and during the war. In this respect the 1787 premiere of Royall Tyler's *The Contrast* was a landmark, probably the first professionally written and performed American comedy with American characters. *The Contrast* remains playable, though not quite the masterful satire of New York society it aspired to be. Its lumbering story puts two pairs of lovers, one virtuous and the other venial, through a series of confusions and misunderstandings that (as a reviewer in the *Daily Advertiser* for April 18, 1787, remarked) "wants the pruning knife very much."

Tyler enlivened this clanking plot with a running commentary by the characters behind the footlights on the city surrounding them and the audience in front of them. Jonathan, fresh off his family's Massachusetts farm, instantly proved *The Contrast*'s most popular character, and the progenitor of a long lineage of canny rubes in the big city that led through Li'l Abner, Pa Kettle, and Hazel Flagg to the Beverly Hillbillies. Jonathan is a goggle-eyed sightseer, an alternately baffled and shrewd observer of city life. Looking for a church to pray in, he heads logically enough for the Holy Ground, only to encounter the red-light district we noted previously. According to Patrick M'Robert, who had visited in 1774, it harbored upward of 500 prostitutes—among whom, he said, were "many well dressed women and it is remarkable that they live in much greater Cordiality with one another than any nests of that kind do in Britain or Ireland." But Jonathan sees only beckoning whores posing shamelessly on benches. Shocked (as he tells the lady's maid listening to his adventure), he wanders a block south as darkness falls, searching for "Mr. Morrison, the hocus-pocus man," a street performer famous because "they said as how he could eat a case knife."

Jonathan makes a random left into John Street and comes upon the theater just in time for the 6 p.m. curtain. His description, apparently accurate, is perhaps the most detailed portrait we have of a New York playhouse in the 1700s. "As I was going about . . . to find it," he says, "I saw a great crowd of folks going into a long entry, that had lanterns over the door" (the streets were dark by six, even in April: Benjamin Franklin had proposed instituting a period of Daylight Saving Time in 1784, but his suggestion wasn't taken up until the 20th century). The theater itself was a dumpy, red-painted wooden structure on a back lot, with a 60-foot-long covered and wood-paved alleyway leading from the door to John Street. The two lanterns were lit to announce a show, which usually began at six or seven—a sensible curtain time since even formal dinners were given in the afternoon. The normal performance days were Monday, Wednesday, and Friday: weekends hadn't yet attained their modern status as official playtime.

Jonathan paid three shillings for admission to the gallery. A place in the pit cost five shillings, the two tiers of boxes eight shillings each. A single drawing of the John Street's interior survives, showing the narrow stage and several rows of spectators on benches in the pit, but not the gallery or boxes—which Jonathan describes as looking "just like father's corncribs." Seats were unreserved, though anyone who wanted a box could send a servant at four in the afternoon to hold it till the family and their guests arrived.

As the audience gathered, the auditorium shed its ramshackle character—mercilessly revealed in the drawing—and filled with a scintillating wash of light and sound. The weaving, ductile glow of multiple candles made up in drama what it lacked in wattage. And the air of anticipation wasn't merely innocent: although Jonathan doesn't mention the fact, he would, sitting up in the third tier, probably have been surrounded by prostitutes, their pimps, and their customers.* Theaters tolerated (and sometimes even encouraged) lust in the gallery from the very beginning, maybe because prostitutes were faithful theater patrons, and because they attracted ticket-buying admirers. The phenomenon quickly became nearly universal, and later houses often built a separate entrance to the third tier to appease the box-holding classes.

---

* In later New York theaters, the third tier became almost institutionalized as a haunt for prostitutes, whom respectable theatergoers seem to have put up with as long as they couldn't be seen from the family box. The phrase "Third Tier" stuck, and became virtually synonymous with lewd behavior.

In the pit a dozen or so musicians sawed away until a green curtain lifted and the show began. Ancient theatrical custom, stretching back at least as far as Greek drama, demanded variety, and the John Street complied. Most audiences saw not just a full-length play, but also a farce, some songs and dances, a short opera or musical (the two genres were synonymous in New York in the 1700s), even stand-up comedy routines. Such, more or less, had been the program at Shakespeare's Globe, and relics survived into the 20th century in the double features, serials, cartoons, newsreels, and short subjects once presented by movie theaters. Promotional film trailers and television commercials inherit some fragments from this vaudevillesque tradition even now, though their mercenary intent traduces the spirit of it.

Footlights, amplified by reflectors, brought the intense blues, reds, greens, and yellows of the costumes and stage fittings to vibrant life, though they also threw grotesque shadows onto the actors' faces. Mechanical spectacle, while it became more common over time, was unusual. Scenery seems to have consisted mainly of flats that slid on and off stage, and backcloths to be raised or lowered. But the show put on by the audience made up for any lack in production values, at least according to Charlotte, *The Contrast*'s dizzy soubrette:

First we bow round to the company in general, then to each one in particular, then we have so many inquiries after each other's health, and we are so happy to meet each other, and it is so many ages since we had that pleasure, and, if a married lady is in company, we have such a sweet dissertation upon her son Bobby's chin cough, then the curtain rises, then our sensibility is all awake, and then by the mere force of apprehension, we torture some harmless expression into a double meaning which the poor author never dreamt of, and then we have recourse to our fans, and then we blush, and then the gentlemen jog one another, peep under the fan, and make the prettiest remarks; and then we giggle and they simper, and then the curtain drops, and then for nuts and oranges, and then we bow, and it's pray Ma'am take it, and pray Sir keep it, and oh! not for the world, Sir: and then the curtain rises again, and then we blush, and giggle, and simper, and bow, all over again. Oh! the sentimental charms of a side-box conversation! (*All laugh.*)

Tyler hoped the audience would find this funny and they did: while everybody seems to have disliked the two main characters, who courted like two damp and sluggish mollusks, Charlotte was a popular role and Jonathan, played by Thomas Wignell, got laughs so big that Lewis Hallam and John Henry, who filled other parts in the production (and who, not incidentally, ran the theater) got jealous and struck *The Contrast* from their repertory despite its success.

John Street naughtiness wasn't always hidden up in the gallery or behind fluttering fans in the boxes. Riots were common, and 1796 seems to have ushered in a particularly rowdy season. On November 2 a pair of drunken sea captains at a performance of a Gothic thriller, *The Mysterious Monk,* shouted down the overture and insisted that the orchestra play "Yankee Doodle" instead. Some males from the audience jostled them out of the theater, but they staggered down to the East River waterfront, mustered their ships' crews, and stormed back up John Street. The ensuing disturbance ended in a number of arrests, and an ineffectual plea from the theater (in an ad in the November 9 *Minerva*): "much confusion having arisen from the introduction of Liquor into the house, during the performance . . . gentlemen will not call for any till the conclusion of the First Piece."

Actor troublemakers were less violent, but more inventive. Mrs. Hallam (though she was well known at the John Street, her first name hasn't survived) provoked another fluff the following March. She'd originated the role of Jenny, the maid who listens to Jonathan's stories in *The Contrast,* but had degenerated over the years into an onstage drunk. In a memoir of their epochal feud, the Hallams' archrival John Hodgkinson later alleged that before one performance she'd passed out, sliding off a chair and out from under the wig her dresser was trying to arrange on her head. Only by herculean efforts, including a strong dose of vinegar and green tea, Hodgkinson said, were he and the dresser able to wake her up, slap her into a simulacrum of sobriety, and push her onstage in time for the curtain.

Mrs. Hallam took a brief sabbatical, dried herself out, and returned to the John Street. But then, during an evening performance of *The Fashionable Lover* on March 29, 1797, in which Hodgkinson was acting, she oozed out from the wings in a black silk dress, then began brandishing a sheet of paper. Hodgkinson, engrossed in playing his role, didn't notice her until applause broke out. Then, as he looked back in shock, Henry Hallam strode in, also dressed emphatically in black, pleading that the audience be allowed to hear his wife's apologia. She apparently moved them, because the next evening they hissed Hodgkinson off the stage, and he lay low for the rest of the season. It was a scandal, outshining even the November riot: the foibles of celebrities were on their way to becoming a staple of public entertainment. In time the John Street feud was a century and a half away from the showbiz world of Walter Winchell, but in concept it was identical.

If civilized New York still lagged the European capitals, its evenings were no longer confined to taverns. Some novelty now beckoned every night of the week. For the well off, it was perhaps a life more full and pleasant than any the city has furnished since. Commerce paused for the long afternoon dinner that often sociably continued into evenings at the theater, an assembly ball, an exhibition, or at an institutionalized social gathering like the Hungarians at Todd's. It was pleasure with amplitude, and, as its veterans remembered, around 1800 an established New Yorker could achieve a graceful balance among duty, conviviality, enlivening gossip, and solitary pleasure.*

William Dunlap, who by the end of the 1700s had bought the John Street Theatre and then undertook the building of its glamorous successor, the Park, was a member of this republican aristocracy's cultural wing. Like most men of his ilk, he kept a store: in 1793 he was on Queen Street, where he sold glass and mirrors. But, like his compeers, Dunlap kept moneymaking in its place. It was one activity among many, and to him at least not the most compelling. He'd grown from a curious boy clambering over the wreckage of Canvas Town into a competent portrait painter, adequate playwright (author, in fact, of *The Mysterious Monk,* blown off the stage by the 1796 captains' riot), novelist of some talent, belletrist, and historian—an architect of the early republican leisure activities that helped supply the cement by which a tacit union of rich, close-bound fathers cemented friendships, discussed mutually profitable commercial enterprises, and otherwise perpetuated their influence on the public life of New York.

Later on, once-invisible people would emerge from the shadows and transform the city's nightlife: Irish prizefighters, transvestites, rat-baiting

---

* Decades later, the memory of this world generated a flurry of old-codger memoirs: Abram Dayton's *Last Days of Knickerbocker Life in New York* (1882), John Mines's *Tour Around New York, Being the Recreations of Mr. Felix Oldboy* (1893), and others. All were reminiscences by relics of old merchant class New York, nostalgic over its lost grace.

impresarios, chorus girls, gangsters. But for the moment, at least, however much their opinions might differ over politics or business, a fraternity of public men was in power, would stay there for a century, and would disport itself at night as a sometimes bizarre—and, in one case at least, remarkably effective—way of keeping its hold on the day.

SECRETS OF THE TAMMANY WIGWAM: THE CITY TAVERN, 1790–91

Some men's social clubs, like the Hungarians at Todd's, vanished. But others played an important role in late colonial and early republican New York. And one of them was destined not only for an epochal history, but also for a pivotal if morally dubious role in the next century's explosion of nightlife. Tammany Hall—begetter of Boss Tweed, John Kelly, James J. Walker, George Washington "I seen my opportunities and I took 'em" Plunkitt—grew into New York's overlord in the 1800s, and though it's now remembered chiefly for its corrupt dominance of city government, much of its power—and its origin—rose from the taverns where the city's male moiety headed after dark for evenings of release.

Tammany Hall's ideals were high-minded: it began as an offshoot of a club that seems to have originated in Pennsylvania in the 1770s, its name honoring Tamamend, a chief revered in the folklore of the Delaware tribe for his bravery and love of freedom. The New York chapter formed in May 1789, after Washington's first inauguration. According to one of its early historians, Tammany began as a patriotic fraternity, dedicated to "that honest and generous devotion to country which is removed from radical and fanatical principles on the one hand and from a disregard to the rights of people on the other." And indeed by 1812, when Tammany built a hall on Nassau Street, the club had become a force in both local and national politics.

This was not an isolated phenomenon; the Freemasons, already influential, exemplified it. But in surviving records the Tammany of the 1790s seems also to have resembled humbler fraternities like the Moose or the Elks, anticipating their mix of boy's-gang mystical rites, solemn avowals of virtue, guy-guy partying, and heroic drinking. At first the New York Wigwam (as Tammany convocations were called) was peripatetic, renting temporary rooms or taverns, including Fraunces's, the City on Broadway, and Martling's, at the corner of Nassau and Spruce.

Serious discussion did take place in the camaraderie of the Tammany Wigwam, but even in its early years it was in fact more Shriners than Phi Beta Kappa, more debauch than seminar. The members dressed, at least on ceremonial occasions, as Indians. On July 21, 1790, celebrating a newly signed friendship treaty between the U.S. and the southern Creek Indians, Tammany threw a gala Wigwam for a delegation of about thirty Creek visiting Manhattan. According to one account, William Pitt Smith, the Grand Sachem, strode into the Wigwam, followed by the Sachems who headed and the Brothers who belonged to each of Tammany's thirteen tribes, named after the colonies. Everybody appeared in war paint, feathers, leather leggings, and moccasins, carrying "huge war-clubs and burnished Tomahawks." At some point they no doubt smoked a calumet, the peace pipe, a rite probably more inspiring to the Brothers than it was to the Creek. Grand Sachem Smith then gave a speech, in which he observed "that although the hand of death was cold upon those great chiefs, Tammany and Columbus, their spirits were walking backward and forward in the Wigwam."

Then everybody got up and went off to the theater.

Minutes of the society's Wigwams survive in a manuscript dating from fall 1791, and offer a window into the club's earliest years, long before it came to dominate City Hall (and the saloons where much of the real work of politics got accomplished). The opening motion at the Great Wigwam of October 24, 1791, typifies the sessions through 1795: "agreeable to Law passed this Evening the Society of Tammany Resolved themselves into a Committee of Amusements." Festivities usually began with a formal recitation of American anecdotes, like "A Sailor and His Girl" or "A New York Lady and a Country Woman." Then the members proposed debate topics. Which was happier, a single or married life? Should the Council of Appointment (which distributed desirable posts) be abolished? If it was, who should appoint state officials? At its October 31 Wigwam, the group postponed discussion of these questions and "Resumed Society," declaring the gathering thereafter informal, and getting to the real point of the amusement meetings—songs and bumpers.

Celebratory blowouts occurred on holidays major and minor. On November 25, 1791, the eighth anniversary of the evacuation of British troops from New York, the Wigwam heard a program of songs, beginning with Tammany's anthem, "The Ethah Song," performed tonight by Brothers Rich and Davis:

Are we not sons of Tammany
That Ancient Son of Liberty?
Over the Lake and through the Wood
He took his Sport, and gain'd his food
Straight were his arrows, strong his Bows,
The dread of all his Country's foes,
Freedom he loved, while he had breath
And sought her in the Arms of death.

And so on for six more verses until the conclusion and business end of the song:

Then pass the Bottle with the Sun—
To Tammany and Washington.

They also downed fourteen toasts, one proposed by the sachems of each of the society's thirteen tribes, and a final bumper raised by the Grand Sachem to the "fourteen united fires." Then three cheers.

Such evenings suggest conventioneers on a bender or Saturday night in a lodge hall above a hardware store. But the boundary between frivolity and serious business isn't always a wall; it can be a conduit. And among these men, at least, play and the exercise of power reinforced each other. The Wigwam eventually relocated to Martling's Tavern, a move that marked a deeper involvement in politics and heralded the Tammany hegemony of the 1800s, when the club had grown into the Leviathan of urban political machines. And yet saloons would remain among the chief strongholds where Tammany kept its grip on power and its finger on the pulse of the people. Of course the bars also drew every nocturnal activity that needs defense against the law, from gambling to prizefights to prostitution. But that fit the scheme as well: New York's misfits and miscreants were a mother lode of the payoffs by which the machine supported itself and its hordes of dependents.

By protecting the proscribed and the shady, Tammany gave them the cover under which they could carve out their identities and gradually establish power bases of their own. As the 19th century progressed, they thrived despite attacks by wave upon wave of crusading moralists. And in the end they would burst from hiding and transform the New York night from a few theaters, coffeehouses, exhibit rooms, and candlelit taverns into a vast and exhilarating carnival.

CHAPTER THREE

HEARTHSIDE AND RUSHLIGHT
Old New York at Home

PETER KALM, A SWEDISH naturalist, walked through New York on the late afternoon and evening of November 1, 1748. "I found it extremely pleasant," he wrote, "for it seemed like a garden." Though the population now stood at 13,000, and the city was awash in new streets and buildings, New York's ambience was probably even boskier than it had been in Dutch times, thanks to a planting binge. The black locust and sycamore trees (still common on Manhattan streets), and their nearness to the abundant streams, ponds, and swamps, were magnets for gray tree frogs. On the evening of any warm day, especially if rain was in the air, the frogs set up a cacophony of flutelike trilling and chirping, which became the signature sound of the 18th-century city night. They drowned out the evening birdsong and indeed, Kalm observed, "they frequently make such a noise that it is difficult for a person to make himself heard."

Yet the countrified soundtrack was illusory. By 1799 New York had been through a century and a half of war, riot, epidemic, revolution, and British occupation. Even though mere survival should have stretched 18th-century technology to its utmost, somehow the city had grown impressively. New streets plowed into the brush; personal and civic life acquired urban sheen and intricacy; public buildings went up, including a new City Hall, a prison, and a network of commodity exchanges and markets. Dutch stepped-gable houses slowly gave way to the squarer, blander English town look. And somehow Manhattan had, from a handful of taverns, created something that could without apology be called a nightlife.

Even today most New Yorkers, with a plethora of evening destinations to choose from, still pass most of their evenings at home. But the conditions of pre-19th-century town life made the likelihood of staying put after dusk even higher. The labor, even the danger, of keeping a house lit and warm conspired to send people to bed not long past nightfall. Heat still came from an open fire, water from the back yard or a common neighborhood well, and light from a flame: these were the distinctive pre-occupations of the city dweller after sunset. While New York's climate seems not to have offered extremes any greater than we experience today (though reliable thermometers and scales of measurement didn't become common until the mid-1700s), it was harder to cope with both cold and heat. One couldn't farm the jobs out: the urban home relied on itself for sustenance and protection. And everything in it, from the locks and the hearths to the candles and lamps, was more necessary at night than in daytime.

DRAWING THE SHUTTERS, KEEPING THE FIRE: NEW YORK HOUSES IN THE 1600S AND 1700S

Mere ownership of land and a house in New Amsterdam didn't earn one the rights of residency, nor did the performance of public obligations like paying taxes or serving on the night watch. On the contrary, a 1661 ordinance denied citizenship to "all those who absent themselves from here for four consecutive months, without keeping fire and light." In this New York the evening hearthside resonated with meanings now hidden or lost. Fastening the doors, pulling the shutters to, drawing the curtains, keeping the fire alive and the wicks trimmed, winding the clock—all these may have been cozy rituals, minor chores. But everyone doing them knew they were also necessities for basic safety, for the preservation and continuity of the town's life.

To Cornelis Van Tienhoven—the same Kieft and Damen crony who ended, universally loathed, as a hat and cane floating in the Hudson—we owe a revealing 1650 description of the kind of temporary house settlers built during the early years of the colony, and designed to meet necessity in the simplest way possible. It was, Tienhoven wrote, a pit, often consisting of just one room, dug six or seven feet into the ground. Timbers, with bark as a wall covering, held back the soil. Planks covered the dirt floor, the ceiling was wainscoted, and overhead a gabled roof rose from the ground, shielded by more bark or green sod to keep out rain and snow. There must usually have been a fireplace, with a simple hearth and a clay-lined wood chimney above it to collect smoke. Beyond this, architectural historians have been forced to speculate. Glass was available in New Amsterdam from the beginning: might there have been windows in the gables to shed light into the room below? But if so, what about the wooden ceilings described by Tienhoven? Could there have been a door in one gable end with a stairway leading down? No buildings or detailed records survive.

Later, above-ground homes, modeled closely on Dutch town and farmhouses, were wood, stone, or brick. Most had glass windows, many had several rooms—but none specialized as in a modern house where, say, a bedroom is immediately distinguishable from kitchen, dining room, or office. In early New York, as in much of Europe at the time, a room was a room. If there were several, it often meant that there were several places the family might eat, cook, socialize, or carry on business, moving furniture to accommodate each use. In 1655 Egbert Van Borsum, who ran a ferry service between Manhattan and Brooklyn, contracted for a house near the Brooklyn waterfront (it cost him 550 guilders, about £300 in 1654 English sterling). It was to be 30 feet deep, eighteen feet wide, and built of wood, with seven stout beams crossing the width of the house at four-foot intervals. There were two main rooms, front and rear, each fifteen by eighteen, with a chimney in the wall between them. The contract also called for a pantry and built-in Dutch cabinet bed in each room, wainscoted walls, glass windows front and rear, and a door to the outside (probably in the hallmark Dutch design, with independently swinging top and bottom panels) in each room.

Van Borsum's house also had an attic (reached by a winding staircase from the front room below) and a cellar kitchen with stairs leading down from street level to outside doors: probably the cellar was a half story below ground and the front door of the house proper a half flight above. There seem to have been no windows in the side walls; the dwelling could have been fit without alteration into a line of row houses, a pattern long standard in both English and Dutch town dwellings and common in New Amsterdam as well.

Architecture, building materials, and decoration varied from house to house, especially as Dutch styles mixed with and yielded to English. Gradually a common row house design became typical: a cellar kitchen with a below-grade doorway, a formal entrance above, and two rooms per floor, sometimes with a chimney in the center, but more often in the side walls. Cisterns and wells were typically sunk just behind the house, sewage pits and the outhouses that topped them near the back corner of the lot. A trip to the privy took place in public view, and the smells and sounds, while perhaps not perceptible in the house, were never far from the back door. By the early 1800s the style was Federal. Houses were typically thirty-five or forty feet deep; lots were narrow, converging toward a 20- to 25-foot 19th-century standard that set the width of a typical dwelling.

And specialized rooms were becoming common: a kitchen and family dining room on the half-basement level, a front and back parlor on the entry level (often joined by a wide doorway, so they could either be separated or made into one large chamber), and sleeping accommodations above. But a basic similarity lay under all such evolutionary changes—the room as a defense against danger and discomfort, demanding constant upkeep and vigilance by the occupants, reminding them of their vulnerabilities and the need for self-reliance at least as much as it allowed them to relax. On the other hand they weren't vulnerable to system failures, like New York's 1965, 1977, and 2003 blackouts, about which those affected could do nothing.

Early New York rooms were typically square or squarish, eighteen or twenty feet on a side, small enough to feel protected, big enough to allow for several activities by different members of the household, and to accommodate the storing of furniture along the walls or the moving of it toward the fire as need arose. It would be some time before 19th-century technology invaded these rooms, tying them to plumbing systems, gas pipes, electric outlets, or central heating. In the candle or lamp glow of the 17th and 18th centuries, glassware and plate withdrew into the shelves, gleaming subtly. Tending fire and light or fetching water and taking care of sanitation, disagreeable chores at any time, were more so at night, and affected the rhythms of life after dark—when, for instance, people relieved themselves into chamber pots, to avoid a trip to the outhouse in the back yard. Neither option can have been pleasant at an evening party, which may be one reason why such gatherings became more common after the arrival of water closets.

During his 1697 visit to the city, Dr. Benjamin Bullivant visited some of the city's better Dutch-style houses. They were, he said, sometimes as tall as six stories, of red and yellow brick, with the narrow side and a steeply peaked gable facing the street. A tall garret topped the structure, with a window and a crane jutting from the peak so goods could be hauled up. The lower floors were solidly built, with, as in Van Borsum's house, a ceiling of boards planed down to smoothness and supported by thick wood crossbeams, far more substantial than those found in English-style houses.

The windows were outward-swinging casements, often separated by a transom into upper and lower sections, the glass divided by lead into diamond-shaped or oblong panes. Stout shutters kept out cold in winter, heat and light in summer, and protected against break-ins at night or during a prolonged absence. After dark, with the shutters drawn and fastened, the house presented a blind face to the street, sealing the occupants into quiet isolation. The earliest shutters were heavy and solid, designed for protection against forced entry as well as for privacy and warmth. But adjustable, slatted versions had appeared on the market by the mid-1700s and remained common for nearly 150 years: they're ubiquitous in early photographs, and still survive today on some old buildings. The slats opened to block sunlight while admitting a breeze in summer, closed to fend off the winter cold. Though they shielded the room from view after dark, the slats, if left a little ajar, might offer a few tantalizing glimpses of the furniture and occupants.

Out-of-the-way chambers, those lacking a fireplace or prone to cold drafts, were often closed off during winter. The standard furnishing for any room where people sat and socialized was a set of parlor chairs, usually sold in sets of six, ranged along the walls, and moved out to accommodate whoever gathered by the fire. The squarish rooms in these early houses allowed heat to radiate more efficiently to all the corners, and also offered more flexibility in the temporary arranging of chairs.

All of this applied by day, but it was really only at night that the early New York parlor showed itself radically different from its modern descendant. We still use candles and kerosene lamps for atmosphere and accent. But with artificial light everywhere, it's virtually impossible to re-create either the natural or man-made light of the 17th and 18th centuries. Aircraft and satellites track constantly overhead, the dark is fractured by blinking cell towers, the bluish, radioactive-looking halos over parking lots, or the sky glow from a town miles away. Indoors, it's harder yet to recapture the 17th- and 18th-century ambience of a dark room shuttered and curtained against the starlight, moonlight, cloud cover, rain, snow, or wind. Even if you douse all the lamps, light-emitting diodes glow beadily from telephones, burglar alarms, stereo control panels, and smoke detectors—often even when such devices are supposedly turned off.

Before 1800 the fuel for indoor lighting remained much the same as it was in ancient Rome: it came from plants (pinewood pitch, beeswax, bayberry) or animals. Whaling was an industry whose boom lay in the future, but sperm whale oil could be had in the 1700s, and commanded a premium price because it gave off a clearer and brighter light than competing fuels. Fish oil was common in ships' lamps, while on land the animal fuel of choice was tallow, particularly from fat deposits found above the kidneys of ruminants. In the early years of settlement, while cows and sheep were still few, bear and deer fat were frequent sources.

Turning such raw materials into light was like making gravy: melt the fat over hot water, lift off the scum as it rises to the surface. Then one dipped cotton or linen wicks into the pot, the candle growing thicker with each dunk. Oil lamps lacked as yet the refinements that improved them in the later 1700s. A Betty Lamp, probably the most common source of indoor light in New Amsterdam, is a simple pot of oil with a wick holder. But all such common lighting devices demanded constant labor. Wicks had to be trimmed often, or they burned too hot and guttered, the wax drooling down the sides of the candle, and the flame palpitating, red, and smoky. Enclosing a flame in glass kept it steadier; putting it in front of a mirror or polished metal plate helped to concentrate and direct it. Any tinkerer might have thought of weaving a purpose-made fat wick for a bigger, brighter flame, but it wasn't until the 1770s that the French, then as now leaders in the science and art of illumination, perfected the ribbonlike band wick. And only in 1783 did Aimé Argand, a Swiss chemist, market a lamp with a circular wick that burned brighter and at a higher temperature, thus incinerating many of the carbon particles that made earlier lamps smoke so heavily.

But these were early industrial age innovations. The people of New Amsterdam and early New York lived in a wholly different relationship with indoor lighting after dark. The main meal of the day, and the socializing that preceded or followed it, happened in daylight, though by 1800 it had begun to push first into late afternoon and then beyond nightfall. Candles, rushlights (lengths of cattail steeped in grease that had to be hand-fed through pincers as they burned, lasting only an hour or so), and oil lamps with wicks were all dim. Glass globes were available to keep the flames steady, but they don't feature prominently even in 18th-century advertisements from glass merchants. Student and reading lamps, with a reflector or shade to focus light on a book or paper, made close work possible but not a pleasure.

None of these sources radiated light as later mantled flames and electric bulbs do: they drew the eye rather than pushing it away. Candlelight-era public illuminations meant to dazzle derived their effects from masses of tiny flames, like a 1688 show at Versailles during which the gardens blazed with 24,000 candles. In a room twenty feet square the drama was subtler. A candle or lamp, enough to warm the eye and keep you from running into things, doesn't force its light into and through the air. Reflections seem to rise out of glass, metal, or polished wood rather than being thrown onto them, a pleasing effect. Glass seems to disappear except for an outline that looks more like an optical projection than the edge of a solid object. Light colors look white and darker ones black, showing true only when the flame is a few inches away.

Faces lose their blemishes and irregularities; sharp features soften and flaccid ones take on definition; bodies show life and depth they lack in daytime. By contrast electric light, even when its wattage is low, seems to impregnate the air and set fire to it, neutralizing everything else in the room. Preferences in such things are subjective, and by and large the public acclaimed every new lighting technology that emerged in the 1800s, convinced in turn that improved wicks, gaslight, the refinements that made gas steadier and brighter, and finally electricity, produced an illumination identical to daylight—though in fact no artificial light does this, and even if it were possible, the effect would be horrible—an erasure of night's distinctively shadow-rich and pleasurably artificial light, and of the subdued visual radiance of an open fire.

In early Dutch rooms the chimney often descended through the ceiling, flaring out into a hood over the hearth. Thus the fire was in the room, radiating light and heat to the front and both sides. English-style fireplaces sank both chimney and hearth into the wall. But neither design was very efficient, and chimneys were deemed satisfactory as long as they got rid of the smoke. The earliest, built of wood lined with clay or plaster, were such firetraps that New Amsterdam outlawed them in 1648. But nobody had figured out how to prevent the heat from escaping through them. Fuel, for anyone without money or servants, was exhausting to obtain—as during the winter of 1741, when John Hughson had to plow every day through snowdrifts on Broadway to haul firewood back to his tavern near the Hudson.

By the mid-1700s, wood-burning iron Franklin Stoves began appearing in New York. The *New-York Weekly Post-Boy* advertised a pamphlet with instructions on how to build them in 1744, and by 1761 Peter Clopper was selling them in the Fly Market, and heralding them as "remarkable for making a Room Warm and comfortable with very little Wood." Stoves radiated more heat than an open fire, and prevented warmth from getting sucked into the flue and blown outside. But they too demanded vigilance. In 1798 Hugh Gaine (owner of the *New-York Mercury*, which had printed the most complete contemporary description of the 1776 fire) was still publishing and still living on Hanover Square; his diary suggests that the most common neighborhood news, apart from weather extremes, were blazes that started in fireplaces or stoves. On the night of Monday, January 22, 1798, he wrote, "about 8 o'clock an Alarm of Fire was occasioned by the Pipe of a Stove in the House of Mrs. Ten Eyck's, 4 doors from Ours; it burnt out without any Damage to the Neighbourhood, but the Fright."

Fear was justified: water supplies couldn't be relied upon. New York's first running water arrived the next year, in 1799, but it was primitive, with hollow logs as pipes, drawing its supply from the increasingly unwholesome Fresh Water. The system served relatively few homes, and those erratically: for most families water still had to be hauled up from a backyard well or carted in from purer sources. When he bought it in 1758, Gaine's house had a dug well with a pump in the back yard, and a cistern for rainwater. Both sources made water cumbersome to fetch and sewage could taint the well: contaminated ground water in crowded neighborhoods like Hanover Square had become a major urban headache.

Despite the inconvenience of taking them, baths had become more and more popular beginning in the mid-1700s, but it was still unaccustomed enough as late as the 1830s that public facilities like the Washington Baths on Pearl Street were advertising the "luxury of Warm Bathing"—six tickets for a dollar. But for all the incremental improvements, in Dutch and Georgian New York, heat, light, and plumbing were only beginning the evolution that led to the ingenious (and troublesome) systems we live with today. Nothing truly new had come along to light the streets, heat the homes, speed communication, move people from neighborhood to neighborhood, or even to eliminate the sewage. At night the home, whether rich or poor, severed most links with the outside world with the locking of its outer doors (lock technology was well advanced). When they went to sleep, New Yorkers shut themselves into the cabinet beds the Dutch had imported from the Netherlands, or later under draped English-style canopies. Whatever its style, a 17th- or 18th-century New

York bed was, at least among the prosperous, a room within a room inside a house within a guarded town.

MANHATTAN SEASON: WINTER, 1800–1801

All night, usually, the erratic Rattle Watch or one of its successors patrolled the streets. The next day the city awoke, both for business and pleasure: visiting still began in the morning, continued through afternoon dinner parties and teas, and was often over by dark. After that the chosen gathering places tended to be public: theaters, exhibits, the pleasure gardens, or balls in the city's assembly rooms.

Yet in time the New York fireside became less and less secluded. By the mid-1700s, people were entertaining at home more frequently. It's difficult to reconstruct domestic entertainments: they weren't announced and faithfully reviewed in the press as public diversions were. Parties at home depend for documentation on letters and diaries, few of which supply the small but telling facts that let us reconstruct them. But there are exceptions—notably in a series of letters home written in the winter of 1800 and 1801 by two teen-aged Connecticut girls on a wide-eyed tour of the New York social season. Maria and Harriet Trumbull, fifteen and seventeen years old, were the daughters of Connecticut's then governor, Jonathan Trumbull, Jr., and his wife, Eunice. They left Lebanon, their small home town east of Hartford, in December 1800, and lodged through the New York winter with a down-on-her-luck but well-connected widow, Mrs. (or "Lady," as she styled herself) Kitty Duer.

Duer's entitlement to her honorific "Lady" was shaky: her father, William Alexander, had petitioned the crown for the Scottish earldom of Stirling (claiming an ancestor who'd been an uncle of the first earl), but the House of Lords had long ago rejected his petition. Nonetheless, in the socially fluid years following the Revolution, her friends, at least, put up with her title. But Kitty's first marriage was unlucky. William Duer was rich when she married him in 1779, and she'd been given away at the ceremony by George Washington himself. But ill-advised speculation landed Duer in debtor's prison by 1792; he'd died there in 1799, a year before the Trumbull sisters arrived to help with the rent. The family had shifted from a luxurious house on Broadway to a more dubious location on Chambers Street, just west of present-day City Hall.

Maria and Harriet wrote their parents at least once a week. First published in 1969 by Helen M. Morgan, their letters are eager, generous, full of detail, and—thanks to the clashing perspectives of fun-loving Maria and anxiety-ridden Harriet—three-dimensional. At first the girls sound a note of scared anticipation; later they voice a bubbling enthusiasm for the city's attractions, especially its young men; finally, by early May, they dissolve into longing for Mama, Papa, home, and friends. But the weeks from February through April show a full calendar of pleasures, from shopping to visiting and the new 2,000-seat Park Theatre just a few blocks away, to which William Dunlap had fled from the last bickering days of the old John Street house. The girls went on March 11 to see his translation of *Abaeillino, The Great Bandit*, at which Maria reported they were "tolerably entertained." They also took in exhibits like the Invisible Woman, who held forth from an apparently empty glass box in a house on William Street, answering questions from the audience. But both girls reserved their greatest enthusiasm for the socializing that, in their circle, started as early as 5:30 in the morning and occasionally lasted long after midnight.

By February their parents, fretting over the heated election battle underway between John Adams and Thomas Jefferson, threatened to yank them back home. In response even deferential Harriet's letters became a charmingly devious mix of dutifulness and pleading:

I am sorry you think of having us return so soon, not but what I would be glad to go, even next week, but I wish to make out two quarters in music and drawing, music especially I dislike to leave as it is probably the only time I shall ever have for learning it, Mr. Hewitt [the music teacher] comes very regularly, and says he is well satisfied with my improvement, yet I can make *but* little progress in six months, and *less time* would only be throwing money away; I hope therefore dear Mama that you and Papa will consent to let us stay longer, and not think we don[']t wish to see you for I assure you we do more than any thing.

Riots, however, never actually broke out, and on the evening of Wednesday, March 4—Jefferson's inauguration day—the girls went to a show at Vauxhall Gardens, where statues of Aaron Burr and Jefferson emitted fireworks, including illuminated snakes (touchier observers thought this was meant as satire).

Harriet and Maria attended their drawing school as early as 5 or 6 in the morning, and a round of visits followed, occupying much of the day. The girls looked up old family friends from Connecticut, cultivated new city acquaintances steeped in the social skills they'd come to master, and spent time with a swelling entourage of cute eligible boys. Now, at the dawn of the new century, pleasures were migrating toward and beyond sunset. Dinner parties always started in the afternoon, but often not till four o'clock, just before dusk. Tableware, once upstaged by daylight, was, as darkness closed in, learning to dazzle in the light of candles, oil, and gas. Often, if the dinner was expected to last into twilight, the drapes and shutters were now drawn and candles lit, to forestall the disagreeable darkening of the windows; night was gradually coming to be an attractive time for a social meal.

Federal-era dating, while much of it too went on by day, could be surprisingly unchaperoned, and had begun colonizing the hours after dark. The Trumbulls went to a number of impromptu (and unsupervised) evening parties. On Friday, March 13, Harriet and Maria came home from one at ten o'clock, accompanied by two boys—21-year-old Harry Hudson, and Roswell Colt, the 22-year-old scion of a family later to found the Colt Revolver Company. Nonchalantly, Maria wrote to her mother that the foursome was alone in the house until almost midnight, adding, "I believe it is the first time since we have been here that we have had any of our friends by ourselves and undisturbed by the rest of the family."

This was a proto-tryst. "I hardly know which is best Roswell or Harry," she wrote at first, but by April she'd made her choice, setting out at dawn alone with Harry for a day-long carriage ride around rural northern Manhattan. This was a standard dating itinerary, which meandered northward into the country along the old Post Road up to the Kissing Bridge (it crossed DeVoor's Mill Stream, now underground, at the west side of Second Avenue between 51st and 52nd Streets). Custom allowed the boy to take a kiss as toll, but whatever happened on the ride that day, Maria ended up marrying Harry in 1804.

Chaperoning, which was to become an obsession later in the 1800s, was casual, at least in the Duer household, and the Trumbull girls' parents voiced no concern about it. Lady Kitty often came home late herself, since she frequently spent the evening and half the night abroad, hard at work trying to land a new husband. She seems to have had no desire to play the duenna, and probably could have used one herself, though her nocturnal habits don't seem to have damaged her hunting skills: she married a rich man not long after the Trumbulls had left for home.

Evenings on Chambers Street were often long, convivial, and only enlivened by the frequent absence of Lady Kitty. On Wednesday, March 11, the Trumbull and Duer girls "wrote, read and played cards—till twelve o'clock—we really have got into a bad habit of sitting up very late, we seldom get to bed before twelve—and many of the family sit up much later." The pastimes seem to have been simple, even juvenile by later measures, yet also slightly impish: playing parlor games like Tom Come Tickle Me (in which the object was not to laugh when someone tickled your knee). Board games, a later 19th-century invention, pleased enthusiasts of moral reform by keeping the players separated around a table and eager hands from their desired destinations. But this doesn't seem to have been an issue in the New York of 1801.

OLD MR. DUNLAP:
GREENWICH VILLAGE IN THE 1830S

Harriet and Maria Trumbull's winter season in the city was almost the last of its kind. New York had sprawled up the island as far north as Houston Street, and was on the verge of becoming unrecognizable as the post-colonial town of the 1770s and 80s. A steep rise in population and a ferment of technical innovation were only a decade or so away. The Park Theatre had acquired a working- and trade-class rival, the Bowery, a blue and crimson forerunner of 20th-century movie palaces. A new Italian Opera House opened in November 1833 at the northwest corner of Church and Leonard Streets (it was the brainchild of Lorenzo Da Ponte, the librettist of *Don Giovanni* and *The Marriage of Figaro,* who had settled in New York in 1805; its premiere opera was Rossini's *La Gazza Ladra*). Greenwich Village, though still rural in ambience, had boomed between 1799 and 1822, when a series of cholera and yellow fever epidemics precipitated the city's first out-migration, a rehearsal for later flights to the suburbs. A state prison sprawled along the Hudson from Washington Street to the riverbank between Christopher and Perry Streets—though the prisoners had been moved upriver to Sing Sing in 1829.

William Dunlap's life was nearly over now; he could remember back as far as Revolutionary-era New York, when as a ten-year-old he'd crawled over the charred ruins of the blocks that later became Canvas Town. Yet even as a septuagenarian, Dunlap wasn't predisposed to a cranky rejection of the newfangled. In any case, the new New York, however strange, hadn't wholly obliterated the old, and by now Dunlap had won recognition as one of the pioneers of American fine arts. Despite his age he remained an active presence on the city scene, an even-tempered observer of both the familiar past and the changing present.

He'd ended his long association with the John Street and Park Theatres, but remained a competent portrait painter—one of the founders, in 1825, of the National Academy of Design. He was a prolific art critic (with a particular distaste for Harriet and Maria's painter uncle, John Trumbull). And in his diary Dunlap left a record of city life in the 1830s. Despite money worries and poor health, he seems to have kept his equanimity, looking at the world around him with tolerance and a painter's eye for detail—an alertness to color and texture hard to find in other memoirs and journals of the period. He kept up with friends even in the 1830s, when he had left his old digs at 55 Leonard Street downtown, and moved up to Greenwich Village.

In 1834, engaged in writing what would turn out to be the last volume of his diary (he died in 1839), he was dwelling with his wife, daughter, son, and one servant at 64 Sixth Avenue, between Barrow and 6th Streets. In 1828, at the Park (experimentally gaslit in 1821),* Dunlap had mounted a successful farce, *A Trip to Niagara,* and had recently published his *History of the American Theatre* and the *Rise and Progress of the Arts of Design.* But he was nonetheless living from hand to mouth, with a bank account perpetually at cliff's edge: on June 15, 1834, it shriveled to $1.22: alarming, given that his monthly rent on the house was $26.33.

Yet once the day was over, home life remained much as it had been 100 or even 200 years before. After dark Dunlap entertained only rarely and went out little except for an occasional evening at the theater. His health was fragile after an excruciating operation for a kidney stone, done at home and of course without anesthesia on March 14, 1834. In the weeks of pain that followed he rose early, usually before seven, then painted, wrote, ran errands, or made calls downtown. Tea at about six o'clock in the

---

* The first theater to use permanent gaslights was the Chatham in 1828, with a system that illuminated both audience and stage. In the 1821 experiment at the Park, "the color of the light is whiter than that of oil, & more brilliant," the *Evening Post* reported, venturing to predict that gas would soon replace the oil lamps whose smoke and stinks were "nearly ruinous to the light silk dresses of the ladies."

evening seems to have been the family's evening meal, and the hours after were quiet, with little of the visiting that kept the Trumbulls occupied, and that Dunlap himself had carried on as a young man.

Greenwich Village, on the outer fringes of the city's noise and activity, allowed Dunlap to convalesce more or less in peace. But—though not involved so deeply as he had once been in the city's affairs—he nonetheless wasn't at all averse to accepting the benefits of technological progress. Just before Christmas he spent $45.65 on a Nott Stove (recently invented by the upstate engineering genius Eliphalet Nott, and soon to generate a major industrial boom in Troy, where it was manufactured). This was an energy-efficient anthracite-coal-burning improvement on the Franklin Stove. The Nott Stove and its vent pipe were in the basement, and it kept the whole house warm. Dunlap had also acquired a gadget unknown in 1700, still rare in 1750, but relatively common in the 1830s: a thermometer, which allowed him to measure the new stove's power. He found himself amazed that it could heat the house to a temperature balmy by earlier standards: 52 degrees Fahrenheit, even when the temperature outside had fallen to twenty.

Nevertheless, in one very cold snap, stove or no stove, the rooms on the north side of the house still sank below freezing. The domestic night remained prone to discomfort, and it was often easier to stay put in the family parlor rather than venturing out or hosting a party. But other, newer inventions were luring people out into the streets. From his house on Sixth Avenue, Dunlap took a daily walk and saw the changes. New row houses were going up, and the neighborhood had begun to acquire the present look of its quieter red brick residential streets.

And some of Dunlap's strolls now ended at a bus stop on the corner where Charles crossed Hudson Street, a short walk from home. An omnibus ("bus" didn't become the common term until later) now ran down Hudson Street, Canal Street, and Broadway to a terminus at the corner of Pine and Nassau. The vehicles, drawn by four horses, carried Dunlap southward to visit the banks, clients, publishers, and libraries clustered in lower Manhattan—a commute and a mode of transport unimagined in the Revolutionary era. When they became common in the early 1830s, buses caught the eye: "a ride in it for several days after it started," the *New York Mirror* commented, "subjected the passenger to as much attention as the adventurers in the first ship that approached the shores of the Indians." But to Dunlap it had already become routine. "Ride down town," he wrote in a June

1833 entry, using the now standard but then new New York directional term, "to make calls . . . Go to Library, Clinton Hall, &c. & ride home."

More noteworthy yet was the city's first railroad, the New York & Harlem, now running from a ticket office at Prince Street up the Bowery and Fourth Avenue to Sunfish Pond, near the corner of present-day Park Avenue and 32nd Street.* Trains ran every fifteen minutes from six in the morning through 8:30 at night; the fare was 12½ cents, and the cars stopped wherever passengers requested. At first they were horse-drawn, but by 1834 steam power came to the line, and Dunlap could probably hear an early locomotive laboring up the tracks: contemporaries compared the railroad's anemic new engine to a teakettle, wheezing and gasping as it tried to haul two boxy passenger cars up the slight grade into Union Square. The new trains made news with their sparks, smoke, noise, and an 1834 explosion.

Then there was gaslight, just now beginning to glimmer on Manhattan's streets and behind its curtained house windows. After a series of experimental illuminations, like that conducted at the Park Theatre in 1821, it had formally arrived on June 11, 1824, when the city's first demonstration streetlight went on. In *Disenchanted Night* (1988), Wolfgang Schivelbusch argues that gaslight was a product of early industrial-era exploitation, first designed to keep factories and workers at constant labor from before dawn to past sunset, especially during the short days of winter. But industrialized utilities like gas, electric power, running water, and sewers also revolutionized the city's nonworking nightlife.

Gas began flowing through the pipes to private consumers south of Grand Street on February 14, 1825, but anyone further north was out of luck for the time being: in the early 1830s it wasn't yet available in Greenwich Village. A new company, the Manhattan Gas Light Company, had built a plant to extract gas from coal along the Hudson at 18th Street, next door to a turpentine distillery. The company had run a pipeline down Sixth Avenue by 1834 (and Dunlap no doubt had seen the men laying it), but service still hadn't begun. So at that point, at least, Dunlap was probably making do with candles or oil lamps.

He apparently wrote his diary entries after dinner, toward dusk; he al-

---

* Construction on the railroad had begun with *éclat* in 1832, when crews blasted into the Manhattan schist of Murray Hill, in order to carve out a level passage from 34th to 40th Streets; service through to Yorkville began in 1834. By 1837 the cutting had been roofed over to become the Park Avenue tunnel, still used today by cars and trucks.

most never records anything of interest happening after dark. He was an early temperance advocate, so avoided the still robust drinking rounds that enlivened the night for those bent on socializing. Dunlap's seems to have been a close family: his wife, son, and daughter were still alive, and no doubt spent their evenings in quiet talk, a tea or light supper, perhaps some reading by lamplight, an early bedtime, and an early wakeup. Thus he both lived and wrote an unconscious coda, summing up the themes of the Old New York Night—the gradual enrichment and complexity brought on by a growing population, a slow but steady proliferation in nighttime activities, and an at first leisurely progress of inventions and improvements that made life after dark more convenient and attractive, both at home and away. Steamships and railroads were already starting to revolutionize American life (Robert Fulton's first steamboat left from the foot of Christopher Street on August 17, 1807, bound for Albany), but in the 1830s, though they brought distant places closer together, they didn't do much for urban transit. Their main effect was to make it easier for out-of-town visitors and immigrants to get here—a change that, though destined to be gigantic, took decades to achieve full impact.

William Dunlap lived on until 1839, but no longer kept up the diary that might have recorded the by then apparent revolution in New York life after dark. The invention of nighttown, as New York was to know it in its heyday in the 1920s and 30s, depended on the fortuitous convergence of many forces, technological, social, economic, and cultural. A bigger and more diverse population; the springing up of new neighborhoods with sharply divergent profiles and new forms of group living; improvements in local transportation; 24-hour hospitals; lighting; improved sanitation—all were either functioning or soon to arrive, and all did their part.

Tethered by pipe and wire to the city at large, dependent on reservoirs, pumps, generators, and gas plants the workings of which few individual citizens understood and none could control, by 1900 the city home had lost much of its independence and with that some of its privacy. Now, only night tempers public intrusion into the ever more infiltrated home, when the lights go off, the phone (usually) stops ringing, the alien images and sounds stop streaming in via television, radio, and recordings. Perhaps too this gradual constriction of domestic privacy lures people out onto the streets in search of relief, where night's enfolding cloak frees people to do things they'd never contemplate at home, where they can be visited, spied upon, telephoned, e-mailed, or instant-messaged.

Whatever the cause, nightfall increasingly became the time for the greatest public gatherings, from fulsome spectacles like Italian opera and night baseball to the more anarchic, improvised spirit of after-hours clubs and the Greenwich Village Halloween parade. This volatile and stimulating nocturnal realignment of private and public first came to be in the 1830s. And the place it made its first appearance—of course—was Broadway.

CHAPTER FOUR

BROADWAY AFTER DARK

Pleasures and Horrors of Federal New York

WHEN JAN DAMEN STAGGERED homeward in the company of Philip Geraerdy on that ill-starred April night in 1643, Broadway was a dirt lane, unlit save for furtive candlelight leaking through closed shutters. Silent too, unless a few early-season frogs peeped from the trees.

Now, in 1835, it was aglare with gaslight, walled in by facades of brick, stone, and glass, thronged with party-colored mobs of men and women who probably would have frightened Damen and Geraerdy more than the Indians did. Yet rude, garish, and new-minted though this Broadway seemed, it had, after all, been in existence for 200 years, and thought of itself as having seen everything, from the genteel promenades that began plying it before the Revolution to the devouring flames of the 1776 fire. Its upper limits had moved north as far as Prince Street; gas streetlights, which had first gone on in 1828, now lined it. To someone visiting from the present, it would probably most resemble the flaring, barnyard-smelling vulgarity of a carnival midway. But to early 19th-century tourists and citizens, Broadway was a panorama of light and motion, one of the world's great metropolitan boulevards. Either way, its noise and flash had forever erased the 17th century's silent Broadway of sweet river air and quiet moonlight.

In *New York by Gas-Light,* published in 1850, George Foster combined a salacious eye with a tone of moral indignation—a formula for describing New York nightlife that endured through Walter Winchell and survives today. "Let us start fair with the young night," he begins, "and take our first walk in Broadway, . . . with its gay throng and flashing lights beaming from a thousand palace-like shop fronts, where fortunes are spread out to tempt the eye of the unwary or the extravagant."

On early 19th-century Broadway, Trinity Church and St. Paul's Chapel still rose tallest, and wealthy New Yorkers were still holding on to their staid houses below Chambers Street. But at night the churches sank into the shadows while the homeowners plugged their ears, gritted their teeth, and tried to sleep. At the corner of Broadway and Ann Street, directly across from St. Paul's, Scudder's Museum drew crowds well into evening, a magnet for dating couples and flaneurs as well as old ladies and awestruck grandchildren. As Edwin Williams described the place in his 1834 guide, *New-York As it Is,* its "four spacious Saloons, each 100 feet in length,"* housed the Grand Cosmorama, whose gaslit glass cases displayed views of great cities, volcanoes, and other wonders of the world. There was also a collection of boa constrictors (fed at showtime with live chickens and rabbits), a mummy, a collection of scalps, ostrich eggs, the signature of John Hancock, various mineral samples, and a wax statue of Daddy Lambert, the then fattest ever New Yorker—all for 25 cents admission. Scudder's, and its rival, Peale's (at 252 Broadway, just across from City Hall), offered competing sideshow attractions, like "Miss Honey, aged ten years (the American Prodigy)," or "The Canadian Dwarfs 30 and 32 inches high."

But these were a mere hors d'oeuvre to what followed when P. T. Barnum took Scudder's over in 1841. Barnum's American Museum, as it was now called, overwhelmed Broadway like the stationary circus parade it in essence was. It came most joltingly alive at night, both to the eye and ear. Crowds gathered to hear Barnum's brass band, blaring down from a balcony; a revolving red, yellow, and blue light spun above the scene in a dizzying chromatic whirl; and atop everything a powerful beacon burned proudly from the museum's crown. This was an early-model Drummond lamp—now called a limelight—a gas- or oil-fired device that used lime instead of a wick and gave off a searing bluish radiance, visible in the right conditions more than 50 miles away. Barnum's version shot a "livid, ghastly glare" a full mile up Broadway, intense enough to project grotesquely long shadows north and south from the horse-drawn omnibuses now hauling crowds along the thoroughfare.

Light flooded down to the sidewalks from shop windows and streetlights, and welled up out of the basement oyster bars, each announced by

---

* In the 19th century "saloon" was a word of many meanings. Classically, it denoted any large room with a high ceiling and some claim to grandeur. Only later did it become synonymous with the city's ubiquitous, humble, even down-and-out working-class bars.

a high-hanging red lantern, and serving the city's favorite food (the waters of the harbor and its estuaries teemed with the world's best oysters). The bars hummed until well after midnight, crowded with oyster-slurping, brandy-swilling, cigar-smoking men and sometimes women (the cigar had replaced the clay pipe as New York's favorite tobacco fix). Broadway flickered, sputtered, and hissed, and because its lights often set fires or exploded, they contributed danger as well as excitement. Competing technologies made a mixture of light qualities perhaps more varied than our own— Argand wicks, Drummond flares, fueled by gas or oil or camphene (also called "burning fluid," a volatile mixture used in strange-looking double-wicked lamps, which gave off a searing light but also caused more than its share of dreadful fires).

Philip Hone (1780–1851), a slightly younger contemporary and friend of William Dunlap, owned a house on Broadway north of Barclay Street, and his diary shows increasing frustration with the intrusive scene playing night and day just outside his front door. When Davy Crockett (the famed Tennessee frontiersman and three-term congressman) visited New York in May of 1834, he went to a banquet at the American Hotel, just two doors down Broadway and well within earshot of the Hones. The party, Hone wrote, consisted of "speaking, singing, toasting, and shouting until a late hour; very much to the annoyance of my household, for we are so near that the noise of the carouse disturbed such of us as wished to sleep."

That, of course, was at night, but almost at the same moment John Jacob Astor was driving the Hone family even nearer to distraction by day. Patriarch of one of New York's best-known and richest families, Astor had made a fortune in furs and was now multiplying it in real estate: that same May in 1834 his workers commenced demolishing the block between Barclay and Vesey Streets to make way for the first Astor hotel. Hone sardonically dubbed this six-story granite pile a "New York *palais royal.*" Heavy and mausoleum-like in pictures, it was indeed palatial for the time, with expensive shops at street level along Broadway, restaurants, grand saloons, and 308 guest rooms, all equipped with gaslight, steam-pumped running hot and cold taps, and water closet. When the place opened on May 1, 1836, even normally sober papers like the *New-York Commercial Advertiser* gushed. The rooms were in fact suites, each with a parlor facing the street, and a bedroom across the hall, looking out on an inner courtyard, with one set of chambers bearing the hopeful name "The Duke's Room."

In mid-block rose the imposing Astor House entrance, with its colon-

nade, blue and white marble floor, and the grand staircase which led up
to a second-story enfilade of palatial halls. All had nineteen-and-a-half-
foot-high ceilings and vast high windows—the 40-by-100-foot Dining
Room, the Gentleman's Smoking and Conversation Room, the Ladies'
Drawing and Dining Rooms. Those facing Broadway looked out toward
the facade of Scudder's Museum—a dignified and desirable neighbor, according to a guidebook sold in the hotel, with collections "for the extent
of glasses and magnificence of views, . . . not superseded in this or any
other country."

This serene streetscape changed, however, once Barnum had moved in
with his band, his lights, his Drummond beacon, and acts like Tom
Thumb, who, whether dressed in a pint-sized Yankee Doodle suit, in kilt
and tartans, or as Cupid in tights, drew adoring mobs. Barnum of course
was famous for hokum, but his clash in taste with the posh hotel across
the way sounded the classic dissonance of the Broadway charivari—Astor
against Barnum against St. Paul's and Trinity Church. Teeming with people, lights, and traffic, abuzz as the theaters emptied, alternately dazzling
and louche, the Broadway of 1840 is easily recognizable in today's chaotic
boulevard, but hard to connect with the dirt lane of New Amsterdam or
the quiet residential avenue of the 1700s.

Yet in scale it was in fact closer to Damen's village than today's metropolis. The Astor House seemed gigantic and overpoweringly opulent to
its 1836 admirers; yet in photographs it now looks dumpy, small, and—
thanks to the stone blocks on its facade—rather jail-like. The fabled
stretch of Broadway reached only from the Battery up to Prince Street.
Grandeur is a time-sensitive illusion, measured against a changing tem-
plate. Bigger scales awe their beholders at first, but soon lose their impact,
and what seemed gigantic quickly shrinks to the routine—just as, in the
suburbs, strip shopping centers were dwarfed by enclosed malls, then
malls by big-box superstores.

BROADWAY DELUXE:
GLAMOUR IN THE 1840S

Broadway's cacophony of style and noise alienated those who still remembered an earlier, tamer thoroughfare. In September 1835 a woman wrote
the *New York Herald* to complain. "This beautiful street the pride of New
York, nay of America, the promenade of 30 years, has become so filthy

and encumbered with all kinds of nuisances, that it is no longer fit for a promenade." Specifically, she railed at the accumulation of boarding-houses, fruit stalls, delivery carts and the piles of furniture and boxes that seemed to spill out from them onto the sidewalks.

Worse, according to detractors, the chaos refused to stay put: having laid one old neighborhood waste, then abandoned it, this voracious Broadway galloped northward to devour another. Commenting on his correspondent's letter, James Gordon Bennett, the *Herald*'s editor, remarked that she hadn't noticed that Broadway *à la mode* was moving uptown. From the Battery up to St. Paul's Chapel, he said, the street had transformed itself into a crowded business bazaar, and already acquired the essence of its present-day Wall Street character. "Now," Bennett remarked, "the fashionable parade is above the Astor House, as far as Canal Street."

It took ingenuity and enterprise to create this blocks-long milieu of fashion and luxury in the 1830s. Running water from the Croton reservoir system wouldn't arrive until 1842; a public sewer system didn't even begin to take shape until the 1850s. Thus any big project—not to mention a hotel with 300-plus guest rooms—put architects on their mettle. In the Astor House all the running hot and cold water for the plumbing in every room came from rainwater cisterns on the roof and a well with a hydraulic pump in the courtyard; the guest with demands beyond a private sink and toilet had to walk to a rank of seventeen cubicles with bathtubs and two with showers on the Barclay Street side of the building. All the Astor's wastewater went out through its own purpose-built drain culvert and straight into the Hudson: sewers, where they existed at all, weren't part of a public system but private improvisations.

In this respect the arts were a little better off than the applied sciences. Theater, depending more on ancient forms of illusion than fickle new technologies, drew audiences with popular actors and familiar repertory—still mainly English and heavily reliant on Shakespeare, Restoration comedy, and sonorous 18th-century tragedy, which in the 1830s still drew the masses as well as the elite to theaters like the Park. But in a city where the election of Andrew Jackson had exacerbated interclass tension, wealthier theatergoers had gravitated toward more rarefied (and incidentally more exclusionary) entertainment—like that offered by the Italian Opera House, built in 1833 at the corner of Leonard and Church Streets. Writing in the 1860s, John W. Francis, author of *Old New York: Or, Reminiscences of the Past Sixty Years,* recalled fondly the alternative it offered to more vulgar entertainment. "It captivated the eye, it charmed the ear, it awakened the profoundest emotions of the heart. It paralyzed all further eulogiums on the casual song-singing heretofore interspersed in the English comedy, and rendered the popular airs of the drama . . . the lifeless materials of childish ignorance."

The building, 99 by 150 feet, with large public rooms, was the first theater in New York with fixed seats in the pit, instead of the crude benches used at John Street and the Park. Philip Hone, an enthusiast, was critical of the performances but impressed by the house, which he praised for "a style of magnificence which even the extravagance of Europe has not yet equaled." Apparently, patrons who kept boxes on the second tier were allowed to do their own decorating, which must have made the interior look like a furniture showroom. "Our box," Hone wrote, "is fitted up with great taste, with light blue hangings, gilded panels and cornice, armchairs, and a sofa. Some of the others have rich silk ornaments; some are painted in fresco, and each proprietor seems to have tried to outdo the rest in comfort and magnificence." Still, the Opera failed in its first season—despite the eminence of its begetter and promoter, Lorenzo Da Ponte. The house survived, however, and—renamed the National Theatre—devoted itself to more popular fare until it finally burned in 1839.

More successful than Da Ponte were new impresarios who aimed at a middlebrow audience, like William Niblo (1789–1878), the leading showman of the ante- and post-bellum city, the thinking man's Barnum. Billy, as everyone called him, was Irish, but nonetheless worked his way into the good graces of both the aristocratic and popular audiences. Niblo's Garden, at the corner of Broadway and Prince Street, defined the northern boundary of fashionable Broadway. It was a Jackson-era retake on the pleasure gardens of the Revolution, not as garish as Barnum's American Museum, but not, like the defunct opera house, to be struck down by a mortal case of sophistication.

Niblo's outdoor garden was famous for its fireworks and festoons of light. "The Gardens will be brilliantly illuminated with gas and thousands of variegated [probably meaning colored] lamps," an 1836 advertisement bragged: the place had outshone Ranelagh and Vauxhall* as the city's leading outdoor

---

* The original Ranelagh had been torn down in 1795, though a new tavern and garden with the same name had opened in 1806. The earliest Vauxhall (see pp. 44–45) had moved twice, ending up at its final location near Astor Place in 1805, under the aegis of Joseph Delacroix. Vauxhall closed for good in 1859.

venue. Niblo's could hold 3,000 people in its garden, theater, saloon, and hotel. Special exhibits and performances generated evening crowds along the sidewalks; shows broke in the midst for a half-hour refreshment period; before they began and after they ended private stagecoaches ferried customers back and forth between lower Broadway and the garden.

Smaller competitors vied for business as well—Contoit's, on Broadway just above Murray Street, where a colonnaded entranceway with a lantern above led customers into a compact house-sized garden where, in warm weather, you ate ice cream under light-bedecked trees. Corrie's illuminated ice cream garden on the Battery offered music. And a walkway led over the water to Castle Garden, in the harbor just off the Battery. Once a fort, it now held 10,000 people for balls and concerts, and fireworks. But Broadway found its real center with the opening of the new (and present) City Hall, built in 1812. Improvements to the park just south of it turned what had once been a rural-feeling pasture into a pulsing urban square, often the site of riotous New Year's Eve and Fourth of July celebrations.

While the Park Theatre across the street, Da Ponte's doomed opera house, and the pleasure gardens may have been bastions of urbanity, they never suppressed the irrepressible low life that flowed around them. Just across from the Park, for example, stood Bridewell prison and the city's second almshouse, which at various times housed paupers, persons arrested for disorderly conduct, and the insane. Some elite New Yorkers may have enjoyed the contrasts, but not George Templeton Strong (1820–1875), in 1836 a bookish sixteen-year-old Columbia student living with his family on Greenwich Street. Strong, a young old man in the mold of Philip Hone, liked the new park's design but loathed its crowds, particularly on the Fourth of July. "A shameful spectacle," he moaned in his diary, describing the 1836 version. "The booths lighted up, the people as drunk as dogs, and such a popping of squibs, rockets, pistols, etc., as I never heard. I'm not much given to moralizing, but it did not look much like Sunday evening in a Christian country."

The *Herald* agreed. "During the whole night the city was in a perfect blaze of light and uproar," it reported. "The theatres and gardens are filled to suffocation—concerts and fire-works, music and dancing, while away the evening. . . . Rows and riots were to be seen on almost every corner—bloody noses and black eyes are the order of the night, and with aching heads and bruised bones, hundreds retire for the night, inwardly exclaiming—'what a happy country!—what glorious fun!—what lots of rum!'"

Whenever Strong left for Columbia, then located along Church Street between Barclay and Murray Streets, he had to walk up Broadway, through the thick of the crowds, and he found them consistently unappealing. On a Sunday evening in October, 1840, he strolled the garish boulevard from downtown up to 8th Street and back again, laconically remarking that "the street is always crowded, and whores and blackguards make up about two-thirds of the throng."

His appraisal wasn't inaccurate: crowds were indeed a mongrel mix of rich, brash, and miserable (not unlike today's). Yet the line between high and low may not have been as firm as he liked to believe. Barnum's genteel predecessors weren't really much less vulgar, with their shoddy carnival acts and Believe-It-Or-Not sensations. The summer the Astor House opened, Peale's Museum, floundering with immaculate respectability just up Broadway, exhibited Afong Moy, "The Chinese Lady," every night at eight. The highlight was a display of her bound feet: "the shoe and covering of the foot will be taken off—thereby affording an opportunity of observing their curious method of folding the toes, &c. by actual observation, [proving] the real size of the foot beyond a doubt." Its other attractions that season included Siamese twins, an anaconda, and a juggler, Signor Vivalla.

Small wonder, then, that the crowds were a potpourri. Between ten and eleven, when the theaters disgorged their patrons, Broadway became a chaos of cabs, private carriages, buses, and hired coaches. Only after midnight did the crowds thin and the lights begin to go out, in a burnt-out end memorably described by George Foster:

> One by one the late shops close their shutters, and at length the oyster cellars extinguish their gigantic painted lamps, and shut their inside windows. With the exception of the dim and distant public lamps the street is now dark. Once in a while a belated omnibus rattles furiously homeward, and the side walk sends along a hollow echo beneath the feet of the lonely passenger.

Not only the lonely passenger—pigs (which, as mentioned before, kept the night wanderer occasional company in New Amsterdam days) were still part of the Broadway scene. After the strolling crowds dispersed, the pigs trotted out to scavenge edible litter from the muck. Edmund Blunt, an English observer who described the city in 1818, blamed them for the reputation of New York streets as the filthiest in the United States. A toothless ordinance exacted a $3 fine for a pig found wandering without a ring in its nose, and an anti-pig campaign collapsed when pig owners staged a riot on Houston Street just east of the Bowery, during which they freed a cartload of renegade hogs headed for the pound, and severely beat the drivers. The hogs came back to stay until mid-century.

Nevertheless the city had still not entirely lost all its nocturnal country stillness. When Lydia Maria Child, a Boston educator with no vulgarity in her makeup, spent a season in New York in 1841, neither Barnum's noise and light nor the antics of the hogs impressed her one way or another. But a nighttime visit to the Battery lifted her into rapture:

> Go there at midnight, to meet the breeze on your cheek, like the kiss of a friend; to hear the continual plashing of the sea, like the cool sound of oriental fountains; to see the moon look lovingly on the sea-nymphs, and throw down [a] wealth of jewels on their shining hair. . . . Or go, when "night with her thousand eyes, looks down into the heart, making it great"—when she floats above us, dark and solemn, and scarcely sees her image in the black mirror of the ocean. The city lamps surround you, like a shining belt of descended constellations. . . . And there . . . stands Castle Garden—with its gay perspective of coloured lamps, like a fairy grotto, where imprisoned fire-spirits send up sparkling wreaths, or rockets laden with glittering ear-drops, caught by the floating sea-nymphs, as they fall.

CITY BEAT:
THE MOON IN THE MORNING AND THE *Sun* AT NIGHT

Something else was new to the 1830s. After midnight the streets may have been nearly empty of all but livestock. Yet they had become a source of gossip, fear, and fascination. Nighttime no longer passed beneath the scrutiny of the sleeping majority, because it had been made into news. The sporadic weekly papers of the 18th century had matured into a relentlessly competitive industry. The first New York daily, Francis Child's *Daily Advertiser*, debuted on March 1, 1785, and was still limping along in 1833 with a circulation of about 1,400, bruised by ten fierce competitors—notably Colonel James Watson Webb's hard-nosed anti-abolitionist

Morning Courier and New-York Enquirer. But all of them charged a steep 6 cents, which limited them to wealthy readers whose tastes dictated their content: politics, shipping, and commerce.

They were thus of little interest to a growing but poor reading public. But then, on the morning of September 3, 1833, Benjamin Day launched the city's first penny daily, the morning *Sun.* In its early days the paper clung to life by frail threads in the hands of two male midwives: Benjamin Day himself (recently arrived in the city from Springfield, Massachusetts) and his $4-per-week assistant, an out-of-work printer named George W. Wisner.

Day reported, wrote up articles, and ran the press. Improvements in printing had revolutionized the laborious craft of Benjamin Franklin's day, when a flat bed of type had to be inked by hand and sheets of paper pressed down on it one by one. Cylinder presses, first perfected in 1811, had vastly sped up the printing process: inking was accomplished automatically by rollers, and as many as three sheets of paper at a time could be fed onto the cylinder, which then rolled them quickly over the type. Eventually the *Sun* acquired even more streamlined equipment: a gripper device invented by Richard Hoe, which fed paper into the press automatically, and (in 1835) a steam engine to replace the hand cranks. All these turned printing into a mercurial dynamo, flinging more news out faster to more people than ever before.

Day's real genius, though, lay in creating a demand big and hungry enough to devour this streamlined output. Selling the *Sun* for just a penny put it within reach of thousands of new readers: 10,000 of them within a year, more than twice the circulation of Webb's *Courier and Enquirer.* More shrewdly yet, Day and Wisner either divined, or perhaps just decided, what this new audience wanted to read about, and came up with an inspired innovation: the night beat.

George Wisner thus became the first among a succession of media genius-troublemakers in the popular press of the 19th and 20th centuries by prowling through town in the middle of the night to attend police courts. In existence at least since 1806, these went into session at four o'clock in the morning in local watch houses to process offenders who'd been rounded up the night before. Night courts eventually hired special justices and clerks who, among other duties, examined "all persons apprehended or detained in custody by the night-watch of the city," and were more particularly charged with the supervision of "bastards, apprentices, servants, vagrants and vagabonds."

Their stories were aching to be told, and when Wisner's earliest "Police Office" columns began appearing, the hidden doings of the city night suddenly revealed themselves to morning readers at the breakfast table or on the omnibus. On the night of July 3, 1834, Wisner recorded an intimate story behind the unruly (but hitherto faceless) Fourth of July crowds that so annoyed George Templeton Strong. Most of the people committed were disorderly or violent drunks, but now they came individually alive as Wisner dragged their stories into the light:

> Patrick Ludwick was sent up by his wife, who testified that she had supported him for several years in idleness and drunkenness. Abandoning all hopes of a reformation in her husband, she bought him a suit of clothes a fortnight since and told him to go about his business, for she would not live with him any longer. Last night he came home in a state of intoxication, broke into his wife's bedroom, pulled her out of bed, pulled her hair, and stamped on her. She called a watchman and sent him up. Pat excited all his powers of eloquence in endeavoring to excite his wife's sympathy, but to no purpose. As every sensible woman ought to do who is cursed with a drunken husband, she refused to have anything to do with him hereafter—and he was sent to the penitentiary.

Thus the daily paper became a record of nightly farce and agony, and the tone Wisner set in the 1830s—hovering or veering between fascination and contempt, summoning up the reader's reservoirs both of repulsion and attraction—has persisted in sensational reporting ever since. Pity, schadenfreude, self-righteousness, and a savor for muck may seem ill-sorted ingredients, but in the morning papers they make a cocktail.

As 24-hour news coverage became a reality, the newspaper plants, clustered downtown in the neighborhood of City Hall, became all-night hives of activity. This was particularly true of the morning dailies, where crowds of newsboys—famed night creatures in Victorian New York—congregated. The old six-penny papers had mostly been delivered to subscribers' doorsteps; it was Benjamin Day who first sent a mob of boys out each dawn to peddle the papers by shrieking out the most hair-raising headlines to the awakening streets. When they had enough cash, newsboys started their evenings at a theater. Presses began rolling sometime after midnight, after the shows let out, and by one in the morning the boys were forming crowds outside the printing plants. In winter, they would huddle near the windows to catch warm currents blasting out from the presses and the steam boilers that powered them. Year round, they haunted Butter-cake Dick's, a cheap all-night cellar restaurant prized by poor and well-off alike, and harshly lit by a camphene-fueled Drummond light. Dick's was a Tammany Hall hangout, famed for its hat-sized butter cakes, as well as an upstairs gambling den and downstairs ladies' beer saloon.

Drunks, gamblers, street and bar fights, family quarrels, murder (not unusual, but not yet so epidemic as to seem routine), were commonplace in court records going back to New Amsterdam. But now they had become inalienable public property, and reporters their self-appointed stewards. Publishers like Colonel Webb abominated the *Sun* and its first rival, James Gordon Bennett's *Herald* (which debuted in May 1835). But within months they'd caved in and soon most city papers, even the staid *Morning Courier and New-York Enquirer*, covered night court and the underworld along with the showy milieu of theater, music, exhibits, and balls.

Benjamin Day left a second legacy to the press, perhaps even more epoch-making: the realization that newspaper readers wanted to appease their imaginations as well as their appetite for facts. This lesson struck home in September 1835, when the *Sun* launched one of the most notorious scams in the history of media. The invention of Richard Adams Locke (another of the paper's itinerant geniuses), it began in the August 25, 1835, issue, with an announcement couched in a tone of suppressed excitement. It purported to be an excerpt from an Edinburgh scientific journal, and it promised news of astounding "recent discoveries in Astronomy which will build an imperishable monument to the age in which we live, and confer upon the present generation of the human race proud distinction through all future time."

Sir John Frederick William Herschel (1792–1871) was indeed a prominent British astronomer—an expert on star clusters and nebulae, also the author of a standard textbook, *Treatise on Astronomy* (1833). But when the *Sun*'s story reached him, he was surprised to learn from it that he had built a huge new telescope on the Cape of Good Hope that, trained on the moon, had discovered wonders: mountains, forests, lilac-colored pyramids, and an Eden of living creatures. The latter included blue unicorns and beavers that could not only build houses but also light fires. And, most exciting of all, bat-winged flying humans, described by Locke's fictional discoverer in convincing detail:

We were thrilled with astonishment to perceive four successive flocks of large winged creatures, wholly unlike any kind of birds, descend with a slow even motion from the cliffs. . . . Certainly they *were* like human beings, for their wings had now disappeared, and their attitude in walking was both erect and dignified. . . . About half of the first party had passed beyond our canvas; but of all the others we had perfectly distinct and deliberate view. They averaged four feet in height, were covered, except on the face, with short and glossy copper-colored hair, and had wings composed of a thin membrane, without hair, lying snugly upon their backs from the top of the shoulders to the calves of their legs.

Small wonder that the Moon Hoax—for hoax it was—created a city-wide, indeed global, sensation. Locke had detected that the strange and marvelous aroused a public hunger powerful enough to beguile skepticism. Nor, in the 1830s, did the tale tax credulity: at the time many reputable astronomers thought as a matter of course that the moon was inhabited. Wonder about the creatures that might walk there seemed an exercise of possibility rather than fantasy, and that made the Moon Hoax the most remarkable nighttime thrill since a gigantic meteor shower in November of 1833, during which a strange fall of gelatinous blobs pelted the city's environs. Or was it since the fall of 1824, on another memorable night when fish plopped down out of the sky during a rainstorm? (Of course the latter two events had actually happened.)

Competing newspapers, notably Bennett's *Herald,* instantly pegged the *Sun* story as an imposition; Webb's *Courier* declined to comment at all. But even when the whole bold fraud imploded, the *Sun* made no apologies. Instead Day confessed to some pride in having diverted "the public mind, for a while, from that bitter apple of discord, the abolition of slavery"—the incendiary topic of the times in the New York press. And readers seem to have taken no offense: by 1836 the *Sun* had become by far the biggest newspaper in the world, with an unprecedented circulation of 30,000.

HANINGTON'S VIRTUAL MOON AND THE DIORAMAS OF MONSIEUR DAGUERRE

Benjamin Day's Moon Hoax was not the first instance of New York's love of illusions; his only real innovation was in using newsprint to create them. New York had been welcoming more tangible man-made marvels at least since the 1756 visit by Henry Bridges's clockwork Microcosm, and the fashion endured through the post-Revolutionary era. In 1810 crowds flocked to Broadway to see a panorama of the city: a circular painting, 35 feet high, 186 feet long, and enclosing a circle about 60 feet across, made with St. Paul's roof as the vantage point. Because the panorama required artificial lighting for maximum effect, it opened only at night.

And in September 1835, two new illuminated shows were drawing evening crowds. One, a giant painting of the flight from Egypt, was on display at Niblo's Garden. The other was at Hanington's Diorama on Broadway near St. Paul's Chapel, and it was even more epical: a deluge, a storm and shipwreck, Italian and Indian scenes, and finally "The Conflagration of Moscow." But these were to prove tame next to Hanington's next attraction—a magnificent (or so the ads said) son et lumière presentation of the moon according to the *Sun* and Richard Adams Locke.

Dioramas, long since replaced by other darkened-room magic like movies and now rarely seen, were an early 19th-century rage, invented by a man more widely famed as the father of photography (though he might better be called the father of light-mediated illusions), Louis Daguerre (1787–1851). Dioramas, cycloramas, and panoramas—different types of exhibits often combined with each other—had become a staple of evening entertainment in the 1800s, astonishing patrons with an uncanny mastery of illumination and mystifying effects. At their best they seemed almost supernatural—baffling and delightful, yet also with a diabolical tinge which only enhanced the spell.

Daguerre-inspired dioramas were more elaborate and ingenious than their best-known surviving descendant: the beloved Indian groups still on view behind glass at the American Museum of Natural History. Daguerre began his career as a scenic designer for the Paris theaters, juggling light, shadow, and color to create mystifying displays of impossible things in motion, and his inventions presaged the illusion-making technologies of still photography and moving pictures. Gifted with a genius for deceiving the human eye, and using little more than darkness, natural light, paint, and lamps, he built stage sets that amazed audiences and convinced Daguerre that a few improvements would make them destinations in themselves. In 1822 he and a partner, the painter Charles-Marie Bouton, built the first diorama, in a 52-by-169-foot building near the present-day Place de la République. It opened on July 11 and caused an instant sensation.

Visitors entered a twilit anteroom, then a dark auditorium with small muted lamps on the floor to prevent stumbling. A disembodied voice directed viewers to waiting benches, and as their eyes became accustomed to the gloom, they gradually saw the rest of the audience, all staring at a barely visible rectangle cut into the blackness. As the show started, it began slowly to brighten. Then, so gradually no one could say just when, objects and lights began surfacing out of darkness, and the blank oblong gradually welled up with color and motion, a magic window. Landscapes appeared, seeming to spread behind and beyond the frame. Streams flowed, lakes shimmered in sunlight, clouds changed shape and shade as they floated across the sky.

In one of Daguerre's most famous effects, daylight seemed slowly to sink, the leaves on the trees appeared to shimmer, the sky went dark, lights went on, candelabras could be seen flickering through miniature house windows. Logic, of course, told viewers they were looking at painted cloth. But their eyes refused to accept this; too many objects in the painting looked real. And no scene was long enough for its illusion to fade: before the viewers could quite grasp the spectacle, they heard a grinding rumble beneath their feet and the entire auditorium began to revolve. The window, rotating with it, gradually centered itself on a second scene that equaled or surpassed the first. Even in Paris, city of the super-sophisticated, the diorama created a wave of astonishment and uncorked a champagne-bottleful of honors for Daguerre, well over a decade before he made his first daguerrotype.

In an early report on Daguerre's diorama, a writer from the London *Times* observed that it played not just on the senses, but on thought and emotion as well. "The most striking effect is the change of light," he said:

> From a calm, soft, delicious, serene day in summer, the horizon gradually changes, becoming more and more overcast, until a darkness, not the effect of night, but evidently of approaching storm—a murky, tempestuous blackness—discolours every object, making us listen almost for the thunder which is to growl in the distance, or fancy we feel the large drops, the *avant-couriers* of the shower.

The *Times* writer praised the illusion, but also voiced a shiver at its hint of cold, black magic: was it an enchantment or a malignant hex? "You have," he noted, "as far as the senses can be acted upon, all these things (realities) before you; and yet, in the midst of all this crowd of animation, there is a stillness, which is the stillness of the grave. The idea produced is that of a region—of a world—desolated; of living nature at an end; of the last day past and over."

Daguerre would do anything to put an illusion across, once installing a live goat in a diorama of Mont Blanc. But his arch-deceiver was light. A daylight scene was painted on the front of a thin, nearly transparent calico scrim and the night scene (in mirror image) on the back. Floodlit from the front, the cloth showed noontime, but if light from the front were slowly damped and the calico gradually backlit, day would dissolve imperceptibly into night. Small holes pricked through the cloth made convincing candle flames. And tinted filters, trained on the cloth either from the front or the back, yielded even more ingenious effects: a red filter would turn blue paint purple and make green look black. Add to all such tricks the disorienting, redimensioning effect on an audience first plunged into darkness, then overwhelmed by Daguerre's concerts of luminosity, and it's hardly surprising that people were awestruck and a little disturbed.

Natural rather than artificial light was the engine of Daguerre's first Paris diorama. Its walls consisted mostly of huge glass windows and Daguerre simply trained the light coming through them according to his will, moving shutters, masks, lenses, and mirrors into place to filter, tint, redirect, magnify, reduce, or even douse it. Thus performances were limited to daytime, and dioramas built on this plan often shut down completely during the short days of the northern European winter. But in New York, the lighting was more often artificial: oil or gas lamps, though harder to tend, were indifferent to the weather, and in any case New York, by the 1820s, liked its amusements to play in the evening. It was, after all, a working town, still without the large leisured populations of a Paris or London.

Indeed night in the city was becoming as dependent on human manipulation and cultural attitudes as on the natural facts of astronomy. The Moon Hoax is an apt illustration. Late in August of 1835, just before the *Sun* sprang its trap for the unwary, two Yale astronomers announced that they had, using a large telescope, caught a first glimpse of Halley's still distant comet, on its long-predicted return. A brief notice to that effect appeared in the *Morning Courier* on September 4, 1835, and in the *Sun* on September 7. Yet the comet, visible for weeks, drew little attention, at least in the press: New York seemed more interested in its virtual sky than its real one. Somehow the night had grown from being a natural condition of life to a phenomenon based on nature but not confined to it, and best experienced in the man-made metropolis. In Lydia Child's encomium, the beauty of the Battery at night came from its contrast with the jewelry of man-made lights sprinkling the streets beyond.

In 18th-century theaters, in any performance that required a transition from day to night, the stage lighting had been abruptly cut down, and this was a convention so accepted as to pass almost without remark. But now, as if humans were claiming a power over day and night once reserved to nature, the art of illusion could compete even with magisterial and mysterious natural spectacles like the sunset. Much of Louis Daguerre's early fame arose from his ingenious methods for making apparent sunlight melt gradually into gloom and darkness; he was a pioneer in the creation of convincing stage moonlight.

Nightfall, always an occasion, became even more so once people could play with it artificially; yet if the heavens were taking on a human dimension, they lost some grandeur in the process. In a curious editorial on the reappearance of Halley's Comet, Bennett—writing in the *Herald* on September 17—bemusedly noted the gradual dispersal of the universal terror that astronomical anomalies had once occasioned. Now panic was confined to the foolish. "Were those who indulge in these fancies to bestow half the time which they employ in giving them publicity, in studying correct principles, they would perceive that the appearance of the Comet is nothing more than any other phenomenon, the future exhibition of which may be inferred from what has passed."

Even after the *Sun* owned up to its moon fraud, Day exploited instead of dropping it, apparently deciding it had even more publicity value as a joke on the competition than it did as a scientific wonder. Later that fall, Hanington premiered a new grand panorama (no doubt in cahoots with the *Sun,* which relentlessly hyped it) in the grand saloon of the City Hotel, at 115 Broadway. The doors opened every evening at 6:30; the performance began at 7:30 and crested with a "grand moving panorama of the Moon, painted on upward of one thousand feet of canvas, being a brilliant illustration of the scientific observations made by the most eminent astronomers, of the surface of the Moon, showing its various mountains, volcanoes, lakes, rivers, etc., to which will be added the reported Lunar Observations of Sir John Herschel, in which will be seen the animals, birds, forests, etc., with their natural motions, to resemble life."

Hanington, originally a sign-painter, still kept a shop further north on

Broadway. But his dioramas were ambitious. Unlike Daguerre's, his audience sat still; it was the scenes that moved. And the moon show, at least, featured animations as well as purely optical effects. All that fall, the *Sun* bent itself into knots in praise of Hanington's erupting volcanoes, plunging waterfalls, and cavorting golden pheasants. At the Monday, September 21, performance, a Newfoundland dog started baying at the flying man- and woman-bats, which at one point took to the wing and gathered in a green valley for a picnic. When, in the real sky, Halley's Comet finally appeared above the city at the beginning of October, the *Sun* dryly noted its appearance, but advised readers "not to gaze at the Comet for a few evenings, for it can scarcely be seen with the naked eye, but go to Hannington's [*sic*] Lunar Panorama at the City Saloon, which is the most unique and beautiful spectacle ever beheld."

The *Sun* was without shame but its eye for virgin territory unerring. Nighttime, still the half of life largely empty of salaried work, trade, or religion, had, at the call of progress, succumbed to illumination and the illusions it could create. Pushed along by transit, mass-market publishing, and other technologies, it came to life and generated an unprecedented amplitude for activity (including new kinds of salaried work, new trade, and even new religious establishments). Benjamin Day, George Wisner, James Gordon Bennett of the *Herald,* and soon Horace Greeley (who launched the *Tribune* in 1841), created, through night reporting, an eager market for their daily papers, and with it a new awareness of the urban dark hours as an expansion of the human realm, a time of unprecedented opportunities and dangers. In the hushed octagonal tower of the Yale observatory, Sir Edmund Halley might be the moment's demigod. But on the new Broadway, a cotillion and circus combined, it was Hanington who showed you the night sky, complete with exploding volcanoes, waterfalls, and airborne homunculi.

In New York art hadn't just imitated nature; it had yanked it offstage with a hook.

"AWFUL CALAMITY—UNPRECEDENTED CONFLAGRATION!!"
THE GREAT FIRE OF 1835

Day's Moon Hoax was, in all its silliness, a fit emblem for the prosperous and exuberant New York of the early 1830s. But change lay ahead in the middle distance: the Panic of 1837 and a floodtide of new immigrants into the packed slums northeast of City Hall. And in the immediate future, a catastrophe loomed: the Great Fire of 1835. Broadway, up which the 1776 fire had roared, had recovered to be a marvel as impressive in its way as the flames that had once devoured it, and gained recognition as one of the world's great thoroughfares. But fears of conflagration had remained a New York bugbear. Even in the midst of the excitement over Herschel's telescope, it kept recurring, like a premonition.

That August the *Commercial Advertiser* had published a thoughtful article about "the numerous fires with which our city is afflicted, probably beyond any other in the world, except Constantinople." Both cities relied heavily on wood construction, but the *Advertiser* noted a further hazard in Manhattan. Increasingly, as downtown became more and more dominated by business and entertainment, merchants were moving out of the upstairs living quarters they'd formerly maintained above their shops and warehouses (which were usually one and the same). "After being closed at night, frequently the duty of the youngest apprentice, or of a common labourer," the writer observed, the buildings "are left to their fate." A lamp still burning, or a flammable item forgotten on a still hot stove, repeatedly caused fires, wiped out merchants, and frightened neighbors.

It was impossible not to know when fire broke out—a bell had been placed in 1834 atop City Hall, audible everywhere. It was more effective than the old system: a lantern hung on an arm off the cupola of the old City Hall on Wall Street, pointing in the direction of the outbreak. The new bell sounded one to six peals to identify in which of the six districts radiating from the belfry the fire had begun. "It gave a somber, ominous tone, appropriate to the message it conveyed," according to Charles Haswell, a retired president of the Board of Councilmen, recalling in 1896 how it had sounded to him as a child.

All through the summer and fall fires were rarely out of the news. Some, of course, happened in daylight: at one in the afternoon on September 17, Niblo's diorama building (also unwisely used for fireworks storage) went up, destroying the giant painting of the flight of the Jews from Egypt, supposedly worth $5,000, and killing Isaac Freeman, a black waiter. Trapped by the blaze when he rushed inside to rescue some furniture, he made his way to an upper-story window. But the ladders were too short to reach it, and just as he was steeling himself to jump, according to the *Sun,* "a sheet of flame struck him full in front, and he fell backward to the floor, enveloped in fire, where he perished alone."

Most of the fires conformed to the pattern noted by the *Commercial Advertiser*: an outbreak in a store left unattended at night. These often didn't result in injury or death, but were worrying because of lower Manhattan's close-packed buildings, the narrowness of its streets, and inadequate firefighting equipment. On August 12, 1835, the major fire that alarmed the *Commercial Advertiser* killed five and destroyed 31 buildings around Fulton Street. And less destructive blazes—like one that broke out at a quarter to eleven during a strong northeast gale on the night of September 21 at the corner of Prince and Mercer Streets—were a weekly occurrence. Theaters, full of gaslights, lanterns, and flammable scenery, were particularly fire-prone, and few escaped: the Park had burned down in 1820, though it was later rebuilt. But nothing had yet happened to match the 1776 fire until a bitter attack of cold struck in December 1835.

It was particularly frigid on the 16th, when the thermometer sank to seventeen below zero. All by itself this could have been read as an omen: intense chill has often coincided with some dark or terrible event in city history, and tonight the pattern held true. A watchman spotted fire around nine in the evening, in a five-story warehouse near the northern end of Hanover Square. The culprit was a relatively new one: lighting gas, leaking from a pipe and ignited by coals left burning in a stove. Just as in 1776, there was a merciless wind abroad, this time rampaging across the Hudson from the northwest (in the end this may have been a stroke of luck; the winds drove the fire toward the East River and the bay rather than over to the Hudson or uptown). The weather made firefighting close to impossible: water froze in the hoses and pumps, the winds spread the flames from building to building in neighborhoods built far denser and higher than in 1776.

Writing in his diary at the family home at 108 Greenwich Street, behind Trinity Church, George Templeton Strong recorded the first alarm. The house itself was never in immediate danger, though its rear windows faced the Hudson, which, as the blaze grew, flickered in a ghastly reflection of the flames. Strong's father, however, was a lawyer who kept an office on Wall Street. This was downwind from the outbreak, and the family was worried.

Evening. At about nine o'clock there was an alarm of fire. Papa went to bed notwithstanding it looked near the office. The fire is evidently an extensive one and shines splendidly on the shipping and houses in the rear. Mr. Havens has just come to call Papa up, as the office is in danger. It is a tremendous fire, by his account. They have just left. *Eleven o'clock.* Mr. Lambert has just come in. He thinks the office out of danger, but the fire is still raging in Exchange, Pearl, Front Streets, etc. It is very cold—mercury at zero—and by his account the fire is yet unchecked. Twelve o'clock. The fire as we can see from the front windows is still raging, and Papa has not returned. I would give a good deal to be there. I shall turn in notwithstanding, as my anxiety for the office cannot prevent me from feeling very sleepy.

By the time his father woke him, at five the next morning, the fire was still roaring, and the family was beginning to fear not just for the Wall Street office, but for the house on Greenwich Street. When George left at eight, to go to class at Columbia, smoke shrouded the blocks just to his west and the city was in an uproar. For there was, as there hadn't been in 1776, a competitive daily press to hammer the disaster into the public mind. Screaming headlines, a commonplace in later popular newspapers, made one of their earliest, and by later standards rather tentative, appearances. The *Commercial Advertiser,* an evening paper, went to press on the afternoon of the 17th, announcing that "New York has been for fifteen hours in flames! They are not yet extinguished." On the morning of Friday the 18th, the *Sun* branded its lead story with "AWFUL CALAMITY—UNPRECEDENTED CONFLAGRATION!!"

Thanks to the loud reverberating chamber constructed by the penny *Sun* and *Herald,* fire had become a nighttime spectacle as well as a dire threat—a perverse form of entertainment that at times seemed to drown out the catastrophe. "During the night," an aghast *Commercial Advertiser* reporter wrote, "all descriptions of carriages were in the immediate [area] of the fire, either waiting to remove books, driving away with merchandise, or in attendance upon those who were watching the progress of the flame."

But this conflagration was gigantic on a scale not seen before. The 1776 blaze had taken 493 buildings; the 1835 fire devoured 674, and while it was at its height the sky glow could be seen as far away as Philadelphia. Thirteen acres of buildings and streets fueled a bellowing red inferno, surrounding Hanover Square and bounded by the East River, Wall Street on the north, Broad Street on the west, and Coenties Slip on the south. A stock of turpentine, ignited in shoreline warehouses, flooded in sheets of flame out onto the frozen East River and set several ships on fire. On the morning of the 18th, the *Sun* strove to put into words the impact of the spectacle on eye-witnesses. The whole district, the paper said, was

> like oil to the appetite of the voracious elements which shot its pyramids of flame high in the heavens, illuminating the earth, the rivers, and the distant sky, and wrapping in one vast sheet of fire every object within its destructive grasp. The scene was awfully magnificent and sublime. It seemed as if a God were moving in his anger, and sweeping away with the bosom of his wrath, the proud-est monuments of man. Destruction travelled and triumphed on every breeze, and billows of fire rolled over and buried in their burning bosoms the hopes and the fortunes of thousands.

The *Sun*'s tone is apocalyptic, but the facts were less so. Only two peo-ple died, as against the five who lost their lives in the much smaller August 12 blaze in nearby Fulton Street. The 1835 fire struck the city most sharply in its pocketbook, and despite the huge swath of physical de-struction it left, the laments in the 1835 papers seem somewhat unmov-ing now because they were chiefly wails of anguish for lost property and the frustration of merchants. In fact, though the *Sun* remarked the loss of the Dutch Reformed Church on Exchange Place, the great lost treasure of the fire was the Merchants' Exchange on Wall Street. Because it was supposed to be fireproof, a number of merchants had moved their goods into it in the early stages of the fire. But it caught anyway, its dome exhaling a spec-tacular column of fire up into the sky before crashing down into the building's rotunda, landing on a newly erected statue of Alexander Hamil-ton—beloved patriarch of New York's mercantile culture—and knocking it off its pedestal. If God was indeed angry, he seems to have had it in for wealth rather than the sins of nocturnal passion. And even in the midst of the blaze the beleaguered firefighters were outnumbered by frantic shopowners trying to save their goods, looters trying to steal them, and gawkers.

The fire carved a black smoking waste into the city's commercial heart and revealed the inadequacy of New York's firefighting system. The money damages amounted to tens of millions, more than the cost of the Erie Canal. There was no repetition of the 1776 fire's rampage up Broadway; Trinity Church was spared; the residential blocks between Broadway and the Hudson were left intact; Scudder's Museum and the Park Theatre, undamaged, still overlooked City Hall. The nighttime entertainment district was largely untouched. Moreover, the 1835 fire put no crimp whatever in the city's growth: the economy was booming, and reconstruction almost instant, with newspapers voicing amazement at the speed with which new buildings sprung up on the ruins. It had taken the better part of two decades to clear Canvas Town and make a respectable neighborhood out of it after the 1776 fire, but in 1835 the whole burned district had been rebuilt, taller and solider and richer, within a year. In 1836 Philip Hone noted that rents were going up at a rate of 50 percent per annum.

MANSION, SLUM, AND BOARDINGHOUSE

On November 4, 1825, a spectacular extravaganza celebrated the just finished Erie Canal. City Hall, brilliantly illuminated, proudly overlooked a fireworks display in the park. There was good reason to celebrate: the canal was the match that lit the fuse that detonated the boom of the 1830s. But the gigantic workforce needed to build it also fatefully transformed New York into a huge magnet for immigration, particularly among the Irish, who now became an important presence in the city, both in numbers and in the public mind—though not, at first, in influence. Disproportionately poor, Catholic, and overrepresented in the slums, they became an inevitable target for the fears and suspicions of 19th-century native New Yorkers. More waves of immigration, in the famine years of the 1840s, brought the Irish to nearly a quarter of Manhattan's population in the 1850s, and by then they had surpassed blacks in the public mind as the scapegoat of choice for dirt, lewdness, drunkenness, uncouth manners, and crime. They came in for particularly contemptuous treatment both in the establishment and the popular press, particularly Bennett's *Herald*.

But they weren't by any means the only group that transformed the city and the social map of night. Apart from the ethnic surges (and cutting across them) these decades witnessed a huge influx of young people from everywhere—not merely everywhere in the world but everywhere in the United States. They'd already begun to be visible on the streets even in 1800, when Harriet and Maria Trumbull spent their season in an intimate Manhattan where almost everyone they saw on the sidewalk could be recognized by name or at least placed and bracketed. New York, after all, had only about 60,000 people in 1800: though no longer a village, it was still small enough to feel knowable. But by 1840, the population had multiplied fivefold, to more than 300,000, and the streets were full of foreign-looking crowds with inscrutable faces, unintelligible voices, and alien customs, circulating among the jammed, rented rooms of teeming neighborhoods like the Five Points. Press stories of the immigrants carrying beds from room to room, sleeping in twos and fours, males with males and females, females with females and males, no longer seemed strange or surprising. People wandering mysteriously in and out of the city had become part of its texture and made it seem like a Joseph Conrad novel, all random arrival and furtive departure, all moral drift and sinister uncertainty.

Nor was it just in the slums that the city's population had begun to abandon the owned or rented single-family houses that, while they were dominant, served as easy-to-classify social pigeonholes. Boardinghouses, familiar since Rebecca Hogg and long before that, were sprouting up everywhere, in the good as well as the shaky neighborhoods. Early in the 1800s, a few began appearing in city guides as eminently respectable—places nobody need be ashamed of living in, ranging in 1817 from a moderate $2 a week to a very expensive $2 a day and even higher. Asa Greene, a businessman (and acerbic commentator), said in 1837 that "there are many of great respectability in different parts of the city." But he noted too a severe shortage of lodgings in New York, sardonically recommending that somebody who couldn't find one spend the night in City Hall Park. There was good reason for the crowding: the population was surging almost without letup, and had outpaced even the building boom fostered by the general prosperity of the 1830s. And in the depression that began in 1837, construction weakened while immigration increased.

Unlike the Great Fire and the rebound that had erased its scars within months, the 1837 Panic ruined economic conditions into the early 1840s and affected everybody. A rash of Wall Street failures mowed down the rich (Philip Hone, for example, lost a good part of his fortune). Unemployment—striking a third of the city's manual laborers—destroyed the poor; many died of starvation. The post-fire construction binge came to a halt, and improvised accommodations became the fate of the city housing market, a pattern that has tended to persist up to the present.

Boardinghouses, as they became more numerous, catered not just to daily or weekly transients, but to young women and men drawn to the city out of restlessness, ambition, or inklings of desire that couldn't be acted on in small towns or the country. Work for such people, once typically a permanent or semipermanent attachment to a tradesman or merchant, had become as ephemeral as they were. Now a job was an interchangeable thing that one might quit or be fired from in a moment. Boarding was an answer to the vagaries of employment: one could move in, settle down, and move out again in a matter of weeks. New York's renters had always been highly mobile (May 1, the traditional moving day, had become famous as early as the 1600s for its parade of furniture-jammed carts clogging the thoroughfares). But in the era of single-family houses, tenants tended to stay put for at least a year. The boardinghouses were more transitory, nomadic campsites for the footloose and mercurial young, who were becoming a volatile presence among the crowds on the streets at night.

By the 1840s, the New York boardinghouse had become a phenomenon famous enough to provoke literary attention. Lodgings ranged from genuinely genteel to falsely genteel to hardscrabble to desperate; but, as Junius Browne observed in 1869,* "Boarding-house existence is a doom and distress here. Men are born to it, and, through narrow circumstances, compelled to continue it when every instinct and taste revolt at it." The buildings were often spacious old houses that northward expansion had left dry-docked in incipient slums, and their reincarnation as boardinghouses often gave them an atmosphere of decrepit luxury, dirt, and frayed manners. The tenants were an ill-defined population, and not confined to the young: they included men and women of all ages, families and single people, fishmongers and stockbrokers.

In 1857 Thomas Butler Gunn, a veteran resident of them, remembered a six-by-eight-foot cubicle in a lodging house hammered into existence among the noble rooms of two old mansions that had been joined together. "It was just possible to open the door to sufficient width to obtain ingress, the bed partially blockading it, and upon this we could recline, poke the fire in the stove, and touch three sides of the room with perfect facility." The only surviving relics of opulence were the wide, heavy oak staircases. "Many a powdered beauty has, without question, in ante-revolutionary days, tripped down them, and many a red-coated, cocked-hatted officer of

---

* Browne's *The Great Metropolis: A Mirror of New York* (1869) contains many passages virtually duplicated in James McCabe's *Lights and Shadows of New York Life: Or, the Sights and Sensations of the Great City* (1872), and a reissue of the latter with added material, *New York by Sunlight and Gaslight: A Work Descriptive of the Great American Metropolis* (1882).

King George as an escort," Gunn wrote. "If such a couple could, by the pale moonlight peering in at the skylight above, and stealing down on the shabby, cracked, dirty plastered wall, revisit the scene now—!"

Ellipses were warranted: the boardinghouse was a natural resort for the demimonde and often gave respectable cover to a brothel.

"DREADFUL MURDER ON ANTHONY STREET": The Surfacing of the Criminal Underworld

Scintillating though Broadway may have been between the Astor House and Niblo's Garden, it also ran deep with undercurrents of desperation and squalor. The misery emerged more clearly in the aftermath of the 1837 Panic, but the harbingers were visible years before. Five Points, the hub of New York's most hyped slum ever, was spreading to the north and east of the filled-in Fresh Water, and was already a subject of scandal in the 1830s. It was, surely, a trouble spot, and its furtive life percolated through the pages of the daily press throughout 1835, as New York coped nervously with its fear of immigrating Irish and undiminished hostility toward native blacks. In the six-penny press, this often took the form of ostensibly high-minded political debate about race and the city's exploding non-native population; here, even the most poisonous sentiments hid themselves in the costume of reason. But the penny press vented its passion in lurid stories about the crime and misery of the slums.

While not yet the newspaper obsession it would later become, crime, of course, was constant in the city's life, and two particularly harrowing stories garnered sustained attention during the weeks of the Moon Hoax. One involved foreigners, the other involved race. They happened within days of each other, one near and the other in the Five Points. And neither, as the stories unfolded over the next few weeks, was quite so simple as it had seemed when first reported.

On Friday, September 4, at about a quarter to midnight, three people were talking in a boardinghouse at 6 Monroe Street, just east of the Five Points: Harriet Shultz, Richard C. Jackson, aged 30, and John "Little Jack" Roberts, 40. Mrs. Shultz took in lodgers and did laundry for a living; Jackson and Roberts were sailors who sometimes stayed with her when ashore. The two men had passed the evening together, laughing and talking. They decided to spend the night, and Shultz set up a makeshift bed for them. For a while the party continued amicably.

At about a quarter to twelve Roberts was sitting on a bed in the room, and Jackson on a chair. Then, according to Harriet Shultz's later testimony, Jackson suddenly jumped up and began to pace silently back and forth. She saw something in his hand, and heard a snap, not realizing it was a pistol until he strode up to within about three feet of Roberts, raised it, and shot him through the left eye: Roberts collapsed to the floor, never spoke again, and died within minutes. The night watchman, Richard Hockman, heard the shot from his post across the street, and then Harriet Shultz screaming, "Watch!" He clambered up the stairs to find Roberts dead and Jackson seated on a chair, calmly smoking a cigar.

When Hockman asked why he'd done it, Jackson replied only that Roberts had "taken away my comfort," then chomped down on the cigar and relapsed into silence. "So cool and deliberate was the prisoner," according to the *Commercial Advertiser,* that he "never took it from his mouth, till his arrest and delivery at the watch house." Toward six in the morning, with the guard outside his cell off on a short break, Jackson hanged himself from the cell door with a silk handkerchief. He was unconscious when the guard came back, but within twenty minutes he'd been cut down, resuscitated, and tied up. Left alone again, he worked his way free of the cords that bound him, but was caught again and taken back to 6 Monroe Street, where Roberts's body still lay inert on the floor. Jackson, according to the *Sun,* closed his eyes and refused to look at the corpse during the inquest, but admitted to committing the murder with a brass pistol, adding that he'd meant to kill Harriet Shultz as well.

Justice was swift by modern standards. Jackson went to trial at the Court of Oyer and Terminer* on September 22; was pronounced guilty by the jury at ten in the evening, and sentenced to death, with an execution set for Wednesday, November 19. It was a straightforward case, not the kind of baffling mystery that would soon become the sought-after drug of papers and readers alike. But it sustained the city's interest, and in the weeks before the hanging its compelling backstory emerged in the pages of the enterprising *Sun.* It was—of course—a love triangle. Jackson was Portuguese by birth; his real name was Manuel Fernandez. Though leading a sailor's itinerant life, he had come to regard New York as his

---

* "Oyer and Terminer," old Anglo-Norman legal terms, mean "hear" and "determine." The Court of Oyer and Terminer was, in the 19th century, a division of the New York State Supreme Court charged with trying criminal cases.

home base, and had begun, years before, a passionate affair with Shultz. When, after a long and eventful series of voyages, he came back to New York aboard the *Samuel Robinson* in 1831, he found her married, but they resumed relations as before. After another voyage, when Fernandez returned in 1835 to work as a rigger on the East River docks, he picked up rumors that Harriet Shultz had abandoned her husband to run the boardinghouse on Monroe Street and was keeping company with another sailor—and friend of Fernandez—John Roberts (also an Americanized name: in fact he was Prussian).

According to a series of interviews Fernandez gave the *Sun* before his execution, he'd become increasingly seized by jealousy, and it boiled over on the night of Friday, September 4. In fact, according to Fernandez, when he climbed the stairs at Monroe Street, he witnessed the sort of disturbing tableau for which the Five Points was becoming notorious, and which Harriet Shultz had good reason to want kept quiet. There were two beds in the room, and Shultz, Roberts, and Fernandez began a tense negotiation about who would sleep where. Eventually Shultz climbed, fully clothed, onto one bed—alone until a lodger, a Miss DeBruce, "came in from some nocturnal excursion" and joined her. Fernandez apparently lay down on the floor and tried to sleep; but then, just before midnight, Roberts crept into bed with the women and began having sex with Harriet. "Rising from the floor, [Fernandez] took from his pocket a pistol which he had put there," the *Sun* reported. "He presented it close to the head of Roberts, but it missed fire; yet by the time his rival had sat up on the side of the bed he had fixed on another percussion, and it now discharged with fatal effect. The ball having entered one of Roberts' eyes and passed through his head, he was dead in a few moments."

By the time he climbed the scaffold, Fernandez had emerged, at least under the spin given the case by the *Sun,* not as a wicked example of slum depravity, but as a dark hero, a victim of the hard and unforgiving life of a sailor in the early 1800s, a case of the unsettling paradoxes of crime. "He was," the *Sun* interviewer concluded, "a man abounding in many good and even refined feelings, notwithstanding his last dreadful act. His understanding, though uncultivated, was naturally shrewd; and we should suppose that in social life he was distinguished by mirth and humor rather than any malignant or gloomy passion."

At six o'clock on the morning of his execution at Bellevue Prison, a reporter for the *Journal of Commerce* found Fernandez lying on his bed, calmly smoking his habitual cigar. "He appeared to be in a debilitated state of health, and bore on his features the impress of one who had suffered considerable mental or bodily agony." He said only, "May God pity my poor soul," asked for a last drink, and marched out to the gallows flanked by two Catholic priests. The reporter for the *Journal* echoed the *Sun*:

> When a man murders his fellow man, the world generally endeavour to discover—and if not they ascribe to him—some peculiarity of person or features. In the present case, however, the criminal's person and countenance were of the most ordinary description, and bore no marks whatever of an atrocious or blood-thirsty disposition. He was below the middle size, delicately made, of a swarthy complexion, like most of his country, and with sharp features, and rather an intelligent cast of countenance.

Cut down from the gallows, Fernandez's body went directly over to the Columbia College of Surgeons, where, the *Courier* reported, "we understand several interesting galvanic experiments were tried on it."

Race too was a nagging issue in the pages of the dailies. The subject still caused deep unease; New York was in the midst of a wave of unrest, provoked by a fierce debate over abolition, with the establishment mercantile papers, the *Courier* and the *Commercial Advertiser,* rabid in their opposition to the abolitionist cause, and their competitors either moderately or passionately in favor. Tensions had already boiled over during the summer of 1834, in a destructive white riot against blacks living in the Five Points and a series of related disturbances that troubled the city throughout 1835.

The *Sun* caught the city's anxious ambivalence perhaps more diagnostically than any other paper, partly because of tension between its two leading lights. Benjamin Day was, while firmly against slavery, also highly critical of what he saw as excesses in the abolitionist movement. But George Wisner, his star reporter and partner, was a dedicated *anti*-abolitionist. As a result the paper was in its early years often revealingly unsettled, even schizophrenic, when it wrote about race. An October 1835 police column, probably written by Wisner, recounted the arrest of a white Rivington Street coach-painter named Charles Jones at the corner of Broadway and Howard Street. It was about half past ten on the evening of Thursday, October 1; the Watch charged him with harassing two black women, and almost no fact in the story escapes a race-baiting twist. Jones, in a sneering allusion to his trade, is called "an amateur of dark colors," who "undertook to attach to his easel a certain dark-colored damsel, named Catherine Hamilton, who with another female darkey, was wending her way along the street." Hamilton roused a watchman, and Jones was kept overnight in the watch house "to mourn over his dark propensities"; the police justice who arraigned him issued Hamilton the equivalent of a protection order against him. New York had finally abolished slavery in 1827, and the abolitionist cause legitimized white sympathy for blacks: to that, probably, Catherine Hamilton owed her restraining order against Jones. Yet racism persisted in the snide slurs like those in the *Sun* piece.

And it often broke out in violence. A second celebrated Five Points crime in the fall of 1835, unfolding at the same time as the Fernandez case, was the racist murder of John Van Winkle in the early morning hours of Saturday, September 19. Van Winkle, an African-American, worked as a scavenger, combing the streets at night for salvageable junk. This was a humble but vital trade in the decades before the establishment of municipal garbage collection. It was licensed, supervised, and highly necessary to the city's appearance and its health. And it was grueling work. Van Winkle, who lived on Anthony Street, was on his way home at about 3 a.m., after cleaning out a cesspool on Robinson Street. Arriving home, Van Winkle and his two assistants sat down on the front stoop to remove their soiled clothes.

Just as Van Winkle was about to go inside, his white next-door neighbor, William Newman, turned drunkenly into Anthony Street from Broadway, on his way home from a minor race riot on Catherine Lane (these were common at the time). He accosted Van Winkle, slapped him, threatened to flog him, and disappeared briefly into 105 Anthony Street, emerging almost at once, coatless. Van Winkle and his companions first backed off nervously, then broke into a run toward Centre Street, but Newman caught up with them and backed Van Winkle out into the middle of the thoroughfare. Van Winkle suddenly yelled, "he has got a knife in his hand, take care boys." They ran away again, turning up into Orange Street, where Van Winkle fell, saying he'd been stabbed. His companions summoned a watchman from Chatham Street, who, not having seen the wounded and dying man, found Newman with knife in hand but let him go home. His two assistants carried Van Winkle, stabbed through the heart and covered with blood, back to 103 Anthony, where he expired: the wound, though lethal, was so small it had taken an hour for him to bleed to death.

It was a grisly week in general. Thursday night, on Avenue D, three-year-old Edward Foley's mother had locked him into his room while she tended her nearby fruit stand; his clothes caught fire from a candle and he burned to death as his five-year-old brother looked on. George Eldred, a produce-seller, fell out of his boat, drowned, and was found floating in the Hudson. Yet it was Van Winkle's death that riveted the press, pro- and anti-abolitionist alike. The anti-abolitionist *Courier* called it a "dreadful murder," and its account, while differing in detail from the *Sun*'s (as papers almost always did in this early era of reporting), voiced sympathy for Van Winkle as the victim of a vicious crime motivated simply by race hatred.

If the murderer or the victim were higher-class, the more damning facts were either repressed entirely or treated gingerly, even by the aggressive *Sun,* and the story downplayed the elements of raging passion, finding chivalrous tragedy instead. On Tuesday, September 8, a (significantly) unnamed young man, "a student at one of the liberal professions, a person of some talent, personal advantages, and prospective property," nearly murdered his rival for the affections of "an accomplished and amiable young lady in her twentieth year." The unnamed young man challenged his competitor to a duel, presumably the next morning, but that night they readied themselves for it by comparing their heights, standing back to back. Suddenly, the challenger pulled out a gun, stuck the muzzle into his mouth, and attempted to shoot, apparently meaning to blow out both his own brains and those of his rival.

Luckily it misfired, whereupon the perpetrator fell into a dead faint. "For a long time," the *Sun* reported, "he refused either to speak or to hear those about him; but at length, in anticipation that he would be made a prisoner, exclaimed that he was at their mercy, and they might dispose of him as they pleased. Nothing of the kind, however, was intended; and in pursuance of a more humane, though perhaps not more just arrangement, made by the parties and visitors during the night, he yesterday morning left the city for his home in Delaware."

Then there were, most notoriously, the crimes of the demimonde, in a milieu everyone knew about but looked at only from the corner of an averted eye. The most infamous and famous of these happened a few months later. It hasn't even now lost its place among the greatest sensations in New York history, and some features of the crime remain mysterious today. On the morning of April 9, 1836, toward the end of the brutally cold winter that had begun so terribly with the Great Fire, Helen Jewett, a young and famously beautiful prostitute, was found murdered in a house on Thomas Street, west of Broadway.

Actually this was a brothel run by a relatively high-class madam, Rosina Townsend, but it masqueraded as a boardinghouse, since—in common with many of New York's stews—it belonged to a leading New York family, the Livingstons, whose clan included Philip Livingston, signer of the Declaration of Independence, and Edward Livingston, a former mayor and U.S. secretary of state who lived just down the block. Helen Jewett's appearance, when she was discovered, was horrifying. Her bed was smoldering and wreathed in smoke; Jewett lay on it in a lake of blood. Her nightgown had burned away, half her body had been charred, and her head had been hacked nearly to pieces, apparently by blows from a hatchet.

It was a sensation, and the reporters and editors fell upon it like hyenas. Newspaper photographs were more than a half-century in the future, but that left room for the artistic imagination to run wild. Drawings of the murder scene showed hints of gore, but the overall impression most gave was ghoulishly erotic. The *Herald's* James Gordon Bennett elbowed his way into the death chamber itself to report the scene to his readers. Not only did the police not interfere with this press busybody; one cop stripped away the linen shroud from the corpse, now on the floor, enabling Bennett to record his rapture and horror. "Slowly I began to discover the lineaments of the corpse, as one would the beauties of a statue of marble," he wrote.

It was the most remarkable sight I ever beheld—I never have, and never expect to see such another. . . . Not a vein was to be seen. The body looked as white—as full—as polished as the pure Parian marble. The perfect figure—the exquisite limbs—the fine face— the full arms—all surpassing in every respect the Venus de Medicis.

According to Patricia Cline Cohen, who has told Jewett's story in remarkable detail in *The Murder of Helen Jewett* (1998), Bennett's transport somehow allowed him to ignore the surely nauseous results of an autopsy performed on the corpse a few hours before he saw it, though he did describe the head wounds and seared skin, "bronzed like an antique statue."

Jewett's murder led almost instantly to the arrest of her lover, Richard Robinson, a nineteen-year-old from Connecticut trying to make his way in the business world and living at a boardinghouse ten blocks south on Dey Street. He denied his guilt vociferously, and thanks to a groundswell of support from a cadre of similar footloose young men from the boardinghouse culture—and, even more, a vigorous defense from a crack three-lawyer team led by Ogden Hoffman—he was found not guilty at his trial in June 1836, though both the evidence and the preponderance of later opinion suggest he had in fact committed the murder.

Thanks to Cohen's exhaustive research, we now know a great deal about both Robinson and the woman who was probably his victim. Both were utterly typical of the rootless swarm of young adults, moving restlessly through the Manhattan boardinghouses of the era, determined to shake off the idiocy of the rural origins from which they'd fled in search of success. Helen Jewett, Cohen discovered, had been born Dorcas Doyen in Temple, Maine, in 1813. As a child she'd become a servant, and from there on her story was a classic one. Seduced by some young man, she'd changed her name to Maria Stanley and begun working in a Portland brothel; it was a familiar tragic arc that brought her as Helen Jewett to the great city and Rosina Townsend's establishment on Thomas Street.

Such was Dionysian Manhattan in the decades before the Civil War, a metropolis of migrants and strangers passing, joining, parting, anonymous; yet a metropolis still small enough that the most furtive of lost lives could cross paths with the most prominent. Helen Jewett, for example, had—before her move to Townsend's establishment—lived at 55 Leonard Street, the house occupied by William Dunlap before he'd decamped for Greenwich Village. New York was beginning to assemble the components of a nightlife that would survive into the 21st century, the dance of stranger and native, low and high, rich and poor, the constant influx of new migrants—evil, good, or just confused.

And also there was the outflow. Freed after his trial, Richard Robinson fled the city, changed his name to Richard Parmelee, and eventually fetched up in Nacogdoches, Texas, where he became clerk of the county court, married, and died of yellow fever on an Ohio River steamboat in 1855. According to the black woman who attended him on his deathbed, in his final hours he raved deliriously—about Helen Jewett.

CHAPTER FIVE

"BOWERY GALS WILL YOU COME OUT TO-NIGHT?"

Nighttime on the Bowery Before the Civil War

BY THE MID-1800S New York could boast not one but two internationally famous boulevards, each within a flew blocks of the other; between them they epitomized the contrasts for which the city was already notorious. Broadway was rich (or looked it), highbrow (or affected it), and elegant (or tried to be). The Bowery, just to the east, was a world away in atmosphere—poor, but loud, free-spending, and lowbrow—a mob scene to defy Broadway's measured promenade.

Broadway saw refinement as its birthright: both before and after the Revolution the well-off had lined it with substantial houses, and its commercial buildings were at first solid and discreet—like the City Hotel, built at 115 Broadway in 1796, and where Hanington presented his moon show in 1835. In February 1798, Gilbert Stuart's already famous portrait of Washington went on display there; the hotel's Assembly Room hosted a posh Washington's birthday ball, with the painting lavishly illuminated for the occasion. Philip Hone held on in the neighborhood until 1836, when commercial development finally drove him northward to Broadway near Astor Place; George Templeton Strong remained in his old family house a block away on Greenwich Street for more than a decade afterward, though he found Broadway increasingly tawdry. At the turn of the 19th century, the Bowery made for a contrast: until recently, it had remained a sleepy farm road, lined by large agricultural tracts. It didn't even acquire sidewalks until 1802 (Broadway at that point had had them for fifteen years). Then came the massive population explosion of the 1800s (which took the city from 32,000 people in 1790 to 515,000 by 1850). As the immigrants surged into nearby neighborhoods, the Bowery rapidly became their outdoor living room, shopping center, and nightclub.

If George Templeton Strong, aristocratic and a strenuous practitioner of good taste, represented the ideal (if not real) Broadway, Ned Buntline (1823–1886) was the laureate of the Bowery, and Strong's polar opposite. Born E. Z. C. Judson in upstate New York, Buntline was a scourge of snobbery; he was intelligent, temperamental, and innocent of all shame. He ran away to sea as a child, and by the age of fifteen, he'd been cited as a hero by the navy: he saved his shipmates from drowning one night when the Fulton Street steam ferry struck the boat they'd been rowing. He published a story, "The Captain's Pig," and later began writing for the highbrow *Knickerbocker Magazine*—an anomaly considering his career as a proud plebeian hack. He won a $600 reward for single-handedly catching two wanted murderers in Kentucky in 1845. But a year later, in Nashville, he showed his outlaw side: he had killed the husband of his then mistress in a duel, leaped out the jail window in an escape attempt, and finally fallen into the hands of a lynch mob. They had gotten so far as to string him up in the public square when, just before he strangled to death, a friend intervened and cut him down. The grand jury set him free, and he headed for New York.

Once arrived, Buntline gravitated toward (and lived near) the Bowery, railing against the studied refinement, snobbishness, and Anglophilia of the city's merchant class and its admirers. He made a career of rousing the Lower East Side workingmen to causes, a habit that would, as we will see, reach a climax in 1849, when Broadway met the Bowery in a bloody riot on Astor Place. As an agitator, Buntline helped widen a crevasse opening up in the city as new people flooded in—between rich and poor, educated and illiterate, populist and elitist, highbrow and lowbrow.

BOWERY PEOPLE:
B'HOYS AND SPORTING MEN

The Bowery was fertile territory—a chortling proletarian hell that refused to apologize for itself, an anarchic funhouse for workers and the underclass. Tourists marveled at Broadway's operatic glamour, but dropped their jaws at a first glimpse of the Bowery. It was (and still is) a wide and spacious street, but by the 1840s it was no longer sedate and verdant. If Broadway was a circus, the Bowery was an unhinged urban hoedown, triumphantly seedy, shameless, thumping with music and steamy with the scent of hot corn sold by pretty young women:

> Hot corn! Hot corn!
> Here's your lily-white corn.
> All you that's got money
> Poor me that's got none—
> Buy my lily-white corn
> And let me go home.

Street performers sang and danced and juggled. Peddlers shouted curb to curb. Motley crowds swept into and out of saloons (as many as a dozen on every block) and cellar oyster bars. For years a huge sow ambled about every evening among the crowds in Chatham Square, the Bowery's southern terminus, with a card tied to her tail announcing, "I'M PADDY DOYLE'S PIG. WHOSE PIG ARE YOU?" Stores stayed open late and didn't wait passively for customers: one stroller made the mistake of glancing into a shoe store and fell into the clutches of a typical salesman. "Set down. On that stool there. Try these. They don't fit? The devil they don't. Never was better fit; was there, Jake? You don't know anything about it. Come, come, old boy. Pull out your pocket-book. Let her bleed for $7. CAN'T WEAR 'EM OUT! You must have 'em."

Everyone came to the Bowery sooner or later, but it was best known for two near-mythical male types, both hovering between respectability and outcast status, and sworn enemies to each other: the Sporting Man and the Bowery B'hoy. The first was an aspiring rake with a veneer of manners and enough money to ape if not duplicate the airs of the well-off man. The second was a proudly jingoistic American worker, usually in a trade that demanded brawn (often he was a butcher; in the earlier 19th century the city's major concentration of the meatpacking trade lay east of the Bowery). The Sporting Man scorned the Bowery B'hoy's proletarian swagger, and the B'hoy despised the Sporting Man's affectations of culture.

Both the B'hoy and the Sporting Man, at least in popular imagination, lived in boardinghouses, though not, if they could help it, in the same ones. Apartments being as yet almost unknown, most such young men wound up as lodgers, as long as they remained adrift between homeless poverty and the wherewithal to buy or rent a house. There were rough-and-tumble boardinghouses for the B'hoy and approximations of gentility for the Sporting Man. But most of them took in anybody who could keep up the rent. They grew thickest near the Bowery and the East River, more thinly in the better-off residential neighborhoods along Broadway and the Hudson.

Boardinghouse life had become a familiar feature of the cityscape by the 1830s and 1840s. The classic account was Thomas Butler Gunn's 1857 book *The Physiology of New York Boarding-Houses*. Alternating between slapstick and satire, Gunn sometimes presents a house as engagingly bohemian. But far oftener they're ratty, with two, three, or even five wobbly beds jammed into a single room.

Lavatory arrangements are mostly of an imperfect description, generally compromising a frail and rickety washing-stand—which has apparently existed for ages in a Niagara of soap-suds—a ewer and basin of limited capacity, and a cottony, web-like towel, about as well calculated for its purposes as a similar-sized sheet of blotting paper would be. In rooms which have not recently submitted to the purifying brush of the white-washer, he will notice the mortal remains of mosquitoes (not to mention more odoriferous and objectionable insects) ornamenting ceilings and walls, where they have encountered Destiny in the shape of slippers or boot soles of former occupants.

For Gunn the hallmark of boardinghouse life was a cramming together of ill-assorted humans guaranteed to antagonize one another—beer-guzzling young lout and aging spinster, laborer and clerk, shrieking brat and child-hating retiree, Sporting Man and Bowery B'hoy. Gunn describes, in Balzacian repletion, an East Side boardinghouse one flight up above a dry goods store, run by an Irishwoman and her policeman husband. The renters, in addition to Gunn, included a doctor who worked in a dispensary and drank himself into a stupor on weekends, a clerk in the store downstairs, and two laborers who shared a room, a banjo, and a bed, in which they often loudly fought one another.

The landlady was a slattern: "no good man could look at her without a wish to put her under a pump." Her children were interested only (but boundlessly) in "dirt-pies, candies, dead cats, and the gutters of the vicinity." The house was a warren of shacklike bedrooms tended by a dimwitted maid who often set herself on fire with the pipes she smoked. Gunn reported holes in the blankets, towels made from recycled coffee bags, grisly meals, and depressing views—his room faced another window across the airshaft with two panes the occupant had removed in order to stick his feet outside while sleeping on summer nights. Dinner forks revolved on their handles; broken dishes were stuck together with putty.

All this, of course, rankled with the Sporting Man, who ached for better, but the B'hoy was less fastidious. He and his girlfriend and sidekick, the Gallus* G'hal, became working-class idols—a legend of heroic but amiable vulgarity that endured into the 1920s. The B'hoy took especially great pains to be recognized; his dress was unmistakable, as a newspaper reported in 1841:

> He was arrayed in a round jacket with a black velvet collar, his lower extremities were swathed in a coarse pair of serge pantaloons which from the knee down branched into an immense width around the bottom; vest he had none (as that, to him, unnecessary garment might have concealed the gaudy red shirt which bore in patent leather figures of his favorite *"machine"*), and on a bullet head shaved almost naked behind, while a pair of shining well soaped locks deepened over his cheeks in front, set a flossy silk "chimbley pot" with a brim exactly round and stiff as the brass circle on a portable globe.

"Soap-lock" in fact became a nickname for the B'hoy, and indeed it was a coif like no other: close-clipped in back, with bushy sideburns down the cheeks, and handfuls of long hair teased upward and forward over the brow, then glued into towering waves by an application of wet soap. The look also required a top hat worn askew, a cigar clamped between the teeth and tilted heavenward, and a coat, never worn but always carried over one's arm. The pants, though clinging at the hips, were loose in the legs, so they could be easily rolled up over skintight firemen's boots.

Every aspiring Bowery B'hoy also wore an insignia with a real or pretend fire-engine number, because the B'hoy sometimes was, and always wanted to be, a volunteer fireman—a job for which one qualified only through bravery and the muscle that came from hard labor in another trade (the city had no paid professional fire department until 1865).

---

* "Gallus" seems to have been an import from Scots English dialect; it means "wild," "daring," "mischievous," or "cheeky."

B'hoys called firefighting "runnin' wid de machine," because each brigade was attached to a fire engine, which the men themselves hauled at a breakneck run through the streets and then manned when they reached a blaze. In 1845, when another major fire broke out near Wall Street, the machines had one of their great moments. This fire, though huge in extent, was less devastating than in 1835, in part because the city now had an ample supply of high-pressure water from the three-year-old Croton system. George Templeton Strong, who had become an aficionado of blazes since the 1835 fire, saw it as a show. On July 19, he wrote, after coming home from a rubbernecking expedition, "the fire had reached Bowling Green, all the east side of Broadway from Exchange Place to Whitehall Street was burned or burning. The Adelphi Hotel was a magnificent sight, blazing from roof to cellar. . . . At the south end of Broad Street the sight was grand." But the men of the engine companies still needed their old speed, bravery, and brute strength.

And they displayed these attributes between fires as well as during them. Brawls were daily, hourly, sometimes continuous occurrences, one shading imperceptibly into another, and not always the result of bad humor or inebriation. The companies—a hybrid of family and gang, proud of their strength and nerve, and repositories of legend about famous fires and firemen—took names like "Black Joke" and fell into passionate rivalries and battles (often over which brigade would be first at a fire). Fights, also often motivated by politics, religion, race, or ethnic rivalry, usually happened at night, and drew crowds. At first they were more or less impromptu, but as time went on, word of mouth in the streets and saloons publicized them; eventually they were staged openly. Thus they were among the earliest of urban nighttime sports exhibitions, attracting crowds of onlookers and bettors. (Eventually, such fights moved indoors and became an officially scheduled addition to the entertainment scene.)

Who, ethnically and socially, were the B'hoys? This is a matter of doubt and some disagreement. In his recent book *Five Points* (2001), Tyler Anbinder notes that they seem, apart from their identification with volunteer fire brigades, to have lived off lower-status trades, working as apprentice butchers, printers, and grocerymen. The classic B'hoy seems always to have been a vocal American patriot, but by the 1840s and 50s, a jingoism once perhaps harmless had twisted itself into violent anti-Irish and anti-Catholic mob prejudice, and many earlier Bowery historians thus assumed that B'hoys were native-born Americans with a strong anti-Irish stripe. That, certainly, was Buntline's view: he saw the group as a natural constituency for his militant nativism.

Sporting Men were far less celebrated figures than B'hoys, and never attracted cheerleaders like Buntline or an admiring public. The Sporting Man, his many detractors said, was thin, pasty, foppish, false, and degenerate. Perhaps the most infamous model of the type was Richard Robinson—the young man who, as we've seen, probably murdered the prostitute Helen Jewett in 1836. In appearance the antitype of a Bowery B'hoy, Robinson was (in at least some of the engravings that appeared in the press) strikingly handsome, slender, and sensitive. He also had a reputation for dressing well. He'd grown up in a solid family in Durham, Connecticut—his father was a farmer, locally important businessman, and eight-term state legislator.

Setting out for New York in pursuit of a career, Robinson settled into Mrs. Rodman Moulton's boardinghouse at 42 Dey Street. He took a job with Joseph Hoxie, a dry goods merchant who paid him $60 a year. It was his attempt to cut a dashing figure on this niggardly salary that got him into trouble: he was, like most Sporting Men, hard pressed in his attempt to achieve city-slicker style. He lived a discount existence, and entertained himself with cheap amusements, including brothels he could afford and a few—like Helen Jewett's—he really couldn't.

Though, not having murdered anybody, they never became notorious, there were thousands of young men like him in New York, devoted to bets, prostitutes, fights, plays, and races, striving to bring life off with flash and even sophistication. Robinson and his type aped the moneyed rakes, the irresponsible young men of good family and leisure who had been a fixture in the city since the 18th century, when they made their first American theatrical appearance in Royall Tyler's *The Contrast*. But unlike the socially prominent idlers, the Sporting Men were transient, anonymous, numerous, elusive of control and consequently a source of disapproval and some fear among the religious and civic-minded.

Yet, for a couple of years in the early 1840s, the Sporting Men were a powerful enough cohort to generate a mini-media empire of weekly newspapers that catered to them. The sporting press was a fly-by-night enterprise—editors absconded and resurfaced almost as frequently as offices closed and reopened; the papers themselves bore a bewilderingly interchangeable variety of banners—the *New York Sporting Whip,* the *Weekly*

Rake, The Flash, or *The Whip and Satirist of New-York and Brooklyn,* among others. They served up steaming platters of scandal and tossed incendiary accusations against each other in a parody of feuding mainstream editors like Colonel Webb of the *Courier* and James Gordon Bennett of the *Herald.*

Until 1843, when the authorities suppressed them, the sporting papers trained a searchlight on the Sporting Men and consequently the city's nightlife in the early 1840s. Their themes were sex, gambling, sex, racing, sex, theater, sex, drinking, sex, whoring, sex, and sex. The articles in all of them are tonally volatile in the classic 19th-century journalistic mode, most often couched in huffing outrage at flagrant immorality, yet careful to include accurate names, addresses, details, and prices: consumer guides disguised as calls for intervention by the police (who tolerated commercial sex at the time and could thus be trusted to ignore both hints and outcries).*

But they were always frank about what seem to have been the Sporting Man's daydreams. In the *Weekly Rake* on September 3, 1842, for example, one writer enthused about his visit to an expensive brothel catering to jaded appetites. Here he found a brand-new pleasure, an offshoot of the boon the city was celebrating that year—the arrival of clean running water through the monumental aqueducts and reservoirs of the new Croton system. After gluing an "additional curl" onto his head, which, he says, "imparts an unique and distingué tone to our appearance," he headed on a moonlit evening for a brothel on Broome Street in the city's newest high-end red-light district—today's SoHo.

Attracted by a girl "who sat alone at the window with a most spiritual and tender smile upon her lip," the writer buys her some champagne, and she leads him from the public rooms to a closed door somewhere in the innards of the mansion. "She opened it, and we were in the midst of the most brilliant scene that it has ever been our lot to witness. Baths of the purest transparency stretched out their liquid radiance before us." The room was

---

* As a marketing concept, sporting papers must have been irresistible. The papers would appeal to the innocent but curious, to the depraved looking for names, addresses, prices, and ratings, to those after blackmail money, and to people with secrets shameful enough to make them willing to pay it. In the fluid legal climate of the era, which Helen Horowitz has documented in *Rereading Sex: Battles over Sexual Knowledge and Suppression in Nineteenth-Century America* (2002), the proposition surely seemed worth the risk, even if it wasn't wholly safe. But the papers seem to have struck a nerve: prosecutions for obscene libel, a criminal rather than a civil offense, had put them all out of business by 1843. This was part of a gathering moral crusade against vice that would crest after the Civil War, and the sporting press wouldn't be equaled for scandal until the 1890s, when New York encountered the all-time world champion of tattletale periodicals, Colonel William d'Alton Mann's *Town Topics.*

lined with mirrors, which added to the effect. "We closed the door that was to shut us from intrusion," the reporter lubriciously writes. "We were alone—our forms were laved in the delicious waters. . . . We will say no more; we cannot reveal to vulgar gaze the rapture that ensued."

Such were the aspirations if not the daily realities of the Sporting Man: addled licentiousness brought off with an air of connoisseurship, self-conscious masculinity not averse to cosmetics and hair extensions, and a weakness for perfumed—indeed rather Pepé Le Pew–sounding— literary effusion. Murderer or no, Richard Robinson wrote letters to Helen Jewett in a comparably florid style. At this remove the Sporting Man may seem both quaint and unwholesome, but he became a permanent figure in the city lore—the lonely young man in the seamy boardinghouse room or apartment, drudging away at a subsistence job, hanging on at the edges of whatever scene has seized the moment, and with great effort fadging up a credibly fashionable manner and appearance.

A Sockdoliger in the Bellows-Mover: The Bowery Steps Out in the 1840s

When civilized New York went out, the Park Theatre, overlooking Broadway and within view of City Hall, remained its premier destination— even though the management quietly reserved its third tier for prostitutes and their johns (who are clearly shown in the best-known picture of the theater, John Searle's 1822 drawing of the stage, pit, and boxes). This was where gentility halted, and where scenes unfolded that were more gripping than anything on the stage—such as the night in 1842 when two tough prostitutes, Windy Green and English Sal, got into an altercation about something. According to a witness familiar with boxing terminology, Green lost the bout when English Sal "sent a sockdoliger into her bellows-mover, and followed it up by a grab, which caught Windy's wardrobe, which came half away from her person."

So, despite its pedigree, the Park's grip on civility was unsure. And even though it was in a distinctly proletarian neighborhood just south of Canal Street, the new Bowery Theatre, when it opened to compete with the Park in 1826, presented plays every bit as arty as the Park did. Its decor was more ambitious—the boxes gold-painted and exuberantly decorated, the roof a blue and gold dome, the stage curtain rich crimson and opera-style, swagging up and to the sides when raised, the lighting fixtures of cut glass. It was technologically far in advance of the Park, boasting the city's first gas footlights. And early on, at least, it drew sophisticated theatergoers. Walt Whitman celebrated it as a temple for the decent male proletariat, "pack'd from ceiling to pit with its audience mainly of alert, well-dress'd, full-blooded young and middle-aged men, the best average of American-born mechanics, . . . no dainty kid-glove business, but electric force and muscle from perhaps 2,000 full-sinew'd men."

But the half-dozen blocks that separated the Park and Bowery Theatres, short in distance, crossed the city's social and economic Maginot Line, and the upper strata of the town soon rebelled at the prospect of evenings at the Bowery. Philip Hone, serving as mayor the year the Bowery Theatre opened, raised a furor among his snobbish cohorts just by attending the cornerstone ceremony: "no act of my public life cost me so many friends." Eventually, the Bowery reverted to the character of its neighborhood. Even diehard admirers like Walt Whitman lamented a deterioration in the house by the 1840s. Contemporary accounts corroborate this to some extent: *The New York Sporting Whip* reported "[o]aths, shouts, shrieks from the throats of drunken outcast bands, and leprous male prostitutes, saluted the ear." And the misbehavior spilled beyond the third tier, with "males and females in strange and indecent positions in the lobbies, and sometimes in the boxes." The crowd seems to have become particularly unruly after 1840, the years that provoked the most vociferous condemnations.

But the *Whip* can't be trusted: its editor was, at the time, feuding with the Bowery management. And Whitman wrote his reminiscence of the house as an old man a half century after its (and his own) heyday: his belief that it had gone downhill may reflect the bent of mature memory to view all change as for the worse. At-the-moment accounts suggest that the Bowery always mixed high and low, vulgarity and sophistication. Like any commercial theater, it stuck at nothing in bad times and would do anything to fill its seats, booking circus acts during threadbare stretches and flooding the stage with water during the summer of 1840 for a run of aqua-dramas with titles like *The Pirate's Signal* and *Yankees in China*.

And if by the 1840s the Bowery had lost its elite patrons, it and likeminded theaters had begun to serve lowbrow audiences with new kinds of entertainment. In 1848, for example, the B'hoys and G'hals got to see a landmark stage portrait of themselves. It happened in February at William

Mitchell's Olympic Theatre, a new house on Broadway between Howard and Grand Streets, with the premiere of a smash hit by Benjamin Baker (1818–1890), *A Glance at New York*. Mose and Lize, the beloved and long-lived archetypes of the Bowery B'hoy and G'hal, were played by Frank Chanfrau and Mary Taylor; *Glance*, a two-act musical farce, remains an entertaining panorama of one New York night in 1848.

Word of the show's Bowery hero got around weeks before it opened. Baker had been presenting short skits based on the Mose character for several years, but for some reason the B'hoys were girding themselves to take offense at the prospect of Mose in a full-length play. According to one reminiscence, Engine Company 28 on Laight Street had sent a letter threatening to "gut the theatre." Chanfrau, Baker, and Mitchell were, in these accounts, terrified at the prospect of a mob of angry firemen in the audience. The Olympic was tiny, only 25 feet wide, with a cramped underground tunnel leading to the pit, which, as always, was the gathering place for rowdies and a scene of pandemonium even on normal nights. Late-arriving patrons would clamber up from the tunnel to be grabbed, passed hand over hand across the front row, and finally squeezed down onto the bench—which pushed men off the far end, who then ran to the back and (launched by a mighty shove from patrons on the rear benches) vaulted over several rows and crashed back down somewhere near the front.

February 15, opening night, matched the general mood by turning out stormy. Baker and William Mitchell cowered in the wings as curtain time neared. Chanfrau later recalled he was "trembling like an aspen leaf" when he made his first entrance and saw the faces of Company 28 glowering up at him. Recollections differ as to whether the men warmed as they saw Chanfrau stomp onto the stage in B'hoy costume, upturned cigar planted between his teeth. One legend has it that the theater burst into instant applause, but other memories disagree. According to a first-nighter, William Cauldwell, who recalled the event more than half a century later, the pit remained ominously silent, though T. Allston Brown, a theater historian, insisted that the silence reflected not hostility but sheer delighted amazement at the accuracy of Chanfrau's costume and impersonation.

This first production of the play featured only Mose, and went through a cycle of 24 performances, ending on March 14—whereupon Baker replaced it with an expanded version, now adding Mary Taylor to the cast as Lize. By this time, *A Glance at New York* had become a sensation, doing so much business that Chanfrau—in one of the great feats of New York theater history—produced a brand-new Mose play, *New-York As It Is,* further downtown at the Chatham Theatre. For nearly two months, while the two productions were running simultaneously, Chanfrau played Mose in *both* of them—exiting one theater, tearing nearly a mile across Manhattan, and arriving just in time to make his entrance at the other.

A Glance at New York's expanded version opens innocuously, with a rousing chorus that greets the Albany steamboat as it pulls in to its Hudson River berth. Fresh from his upstate village, a rube named George debarks and falls instantly into the clutches of two swindlers. Then Chanfrau appears as Mose, announcing he's foresworn his machine because the chief "hit me over de gourd" with the company trumpet, and that he's been devoting the time thus freed to brawls: "I'm bilein' over for a rousin' good fight with someone somewhere." Then the script called on Mose to show his sentimental side, in a scene that has him enthusing with Lize over a weepy romance novel, *Matilda the Disconsolate*: "Have you come to where Lucinda stabs the Count yet?—ain't dat high?" But the great moment is when Mose bursts into tears at the memory of having rescued a baby* from a fire: "The fire-boys may be rough outside but they're all right here [*Touches breast*]." In one theatergoer's recollection, "it was the baby that saved the play."

Between them Baker and Chanfrau had saved the Olympic from wreck: Mose's pluck and heart flattered the firemen into cheers, and from then on it was a mounting triumph. Mose, George, and a motley entourage battle their way from high places to low. In drag, they pay a visit to Mrs. Morton, a dowager and Margaret Dumont prototype who has opened a Ladies' Bowling Alley, complete with bar: "I have found that card-playing, dancing, theaters, &c. were a bore; and the continual cry of the doctor was 'You should take exercise!' So I determined on a bowling alley."

Mose finds the fight he's been seeking at the Loafer's Paradise, a Bowery bar patronized by "foo-foos"—people who can't or won't spend "three cents for a glass of grog and a night's lodging," according to Mose, who defines them thus: "Foo-foos is outsiders and outsiders is foo-foos." He happily wrecks the bar, and the melee, boiling over into the street, brings down the first act curtain.

---

* Some versions of *A Glance at New York* show Mose actually rescuing the baby; others only show him remembering the event.

In the final act, Mose and Lize make a date to meet at Vauxhall Gardens. "What's goin' on?—is de wawdeville plays there?" Lize asks; Mose says, "No—there's goin' to be a first-rate shindig; some of our boys'll be there." *A Glance at New York* closes in the Gardens as Lize sits down to a cup of coffee and nine doughnuts, while Mose, rushing off to join a street brawl, delivers his farewell address to the audience:

> Look here, ladies and gentlemen—don't be down on me 'cause I'm goin' to leave you—but Sykesy's got in a muss, and I'm bound to see him righted, 'cause he runs wid our machine, you know—and if you don't say no, why, I'll scare up this crowd again tomorrow night, and then you can take another GLANCE AT NEW YORK!

The play was so popular that it fathered a brood of sequels (inevitably a Little Mose appeared—a child actor with a miniature cigar and B'hoy getup). New York theatergoing, dominated by English plays from Shakespeare to the 1700s, had begun giving way to popular fare on familiar, contemporary, and American subjects, with the city now taking a prominent place on its own stages. *A Glance at New York* made a star of Frank Chanfrau and broke down an old wall between the theater and the city's streets. Mose and Lize remained fixtures of popular culture for half a century or more, and even today it's not difficult to understand their attraction.

Not all popular performance traditions, however, are so easily appreciated now, and chief among these are the minstrel shows and the sprawling blackface performance industry to which they belonged. Their racism is, of course, the root problem, but blackface also makes us uneasy because it was amazingly durable and its departure from the American scene uncomfortably recent—it endured well into the 20th century. Irving Berlin, the cynosure of American songwriters, began as a white writer of pseudo-black songs as early as "Alexander's Ragtime Band," and even in the 1940s was still working the genre: in his 1942 score for the movie *Holiday Inn,* he wrote a surpassingly strange blackface number, "Abraham," for Bing Crosby and Marjorie Reynolds. Joan Crawford, of all actresses, sang in blackface as late as 1953 in one of her most dreadful films, *Torch Song.*

Face painting, of course, is ancient, and the change it wreaks in the wearer's countenance can have effects both functional (as war paint scares the enemy) and magical (as a mask seems to free a person from his or her usual identity). The practice isn't by any means always a comment on race. Yet it became so in early 19th-century America, when Thomas D. Rice (1808–1860), a white actor, appeared at the Bowery Theatre in 1832, in blackface and performed his phenomenally popular song-and-dance act as Jim Crow. Other actors had done blackface routines before, but Rice turned it into a mainstay of 19th-century American theater.

In a Catherine Street boardinghouse four unemployed white men with a violin, banjo, bones, and tambourine became the Virginia Minstrels. They first appeared in February 1843 at the Bowery Amphitheatre (an indoor circus venue at 37 Bowery), and within months had become a favorite act at the Bowery Theatre—which also put on a dramatization of *Uncle Tom's Cabin* in 1854, with Rice in the title role. The ensuing Uncle Tom craze, which eventually had cobbled-together dramatic versions of Stowe's book galumphing across stages everywhere in America, spurred still further the popularity of "coon" shows. And thus the Bowery, which in its early years had mounted such superior productions of Shakespeare, was at length reduced to fare like a blackface travesty of *Othello,* in which Desdemona—when the distraught Moor demands the missing handkerchief—answers, "Blow yah nose on yah sleeve, nigger, and git on wid de show."

Yet minstrel shows, despite such crudeness, sometimes hid meanings more subtle and disturbing than present-day sensitivity about race is comfortable acknowledging. This is a point made perceptively in Eric Lott's *Love and Theft: Blackface Minstrelsy and the American Working Class* (1993). What, for example, was the real source of the Virginia Minstrels' appeal? Real performances by real blacks of black material had been a feature of New York life at least since the colonial period, perhaps most powerfully in the funeral songs and dances Africans performed as they carried their dead to the Burial Ground. The effect on whites, as we know from their reactions, was disturbing but unmistakably forceful. And in the 1830s the Bowery was full of black musicians and other performers, though their venues were low-profile—small transient theaters, bars, and the street.

Blackface, significantly, rose to mass popularity at a time of inflamed race relations in the city. Its uncouth mockery pleased poor whites and gave them a feeling of superiority over the blacks whom they saw as economic and social rivals in the hard times that followed the 1837 Panic. That the actors were white put them in the role of commentators and judges, reinforcing the white conviction of superiority. Yet, as Lott has remarked, blackface also betokened a fascination with black culture, and particularly with black men, so complex in its blend of repulsion and attraction that it defies easy explication. Minstrelsy was perhaps a newly opened—hence understandably rough and unpleasant—channel between the races, even as it reinforced racism. It was, from one perspective, an act of cheapening and exploitation; from another it marked the dawning of interest, an early herald of a possible accommodation, even a merging, of once hostile cultures.

In surviving transcriptions, indigenous African-American music is often stark and moving, rooted as it was in the music of a people caught in a daily struggle for existence. In the years before the Civil War, entertainers borrowed and imitated some of these motifs, packaging them as commercial products, often minus their edges and depths, and with an addition of harmonic, structural, and decorative effects that branded them as the property of a particular composer.

Stephen Foster was the acknowledged master of this trade. But also among the popular minstrel songs of the 1840s was "The Bowery Gals," and it reveals how easily such songs could blur the lines of racial division. Its history is obscure: it seems to have been written in 1844 by John Hodges, a minstrel performer who used the stage name "Cool White," and sang with a five-man group known as the Virginia Serenaders. Apparently the song was first called "Lubly Fan," but it's been known under a number of titles (most commonly "Buffalo Gals"). In 1845 it came out as "The Bowery Gals" in a sheet music version arranged by William Clifton, published by Thomas Birch from his music store at 291 Bowery, and billed as a specialty of the Serenaders.

> De Bowery gals dey come out at night,
> Dey come out at night,
> Dey come out at night,
> De Bowery gals dey come out at night,
> And dance by de light ob de moon.

Apart from the dialect, little in the content, either of chorus or the seven verses, seems in any way race-particular (as the easy movement of the song into other contexts demonstrates). Rather, it's a celebration of courtship and the Bowery by night:

I stop'd awhile and had a talk.
Had a talk, had a talk;
Wid a pretty gal on de side walk
She was so neatly dress'd. . . .

I ax'd her would she dance wid me;
Dance wid me, dance wid me;
She answer'd yes, if I'd agree
To meet by de light ob de moon. . . .

I'm bound to make dat gal my wife,
Dat gal my wife, dat gal my wife,
Den I'll be happy all my life,
Wid her by de light ob de moon.

Birch's sheet music included an easy piano accompaniment, and was plainly aimed at the middle-class living room, even though the song itself was a Bowery staple. The lyric seems at once race-bound and generic; it's easy to imagine a white singer enjoying it as a sweetly universal courtship song and slipping unconsciously into a human solidarity that unstrings the racism manifest in the dialect and the blackface mise-en-scène. Foster's white minstrel songs share this same vacillation between exploitive condescension and a simplicity of emotion that makes them seem harmless and communal—everyone's property.

Bowery-area brothels also hinted at hidden interracial harmony in a landscape where hostility was more visible. Rough and geared to poor clients, they were clustered in the Five Points and to the east in Corlaer's Hook, and especially near Chatham Square in Orange Street, Cow Bay, and Squeeze Gut Alley. Some were exclusively white, some black. But many were interracial: vice sweeps often picked up a number of prosperous white men in the mixed-race houses—a phenomenon that may have surprised the naive, but which is of the night's essence. The sneering piece in the *Sun* about Charles Jones's altercation with Catherine Hamilton, the black woman he was soliciting on Howard Street, was also a barometer of the attraction and hostility that tangled with each other in antebellum New York.

Legend (with a powerful boost from Herbert Asbury's exciting but not wholly reliable 1928 classic, *The Gangs of New York*) has given the Five

Points durable notoriety as a hell of vice, misery, and degradation. Imaginative or imaginary reconstructions sometimes make every crowd a gang, every meeting a battle, every house a brothel, rotgut bar, murderers' den, or flophouse. These were plentiful, but in fact the neighborhood was, as historians have recently been discovering, a far more complex and layered environment. It housed, for example, a complement of ambitious, hardworking, hard-pressed families and small businessmen.

Running a bar or restaurant in the area was one of the earliest prospects open to a black man in the New York economy, and a number of such men became rich and put together small real estate syndicates in the Five Points vicinity. And though court records do indeed reveal plenty of forbidden behavior in and around the Five Points' Paradise Square, they also record complaints by homeowners, appealing to the city to help them clean up their neighborhood. In 1826, for example, a group of Anthony Street citizens complained about the rising number of brothels and bums, saying that it had become "intolerable to the inhabitants and dangerous for people to pass through the streets"—a concern shared by better-off families near Broadway who had to close their windows at night, lest they overhear "the blasphemous language that nightly would salute their ears uttered by the harlot and her companion."

Even acts of violence, seemingly transparent in meaning, were often more complex than they first appeared. Black John Van Winkle, living on Anthony Street and murdered in 1835 by William Newman, his white next-door neighbor, eked out an honorable living as a scavenger. Newman's attack was, as we saw above, a racist hate crime. But Newman's Yankee-sounding name was misleading: he was an Irishman who had lived in the city only six months, and apparently learned (or at least perfected himself in) his hatred of African-Americans under the tutelage of American nativist mobs—groups who were already turning violently against Irish immigrants. In press accounts of the killing, the anti-slavery *Sun* praised Van Winkle as the hardworking innocent victim of an inebriated thug. But so, surprisingly, did the rabidly anti-abolitionist *Courier,* apparently deeming the Irish immigrant a worse threat to civility than the native black.

Squalid, loud, and sometimes violent though it was, the Bowery might just as fairly be dubbed the boulevard where all the cliques, claques, classes, and cabals that repelled each other by daylight met on equal terms at night. Here, a black man like Van Winkle might be viewed as a respectable tradesman while white William Newman was seen as a sodden Irish street brawler.

Anthony Street and the Five Points were poor, but not ghettos in the later 19th- and 20th-century sense that implies isolation and a homogeneous population. New York was still too small to be wholly balkanized. It was a place where every human type lived a short walk from its antitype.

In her 2000 book about the 19th-century Paris night, *The Twelve Dark Hours,* Simone Delattre viewed this restless nocturnal dance of fraternization and fratricide as an essence that distinguished a great capital from a provincial town, quoting a palpitating but evocative passage by Alphonse de Neuville (1835–1885), written to celebrate the 1867 Paris Exposition. The streets at night, Neuville rhapsodized, were "the life of the imperial city, the life of all advanced civilizations—in a word, modern life, with pains so intense they stun, joys so powerful they make one dizzy, beauty pushed to the brink of horror and horror driven to the edge of the sublime. . . . [This life] is a pleasure beyond definition, undefinable, leading not to the satisfaction of any of the senses, but rather to the satisfaction of one's deepest, instinctive, animal essence."

In pre–Civil War New York, Broadway and the Bowery, a few blocks apart in fact, a world apart in image and reputation, embodied this sublime dance of horror and beauty. One radiated the studied dignity of wealth, the other the anarchic sprawl of poverty, and with the rise of the Bowery, the city's high life and low life began to evolve cultures of their own. For a time they coexisted; but tensions were on the rise as early as the 1830s. On New Year's Eve in 1829, for example, a mob of about 4,000 gathered on the Bowery between eight and nine in the evening, and their increasingly disorderly revelry spilled over into Broadway, drowning out the dignified high point of the holiday—the midnight ringing out of Trinity Church's bells. By sometime after two in the morning they'd surrounded the City Hotel and trapped the cowering ball guests inside until dawn.

It was a prophetic moment: the lowbrows were giving the captive highbrows a foretaste of the clash between brilliance and savagery toward which New York would head within a generation.

SEX AND THE ANTEBELLUM CITY:
GAY, STRAIGHT, WHITE, BLACK, AND CHARLES DICKENS

In spring 1842, New York welcomed an eminent foreign visitor, the writer of books—recently including *Oliver Twist* and *The Old Curiosity Shop*—that had sent the city, indeed the whole nation, into transports.

His readers laughed, bawled, shivered in suspense, steamed in moral outrage at harrowing evocations of innocent poverty and sneering villainy.
The writer, of course, was Charles Dickens, and he found much to criti-
cize in both New York and the U.S. at large, venting his thoughts in another bestseller, *American Notes*: a book full of detail, as Dickens always is.
But he neglected to include a complete account of his New York sightsee-
ing—a gap that can be at least partly filled from the ragged and deteriorating pages that survive from the sporting newspapers.

Dickens was staying near the heart of nocturnal New York, at the Carlton House on Broadway at Leonard Street, a few blocks away from
Chatham Square and the Bowery. Somebody apparently suggested a taste
of New York grit, promising it would offer sights not to be found even in
Victorian London. So on a Friday evening, March 4, 1842, a poker-faced
cop and an alderman, well-informed guides, conducted the novelist on a
tour of low-down New York. Luckily for posterity, a reporter for *The
Whip and Satirist of New-York and Brooklyn* was tagging along when they
turned off Broadway onto Anthony (now Worth) Street.

Posh though the Carlton House was, it was only a few hundred feet
from their destination, Frank McCabe's roughhouse tavern. McCabe's
was not, apart from its owner's name, an Irish saloon in the classic mold.
Once inside, Dickens, according to the *Whip,* shrank back in horror
when he came upon five blacks, male and female, all stark naked and
sweatily entangled in mid-gangbang. The cop and alderman, who in theory should have padlocked the place and hauled everyone off to the ward
house, chatted amiably with the orgiasts in between their spasms of ecstasy, as if this were an encounter between old friends. Dickens, the
Whip said, nearly fell into a swoon and fled the place: it was stronger
stuff than the blacking factory of his childhood. As a matter of fact he
did write about McCabe's in *American Notes,* but without giving its
name or address, and only as a sordid lodging house, without a hint of
the smoking sex on its entertainment bill. He kept safely to generalized
misery and rhetoric. "Where dogs would howl to lie, women, and men,
and boys slink off to sleep, forcing the dislodged rats to move away in
quest of better lodgings" was the worst Dickens could bring himself to
say in print.

Sex, of course, was everywhere, but to Dickens New York must have
seemed a stewpot of unmatched excess. Abortion remained legal, as long
as it was performed before the fourth month of pregnancy. Abortionists

flourished and advertised in the newspapers. The most famous of them all, Madame Restell, grew rich in defiance of outcries from moral reformers, and came to cut a considerable public social figure. In 1839 she set up headquarters at 148 Greenwich Street (just two short blocks from the home of George Templeton Strong, at the time still a Columbia undergraduate), and practiced openly, drawing clients from among both the rich and the poor. In the 1830s and 40s, she was an institution, if a queasily accepted one.

Prostitutes too could be wealthy and suave, like Julia Brown, whose luxurious Leonard Street brothel, another Carlton House neighbor, was among the most select. "Princess Julia," as admirers called her, circulated familiarly among the city's elite, as unashamed as Madame Restell. Yet soigné as she was, she was also tough, according to the *Weekly Rake*, and apt to "revel in her two-thousand dollar parlor—play upon her piano, and exclaim, 'God damn it, girls, why the hell don't you dance?'" Beginning in the 1820s such brothels became the targets of frequent vigilante violence. Though the attackers often claimed they were motivated by moral outrage, class resentment was clearly a factor,* since they tended to wreck only the better houses catering to—and frequently leased from—the city's property-owning elite. Brown herself was a victim in 1834 at a house she ran on Chapel Street.

Often hailing from modest origins, women like Julia Brown perhaps seemed, to their old compatriots, to be rubbing their success in; for whatever cause they certainly aroused disproportionate hatred. Ned Buntline, always on the lookout for ways to stir working-class vigilantism, was, among his many paradoxes, a vitriolic moral reformer, and nursed a particularly acid grudge against Caroline "Kate" Hastings, one of the period's most famously beautiful prostitutes. In 1849, after encountering her in the street, he sent her a poison-pen letter, signed "One who knows something." It was scorching: "You will probably spend a full year at Sing Sing for which everybody will rejoice—you corrupt young men by sending out your dirty filthy girls into the street and bringing these young men into your house—you cause rows at night and in fact you are nothing but a *damned whore*. You are *fucked* every night by Sporting Men."

But the police still left brothels largely alone, and courts rarely con-

---

* The trades of the attackers are suggestive: mariner, apprentice, ship carpenter, milkman, paver, cartman, butcher, laborer, bartender.

victed anyone accused of running a disorderly house: the institutions
charged with suppressing vice were (not for the first time in history)
among its patrons and protectors. And the vigilantes weren't motivated
solely by the hatred of vice: they sometimes demanded sex with the
women whose houses they'd broken into. All cities are a tissue of contradictions that defy logic or moral analysis, too tangled ever fully to tease
apart. But the New York of this era was more so than most: the truth of
this emerges forcefully in Timothy Gilfoyle's 1992 classic *City of Eros:
New York City, Prostitution, and the Commercialization of Sex, 1790–1820.*
In 1857 the rector of Trinity Church, William Berriam, announced in his
Sunday sermon that "During a ministry of more than fifty years I have
not been in a house of ill-fame more than ten times!" Startlingly, nobody
in the congregation seems to have been in the least taken aback by this admission.

Lewdness had become blatant and debates about it public; the whole
metropolis seemed to have become a glass house. The sporting papers featured regular columns called "Wants to Know" and "Free Advice." These
columns pinioned anonymous New Yorkers in embarrassing behavior,
and the individual items are always intriguing, sometimes baffling, often
both. In its July 30, 1842, issue, *The Weekly Rake* Wanted to Know "who
those young men are who danced on the corner of Grand Street and Allen
last Monday night? They come the Diamond touches and no mistake."
The latter phrase is obscure; could it offer an early whiff of gay nightlife?

It probably could. It's become a commonplace idea that homosexuality was a cultural invention of the later 19th century, and came into its
own only in the 20th century. But this would have surprised the sporting
press of the 1840s, which was obsessed with sodomy. On September 10
the *Rake* demanded, "Is there a man in town that requested another to
shave his legs? Why did he make such a strange request? We have received a detail of the whole affair. Shall we publish it?" Such items could
be inserted (in the *Rake* at least), for a quarter, and the threat of further
details unmistakably suggests blackmail. Warnings of imminent disclo-
sures also abounded in both feature articles and letters to the editor, but
the promised revelations rarely appear. This suggests victims routinely
paid the papers off—as well, perhaps, as the blackmailers who had
planted the tips.

Homosexuality seems to have been the biggest-uddered cash cow in
this market of extortion. The papers mounted intermittent crusades, in-

valuable now because the loaded allusiveness of the articles allows the reader to infer raw details, and also suggests that male-on-male sex by no means passed beneath early 19th-century American cultural radar, at least among urbanites in New York. It was plainly familiar as an organized activity on the boulevards and in some taverns—though, as with the sporting papers' alternate celebrations and attacks on female prostitutes, it's often hard to tell whether the anti-gay articles originated from the papers' tourist guide, muckraking, or blackmail functions.

Of the dozen or so surviving articles, squibs, and letters to the editor, the most remarkable appeared in the *Whip and Satirist*'s February 12, 1842, issue, and disclosed the existence of a cabal of gay men in New York's otherwise wholesome nightscape of brothels and riots. Moreover it identified the spider who minced delicately along the wide-flung strands of the sodomitical web. "There is not one so degraded as this Captain Collins, the King of the Sodomites." He was a foreigner, an Englishman, in the long tradition of blaming homosexuality on the influence of aliens. Among the syndicate of perverts, the writer announced, "we find no Americans as yet—they are all Englishmen or French" (the English called homosexuality the French vice and the French the English vice; for the *Whip* it was the French *and* English vice).

It was Collins, the writer says, "who it will be recollected formerly kept the Star House in Reade Street, about a year since." An 1840 city directory does indeed list a Robert A. Collins as the proprietor of the Star House, at 34 Reade Street, at the corner of Republican Alley, which started at Duane and then turned right to end at Elm (now Elk) Street—an intersection that remained in existence until the construction of the bunkerlike federal office building now at the corner of Broadway and Reade. The premises lay, probably, over the old African Burial Ground, covered over when the hill to the north was plowed down to fill in the Fresh Water (a gangway that runs behind a preserved swath of the Burial Ground on Reade follows the old path of the alley). Such was the obscure location of what seems to have been the earliest New York gay, or at least gay-friendly, bar, long before mainstream papers began routinely attacking such places.

The Star House seems also to have doubled as a gay brothel. Collins, the writer continues, "has been the instrumental cause of the death of a young man, who was employed by the monster as barkeeper; who was forced to nightly lie with beasts in the shape of men. . . . A number of young men, who are now in the city, . . . have also felt the inhuman embrace of this monster." Worst of all, the *Whip and Satirist* concluded, such behavior was not random but the product of a conspiratorial agenda. "We have received a number of letters from friends of these brutes threatening us with violence, if we persisted in our strictures upon these *'harmless'* young men."

Impossible, of course, to say how widespread was this forerunner of the modern gay metropolis. One can't rule out a hidden agenda behind such attacks—they could, for instance, have amounted to an exaggeratedly macho defense against whisperings about or accusations against the writers or editors. But they presume, at least among Sporting Men, acute awareness of sexual depths suddenly appearing underneath traditional customs of heterosexual male fraternizing. The sporting press was in appearance aggressively, perhaps hysterically, heterosexual, and yet rarely does a month pass without a flurry of sodomy alerts, most of which presume that all the readers are familiar with gay men as common on the streets, visible and even advertising themselves as a distinct and recognized subgroup.

Captain Collins was not the only target of attack. The papers went after others as well, including the pianist at Palmo's Concert Saloon, at the corner of Broadway and Reade Street (three blocks from the Carlton House), whom the *Whip and Satirist* began hounding in the winter of 1842. The campaign succeeded: Palmo fired him that summer. Interestingly, Palmo's Saloon (whose actual, precious-sounding formal name was the Café des Milles Colonnes) was a mere half block from the Star House. Thus the sporting papers' persistent snipings at Palmo may suggest a reputation as a gay magnet.

John Emanuel, who suffered even worse opprobrium because he was a Jew, came within the *Whip and Satirist*'s sights the same year. The paper's account of his history is garbled; he seems to have come from Boston. Once in New York he set up as a wholesale and retail liquor merchant, but his business, the *Whip* maintained, was a front. The place was really a house of male prostitution.

At dark, the shutters are put up and the store closed, but it is opened again in a few minutes after to admit a boy who has either just been picked up in the street, or has been in the place before. Decency draws the veil over what follows. In the morning, an emaciated lad, of about twelve or fourteen, may be seen stealing forth with tottering limbs and pallid countenance. . . . Jem Barnes is one of the lads thus foully ruined. . . . Where are the police officers who send unfortunate females to the penitentiary for a far less crime?

Yet the city's law enforcement apparatus seems only to have yawned at such outrage. When a "miserable beast" was brought up on sodomy charges in October, he was, the *Rake* said, "a horrible looking being, as was his accuser," but the police justice who arraigned him declined to press charges. The sporting press sometimes insisted that sodomy was infrequent. But this was not consistent: a letter to the *Flash* denounced "man-monsters," complaining that "they are continuously parading our streets of an evening watching for their prey, and hundreds of young boys, yes, sir, boys as young as twelve years to eighteen, are victims of their foul and disgusting deeds. I venture to say none of them are married, but hire rooms in various parts of the city for the purpose of bringing their victims to."

Reports of nefarious gay doings soon began to appear in sources outside the short-lived sporting press of the early 1840s. One such event happened on Cedar Street. Sometime between midnight and one in the morning on February 15, 1846, Thomas Carey was walking home after spending the evening at a friend's house on Washington Street. Mildly drunk on beer, he turned into Cedar Street to relieve himself against a wall, when he saw that a cop had rounded the corner and was bearing down on him. The officer was Edward McCosker and, according to Carey, "he made use of very gross, indecent language to me, and directed me around the corner in Thames St." Then, according to the clerk who took Carey's deposition, McCosker "took hold of deponent by the privates and at the same time requested the deponent to feel his privates, at which deponent became enraged and called him names, that he was a 'pretty policeman' and words to that effect."

This happened just off the lower reaches of Broadway, quieter at night in the 1840s as the hub of activity moved north, but not dead. James Rees kept the Shady Tavern on Thames Street, and overheard some of the encounter. Cops were a new presence on the streets at night. In 1834 the force numbered 550 men, 245 of whom patrolled every night, but they were still most often called the Watch. By 1845 they numbered 800 and had formally become the police: the first commissioner, George W. Matsell, had been appointed on June 17. Members of the force wore—for the first time—a star-shaped badge, not out of pride but so that supervisors could keep track of what individual cops got up to on their beats.

McCosker's alleged misbehavior thus triggered an early department inquiry, in the course of which several other witnesses testified. Michael O'Brien, a tobacconist living at 135 Washington Street, said he too had had a run-in with McCosker a few weeks earlier, on the night of January 12.

I am setting on a spar at the corner of Rector and Washington P[lace]. He came up to me and spoke to me and asked me what I was doing there; and after talking some time about females, he put his hands two or three times towards deponent's privates in a very indecent manner and making very indecent expressions, and finally put his hands on deponent's privates; after awhile he asked me to go over to the Porter House of Dennis Mullins, where he treated me to a glass of beer.

Other witnesses came forward to defend McCosker, and the record as it survives doesn't make it clear whether the accusations were straightforward or an act of revenge rising from some feud (gay or straight). Nor—characteristically for these earliest faint traces of evidence for the existence of a 19th-century gay subculture in the city—is it at all plain what any of those involved thought they were doing. Were McCosker's assaults a sadistic form of machismo, or was he frankly cruising? If O'Brien was just sitting insouciantly on Rector Street, and McCosker's gropings were unwelcome, why did they end up sharing drinks at Mullins's tavern?

Homosexuality was nothing new, was in fact ancient, but not (in Federal New York at least) public, until the newspapers illuminated corners and alleys once left dark, sometimes perhaps not fully conscious of what they were reporting. Such was the case of brothels, mainly straight ones, which may sometimes have harbored male as well as female prostitutes, though the evidence is ambiguous. The most famous case was Peter Sewally, a black transvestite arrested in June 1836 for stealing a man's pocketbook (both sexes still carried them at the time). Sewally, however, normally called himself Mary Jones, and worked—as he said when examined by the grand jury—as an attendant and servant in a brothel at 108 Greene Street. Asked to explain his alias and his clothing, he replied that the residents and/or customers of the brothel "induced me to dress in women's clothes, saying I looked so much better in them and I have always attended parties among the people of my own colour dressed in this way—and in New Orleans I always dressed in this way."

Sewally was convicted of theft, but the jury didn't pursue the possibility that he sidelined or perhaps even specialized in hustling customers as well as serving their breakfasts. Most civic attempts to control the sex trade took the form of indictments for keeping a disorderly house, and the language was usually vague: the charge accused the owner of bringing into the house for profit "certain persons, as well men as women, of evil name and fame, and of dishonest conversation, . . . as well in the night as in the day, . . . drinking, tippling, gambling, whoring, and misbehaving themselves." This covered all kinds of behavior without resort to particulars, and gave the authorities wide latitude both for intervention and a neglect born either of toleration or greed for payoffs.

Brothel madams were sometimes accused of harboring boys in disorderly house depositions, but the language is vague as to whether the boys were there as customers, prostitutes, servants, or merely house mascots. Disorderly house convictions seem to have been rare, and by the 1830s the sex trade was becoming a business, even showing early signs of diversification. The people who lived and worked in the brothels, gay or straight, made their mark on the nightlife of the city: they were the first generation of night people, living during the day at a cliff's edge of survival but emerging after sunset to reclaim the city as their own.

Whether because they wanted nothing to do with forbidden sex, tacitly condoned it, or simply treated it to a worldly shrug, New Yorkers, at least into the 1850s, exercised a degree of sexual tolerance they wouldn't approach again until the 1920s. Moral reformers, though destined to play a much bigger role in the century's closing decades, were not yet on a rampage. Everyone else seemed, for a while, content to live with if not approve of such contradictions. Broadway was genteel, the Bowery was louche, yet the louche paraded proudly up Broadway and the genteel couldn't keep themselves off the Bowery.

Instead conflict rose from more visceral and violent oppositions. Fanned by the press, the city, in the furor over abolition, divided sharply, and often along class lines, over questions of race and slavery. The moneyed classes despised the poor and vice versa; the Irish and blacks were at constant loggerheads with each other, united only in the scorn heaped on all their heads by the rich. Even the Irish, with every incentive to stick together, were split by rivalries personal, political, or rooted in interregional hostilities brought westward from Ireland. Small wonder that historians have often branded the decades before the Civil War as an age of riot: the streets nightly attested to it, and a common note in the newspaper accounts that recorded the unrest month by month was bafflement and contradiction as to who was fighting whom and why. Even the participants often didn't seem to know.

Showdown at Astor Place, 1849

As the booming 1830s gave way to panic and mass unemployment, then melted into the busted 1840s, new people were still pouring into New York, ever more numerous and more visible. Superficially Broadway may still have resembled the grand, orderly boulevards of great European capitals. But no such mistake was possible on the Bowery, polyglot yet entirely American and quintessentially New York. "Order, and form, and caste, and deference," Junius Browne wrote, "shaken and confused on Broadway, are broken into fragments in the Bowery, and trampled under foot. 'Who are you?' 'I am as good as anybody.' 'The devil take you.' 'We are for ourselves; Look out for your own,' are written in every passing face and flaunting sign."

By the late 1840s the local economy was steaming ahead again. Broadway and the Bowery, diverging to the west and east near City Hall, gradually pushed their crowds ever further up island, first through today's TriBeCa, then SoHo, then Greenwich Village. The city's two nighttime boulevards were on a cultural collision course, the crack-up finally coming in 1849 at Astor Place, where the Bowery ended, mixing its crowds with Broadway's in the Vauxhall Gardens, which stood between the two thoroughfares.

It was the Astor Place Opera House that detonated this explosion, though its opening might have appeared uncontroversial: it was merely the latest in a string of ill-fated attempts to give grand opera a permanent home in New York (an ambition that wouldn't be fulfilled until 1854, when the Academy of Music opened on 14th Street with Bellini's *Norma,* and broke a jinx that had lasted since Lorenzo Da Ponte's failure in 1833). Opera was ambrosia to a self-professed elite but chloroform to the masses and the casual audience because of its demanding music and exacting performance standards (compared to the "operas" of early New York theater, which were really plays punctuated by unchallenging renditions of popular ballads).

Like the vanished Italian Opera House, the Astor Place theater exuded luxury, both in its ambitious early programming and lavish appointments.

Fixed, reserved, red-covered chairs instead of benches lined the pit, low walls in the two tiers of boxes improved sightlines, and, oh yes, there *was* a cramped 500-seat gallery for the nobodies willing to pay fifty cents for a seat and almost no view of the stage (though an excellent one of the chandelier). Astor Place opened with Verdi's *Ernani* in 1847, but failed even faster than the old Italian Opera House had—in fact, before its first season was over. William Niblo, idle because his pleasure garden was undergoing reconstruction a few blocks south at Broadway and Prince, took over as house manager, and tried to save the place with a bill of crowd-pleasing straight plays.

In contemplation, this must have seemed promising. Vauxhall Gardens, just down Lafayette Street from the Astor, had fallen on hard times, partly because of its increasing attraction to the Bowery crowds. For Mose and Lize, it was the finale of a high night on the town, but for Mose, at least, that meant the happy and likely prospect of a brawl (and in truth Vauxhall had gone threadbare; it would shut down for good in 1859). Niblo decided to make an advantage of the neighborhood's hybrid character and to put on a play that would interest everybody and garner an avalanche of profitable publicity. He settled on a production of *Macbeth* starring the world-famous English actor Charles Macready.

But Niblo had miscalculated: his plan touched a match to the long-smoldering hostility between the popular audience and the city's elite. He had pitted the upstart and aristocratic Astor Place Theatre against its by now revered neighbor, the old workingman's Bowery, a few blocks south, and the highly popular Mitchell's Olympic, in between them on Broadway. Checkered history or not, the Bowery had become the theater of the people, and had nurtured and made famous a legendary Shakespearean actor of its own, this one an American, with a flamboyant patriotism to match and exceed the fervor of the B'hoy: Edwin Forrest (1806–1872). Sensing a profitable opportunity, the Broadway Theatre (just south of today's Worth Street) scheduled its own competing production of *Macbeth* starring Forrest, and the Bowery, not to be outdone, scheduled a third production starring another popular actor, Thomas Hamblin.

As the May showdown loomed, the newspapers whipped it into a press frenzy, with Hamblin edged out of the limelight because Forrest and Macready made better copy. They were, after all, combatants in a transatlantic rivalry between England and the United States. Also, they bore considerable personal animus toward each other, supercharged by the histrionic egos of both participants. Their feud dated back to the 1830s and had flared into open warfare in 1846, when Forrest attended a performance of *Hamlet* at the Theatre Royal in Edinburgh with Macready in the title role. At the moment in Act II when Hamlet is readying himself for the play within a play, Forrest lost his composure and loudly hissed Macready, who was prancing around the stage while swishing a handkerchief above his head (a fellow actor later reported that on this particular occasion Macready was also for some reason wearing a dress, whose waist hovered just under his armpits, like a prototype Shirley Temple costume).

Macready was famous for the subtlety and nuance of his acting. Forrest, a powerfully built man with calves like Popeye's forearms and the general contours of an old-fashioned combination safe, had made himself rich and famous in America thanks to his not-to-be-outdone patriotism and, in performance, an eruption of passion, emotion, and sheer physical incandescence that blew out into the auditorium like a tornado. Forrest became the idol of the B'hoys and the Bowery Theatre. In photographs and engravings, whether he's costumed as Spartacus, Othello, an Indian brave, or Macbeth, he always looks defiant, his face a mask of chin-jutting pugnacity. He bore some resemblance to Frank Chanfrau of Mose fame, but Forrest embodied the working man's idealism where Chanfrau evoked the tough camaraderie of his daily life.

Forrest's bruiser's mien, however, antagonized the box-holders at the Park, and as his career matured, he played there less and less, discomfited by the scorn of upper-class patrons like Philip Hone, who thought him "a vulgar, arrogant loafer, with a pack of kindred rowdies at his heels." Forrest and Macready realized onstage the collision of values represented in life by George Templeton Strong and Ned Buntline, with Forrest the people's self-appointed but enthusiastically followed tribune and Macready the cultured voice of the establishment.

Newspapers anticipated the Forrest-Macready showdown as an occasion of high social comedy as well as an incomparable moment in the history of the New York theater. But they had missed the undertow. In the weeks before Macready's debut at Astor Place, the newly organized police force had been picking up rumors of coming violence from the neighborhoods abutting the Bowery. Not that it took much investigation: Ned Buntline had, in his eponymous weekly newspaper *Ned Buntline's Own*, been stoking populist passion with the energy only he could summon.

As the opening of Macready's Astor Place *Macbeth* neared, it was no surprise to find Buntline siding with the Forrest fans. But he had a passionate if confused political agenda, and a megaphone in *Ned Buntline's Own*. He'd become a determined provocateur. His portraits of down-and-out New York in his long series of trashy novels, like *Mysteries and Miseries of New York* (published in 1848 and modeled, as its title indicates, on Eugène Sue's *The Mysteries of Paris*), were Dickensian in their gushing sentiment and their outrage against the exploitation of the urban poor.

But unlike Dickens, whose visit to McCabe's had provoked him into ashen-faced retreat, Buntline was at home in the underworld, as he'd shown in the rabid poison-pen letter he'd written only a month before to Kate Hastings. His rage at her was part of a broader campaign to defend the native American against predators sexual, economic, and cultural. The energies he directed into rebellion were bottomless, and authorities targeted Buntline as a chief instigator of a handbill plastered all over the city on the eve of Macready's opening.

WORKINGMEN,

SHALL

AMERICANS OR ENGLISH RULE

IN THIS CITY?

The Crew of the English steamer has threatened all Americans
who shall dare to express their opinions this night,
at the English Aristocratic Opera House!
We advocate no violence, but a free expression
of opinion to all public men!

WORKINGMEN! FREEMEN!

STAND BY YOUR

LAWFUL RIGHTS!

American Committee

This broadside ratcheted a feud of fans into warfare between people who looked across the Atlantic for their aesthetic models and those who defended the cultural purity of the Bowery and Paradise Square. When Macready played *Macbeth* at the theater on Monday, May 7, a disturbance had marred that performance: a volley of rotten eggs, potatoes, old shoes, a stink bomb, and finally, in Act III, a meteor shower of chairs from the gallery, at which point Macready fled the stage (the orchestra had scattered when the first chair landed in the pit). But it took three more days before tension rose to riot level. The earliest sign of real trouble was in the crowd that gathered ominously outside the theater on the evening of May 10. Bowery audiences were particularly galled by Astor Place's exclusionary dress code, and one man in the crowd shouted, "You can't go in there without kid gloves on. I paid for a ticket, and they would not let me in, because I hadn't kid gloves and a white vest, damn 'em!" All that afternoon Ned Buntline, in a blue frock coat and top hat, raced back and forth across the city urging people to the protest; at night he changed into a short jacket and cap, so as to look more working-class, and joined the crowd.

At seven the management opened the house doors. The white-vested and kid-gloved Upper Ten, as the fashionable classes were beginning to be called, apprehensively rode up and down Broadway in their carriages, trying to decide whether or not it was safe to go in. By 7:15 a mob of angry B'hoys and gawkers was pouring up the Bowery and the crowd became thicker and thicker. The management had sold more tickets than it had places (reserved seating was still not yet customary, even at high-priced houses). But, whether patrons had been frightened off, or the apprehensive management had closed the doors early, the house wasn't full at curtain time. The mood inside was ominous. The building was peppered with nervous cops, and while everybody in the audience was indeed wearing the required gloves and vests, a sizable and tough-looking contingent looked ready to peel them off at a second's notice.

Apparently prompted by intelligence of a major riot in the offing, Mayor Caleb Woodhull, Police Chief George Matsell, and Major General Charles W. Sandford (head of the Seventh Regiment of the New York County Militia), had held an emergency meeting at 11 a.m. But Macready was oblivious. "I went gaily, I may say," he wrote in his diary, "to the theatre." As he walked eastward down Astor Place, he caught a glimpse of the Bowery, just where it turned into Fourth Avenue, and "saw one of the Harlem cars on the railroad discharge a full load of policemen; there seemed to be others at the door of the theatre. I observed to myself, 'This is good precaution.'" He was, he said, far less disturbed by the crowd and the police than his hairdresser, who hadn't shown up.

Richard Moody has described the tragedy that followed in *The Astor Place Riot* (1958). At 7:40 the curtain rose and Macready strode confidently onstage (though armed with a truncheon). This was appropriate to the character, but when a loud chorus of moans, hisses, and competing cheers flooded down on him, he brandished it to point out jeerers to the police. That proved the last comic moment of the evening. Just as Act I, Scene iv drew to a close, the cops, led by Chief Matsell, moved in on a crowd of hecklers in the pit, beat them up, nearly stripping them in the process, and dragged them one by one into a locked room in the basement.

Doggedly, Macready played on. Outdoors, darkness had fallen and the streets surrounding the building were now mobbed. Stones were beginning to sail and smack against the precautionary boards nailed earlier over the theater windows. Somewhere among the crowd stood Ned Buntline, urging it on. Anybody who lived in the prosperous neighborhood had either decamped or was watching and listening with sharpening unease (this number included Herman Melville, living just three blocks away on Fourth Avenue, near 11th Street, but despite his affinity for the strong young American working man, he'd sided publicly with the patrician supporters of Macready).

A pile of heavy paving blocks had been pulled up for sewer construction, and the increasingly noisy crowd seized them. Jumpy theater patrons, trapped inside, heard the stones thud sickeningly against the wood, then splinter it, then crash through the glass into the lobbies. A stone hurtled into the middle of the air over the seats and smashed the chandelier; a plank, violently dislodged, shot into the auditorium, sailed over the balcony, and plunged down toward the pit (luckily it bounced off a railing on the way and someone caught it before it struck the crowd below). The audience, too scared to head for the exposed lobbies, now loud with projectiles, huddled in the auditorium as if a tornado were bearing down on them.

The rioters locked in the basement tried to start a fire (they were foiled). Outside the crowd now peaked at somewhere between 10,000 and 15,000, though a few hundred teenaged boys seemed to have heaved most of the stones. The National Guard moved into the area around nine o'clock, as Macready forged through Act III. Around ten o'clock the soldiers began firing, at first a warning volley, with the balls smashing into the walls of the theater and clattering to the pavement. The crowd retreated, then surged back, with Buntline in front, now waving a sword and shouting, "Workingmen, shall Americans or English rule? Shall the sons whose fathers drove the baseborn miscreants from the shores give up their Liberty?"

Macready played on at warp speed through the fourth and fifth acts, but most of the audience had slipped away into the lobby, hoping for a chance to escape. After the banquet scene in the fourth act, Macready raced back to change, but "water was running down fast from the ceiling to the floor of my room and making a pool there. . . . The stones hurled in had broken some of the pipes." Bravely or heedlessly, he went back on and finished the play, to applause from the few patrons remaining in the auditorium. In his nearly wrecked dressing room, Macready now began changing his costume. "Suddenly," he recalled, "we heard a volley of musketry."

Outside, the militia and the police had more or less secured an escape lane from the theater along 8th Street; Macready left in nondescript dress and made his way to lodgings on Broadway. Most, if not all, of the street-lights had been smashed, and this no doubt helped him escape the notice of the crowd. Lack of light had also accentuated the vivid red gun explosions that had, within seconds, killed or mortally wounded nearly three dozen people.

Ned Buntline had sold the riot as an outpouring of just indignation against snooty English hams and their servile New York admirers. George Templeton Strong, who also commented, predictably took the side of the supposed snobs: "Some of the cavalry were badly hit by paving stones, but as soon as the Unwashed were informed that unless they forthwith took themselves off they'd be treated with a little artillery practice, they scampered." But neither Buntline nor Strong suffered a scratch: the first person to die in the violence was Thomas Kiernan, a 21-year-old Irish waiter from 13th Street, who fell to a ball fired through his eye and into the brain. The 31 dead and the many wounded included laborers, clerks, a Wall Street lawyer, and a small boy, Frederick Gillespie, shot through the feet. Medical rescue was still haphazard: some of the injured were carried to New York Hospital (then at the corner of Broadway and Anthony Street), to precinct houses, or to drugstores and dispensaries, which served in lieu of emergency rooms.

New York awoke on Friday morning to a day of shock and anger, a sensation probably worse than the aftermath of the 1835 fire, because it wasn't buildings that had been destroyed, but people. Buntline was arrested as an instigator and eventually convicted: he spent a year in jail on Blackwell's (now Roosevelt) Island. Yet the punishment was far from severe: with plenty of money and support behind them, prisoners like Buntline could, at will, bring in their own furniture, food, liquor, cigars, and visitors. And when Buntline got out he was cheered home in a celebratory parade and given a blowout banquet by the nativists.

Riots, common since the 1830s and culminating with Astor Place, had exposed the city's smoldering tensions—rich against poor, Protestants against Catholics, Whigs against Democrats, native-born whites (poor and rich) against the Irish and the blacks. Yet those rivalries, violent as they often became, may well deceive the modern observer schooled to think of such conflicts as clashes of well-defined and separated interest groups, clearly segregated by class, race, ethnicity, customs, and neighborhood. Looked at more closely—and in the city after dark—the New York of 1850 was far more confused. Group lines dissolved as soon as you followed their members out of their shops, offices, and homes at night.

If he could scrape together enough cash, the boardinghouse dweller might join the clergyman at a well-appointed brothel run by a woman, like Julia Brown, who moved familiarly among men of the merchant class. As Timothy Gilfoyle has shown in *City of Eros,* brothel-keeping offered an unprecedented opportunity for women to become well established in business. Roughneck prostitutes exchanged blows in the third tier of the Park within earshot if not sight of the staid families in the boxes; Philip Hone or Walt Whitman, at least through the early 1840s, could be seen at the Bowery Theatre along with locals from the Sixth Ward.

Broadway and Bowery night scenes, rushed forward by complex human currents and the whirlpools they created, are a snapshot of antebellum New York as recent historians have often depicted it—a stressful tangle of interwoven social threads. Sean Wilentz, in *Chants Democratic: New York City and the Rise of the American Working Class* (1984), observed that New York's sharp increase in wealth and population coincided with a steady worsening in living conditions among the working people of the Fourth, Sixth, Seventh and Tenth Wards, the neighborhoods bordering the Bowery. Yet just a few blocks west—despite rapid commercialization and a peppering of brothels—the neighborhoods between Broadway and the Hudson retained much of their economic value and social cachet. Such close proximity between opposites implied collision: the Astor Place riots were no anomaly. Nor was their location, just where genteel Broadway met with the raucous Bowery.

New York's unrest was part of the nation's, particularly as the nagging issue of the 1840s—the Mexican War and the problematic annexation of new territories like Texas and California—gave way in the 1850s to the increasing tensions over slavery. As civil war approached, the city found itself wrestling even more strenuously with its already envenomed social relations. Many of New York's merchants and financiers were sympathetic to the South because they depended on it for profit and trade, and they fell out with well-off abolitionists without southern affinities, like the *Tribune's* Horace Greeley. And New York's already tense interracial and class strife fractured even more under the pressure, with black Republicans, for example, pitted against the Irish. On the waste ground later to become Central Park, black and Irish squatters had set up shantytowns, in which they lived together amicably, sometimes intermarrying, an exception to a general pattern of anti-black hostility among the immigrant Irish, who associated the abolitionist cause with the nativists: Archbishop John Hughes, the strong-willed, powerful, and shrewd leader of the immigrant Irish Catholic community, opposed emancipation. Buntline's rabble-rousing placards may have looked like spontaneous expressions of popular fury, but in fact he wanted to herd the rioters into a nativist political movement, the Know-Nothings, and their political arm, the American Party. And Tammany Hall was also keen to exploit nativist passions: Isaiah Rynders, the legendary Tammany strongman, was as deeply implicated in the Astor Place riots as Buntline.

Gangs were—and of course remain—fluid, their composition unstable, driven by random events and ricocheting passions. John W. Ripley, an engraver who had been a B'hoy, described later in life the Five Points gang landscape with firsthand authority. Gangs had, he wrote, "no organization, but were a crowd of young men of different nationalities, mostly American born, who were always ready for excitement, generally of an innocent nature." Generally, perhaps, but not always: gang energy readily lent itself to partisan rage, and sometimes even to wanton violence if a cause were lacking.

The Bowery Boys gang, for example, were Irish Democrats from the northeast sector of the Five Points, active in the 1850s, and their most famous imbroglio was an 1857 battle not with nativists but with another Irish Democratic gang, called—in legend and in Martin Scorsese's *Gangs of New York*—the Dead Rabbits (though in fact the members denied any such gang had ever existed; the police called them the Mulberry Boys and they dubbed themselves the Roche Guard). Bizarrely, the Democratic Bowery Boys found themselves defending members of a reformed police force that had been purged of Democrats and filled with nativists.

Whatever the 1850s Manhattan nightscape lacked in height, extent, and wattage, it was never exceeded in drama and surprise, possessed as it was of an intimate immediacy of scale the modern urban behemoth can't duplicate. The lights still hissed and smoked and smelled in your very face, with the lability of flame rather than the controlled evenness of electricity. Actors and actresses were living presences, not only on the stage but on the street; audiences expressed approval with unbridled emotion and revulsion with flying furniture. Differing convictions, political and otherwise, met fist to fist on the streets.

As the Civil War approached, the population and the nighttime entertainment districts pushed relentlessly northward. Increasingly, "high" culture tried to divorce itself, at least in appearance, content, venue, and personnel, from low-life doings. This marked a loss: the city's nightlife, though it grew in scope, never quite duplicated the explosive democratic inventiveness of the pre–Civil War era. The educated gravitated to the New York Philharmonic's concerts (the orchestra had begun playing in 1842), or grand opera, first at the Academy of Music on 14th Street, finally (beginning in 1883) at the Metropolitan Opera on Broadway at 39th. In the immediate aftermath of the riots, however, it was popular culture that triumphed on Astor Place. Pockmarked by bullets, and now bearing the nickname "Massacre Opera House," the Astor Place closed for six months after the riots; Sanford's New Orleans Minstrels played it in 1850. In 1852 the quintessential stage Bowery B'hoy, Frank Chanfrau, took over the building for a season of mixed fare, from Mose and Lize to classic drama. A year later the place was on the block again; it reopened as Clinton Hall for a series of evening lectures and spiritualist séances.

But by now New York was not alone in conflict. Beginning with the uprisings of 1848, Europe had begun toppling its kings and counselors, and the United States was well on the way to its own apocalypse. The Republican Party formed itself in 1853 on an anti-slavery platform; in 1857 the Supreme Court handed down the Dred Scott decision. The whole nation was edging toward catastrophe.

CHAPTER SIX

"UNDER THE RAIN OF GASLIGHTS"

From the Civil War to the Gilded and Gruesome 1870s

S HORTLY BEFORE DAWN ON Friday morning, April 12, 1861, Confederate troops in Charleston fired on Union-held Fort Sumter. The news traveled faster than could have been imagined even twenty years before: Morse had sent his first telegraph message in 1844. Now, despite the confusion of the day, the first telegram reached New York at five that afternoon: "WAR HAS BEGUN." Contradictory wires quickly followed, however (perhaps the Confederates were trying to confuse the enemy), and anxious crowds gathered at the telegraph offices and in Printing House Square, waiting for news.

Walt Whitman was in Manhattan to see a performance of Donizetti's *Linda di Chamounix* at the Academy of Music, where a popular soprano, South Carolina–born Clara Louise Kellogg, was to sing the title role. As night fell, he sat in the Academy on 14th Street (famous for its excellent sound, ugly decor, and terrible sightlines), listening to Kellogg's celebrated rendering of the opera's second act, in which Linda, after one anguished confrontation with her lover, Carlo, and another with her father (who accuses her of being a kept woman), has a Donizetti mad scene, à la *Lucia di Lammermoor*.

When the performance was over, Whitman turned down Broadway, on his way toward the ferry landing. Just before midnight, he recollected, "I heard in the distance the loud cries of the newsboys, who came presently tearing and yelling up the street, rushing from side to side even more furiously than usual." At Prince Street near Niblo's Garden (Nixon's Royal Circus was playing there; it featured equestrian acts and an Oriental Scene, "A Night with the Celestials"), Whitman bought a newspaper and stopped, "where the great lamps were brightly blazing," trying to absorb the tragedy:

With a crowd of others, who gathered impromptu, [I] read the news, which was evidently authentic. For the benefit of some who had no papers, one of us read the telegram aloud, while all listen'd silently and attentively. No remark was made by any of the crowd, which had increas'd to thirty or forty, but all stood a minute or two, I remember, before they dispers'd. I can almost see them there now, under the lamps at midnight again.

As he continued downtown the crowds would still have been thick. At Howard Street, Mitchell's Olympic Theatre had become the popular American Music Hall, "Old 444" (a working man's place if ever there was one, with a 15-cent gallery admission and cigar vendors plying the audience; even the violinists in the orchestra could be seen smoking cigars, cigarettes, and pipes as they played). Further on, just south of Canal Street, Spaulding and Rogers's Circus was at the Bowery Theatre. And the Brooklyn ferry slip at Fulton Market was always alive all night, with passengers boarding and leaving the ferryboats, pickpockets preying on them, and rows of 24-hour oyster restaurants (the best known was Doilon's on Fulton Street).

But tonight everyone must have been subdued, contemplating the agony ahead. And four years of trouble and calamity would indeed follow, both for the nation and the city, and not from war alone. William Marcy "Boss" Tweed of Tammany Hall, now the biggest and perhaps most corrupt of all big-city political machines, began his rise to power. Draft riots exploded in 1863, leaving 105 New Yorkers dead. Construction came nearly to a halt and a housing shortage followed. Inevitably, leisure and nightlife shared the universal melancholia. Edwin Christy, the originator of the popular Christy Minstrels, jumped to his death in 1862. On November 25, 1864, while John Wilkes Booth played in Shakespeare's *Julius Caesar* at the Winter Garden, a cabal of Confederate agents slinked through Manhattan, setting five hotels and Barnum's Museum on fire.

All the blazes were doused before they spread, but even an unsuccessful act of terrorism served as a metaphor for the times—indeed a mild one compared with horrors like the more than 20,000 casualties in one day at Antietam in 1862, or the Lincoln assassination. And yet, once the war was finally over, the pall of the tragedy may still have darkened minds, but ambition recovered with unseemly haste: New York resumed its impetuous rush for money, pleasure, and novelties both imaginative and technological. By the late 1870s—one short generation after the Astor Place riot—Manhattan's dark hours had remade themselves yet again. Contrasts, always the dominant urban note, had become a loud ostinato.

By the 1870s the gulf between Gilded Age swagger and racking poverty were astounding even veterans of the tense 1850s. New inventions, already common back in William Dunlap's old age, had invaded the city and seemed to be taking over. Steam trains lumbered down the streets or hooted, clacked, and squealed overhead on iron skyways. The air grayed and sagged with its burden of fumes from coal and wood smoke, from the gashouses along the rivers, and from raw industries everywhere. Telegraph wires swung overhead by the thousands—spaghetti swooping on thickets of pasta-fork telegraph poles, leaning crazily as they charged down thoroughfares and around corners, as if the masts of the old sailing vessels, crowded ashore by the steamships, had clambered onto the streets.

Patrician Philip Hone had died in 1851, man of the people Edwin Forrest in 1872. George Templeton Strong lived on until 1875, and Ned Buntline—eternally irrepressible—until 1886. He had rusticated upstate to Delaware County, having accumulated countless enemies and seven wives (he was married to two, possibly three, of them at the same time). New York City, full of unexpected encounters and eager lawyers, was too hot for him.

Eventful though the 1850s had been, the years following the Civil War withstood their own succession of shocks. After a postwar boom, panic and depression had struck again in 1873. William Tweed lost his adamantine grip on Tammany Hall, and ended up languishing in prison for his misdeeds. But the city's growth only accelerated. Between 1870 and 1880 the population soared from about 942,000 to nearly 1,170,000. Harlem and Washington Heights remained semirural but the poor of lower Manhattan massed together in the thickest population density on earth, in conditions of crowding unknown to the 21st century outside the Third World.

Yet the bigger it got, the more this teeming new New York seemed intent on balkanizing itself. No longer did brothels abut mansions on the left and butchers on the right. Sailmakers no longer routinely lived a few yards away from merchants and opinion-making publishers, as they had in 1800. The rich had fled lower Manhattan. Homes had fled from the shops and countinghouses they once shared premises with, wealth fled from poverty, vice from virtue, and virtue from vice. Entertainment ricocheted from vicinity to vicinity. Broadway, as it had since the days of Jan Damen, continued to carry New York and its nightlife triumphantly northward. The Bowery, though it came to an end at Astor Place, retained its proletarian energy. Yet New York was de-coagulating into an archipelago that even the fastest surface trains of the 1850s couldn't expeditiously bridge: they took forty minutes to steam from Chatham Square to east Harlem.

By Owl Train to Harlem

Rapid transit revolutionized urban travel. The advent of one of the world's most remarkable transport systems, the steam-powered elevated railroads, made a night journey through the million-strong metropolis an urban lure and a tourist must. The els shamed the lurching horsecars and outclassed the exploding steam engines and bone-knocking rails of the old surface lines. By the end of 1878 the Third Avenue elevated railway was running 24 hours a day. Between midnight and 4:45 a.m., Owl Trains departed South Ferry for 129th Street every fifteen minutes.

One night, as the clocks struck one, a *Herald* reporter boarded an Owl Train at the deserted foot of Whitehall Street. The engine, steaming aloft just 500 feet from the site of Geraerdy's long-gone Wooden Horse, labored past blocks once draped with the wilted tarps of Canvas Town, past the surviving Fraunces Tavern and the vanished Stadts Herbergh. "On we go, slowly at first," the *Herald* reporter wrote, "over the tangle of switches, and then as the gleaming track stretches out before, we gain headway and go rushing into the shadow of the silent tenements and the deserted workshops of down town." The train's lit windows made a light show new to the streets—a gliding serpentine chain of glass oblongs, oblivious to the city sleeping or working below. The line flew a tight S-curve—first left into Coenties Slip, then sharp right onto Pearl Street, passing the forest of masts along the East River wharves, then up to Fulton Street and past the fish market.

In the 1870s, the southern tip of Manhattan had lost its once glamorous reputation to the uptown migration of nightlife. Few people lived there anymore. Only beyond Hanover Square, where "odd clusters of houses . . . swarm down to the river's edge," did lit parlors and kitchens begin disclosing themselves, with "human lives crowded together in so many uncouth shapes with a stray light struggling through the panes, and the lines of the narrow streets broken and almost lost among them." Continuing north, the Owl Train bucked over more switches, jerked into Chatham Square, then headed up the Bowery, whose rowdy life and noise contrasted sharply with the silence further south. The neighborhood had grown more ragged after the Civil War, but lost none of its brio. "There is nothing in this glare of light, nothing in this swarming pavement to indicate that midnight has passed," the reporter wrote.

The Bowery B'hoy look of the 1830s had faded by now, but the cheekiness survived. "The windows gleam, the saloons are all aglare, a half-score pianos and violins send as many airs floating into the night to blend into an instrumental discord that attunes itself fitly to the roysterer's song, the brawler's oath, and the hundred strange voices of the night."

Bowery music had enriched the sound texture of the urban night. Its clunking pianos and squawking strings were not so loud as modern amplified sound. But neither had they been electronically laundered of density and edge, and as a result the music jolted like a living thing, a carnival for the ears, with the dull thunder of the el as a backdrop heard everywhere. By 1880 four lines plied Second, Third, Sixth, and Ninth Avenues, shedding smoke, sparks, cinders, and crowds of disembarking passengers to the streets below. Once, steam engines had been banned south of 32nd Street, but now the els added their roar to the carriage wheels jarring over the cobblestones, clopping horse hooves, shouts, and laughter.

At 6th Street, the tracks bore right onto Third Avenue, passing a block east of the site of the Astor Place riot (the old opera house, renamed Clinton Hall, now housed the Mercantile Library). Next the line traversed neighborhoods like Gramercy Park, newly developed as an enclave of wealth: George Templeton Strong, long a holdout on ever-grubbier Greenwich Street, had fled after the Astor Place riot and lived at 113 East 21st Street until his death. "Closed shutters, draped windows, darkened rooms—everywhere a recognition of the hours of slumber, only the street lamps beneath, and only a semi-occasional by-passer." Here Manhattan burrowed again into sleep, and the train echoed louder in the silence.

A few years later, in his 1890 novel *A Hazard of New Fortunes,* William Dean Howells evoked the night magic of the Third Avenue line through the eyes of his principal characters, Basil and Isabel March. Urban technology, as Howells perceived, had leapt past convenience and wonder into romance.

Night transit was even more interesting than the day. . . . The fleeting intimacy you formed with people in second and third floor interiors, while all the usual street life went on underneath, had a domestic intensity mixed with a perfect repose. . . . [Basil] said it was better than the theatre, of which it reminded him, to see those people through their windows: a family party of work-folk at a late tea, some of the men in their shirt-sleeves; a woman sewing by a lamp; a mother laying her child in its cradle; a man with his head fallen on his hands upon a table; a girl and her lover leaning over the windowsill together.

For the Marches, the el cast its deepest spell at 42nd Street, where a short branch line took passengers two blocks east to the old Grand Central Terminal.

At the 42nd Street station they stopped a minute on the bridge that crosses the track to the branch road for the Central Depot, and looked up and down the long stretch of the elevated to north and south. The track that found and lost itself a thousand times in the flare and tremor of the innumerable lights; the moony sheen of the electrics mixing with the reddish points and blots of gas far and near; the architectural shapes of houses and churches and tow-ers, rescued by the obscurity from all that was ignoble in them, and the coming and going of the trains marking the stations with vivider or fainter plumes of flame-shot steam—formed an incom-parable perspective.

Strolling at night into the old Grand Central—a mansard-roofed pile about half the size of the current terminal—the Marches saw yet another city revelation in the 100-foot-high glass and iron arch that soared over-head. It was huge—652 feet long, 200 wide—and it "looked down upon the great night trains lying on the tracks dim under the rain of gaslights that starred without dispersing the vast darkness of the place. What forces, what fates, slept in these bulks which would soon be hurling themselves north and east and west through the night!"

Perspectives, no longer unfolding 1830s-style at eye level and the pace of a walk, opened up beneath the watcher like a moving panorama, more diverting than anything at Hanington's or Niblo's, seen through a window in flight, atop a grid of iron, sweeping past scene after scene at the then breakneck speed of twelve miles an hour. As the train left midtown, it passed building sites, factories, and vacant lots. St. Patrick's Cathedral was rising on Fifth Avenue at 50th Street. Still without steeples, it looked squashed and belligerent. Toward Harlem, lines of gas lampposts trailed down unbuilt and unpopulated streets. To the west lay the rounded hills of "the" Central Park (as it was first called). To the east, across the river, one saw a few lights still burning in Astoria.

Among these empty blocks, silently awaiting an imminent building boom, scattered structures reared up, stark and monolithic. One such, at the corner of Fifth Avenue and East 52nd Street, was a grand brownstone, reached by a heavy staircase from Fifth and pierced by rows of huge plate glass windows. This was the new mansion of a wealthy woman who was also an outcast, indeed an emblem of New York's now fractured and confusing class landscape. Her name was Ann Lohman; we have met her before under another name, and we will hear more of her shortly. It was no happpenstance that she had staked her claim on this desolate urban frontier—scattered islands of privilege and misery, seemingly sealed off from each other, were the trend of the times.

Yet they were not so isolated as they looked. Money and real estate separated, but restlessness, the els, and the power of human magnetism reunited them; they were perpetually infiltrating each other. By the 1840s the brothel district was migrating uptown. It reached present-day SoHo during the 1850s. By the 1860s it had crept up to the West Side between 23rd and 34th Streets, where it acquired a name ever since synonymous with New York sin: the Tenderloin. A cop on the take, relocating there, baptized it with the famous remark "I've been having chuck steak ever since I've been on the force, and now I'm going to have a bit of tenderloin."

Of course respectable people kept on trying to restrict their evenings to neighborhoods of virgin civility, but it was easier to pack up and relocate a brothel or saloon than an opera house; attempts at balkanization somehow never came off. Ann Lohman, owner of the fortlike house on Fifth Avenue at 52nd Street, was in fact the infamous Madame Restell, New York's most notorious abortionist. Her trade had always been disreputable. It had always exposed her to condemnation, once sent her to prison, and had more recently become the target of indignant anti-vice crusaders. In 1878 her front windows looked across to a vacant lot and thence to the heavy pillars and girders of the brand-new Sixth Avenue el, which hadn't yet started running. Yet two socially ruthless Vanderbilts— William Henry and William Kissam—had bought land directly across the avenue from her and were, undeterred by their sinister neighbor, about to build two mansions of unprecedented opulence.

Down on the Rialto, as 14th Street was called, the situation was no different. Lester Wallack—the only actor the Upper Ten admired and invited into their homes as a peer rather than a human curiosity—headed a highbrow repertory company in his own theater, Wallack's, at Broadway and 13th Street. But even his once immaculate near neighbor, the Academy of Music, had begun, in between opera performances, hosting masked balls put on by the Cercle Français de l'Harmonie. The name was ethereal, but the parties were in actuality bibulous orgies between the city's richest parvenus and most notorious courtesans.

BLAZING CITY, HIDDEN CITY

New York's lights had become brighter since the war. But many of its moods grew darker as the city shed the last remainders of its old, rural-feeling Federal-era self. The Kissing Bridge, where Harry Colt took Maria Trumbull in 1800, was no more. De Voor's old mill creek had been boxed into a sewer and paved over—it now lay under the corner of Second Avenue and 52nd Street, just downhill from Restell's house. In between there now crowded a Schaefer Brewery, the Steinway piano factory, and the wasteland of railroad tracks along Fourth Avenue. This was the current incarnation of the once quaint old Harlem line, which had bridged the Harlem River and reached far up into Westchester County by the 1840s; even at the beginning of that decade it was carrying a million passengers a year in Manhattan alone.

Now, once the sun set, one could climb the el stairway, speed above streets, parks, houses, and reappear in a new little world. Downtown, among the three-and-a-half-story brick row houses that survived, some held on as one-family dwellings. But in the Lower East Side slums, they (along with warehouses and abandoned breweries) had been cut up into cramped rooms—miserable lodgings for the poor, who packed them to the very walls, often without running water, heat, and sanitation. The photographs in Jacob Riis's 1890 classic, *How the Other Half Lives,* derive much of their impact from the contrast between the still dignified, still elegant forms of old row houses and the beaten-down women, hollow-eyed men, and dazed-looking children posed in front of them: the misery of existence inside emerges only from interior shots.

Purpose-built tenement housing was no better. Gotham Court, on Cherry Street and just south of an eight-foot-wide thoroughfare called Murderers' Alley, had gone up in 1850. Six stories high, it was a block of ten-by-fourteen-foot apartments, each divided into two minuscule rooms, with windows looking out east or west on the two narrow blind alleys through which you entered them. A series of narrow staircases opened into each alley, with two apartments on each landing. The only amenities were two rum shops facing Cherry Street and—at cellar level, underneath the alleys—a long row of subterranean water closets and sinks. It smelled filthy, it was filthy, and by 1879 as many as 240 families were living miserably in it.

Demolished in 1895 in the aftermath of cries for tenement reform, Gotham Court was an archetype of the squalid tenement rooms inhabited by the immigrant poor, an atmosphere caught by Stephen Crane's *Maggie, A Girl of the Streets* (1893), in his description of the tenement house where Maggie and her family live,

> a dark region where, from a careening building, a dozen gruesome doorways gave up loads of babies to the street and the gutter. . . . Long streamers of garments fluttered from fire-escapes. In all unhandy places there were buckets, brooms, rags and bottles. In the street infants played or fought with other infants or sat stupidly in the way of vehicles. Formidable women, with uncombed hair and disordered dress, gossiped while leaning on railings, or screamed in frantic quarrels. Withered persons, in curious postures of submission to something, sat smoking pipes in obscure corners. A thousand odors of cooking food came forth to the street. The building quivered and creaked from the weight of humanity stamping about in its bowels.

Tenements were awake 24 hours a day, whether with violence, suffering, socializing, or labor. Cigar-making was a common work-at-home industry, and ground on constantly, as Theodore Roosevelt noted in 1885 when, as a state assemblyman, he toured the slums:

> The work of manufacturing the tobacco went on day and night in the eating, living, and sleeping rooms. . . . I have always remembered

one room in which two families were living. On my inquiry as to who the third adult male was I was told that he was a boarder with one of the families. There were several children, three men, and two women in this room. The tobacco was stowed about everywhere, alongside the foul bedding, and in a corner where there were scraps of food. The men, women, and children in this room worked by day and far into the evening, and they slept and ate there.

Endlessly publicized, such hideous conditions had made multifamily dwellings synonymous with poverty at its worst. But by the 1870s, developers began to fight the bad reputation of apartment buildings by aiming them at wealthier tenants. Madame Restell and her husband, Charles Lohman, were among the pioneers in this movement. In 1876, on a lot just north of their mansion, they'd built a six-story elevator apartment house, the Osborne. Architectural critics called it "the finest apartment house in New York," and it was indeed imposing, with two spacious nine-room apartments on each floor. Still, like many early luxury apartment houses, the Osborne suffered from a high vacancy rate. Prospective tenants, acclimated to row houses, were squeamish about communal living and the bohemianism it suggested. And Restell's notoriety couldn't have helped matters.

Evenings at home in the cosmopolitan New York of the 1870s now included multiple styles of both wealth and poverty. A few old families with money still hunkered down in their old row houses; others joined the free-for-all of dueling Gilded Age mansions that had caught up both the Lohmans and the Vanderbilts; still others chose the novelty and convenience of a luxury apartment. For the poor, the alternatives were all bad: the jerry-built hovels that characterized the city's earliest attempts to accommodate a flood of immigrants, or the supposedly improved but often dreadful tenement house designs that appeared with each attempt to improve housing law, or—and these provoked the worst dread—the hospitals, poorhouses, and prisons.

Foremost among these was the jail that still outranks all others in city legend, the Tombs. The massive architecture of ancient Egypt had fascinated western architects for some time, but the fad took a fateful turn when the city jail commission fell in love with an illustration of an Egyptian tomb in a travel book by John L. Stephens. The result, which opened in 1838, was a barbaric mausoleum for the living dead. The former city prison, the Bridewell in City Hall Park, was grim inside, but from the street it looked, at its best, like a trim municipal building on a well-kept green. The Tombs stood on the block bordered by Centre, Franklin, and Leonard Streets, atop the old Fresh Water, drained then buried under piles of garbage-laden fill in the early 1800s. The new building, officially the Halls of Justice, had been consciously engineered to radiate menace, even before the arrival of its 200 anticipated male and female inmates. Four squat Egyptianesque columns guarded the Centre Street entrance. The walls and front windows sloped in as they rose upward, adding to the aura of sepulchral tonnage crushing the earth and interring the prisoners.

A sewer line had been run beneath Centre Street from Canal to Pearl in order to drain and stabilize the soil. But nonetheless the Tombs instantly began burrowing into the feculent mud. Four-inch-wide cracks split the walls, which sank visibly, as if sucked into quicksand. Dampness seeped up into the masonry from the buried pond and the drains periodically erupted, spraying up geysers of sewage. In the mid-1800s a model prisoner named Duffy served as the Tombs's plumber, happy to thrust his arm up to the shoulder into the filth of a backed-up drain. Twenty years' confinement had inured him to this sickening potion, riddled with liquefied garbage, ooze from the old slaughterhouses along the East River, and runoff from the African Burial Ground.

The Tombs was particularly terrible at night. Cells were dungeonlike (six by eight feet, but with eleven-foot ceilings), and unlit, except for such light as filtered through three-by-twelve-inch grates or the four-foot-high doorways. But the drunk tank was noisiest and grossest, the Ninth Circle of the place. Typically sentenced to ten days in the Tombs, hungover drunks spent their mornings and afternoons in a stone-floored hall that reeked, according to one veteran, of "tobacco spit, vomit and filth." From seven at night to 6:30 in the morning a guard, often as drunk as or drunker than his wards, herded them into sleeping cells on the ground floor. An enterprising investigative reporter deliberately got himself committed around 1870, and described a night in these dungeons.

> You enter a wide, arched gloomy hall, on one side of which are three large cells, about fifteen feet square, with open barred grates the whole front of them. . . . [The jailer] feels his power, and now his mean, cruel spirit creeps out; his cold, leaden gray eyes emit a fiendish glare; his hyena nature gloats, pur[r]s and grunts out its inward satisfaction. He yells, "get in there!" but it is full. "Get in there, I tell you!" He packs

one cell full, the other two only comparatively; he locks the doors, rattles the bars and chuckles aloud. Now commences a perfect pandemonium—the prisoners rave—they ask to be put into the less crowded cells; the more they growl the louder he chuckles; they abuse him, curse him, and call him all the bad names known to obscenity and profanity. . . . They yell and hoot at him. He yells and hoots back. For hours it is a miniature hell—there is no such thing as sleep—vermin of every kind crawl over you and *eat* you. You are on fire, you tear your flesh with your nails; huge rats rush between your legs or over your body; vulgarity, obscenity, profanity of every description reigns supreme.

At length the keeper throws his own straw mattress on the floor outside the cells and falls to snoring. A maniac somewhere in the cavernous four tiers of the main men's cell block begins screaming:

Loud and strong as the roar of the lion it reaches to every crevice, even to the outer walls of the prison, and in bitterness, in agony, in passion it resembles the commingled yells of a hundred infuriated demons. . . . Great heavens what power of lungs, what physical strength he must be endowed with; the live long night his horrid shrieks resound. Oh, there is a terrible tragedy connected with him; cold chills creep over me now as I write and think of it. It never can be effaced from my memory.

Other accounts confirm that the Tombs was as bad as the reporter claimed; but his goose-bumpy prose also reveals its fascination for readers. Nurtured by cases like the Helen Jewett murder and the disappearance of Mary Rogers in 1841 (another much-publicized incident), horror had become a staple of the dailies. And it had also infiltrated literature. Edgar Allan Poe (1809–1849) had, when he moved to New York in 1844,* already begun writing stories of nocturnal urban intrigue in 1841, with "The Murders in the Rue Morgue." All this betokened a growing interest in the hidden secrets of the night, its places (like the Tombs) and its people: cops, morticians, detectives, scavengers, gravediggers, and everyone else who worked in the dark to spirit the city's horrors away from the eyes

---

* Poe's first job in the city was to write up yet another headline-grabbing hoax for the incorrigible *Sun* (this one announced that a hot-air balloon had crossed the Atlantic and landed in South Carolina).

of citizens before dawn. Then, every morning, the catlike night beat reporters undid their work by fishing the monstrosities up again and dropping them on the reader's breakfast plate.

Every night and every dawn the straying corpses reclaimed their place in the city, floating to the surface in rivers or discovered in the streets. Most of them ended in a small, vaultlike building near the East River. Above the door a sign, incongruously written in gilt letters, announced "MORGUE." Modeled on its famed Paris predecessor, it had opened in 1866 in Bellevue Hospital, a jumble of asylumlike hulks, bastions, towers, and cupolas piled up along the north side of 26th Street. The morgue was damp, cold, and a mere twenty feet square, with four three-by-six-foot stone tables for the corpses, and a tiled floor three feet below street level. The dead person's clothing drooped from high hooks behind each table, and a shower head dangling from a length of gutta-percha hose misted each sheeted body to chill it; observers peered through a barrier of glass windows.

James McCabe described the place with morbid gusto in *Lights and Shadows of New York Life* (1872):

> The dark waters of the rivers and bay send many an inmate to this gloomy room. The harbor police, making their early morning rounds, find some dark object floating in the waters. It is scarcely light enough to distinguish it, but the men know well what it is. They are accustomed to such things. They grapple it and tow it in silent horror past the long lines of shipping, and pause only when the Morgue looms up coldly before them in the uncertain light of the breaking day. The still form is lifted out of the water, and carried swiftly into the gloomy building. It is laid on the marble slab, stripped, covered with a sheet, the water is turned on, and the room is deserted and silent again.

Nearer Broadway, and safely removed from the riverfronts, Manhattan's conventional nightlife continued to flourish; nor had the rage for refinement that built the Astor Place Opera House abated. As early as 1848 the Park Theatre management, mortified by the evil reputation of its third tier, renamed it the "Family Circle," a final stab at banishing prostitutes.*

---

* This euphemism stuck: the 1883 Metropolitan Opera House dubbed its fifth tier the Family Circle, and the name remains in the new house, which opened at Lincoln Center in 1966. The prostitutes are (mostly) long gone.

Some old houses, long known for rowdiness, closed or changed hands. The Bowery had burned in 1828, 1836, 1838, and 1845. Though instantly rebuilt after each fire, it was sold at auction for $100,700 in 1866 and found new life as a venue for German, Jewish, and Italian ethnic theater (it survived until 1929, when a final blaze erased it forever).

Niblo's Garden survived too, so extensively remodeled and upgraded as to be unrecognizable as the folksy pleasure garden of the 1830s. A hotel had been built on the site, and in the theater the department store magnate A. T. Stewart kept a private box, whose back entry opened on a Versailles-like mirrored arcade. In the gardens a series of stereopticon photographs show a statue of a lady at the entrance, holding a gas globe, poised as if to draw attention to the allée of trees behind her. Tables and chairs receded down a perspective of five gaslit arches, statuary, a fountain, and a large outdoor stage. The grounds admitted carriages after 11 p.m. And in 1866 Niblo's saw the opening of a still celebrated and at the time highly daring smash hit: *The Black Crook*.

Although it has often been labeled the first American musical, *The Black Crook*'s producer, Henry Jarrett, bluntly stated its real inspiration: "Legs are staple articles and will never go out of fashion." Jarrett and his partner Harry Palmer scoured Europe for girl dancers, commissioned costumes, and ferried the lot of them back to New York for a new production of *La Biche au Bois* at the Academy of Music—which, however, burned on the night of May 21, after a performance of *La Juive*. Jarrett went in desperation to William Wheatley, the current manager of Niblo's. According to Joseph Whitton, a Niblo's employee, Wheatley suggested inserting the stranded corps de ballet, clad as scantily as the law would allow, into an over-the-top melodrama. Sometimes, he proposed, the girls would dance, sometimes pose bewitchingly in front of the scenery, with songs and gobbets of plot thrown in between.

Wheatley had found what Whitton called his "clothes-line . . . on which to hang the pretty dresses" in *The Black Crook*, a preposterous melodrama by Charles M. Barras, with a Harz Mountain setting, a pure young hero and heroine, a villainous sorcerer, an "Arch Fiend," Zamiel (to whom Hertzog the sorcerer is supposed to deliver one soul every year), a cast of low-comedy supporting players, and, for good measure, a goddess named Stalacta, "Queen of the Golden Realm." Jarrett, Wheatley, and Barras all knew perfectly well that the story was ridiculous.

But Wheatley saw something better than logic in it. Brandishing the script at Whitton, he declared, "My boy, I have a fortune here," and indeed *The Black Crook* took in $87,000 in its first five weeks. When it opened on September 12, the audience passing under the theater marquee, with its NIBLO'S spelled out in multicolored gas globes, had no idea of the spectacle to ensue. Wheatley had spent $50,000 on the production—including $5,000 just to excavate the basement so as to allow whole scenes to sink beneath the stage. There were machines that produced knock-dead stage illusions, novel lighting effects, and a stupendous climax at the end of the evening—which lasted from 7:45 till 1:15 the next morning. The *Tribune* (whose reviewer said "the scenery is magnificent; the ballet is beautiful; the drama is—rubbish") particularly praised this closing tableau. "One by one curtains of mist ascend and drift away. Silver couches, on which fairies loll in negligent grace, ascend and descend amid a silver rain. Columns of living splendor whirl and dazzle as they whirl. From the clouds [drop] gilded chariots, and the white forms of angels."

The Black Crook introduced several hit songs, including "You Naughty, Naughty Men," sung by Milly Cavendish, a popular English actress making her American debut:

> You may talk of love and sighing;
> My! For us you're nearly dying! . . .
> All the while you know you're trying
> To deceive—you naughty, naughty men!

But the thrill of the production was the 70-member female corps de ballet. They leaped, swayed, and kicked before the audience, clad in a profusion of costumes that always ended at the upper thigh, giving way to pink tights—an unprecedented display of virtual nudity that was the show's real selling point. The aging George Templeton Strong missed *The Black Crook*, but caught its sequel, *The White Fawn*, in 1868. Even the hard-to-please Strong admired the scenic effects (it required a crew of 80 carpenters and twenty gasmen to manage them), but his description summed up the appeal of both shows: "ballet, spectacle, machinery, and pink legs. . . . The whole production," he concluded, "depends for its success mainly on the well-formed lower extremities of female humanity."

The Devil and Anthony Comstock:
Vice and Vigilantism in the 1870s

As the population grew, audiences did too, and cheap mass entertainment more than held its own against the high-end Academy of Music, Wallack's, Niblo's, and the Booth (the era's other select house). Concert saloons—in essence bars equipped with balconies, stages, and often featuring tables in the pit—proved especially alluring to the working-class audience. Prototypes of 20th-century nightclubs, they ranged from vest-pocket to vast in size. Even the earliest concert saloons, like Palmo's old Café des Milles Colonnes—butt of jibes from the sporting press about its gay aura—had been notorious for their mix of alcohol, music, and scantily costumed dancers. They also bore a reputation as markets for prostitution, which continued as a major though changed city industry—a new population of southern girls and women had arrived on the scene, displaced by the Civil War.

Gambling had swollen from impromptu entertainment among friends and acquaintances to big business, sharply divided by class. Rich bettors went to expensive gambling hells (despite their moniker these were often palatial); gullible tourists found themselves lured into gimcrack clip joints; and the poor fell for lotteries and policy rackets on the streets. Race became intricately involved with the latter, one of the few profitable businesses open to blacks, and several became rich running numbers operations. Cheap or giveaway dream books, purporting to be the lore of Gypsies, Arabs, or black clairvoyants, had become popular, and remained so into the 20th century. Ostensibly they were keys to dreams, but titles like *Old Aunt Dinah's Policy Dream Book* revealed their true function as guides to lucky betting numbers. According to Aunt Dinah, dreaming of "a Negro man, or one of very dark complexion, is a favorable token for the dreamer for fourteen."

Post-bellum lower-class nightlife, proliferating and often illegal, revived the fortunes of vigilante vice hawks. New York's vanguard anti-vice movement dated back to the first Society for the Suppression of Vice, founded in 1822. The early society's surviving records, however, voice less indignation against the evil habits of the slums than a growing gap between rich and poor, which of itself tended to multiply vice. "The opposite conditions of riches and poverty," the society argued, "have their peculiar vices which more particularly in large Cities tend to constant increase." Members of the society deplored the already ample trade in dirty books and the ubiquity of prostitution, but devoted most of their worry to alcohol, masquerade balls, and gambling (which, the society said, "favor debauchery and various other vices)." But when the Society for the Suppression of Vice formed anew in 1873, its members found themselves less interested in social ills than dirt qua dirt. The society of course never succeeded in eradicating vice; in fact, like the sporting press of the 1840s, it may have helped publicize it. But its mania for fact-finding left a record more graphic than underworld New York would ever have thought of compiling for itself.

Dragged along by the puffing human steamroller that was Anthony Comstock (1844–1915), the reinvigorated society nosed into low pastimes—especially the trade in Comstock's perennial bête noire, pornography, "cunningly calculated to inflame the passions and lead victims from one step of vice to another." The porn industry was, as it appeared to Comstock's bulging eyes, a million-tentacled creature of darkness ("the men who pander to it, and those who indulge in its enormities, hate the light"). The only remedy was to seize its products by the hundredweight and destroy them by the ton. The society's reports usually commenced with a rhetorical blast and concluded with a detailed table of enormities laid bare and contraband snatched and incinerated. "Above 20,000 pounds, say 100,000 volumes of books, and above 63,000 implements for immoral use have been seized, condemned by law, and destroyed," the society's *Annual Report* announced in 1876.

Those 63,000 "implements for immoral use," not further identified, were probably dildos and the like (one society inventory also listed "lead molds for making the same, seized and destroyed"). Piled up in a storeroom they must have made an impressive sight. Dirty images, particularly "microscopic pictures for charms, rings, knives, etc.," easy to carry about and hide from a patrolling eye, were also high on Comstock's list: he had bagged 6,250 by 1876. Prostitution, gambling, and alcohol also drew the society's fire, but Comstock, at least at this point in his career, seemed more upset by erotic images than flesh-to-flesh sex.

Possibly the advent of photography—and the realistic porn it made possible—contributed to his outrage, but the society was no less alarmed by "indecent playing cards," and conducted a vendetta against nude barroom paintings. Posses would raid a saloon and rip the odalisque from her niche over the bar. In 1875 society vigilantes destroyed 26 such pictures, and by 1886 the total had risen to 74, plus 26,869 confiscated "articles for immoral use of rubber, etc."—though by that era the society had begun to direct more attention to gaming tables, policy books, and betting slips.

Municipal authorities lent support to the anti-vice movement, or at least avoided coming to loggerheads with it. For their part Comstock and the society appear to have gone after the near occasions of sin rather than sin itself, leaving most crimes of vice to the already reluctant attention of the police. The society was prominent in an ever-accelerating attack on abortion and abortionists, but their practical strategy was to seize property (in 1876 they destroyed 3,250 "boxes of pills, powders, etc., used by abortionists") rather than to make direct attacks on practitioners.

WOMAN IN THE DARK:
MARCH 31 TO APRIL 1, 1878

This, however, came to an end in 1878, when Comstock set his sights on Ann Lohman, the notorious Madame Restell. The highest-profile abortionist in New York and indeed the country, Restell had prospered for nearly forty years, and now figured as a prominent Gilded Age nouvelle riche. Like Julia Brown before her, Restell lived in an underworld, but her wealth, the influential connections it won her, and most of all the sheer necessity of her trade, had propelled her to a weird eminence beyond anything an antebellum brothel-keeper might have aspired to.

By the 1840s Restell had expanded beyond her original quarters downtown on Greenwich Street and had opened branch offices in Boston and Philadelphia. Her newspaper ads (on which she spent as much as $60,000 a year), were elliptical but unmistakable in import:

> Madame Restell's experience and knowledge in the treatment of cases of female irregularity is such as to require but a few days to effect a perfect cure. . . . She also sends medicines by mail.

By the 1850s she had become rich enough for a gaudy new mansion, and in 1857 chose her lot, at the corner of 52nd Street and Fifth Avenue (then still a dirt road). She broke ground in 1862, spent $200,000 on the house, and took possession in 1864. By the 1870s the neighborhood was becoming fashionable, but still looked half-baked—a builders' midden, with grandiose new houses looming here and there in naked isolation. Photographs show mud, shacks, factories, excavations, rising mansions, and half-paved streets with spindly gas streetlights straggling over tracts of rubble and vacant land. Grass grew calf-high in front of Elgin Gardens, a botanical preserve only a block south of Restell's front door.

Restell drew condemnation from the beginning. But she survived in the no-man's-land between public moralism and private need. After a periodic firestorm of outrage—which even its shrillest enthusiasts seem to have taken care to curb before it came to any practical consequences—Restell went quietly back to work. In Federal-era New York, abortion was criminal only if done after "quickening," the variable (and subjective) moment at which the mother first felt the fetus stirring; later practice, following this tradition, fixed a limit at the fourth month of pregnancy. But in the 1840s and 50s, opposition began growing. Anti-abortion campaigns originated with the city's medical establishment and soon inspired blaring crusades in the newspapers; New York State's first anti-abortion laws appeared on the books in 1845.

Religious leaders, interestingly, at first avoided the issue, and didn't begin denouncing abortion until the late 1860s; nor did the mounting outcry among doctors and their editor cronies stop Restell. But it did make her life difficult, landing her a full year in the women's prison on Blackwell's Island (a miserable enough place, if not in the Tombs's class). Still—as they had for Ned Buntline—money and pull cushioned her hard time: she quickly acquired two easy chairs, a rocker, a carpet, a night-light, room service (including made-to-order meals delivered on covered trays), and unlimited conjugal visits in a private room with her husband, Charles. On the day of her release in June 1849, she alit from the prison ferry to applause from a small crowd of well-wishers along the East River, then swept with her husband, driver, and footman into her carriage for the short ride home.

Restell resumed business, weathering new attacks by doctors and the two-faced *Tribune* (which vilified her in its columns even as it accepted and ran her ads). Back in the 1840s she'd asked $5 for an office visit, then negotiated a price for the abortion, charging well-off clients up to $100, but far less, occasionally nothing, for poor women. Later she confined her clientele to the wealthy and influential, which made business both safer and more lucrative. By 1878 the *New York Times* estimated her wealth at somewhere between $750,000 and $1 million.

Nemesis struck early in 1878, when Anthony Comstock—posing as a customer and accompanied by an undercover policeman—followed in the footsteps of many heavily veiled women, opening a gate in the balustrade that skirted the house's 52nd Street facade, then going down an outdoor staircase. Clients vented their desperation beneath Restell's grand parlor in a basement consulting room, furnished with incongruously motherly appurtenances like a sewing machine. If the client was female, Restell dispensed a packet of medicinal powder, with instructions to return in a few days if it failed. Most often it did (no effective abortifacients were known at the time). At that juncture Restell seems—though lately she'd begun denying it—to have offered a quick and painful operation with a wire. She then gave a referral to a physician who would, no questions asked, see the patient through the miscarriage that soon followed.

Comstock, imitating most of Restell's male clients, begged a prescription for a distressed lady friend; the cop arrested her as soon as she complied. So hostile had the climate become that Restell, arraigned at the Jefferson Market Courthouse in Greenwich Village, found it difficult to raise bail and spent several awful nights in the Tombs—no trivial ordeal for a woman of 66, despite her stint as a younger prisoner on Blackwell's Island. She was not the only notorious New Yorker in trouble at the moment: Tammany Hall's infamous Boss Tweed had finally fallen under corruption charges. In the county jail on Ludlow Street since late 1877, he was now spilling the details of Tammany shenanigans to a committee of aldermen. Might his well-publicized example have spooked her? Might he even have known and revealed something about how she'd secured the forbearance of the police and courts?

Eventually she raised her bail, but once home she grew morose and haunted as the trial date neared. Her case, docketed for a hearing Monday, April 1, 1878, at the Court of Oyer and Terminer in the Jefferson Market Courthouse, weighed on her intolerably. Her lawyer patiently repeated that he was sure he could keep her out of prison, but reassurances stoked the fear instead of assuaging it. As April 1 approached, the strain mounted, her anguish deepened, and the very luxury of her daily existence became a torment.

Sunday, March 31, 1878, brought a crisis. As the afternoon lengthened, Restell began wandering through the oppressive halls and parlors of her heavy brownstone. Her husband, Charles, who had been at her side through earlier travails, had died in 1876; now she was alone except for the servants, her granddaughter Caroline, and Caroline's young husband, William Shannon, who were living with her. Caroline now stood by helplessly as Restell moaned, "What shall I do? What shall I do?" Nothing Caroline or William said soothed her. Over and over she repeated that agonized refrain: "What shall I do? What shall I do? I never did anything to anybody. Why should they bring this trouble on me?"

That afternoon the skies over Manhattan had been cloudy, the air raw. A dank drizzle fell intermittently. New York's meteorological oracle, consulted universally and reported in the daily papers, was a thermometer at Hudnut's drugstore (five miles downtown on Broadway near Fulton Street): it registered 55 degrees at 3:30 in the afternoon.

As darkness thickened, some activities wound down, others picked up speed. Coal gaslight (natural gas wasn't yet available) was now everywhere, and gigantic generation plants lined both Manhattan riverfronts, belching smoke and blighting their neighborhoods. Volcano-like, they hinted at the Hadean tides of fuel surging under the night city through pipes jimmied in among water mains and sewage culverts. Inside each gashouse stretched a battery of fierce ovens. Frantic three-man crews stuffed their roaring maws with heavy fireproof clay retorts, each one first loaded with 220 pounds of coal, then heaved into an oven. After five hours the coal had released all its gas and burned down to coke. The crew hauled out the spent retort, refilled it, and reloaded it into the furnace. Though one observer, not incidentally a gas company stockholder, said the crews "play about in the fire like salamanders, seeming really to enjoy the burning," the heat was stifling and the labor punishing.

It was also without respite, particularly as dusk descended, lights went on, and homes and businesses inhaled more and more fuel up into their lamps and chandeliers. Fogs of dingy-looking and noxious coal gas, drawn from the furnace by water-powered fans, bubbled through water in an assembly line of pipes that leached out the tar and ammonia. Next, a filter, packed with powdered lime, sucked out much of the sulfur. Iron gasholders awaited, huge bells (some of them 60 feet high and 95 across), suspended by counterweights, with their heavy rims sunk deep into subterranean water tanks. As newly manufactured gas bubbled up through the water, the holders slowly rose, drawing in as much as a half-million cubic feet of it.

Hudnut's thermometer gradually sank through the 40s, and the sun set at 6:28. Now at each gas plant a single watchman kept a constant watch on the pressure gauge. As demand rose, the crews' work became ever hotter and harder: the fumes had been observed to knock down horses on nearby streets, and crewmen in the purifying plant sometimes keeled over unconscious, not to revive until carried outside. The gasholders' great iron helmets now sank back into the water, breathing the gas out at a controlled pressure into the mains and pipes, where it inched along, turning north and south, uptown and downtown, left and right, block after block, threading its way through an underground grid of sewer pipes and watercourses. New York below ground was, even before the subways, an echo—in gas and fluid—of the human traffic plying the streets and the communicative pulses passing through the telegraph wires overhead.

Lamplighters inched their way along the curbs and paving stones, and the streetlights flared up one by one, fan-shaped blobs of red, yellow, violet, and orange. Underneath the 100-foot-high glass and iron arch of the Grand Central train shed, chandeliers puffed into flame in a gentle explosion, but left the trains in semidarkness, at rest in their berths below. Gas flowed noiselessly into Restell's basement, passing through a mechanical meter, through the house pipes, into the fixtures. Three iron and gilt gas lanterns puffed into flame over the door of the mansion's stables on 52nd Street (next door to the present-day site of the French restaurant La Grenouille). Their light flared on a wall across the street belonging to the Roman Catholic Orphan Asylum for Boys (now the home of Cartier). In the mansion, Restell's chandeliers ignited, illuminating her ornate front hall and parlors. Later, these were much publicized, called "vast" by reporters, though the largest was only about 25 feet square. Her interiors flashed briefly to the street before a servant lowered her flower-splotched shades to frustrate prying eyes.

Tonight the house afforded Restell no comfort. As her family looked on helplessly, she paced past the busts of Washington and Franklin, who stared blankly from pedestals at the head of a staircase that led down to the basement kitchens and offices. Heavy wall mirrors shattered the rooms into kaleidoscopes of glass, marble, and upholstery. They caught again and again the distraught face against backgrounds better suited to deluxe receptions than lonely agony. "What shall I do?" Restell kept pleading. "I never did anything to anybody. Why should they bring this trouble upon me?" Her mind numbed by terror, she kept helplessly repeating herself. "Why don't they leave me alone? . . . Two o'clock tomorrow—we'll know then," and, most despairingly, "I wish I was dead, as it would then end all." The harping on "two o'clock tomorrow" puzzled William and Caroline. She hadn't been ordered to appear for her hearing, and in any case it was docketed for morning, not afternoon.

New York began readying itself for the pleasures of a Sunday evening in early spring. Coaches and cabs passed, lamps quavering as they rattled over the cobblestones. Here and there theaters were still using an attention-getter that dated back to Barnum—a Drummond beacon shooting its ghastly blue glare for blocks. The city now boasted nearly 6,000 restaurants, many lit, open, and crowded, even late on a Sunday night. But Restell, exhausted by her ordeal, went to bed at nine—early for her. Her bedroom, on the second floor of the house, faced 52nd Street. To her right, as she lay in bed, the corner sitting room fronted Fifth Avenue. To her left was William and Caroline's bedroom. At the end of the stair hall was a bathroom with a single window looking east.

A few minutes later William found Restell in her bedroom with Caroline. The young couple tried again to ease her. "I feel better tonight," she finally responded. But then, "Oh! How I dread tomorrow! How shall I ever get through that trial?" and, yet again, "Oh, how I dread two o'clock!" Caroline left. William kept watch as Restell slowly quieted herself. At length she muttered, "I'm in a little doze." William crept out and went downstairs to secure the house for the night.

A hall boy went through the mansion, carefully locking the street doors, the pantries, and the cupboards. He then turned the keys over to William, who—as was the family custom—returned to Restell's room. She had an early burglar alarm system; if it was typical of the time, it connected all the main entrances by wire to a set of bells in her bedroom, and from there a private telegraph line linked it to the local precinct and firehouse (the services were offered by security firms still in business today, like ADT and Holmes). William armed the system from the master control panel in her chamber, left the keys on her nightstand, went into the bedroom just behind Restell's, locked the communicating door, and retired with Caroline.

Now the house was soundless—the servants asleep in their third-floor rooms, the basement deserted, the main-floor parlors empty, the darkened billiard room and ballroom on the top floor looking vacantly out over Fifth Avenue and uptown to Central Park. The night, with its respites, pleasures, tragedies big and small, was commencing in earnest. Lester Wallack and his company were preparing for the Monday opening of what would prove the season's most remarkable play, Sardou's *Diplomacy*: a tale of betrayal, with the dominant role of the villainess, Countess Zicka, played by the broad-faced and powerful Rose Coghlan. Along the bank of the East River at the foot of 43rd Street, a crowd of fashionably dressed people gathered. They were awaiting a 5:45 p.m. Long Island Rail Road ferry bound for the last eastbound train from Hunter's Point, on their way to camp out for the night along the brooks and streams of Long Island (the trout-fishing season, a rite of well-bred New York's spring, began at dawn on the morning of April 1).

Just beyond Restell's dining room wall was the stable, where the seven horses lived that drew her carriage through the streets. The rest of the block east to Madison Avenue was given over to mews belonging to other wealthy families: the sounds and odors of the animals were part of the neighborhood atmosphere. Light and street life emerged again only as one neared the Second Avenue surface railway's northern Manhattan station, in the village of Harlem, where a yellow-lit tower clock hung over the street like an artificial moon.

Whether Restell was really asleep or not when William Shannon left her keys on the nightstand remains unknown. So does what happened after midnight, in the small hours of April 1.

William and Caroline said they heard nothing, but sometime during the night, Restell seems to have awakened and disarmed the alarms. They were shut off when checked the following morning. She passed between the busts of Washington and Franklin, descended the stairs to the basement kitchen, and from the drawer where it was kept took a razor-sharp carving knife with an ebony handle. She then returned to the second floor, and entered the bathroom at the rear of the house.

As the *Herald*—in 1878 the most lubricious of the city's major dailies—later described it, this bathroom was "such as is found in all first class houses, nicely carpeted and a marble washstand between the tub and window, which overlooks the yard. Two velvet settees completed the furniture." During the predawn hours the rain stopped, and the sky began to clear. Restell drew a bath, undressed, and got into the mahogany-encased tub (hot and cold running water, not widely thought a domestic necessity until the early 20th century, had been standard in rich houses for decades). She kept the warm water running, the excess gurgling into the tub's overflow drain.

By this time the blocks around her were dead to the world, except for the occasional carriage clattering along the cobblestones on Fifth Avenue. As she lay in her bath, dawn began to filter through the window. Then—around a quarter to six, according to later medical guesswork—she dragged the knife across her throat.

The gash barely bled. She was still conscious; she hadn't used enough force. She tried again, but she achieved only a superficial cut in the skin of her throat. Summoning determination, she made a third attempt, now dragging the knife from below her left ear to her right, slicing through her right carotid artery, then down through her right and left jugular veins. The knife slipped from her grasp, plunged back into the tub alongside her thigh, and came to rest under the water, now pinkening with blood. After what must have been a rush of colliding sensations—pounding heart, stinging pain, a surge of adrenaline, terror, sudden aroused memories, exultation, and finally release—she passed out. Her right arm, spatters of blood still raining on it from the wound, swung over the rim of the tub and hung there.

For the next three-quarters of an hour, the only sound was water running into the bath and out the overflow pipe, gradually carrying the blood away. Restell's face, whatever its expression before her death, now relaxed into a look of unearthly serenity.

At 6:30 a.m. Peggy McGrath, the maid, emerged from her room on the third floor and went downstairs. She heard running water; seeing the bathroom door ajar and a nightgown draped over the settee, she concluded her mistress was taking an early bath and continued downstairs for her breakfast. But when she came up an hour later the water was still running, the nightgown still in place. She peered in the door, and her eyes suddenly took in the blood-streaked arm hanging from the tub. Her screams woke the household.

Within hours, those screams had aroused all New York: Restell's death was the sensation of the young year, a bombshell going off in an already notorious case. Reporters appeared around the house as if from nowhere, hovering like vultures. The police showed no desire to shoo them away, and in fact guided them up to the bedroom hall, where all Monday morning Restell's naked corpse lay in an ice chest outside the bathroom door. With cops looking on placidly, the newsmen drooled out word portraits of it onto the pages of their notebooks, poked into the bathroom, the bedroom, the public parlors downstairs; one of them even took careful measurements of the outside dimensions of the house (it was 45 feet by 70).

All Monday morning they lined up for press tours, while the public gaped from the sidewalk. The murder was gory, and perhaps even more important it was a mystery suited to a public absorbed by news of crimes that seemed inexplicable or even supernatural. Nobody knew for certain how Restell met her death. Fingerprinting did not become a standard investigative tool in New York until the early 1900s, so there was no way of being sure only she had touched the ebony knife handle. Was it in fact Restell who had turned off the burglar alarm, or someone else? And if she had done it, why? What had she meant by exclaiming, "Oh, how I dread two o'clock. . . . Two o'clock tomorrow—*we'll know then*"? She had survived for forty years in part thanks to powerful allies who, of course, kept their friendship with her quiet. Could she have arranged a predawn meeting with a supporter, waiting until William, Caroline, and the servants were safely asleep?

The press blazed with rumors and conspiracy theories. William and Caroline sped the corpse to burial in Tarrytown on April 2. This, people said, was a ruse, and the body really that of a patient who'd died during a botched abortion. Restell herself, incognito, had boarded a steamer bound for Europe. Poe and the newspapers may have started the fad for nocturnal mystery and sensation, but Restell's death was surely a remarkable proof that real-life and imagined horrors had come into their own as staples of commercial public entertainment.*

And Madame Restell's death was far from the only chill arising from the dark hours of April 1, 1878. Indeed the fact that every terror of the city night took place among others was one thing that made the aura of urban crime different from that of the country house murder. As Restell paced her halls, Mary Brown, penniless, without influence, and accompanied by her bewildered five-year-old son, Thomas, was being led into the Tombs, after her arrest Saturday for kicking Frederick Wiegand in (as the establishment paper, the *Commercial Advertiser*, phrased it) "the lower part of the abdomen."

In the crowded First District court, which covered the southern tip of Manhattan and the Five Points, 67 people, mostly Irish, faced the judge—chiefly for alcohol-related offenses. Forty-seven of the arrests were for intoxication, excise law violations, or disorderly conduct. There were

---

* More would soon follow. Sherlock Holmes first saw print in 1887; Bram Stoker imported Dracula from the Carpathian Mountains to an imaginary London wharf in 1897—the same year Jack the Ripper first struck the city in earnest and set its press on a rampage.

six cases of assault and battery, one burglary, two robberies, and the arrest, by officer Peter Kelly, of John Ruffe for keeping a disorderly house on Pearl Street (the ten crimes remaining were a miscellany). Further north, in the Second District, which centered on Chelsea, there was still plenty of trouble (53 arrests, again with drink the prime troublemaker). But the arrested, though still predominantly Irish, here included some Germans and blacks, and tonight, at least, the accused seemed to be richer: more attorneys appeared beside them, and more of them raised bail. In the Fifth District court—Restell's neighborhood and everything else northward to the farms and the forested tip of Manhattan—arrests dwindled. There were only six: four for alcohol, two for vagrancy.

Over in Brooklyn, eighteen-year-old Nellie Dowd set out for an evening walk with two strange men. At the corner of Lefferts Place and Classon Avenue, they attacked and raped her. Closer to Restell, in Manhattan, a two-year-old toddler, May Correll, of 305 East 85th Street, died. A doctor blamed the death on toxic food coloring in some candy she'd been given. And sometime during the night the body of John Schlaeg, missing since January, surfaced in the East River at the foot of East 5th Street.

By Monday afternoon and evening, New York had returned to its daily round, but the Restell story continued to reverberate. When Wallack's production of Sardou's *Diplomacy* opened, the audience heard an eerie echo of the Restell tragedy. At the climax, the evil Countess Zicka suffers exposure as a spy who has stolen a secret government document from the hero and blamed the theft on his innocent wife. Outcast, she utters a last, rafter-raising speech both of defiance and appeal. It was pure theatrical hokum:

> Yes, you can laugh! Pride yourself upon your clever plot! Rejoice, if you will, at the degradation of one who might have been as good as any here! . . . A wicked woman has been trapped and caught! As I have suffered, so shall I suffer still, and there is not one in this wide world to pity or to help me.

And yet, put in Restell's mouth, it would have been a bald statement of fact.

Boss Tweed, discredited, convicted, and imprisoned, followed Ann Lohman into death on April 12, and in similar anguish, in the Ludlow Street jail—though the barred windows of his two-room suite there were decked with flowerpots, and the cells furnished with easy chairs, a book-piled table, a grand piano, and etchings. His loyal black servant, Luke Grant, slept by Tweed's bed with a string tied around his wrist, which Tweed jerked whenever he wanted anything. He'd been suffering from heart pangs and pneumonia, and on the evening of April 11, a fever and severe chest pain seized him, worsening all night.

With the gaslight turned down, Grant mopped his master's forehead with vinegar and water, and Tweed's desperate cries strangely echoed those Restell had uttered little more than a week earlier. "Oh, what shall I do? What shall I do? . . . I can't stand this pain!" He survived through the night, however, dying just as the bells rang out at noon on Friday, April 12.

Ann Lohman knew nothing of this. She lay in a Tarrytown cemetery beneath a statue of a sleeping infant, where she can still be visited today.

CHAPTER SEVEN

ELECTRIC COSTUMES AND BRASS KNUCKLES
Glamour, Crime, Sports, and the Commercialization of Night in the 1890s

AFTER MADAME RESTELL'S DEATH, her granddaughter Caroline and Caroline's husband, William, lived on in the great brownstone sarcophagus at Fifth and 52nd. But by 1883, their parlor windows looked across the avenue not to a vacant lot but to William Kissam Vanderbilt's palatial new residence. This was, in effect, a battering ram, propelled by money and meant to smash through the high-society ramparts patrolled by Mrs. William Backhouse Astor II, the social doyenne of the Gilded Age. Twelve hundred invitations had gone out to society's most envied, and on Monday, March 26, 1883—just five years after Restell's death—Vanderbilt christened his new residence with a grand ball that commenced at 11 p.m.

For the uninvited thousands there was a consolation: Barnum's indoor circus, now performing that same Monday night to a capacity crowd in Madison Square Garden, starred Jumbo the elephant ("he is taller and fatter than he was last year," the *Post* reported, "and is still growing"). The Garden, at Madison Avenue and 26th Street, held 10,000 spectators and looked like a warehouse, but at least it could boast a link to William Vanderbilt: he had owned it since 1879. Nevertheless his imperial housewarming gala had out-publicized even Barnum and Jumbo. A crowd of gawkers had formed at Fifth and 52nd long before the ball got underway at eleven o'clock, oblivious to the once notorious Restell residence behind them, their stares glued instead to the turreted and Gothic-gabled Schloss Vanderbilt.

They'd soon pushed their way up the stairs that led, under twin canopies, to the front door; a phalanx of police arrived to keep an eye on them. By 10:30 Fifth Avenue was jammed with carriages—invited guests peering into the windows, eager to get in but also determined not to show up too gauchely early. An hour later the stately parade of guests had begun flowing inside. The street was mobbed, the house stuffed with hothouse flowers and greenery and sparkling to the roof-beams with light. The third-floor gymnasium had been fitted out as a supper room, its already extravagant furnishings—including even the doors—hidden under ferns and palm trees, laced with blushing orchids, blazing roses, dripping bougainvillea, and lilies of the valley.

A hundred men and women now paraded slowly down the Richard Morris Hunt staircase. A group of debutantes appeared at the top, dressed as hobby horses, wearing glass-eyed costumes made of real horsehide; they cavorted down the staircase in a herd. Another procession carried electric lights (which sputtered out, somewhat ruining the effect). From the foot of the stairs the masquers eddied into parlors aglow with tapestry and paneling plundered from French châteaux, then swept into the showpiece of the showplace—the dining room—and began the dancing.

In tribute to the mansion's profusion of French accents, somebody dressed up as Joan of Arc. There were a hornet, a female devil, a peacock, a Queen Elizabeth, a woodland goddess, a witch carrying a stuffed owl, and a cat, with a skirt made of white cat tails, a bodice of cat heads, and a cat-skin hat. Abram Hewitt, a congressman who would be elected mayor in 1886, appeared as King Lear, "while yet in his right mind" (the *Times* reporter's phrase). William Vanderbilt's sister-in-law, Mrs. Cornelius Vanderbilt, appeared in white satin, brandishing a torch in salute to the soon-to-be-raised Statue of Liberty. But she called her costume "The Electric Light," achieving brilliance with diamonds rather than batteries or a wall plug (though a photograph does suggest that her torch was electrified).

By the late 1870s electric light was no longer a novelty (though the city didn't get its first consumer power grid until 1882), yet candles and gas fixtures hadn't dwindled to mere props in aid of old-fashioned effect. The mansion's everyday system was gas, but tonight the dining room shone under limelight, harsh by itself but here achieving a silvery effect as it struck stained glass windows, deep-toned tapestries, and the swirling multicolored costumes. The main hall quivered under a phalanx of wax candle torchieres. The illumination was a digest of the era—an orchestral harmony of purring gas, flickering candles, oil-fed Argand wicks, Drummond lights, Welsbach mantles,* and electric bulbs. All except the latter smelled, covered the walls and ceiling in grime, and stifled the air with fumes, but they made the atmosphere rich, romantic, and theatrical.

All the newspaper accounts commented on the glory of the Vanderbilt lighting, but the raves spiraled beyond it. Vanderbilt money—William Kissam's was only one of the family palaces—had bankrolled a higher-caliber luxury than the city had ever seen. And the Vanderbilts were only one note in a greater theme: since the early 1800s, newspapers had been flinging one superlative after another at astonishments like the old Astor House hotel, the Park Theatre, the Astor Place Opera House. Nor was this an illusion: grandness had indeed gotten grander. Broadway had dazzled not just New Yorkers but even jaded Europeans when it stretched only the scant 6,000 feet between the Bowling Green and Niblo's. Now it shone for nearly five miles, as far as 42nd Street.

In 1810 viewers had been amazed by the dimensions of a painted city panorama 35 feet high and 60 feet in diameter. In 1853 the grandest urban interior, a republican retort to an 1851 London wonder, was the New York Crystal Palace, a glass and iron structure topped with a dome 100 feet across and rising 149 feet above Sixth Avenue. The building covered more than three and a half acres of what's now Bryant Park. The Crystal Palace burned in 1858, but the old Grand Central train arch, the glory of the 1870s, though close to it in size, enclosed a far greater unbroken sweep of space. And that primordial Grand Central looked cramped and dumpy by the standards of its early 20th-century successor, the soaring concourse that still administers an undiminished adrenaline kick to anyone entering for the first time.†

If the scale of the 1890s metropolis was big, its complexity was huge: many of the technological marvels supposedly distinctive of the 20th century were already commonplace. In 1877 the city's earliest telephones had begun service, and Bell had published its first, one-page directory. By 1878, the Metropolitan Telephone and Telegraph Company had 271 sub-

---

* Welsbach mantles were a recent invention—fabric nets soaked in rare elements and placed above a circular Argand wick in an oil lamp. When first lit the mantles burned into a tracery of ash that remained permanently in place, reaching temperatures so high they consumed most fumes and smoke from the fuel, and burned with a white light that rivaled electricity.

† Though the old Grand Central was unimpressive, it outdid its replacement in one respect: the arched train shed in the earlier depot, though it was 25 feet lower than the concourse in the new building, covered more square footage.

scribers. The new Park Avenue Hotel, between 32nd and 33rd Streets, installed arc lighting as an experiment. The building's windows flared with what appeared to contemporary observers as a harsh and ghastly blue-white moonlight amplified to the power of sunlight, heralding the era of interior electric light that would change once again the appearance of the dark hours.

Each of these innovations was the product of commerce, and each was too complex to be managed by one man, even an Edison: it was an age of networks, syndicates, and companies. And the pattern quickly extended to evening entertainment. Maverick fly-by-night producers like Barnum evolved into impresarios, who built show business into a galaxy of commercial empires, run by moguls whose names became household words—like B. F. Keith and E. F. Albee, who put together a national booking system and by 1904 controlled more than 500 theaters. Nor was corporatization limited to corporations: toughs, not to be outdone, formed gangs far more organized than the firefighters' brawling clubs of the old Bowery. By the 1880s gangs too had begun to recast themselves as syndicates, and were running gambling house chains and organized prizefights.

Under this wave of consolidation, entertainment became more sophisticated and more professionalized. In the process it lost some of the spontaneity that characterized the Bowery in its glory days, when a New Yorker out for the night could (if plugged in to the city's word-of-mouth apparatus and not bound by the Amusements sections in the paper) find not just singing and dancing, but even violence, sex, and death. When the moguls took over they didn't stamp out such performances. But their comparatively hyped and harmless mass-market offerings did in the end help to create a blander and more uniform urban nightscape.

RIALTO MARKET:
THE BUSINESS OF ENTERTAINMENT AFTER THE CIVIL WAR

In 1889 the Four Hundred (the grandees at the apex of New York's social hierarchy) celebrated New Year's Eve with old-fashioned ceremony. Yet the ballrooms into which they crowded were mostly higher, bigger, newer, gaudier, and further uptown than could have been imagined a half century earlier. The Academy of Music had closed after losing its operagoing elite to the huge new Metropolitan Opera uptown, which opened on 39th Street and Broadway in 1883. The new Met had become the site of

the New Year's Ball, the city's bluest-blooded seasonal event. As soon as
the curtain fell on *Lohengrin* the evening of Wednesday, January 1, 1890,
carpenters began sawing and hammering to build a temporary ballroom
floor over the sloping orchestra seats.

While the ball was underway the next evening, the carpenters remained in the balcony, waiting to turn the place back into a theater as
soon as the evening ended, and if they watched the revelers below, they
may have thought the dancing lions and lionesses of diamond-studded
New York were as glorious as ever. But the press was beginning to find socialites inviting targets for ridicule. *Town Topics,* a popular weekly scandal
sheet devoted to the nocturnal peccadilloes of the rich, had been appearing since 1885. Of the New Year's cotillion, its reporter noted cattily that
the Met's gimlet electric chandeliers mercilessly exposed the caked
makeup gaslight had once concealed: "not only . . . fair complexions and
roseleaf cheeks but brilliant eyes and long dark lashes owe a good deal
more of their beauty to outside sources than was ever before imagined."

In fact, by the 1890s, the Four Hundred, though still lumbering
about atop the Olympus of snobbery, were becoming a little peripheral,
like a winter scene in a snow globe—a sealed, jewel-like shelf ornament
in a noisy arcade. The bifurcation into "high" and "low" forms of entertainment that had begun in the 1840s reached a crisis at Astor Place in
1849, and was extreme by the 1880s. The result was an explosion of entertainment alternatives, from the Metropolitan Opera down to the concert saloons, the popular Bowery theaters, and brand-new arrivals, like
the Yiddish, Chinese, and Italian dramas that had begun stirring immigrant audiences on the Lower East Side. Highbrow and lowbrow sneered
at each other's tastes; even men and women, always distinct as audiences,
had created exclusionary enclaves. Such fragmentation complicated the
cultural scene, but led to a profusion of offerings, which in turn led to
commercialization. There was profit in mass-produced shows, shrewdly
tailored to suit every taste. After the Civil War, entertainers and entrepreneurs often succeeded by carefully identifying a neglected or under-
served audience, then either devising a new genre or repackaging an old
one to attract the target market—high, low, male, female, rich, bourgeois, poor, immigrant. Producers created—even themselves became—
brand names.

Genteel uptown drama appealed to audiences that to some extent
overlapped with the Metropolitan, and mixed broader appeal with a care-

ful attention to decorum. *Diplomacy*, the Sardou play being rehearsed by the Wallack company during Madame Restell's last agony, was an example. Such plays avoided naked grief, terror, and rage, depending instead on moral revelations and tormented ethical convolutions for their appeal: they often read like Henry James for the masses. Such was Bronson Howard's *The Banker's Daughter* (1878), so popular it hung on in stock company productions as late as 1914. Howard's heroine, Lilian Westbrook, abandons her impoverished true love, marrying the rich John Strebelow to rescue her father's investment bank from collapse. Years later the abandoned lover, Harold Routledge, dies in a duel, and in the scene that made the play famous, Lilian's grief betrays her to Strebelow, who walks out on her and their small daughter, with an exit line that brought the house down. "Harold Routledge dead! Dead! Leaving her a widow with a living husband, and leaving me a wifeless husband and a childless father."

To anyone who found this either underwhelming or incomprehensible, there were myriad alternatives. The first commercially projected movie—a four-minute boxing match—premiered in a converted storefront at 153 Broadway in 1895. And in 1896 Edison had set up his Vitascope movie projector for its first public show: the audience in Koster and Bial's 23rd Street Music Hall saw a series of short films that included crashing surf, an umbrella dance, and a boxing bout between a short, fat comic and a tall, thin one. Restaurants had evolved from nondescript eating shops or exclusionary institutions like Delmonico's into extravagantly decorated Broadway theme palaces like Murray's Roman Gardens, which specialized in post-midnight champagne suppers for demimondaine showgirls and their well-padded admirers. One visitor recalled Murray's interior as a riot of "fountains, temples, Roman galleys, caryatids, views of the Bay of Naples, Libyan tigers, Egyptian peacocks and Greek Phrynes and Aphrodites." Inebriated guests had to contend with a revolving dance floor and a mirrored lobby lit by a huge chandelier of colored glass—the latter room a particular trap where people found themselves crashing into mirrors they thought were doors or colliding with real statues while maneuvering to avoid reflected ones.

Although the heart of the theater district had moved uptown, many of the old Lower East Side houses survived on shoestrings, with shows staying for a week or so and then moving on, to Brooklyn, Philadelphia, or Albany. The People's Theatre was typical, offering pasted-together *Black Crook* knockoffs like *The Devil's Auction*, which featured the desperate-sounding spectacular scene "The Haunted Dell of the Gigantic Mush-rooms," and an equally grubby novelty act: "Mlle Irma von Roecky in her celebrated Jockey dance."

But such scuffed goods weren't the only fare available downtown. Soon the People's, the Windsor (at Bowery and Canal Streets), and many others were netting new audiences from booming populations of immigrants. Antonio Maiori (1868–1938), a pioneering Italian actor, opened his own tiny per-formance space in a row house at 24 Spring Street. His audience sat indoors on the ground floor; the stage was outside in the back yard. Maiori specialized in Shakespeare, playing Hamlet and Othello in Italian with a passion that thrilled his audience (the few mainstream critics who strayed in tended to call it hammy). In 1895 a small theater opened at 5–7 Doyers Street, specializing in Beijing opera (the theater connected through the basement with a warren of underground tunnels threading beneath Chinatown).*

Not far away the old Bowery Theatre still stood where it had since its last rebuilding in 1845, but it had been renamed the Thalia and now, after years as a first-rank house for German plays, it had become a venue for Yiddish theater. This was a new genre—a recent European offshoot from the mummers' entertainments traditionally performed during Purim in early spring. In Europe, Yiddish theater had only begun to break away from its informal holiday origins to become a specialized undertaking, but for Lower East Side Jews it was a cleansing escape from the hardships of settlement. As theater historian Nahma Sandrow has put it, "to many sewing machine women and men a ticket seemed almost as much neces-sity as extravagance." By the mid-1890s, Yiddish companies had also taken over the Windsor, the People's, and the Orient Theaters.

In the 1890s Hutchins Hapgood (1869–1944), a reporter for the *Com-mercial Advertiser,* wrote a series of remarkable columns on immigrant life in the Lower East Side, scorning the dismissive reporting typical of the high-circulation dailies. In Yiddish theater Hapgood saw a fertile blend of Jewish folk tradition with the passionate socialism synonymous with the 19th-century Russian intelligentsia. Uptown theaters had been forced to choose between high-minded and low-down patrons. At downtown Yiddish plays, however, "the poor and ignorant are in the great majority," Hapgood said, "but the

---

* Part of this tunnel survives today as an underground mall, open to the public. It can be entered from Chatham Square and runs to an exit on Doyers Street. In 1905 the theater was the scene of a gun battle between rival tongs, the Chinese gangs active in New York begin-ning in the late 1800s.

learned, the intellectual and the progressive are also represented, and here, as elsewhere, exert a more than numerically proportionate influence on the character of the theatrical productions." The pioneering Yiddish dramatists of New York gave voice and presence to the hard lots of the 1.3 million Jews who had crowded into New York between 1881 and 1903.

That didn't, however, mean that Yiddish theater sacrificed art to commerce. Moyshe Hurwitz and Joseph Lateiner,* the earliest popular Yiddish playwrights in New York, ran a clanking play factory, ripping scenes wholesale out of other plays, sometimes still frantically assembling the last act of a new offering while the cast was performing the first. Once, when writer's block got Hurwitz into a tight spot, he ran onstage wearing a turban and delivered an improvised harangue to take the place of the fourth act that had up to that point eluded him. This method became known as "play-baking," and Hurwitz, though a master of the technique, had competitors like Israel Barski, whose business card read:

> Tailor, Actor and Playwright.
> Author of *The Spanish Inquisition*.
> Pants altered and pressed.

Later, more intellectually rigorous dramatists, like Jacob Gordin, called such work *shund*—Yiddish for "trash." But *shund* nonetheless made theater gripping even if it wouldn't stand up under critical scrutiny. As Hapgood observed of the Yiddish theater audience, "Great enthusiasm is manifested, sincere laughter and tears accompany the sincere acting on the stage. Pedlars of soda water, candy, of fantastic gewgaws of many kinds, mix freely with the audience between the acts. Conversation during the play is received with strenuous hisses, but the falling of the curtain is the signal for groups of friends to get together and gossip about the play or the affairs of the week."

An otherwise obscure actor named Boaz Young recalled his big scene as a beleaguered king in a Hurwitz concoction. At the crisis, the king's enemies try to finish him off with some poisoned apples:

> For some reason I become suspicious and ask myself, should I eat these apples or should I not? The spectators know that the apples are

---

* English spellings of Yiddish names follow Nahma Sandrow's *Vagabond Stars*.

poisoned and enjoy themselves when I am about to start eating them. . . . Some yelled that I shouldn't eat and some told me to go ahead and eat.

After milking the moment for all it was worth, Young remembered shouting, "No, these apples I shall not eat!" to thunderous applause, and then clambering up on the throne where he delivered his curtain line, "I must and I shall become the King of Israel!"

Like Maiori's Italian company, Yiddish actors also played Shakespeare, unhesitatingly adapting the plots to the audience. Jacob Gordin, who began writing in the 1890s, was, though a scornful critic of *shund,* fond of its audience-pleasing tricks: his *Yiddish King Lear* had Regan and Goneril denying their father not his retinue of 100 knights, but a bowl of soup. At one performance, when the legendary Yiddish actor Jacob Adler (1855–1926) played Lear in this scene, a man in the audience stood up and yelled, "Leave those rotten children of yours and come home with me. My wife is a good cook. She'll fix you up." Performer and audience both took pleasure, even pride, in egging each other on.

Adler was a powerful actor who crossed over successfully onto the English-speaking stage and founded a New York theatrical dynasty,* and the family moved within a generation from immigrant invisibility to a social and intellectual status comparable to Wallack's. Others, however, anticipated a show business phenomenon of the 20th century by turning themselves into celebrities. Such was Boris Thomashefsky (?–1939), perhaps the first matinee idol, worshipped by crazed female admirers two decades before Valentino. Thomashefsky's very name could turn his adoring fans into Lower East Side maenads.

As a teenager Thomashefsky had worked as a cigarette-maker, but soon deserted to the theater, and organized some of the very earliest Yiddish performances in New York. By the early 1880s his curly black hair, liquid singing voice, bedroom eyes, and iron-man calves—clad, *Black Crook* style, in pink tights—had begun to attract adulatory claques. He called himself "America's Darling," and though he started out husky and ended up frankly tubby, this mattered no more to his worshippers than it later did to Elvis Presley's: women continued to faint in his pres-

---

* Jacob Adler's children kept up the family tradition. Celia, Frances, and Luther became stars in their own right; Stella (1901–1992) was a pioneer in the introduction of method acting to the New York theater.

ence, ply him with flowers, and sandbag him in the street beseeching assignations.

Thomashefsky conducted numerous love affairs with admirers, but the plays he performed in were clean. Yiddish drama, whether *shund* or powerful and intellectually challenging, was morally irreproachable, and this seems to have been generally true of the downtown ethnic theater. But Manhattan also offered sleazier entertainment, and had been doing so for decades. Back in 1850, out-of-the way halls put on "Model Artist" or "Living Statue" exhibits. At first these seem to have featured men who posed in pink body stockings, but women soon joined the displays. This raised an outcry, which became even louder once—as soon happened—the tights disappeared. In *New York by Gas-Light,* George Foster described a late-1840s raid on a "hole in Twenty-first street," in which a naked Bacchus escaped out the back window while the nude but slow-on-her-feet Venus wound up in the Tombs.

Entrepreneurs soon found a way to satisfy raunchy tastes while cleaning the performances up enough to make them at least marginally acceptable to the public. Concert saloons, growing ever more popular in the 1850s and 60s, weren't blatant like the Model Artist halls, but nevertheless tested the limits of conventional toleration. Some, like the Gaieties on Broadway, brought sex into the audience by hiring "waiter girls." Women were a novelty as table servers, and at first (though managements always denied it) many if not the majority seem to have doubled as bar girls or prostitutes. Goaded by moral reformers, New York state passed a law requiring that concert saloons acquire licenses, ban alcohol, and get rid of all-female waitstaff. But the saloons proved unkillable: after a wave of raids, they promptly reappeared, and in 1872 there were nearly 80.

Some did fire the girls, but compensated by spicing up their stage shows. Most of these—while not fully nude—followed the strategy of the Model Artist tableaux in claiming that flesh appeared on view only in the cause of Art. Openly raunchy songs and circus acts gave way in concert saloons to an obligatory female "ballet," often a "Grand March of the Amazons," à la *The Black Crook* and *The White Fawn,* and forerunners of the lavish girlie extravaganzas of the 1920s: Florenz Ziegfeld's *Follies,* Earl Carroll's *Vanities,* George White's *Scandals.*

Then, almost as soon as the risqué had been normalized, an entrepreneur materialized to tame, dilute, and dry out the concert saloon formula just enough to spread its appeal beyond loose males to families. Antonio

"Tony" Pastor (1837?–1908) is still a familiar name, and well commemorated in Parker Zellers's *Tony Pastor: Dean of the Vaudeville Stage* (1971). Pastor started performing as a six- or seven-year-old for the Hand in Hand Society, a temperance group that reeled its congregation in with entertainment rather than sermons. Later, he worked up a blackface act, sang a minstrel song, "Stop the Knocking," at Barnum's Museum, toured with a circus, and by the 1860s had become a star act at the leading concert saloon, "Old 444," known for wholesomeness and the patriotic songs of which Pastor made a specialty.*

Eventually he became so beloved a performer (though time turned him, as it had Boris Thomashefsky, from compact muscularity into girth) that he opened a music hall of his own on the Bowery at Spring Street, in an old German theater of the 1850s that later, as the Oriental, turned to Yiddish drama. Pastor's new shows resembled what Lize called "de wawdeville plays" she saw with Mose at Vauxhall Gardens in 1848: a loose assemblage of songs, skits, and specialty acts. But Pastor came up with a way to turn such shows into the slick but harmless entertainment now in demand. From the outset he seems to have tried to keep alcohol out of the auditorium, because it repelled women and children (though drinks were apparently still served in the lobby). Pastor's shows were primitive but careful to avoid offense: mostly variety acts, cleaned up but not gentrified, a hybrid of Broadway, the old garden "wawdeville," and the Bowery. The genre wasn't yet called vaudeville, but in substance it was a wilder and less standardized version of entertainment that made the rounds of the nationwide Albee-Keith-Orpheum vaudeville circuit in the 1920s.

Admission to Pastor's on the Bowery, which called itself "The Great Family Resort of the City, where heads of Families can bring their Ladies and children," cost from 25 to 35 cents. Audiences filed in under a gas-fired TONY PASTOR sign over the sidewalk. Around 7:45, a stagehand lit the footlights with a taper and the show began. There were almost always dancers and singers on the bill, usually including Pastor himself. Following a model already set by the concert saloons, Pastor usually ended with an afterpiece—a short skit, often burlesquing highbrow theater. Pastor's specialized in Shakespeare travesties like "Romeo and Juliet, Or, The Beautiful Blonde Who Dyed for Love." There were also athletic acts—Indian club jugglers, living-statue muscle poses (clothed, of course), and in one

* Its formal name was the American Music Hall; it had opened in 1860 at 444 Broadway, at the site that had once been Mitchell's Olympic.

case a supposedly accurate but blood-free reenactment of a prizefight: an attempt to improve a for-men-only blood sport into family fare.

By 1875 Pastor had become successful enough to make a move uptown. He rescued a cancan theater on Broadway near Prince Street, and the better address and bigger shows drove up profits enough to bankroll a final move to Union Square in 1881. This last Pastor's, in the Tammany Hall building, became the nation's first real vaudeville venue, and survived into the early 20th century, when the vaudeville conglomerates put Pastor out of business: he died in 1908, and the theater became a burlesque house. Decent entertainment had become a franchise of hard-nosed businessmen like Keith and Albee; more venturesome audiences had to turn to surviving individualists like Edward Corey, who ran the Haymarket saloon in the Tenderloin on the corner of Sixth Avenue and 30th Street.

Corey, subject to harassment by vice hawks, had a rougher time of it than Pastor. The Haymarket had been open on and off since 1872, offering a meaty sex smorgasbord (the place was called "the prostitutes' market"). But not without interruption: it had been repeatedly raided, putting Corey's resourcefulness to a severe test. In 1901, after a shutdown and the resulting bad publicity, he had sponsored a prayer meeting with hymns like "All Hail the Power of Jesus' Name" (though a year later a raid found "women flashily dressed, . . . seated at tables or gliding over the waxen floor to dance music," and arrested nearly a hundred of them).

Checkered though its history was, the Haymarket survived until 1911, when it was finally closed; eventually it was torn down. Dance hall sex had taken a fall, but it would never suffer a knockout.

BLOOD UNDER THE GASLIGHTS:
PRIZEFIGHTING AND THE RISE OF NIGHTTIME SPORTS

Not all concert saloons specialized in acrobats, dancers, singers, or sex. Sports too were becoming a staple nighttime entertainment. Harry Hill's on Houston Street, for instance: Hill disclaimed any significance in the waiter girls he hired, or in his saloon's reputation as a haunt for prostitutes and bar girls (some patrons remembered a prominent sign behind the bar that read "LOVERS NOT WANTED, THEREFORE NOT APPRECIATED"). Instead Hill boasted about his prizefighting programs: he organized a series of matches in the 1870s and 80s, charging between 25 and 50 cents for admission.

John L. Sullivan (1858–1918), the great Irish-American heavyweight boxer, fought his first New York match at Hill's in 1881.

In the early post-Revolutionary republic, field sports like fishing and hunting had dominated the urban scene, along with impromptu contests of strength and physical skill. Most of these were daytime and outdoor events. But by the 1820s many taverns had installed billiard tables, and gambling on the matches attracted customers as well as players. Any competitive sport small-scale enough to fit indoors was an attraction, and sometimes patrons would even pay for the show: Kit Burns's saloon, Sportsman's Hall, was famous for performances by a man named Jack the Rat, who would bite the head off a mouse for 10 cents, or a rat for 25.

But the most enduringly popular saloon attraction was the prizefight. Bare-knuckled, often lasting dozens of rounds, these had been violent indeed in their rural origins, where eyes were dug out, ears ripped off, and noses bitten away. Barroom matches, though still ungloved, were slightly tamer, and probably began in spontaneous brawls, with a crafty saloonkeeper organizing the fight and taking bets on the contestants to keep them and the customers from wrecking his premises. Matches proved so popular that they became scheduled affairs, advertised by word of mouth among bar regulars. Favorite boxers became underground celebrities, and in the end the sport became a spectator activity popular enough to begin appearing in theaters.

Pugilism was a special point of pride with the Irish: their indefatigable fighters staked a claim to honor in a city that otherwise seemed bent on dispossessing them. John "Old Smoke" Morrissey (1831–1878) won his nickname in a fight in which he'd scrapped on even after the combatants knocked over a red-hot stove and sent coals skidding out across the floor. Morrissey fell and his clothes caught fire, but still he kept slugging. The clothes burned through, the room began reeking first of smoke, then steam from the water his friends poured over him to douse the flames; he fought on even when bathed in the scent of his own roasting flesh. Morrissey grew up in a family of Irish immigrants in upstate Troy, whose mean streets educated him in the art of bare-knuckle combat. He came downriver to New York, and won fame as a fistic scourge of anti-Irish prejudice. One of his early triumphs was a 37th-round knockout in 1853 of James "Yankee" Sullivan. As his surname suggests, Sullivan was Irish-born, but had been transported to Botany Bay in Australia for murder; once in New York, he had somehow managed to pass himself off as a Yankee nativist.

In a still more remarkable bout at the Amos (now West 10th) Street

Hudson River docks on July 26, 1854, Morrissey fought an American-born scourge of the Irish, "Butcher Bill" Poole, who bit and gouged but won only when his friends joined the fight and kicked Morrissey unconscious. A rematch on February 24, 1855, at the Stanwix Hall (a Bowery saloon) ended when Morrissey and Poole pulled guns on each other and the police intervened. Later a group of Morrissey's friends accosted Poole and shot him dead (Morrissey was arrested for the crime, but was soon released and never convicted).

Though mild by comparison with rural prizefights, early city boxing was much rougher than later matches, which were supervised by more or less independent overseers and fought under the Marquis of Queensberry's rules. These required that the opponents wear boxing gloves, keep the contest within a 24-foot-square ring, and fight a limited number rounds, each three minutes at the longest. Both fans and fighters resisted this. It seemed too tame for a sport rooted in simmering urban ethnic and racial hatreds, staged in dives, and indulging an urge toward riot and insurrection. But mayors, terrified of a breakdown in urban order, periodically instituted crackdowns, and demanded that the reluctant police force, a hotbed of boxing enthusiasts, mount raids.

This might suggest that sports, like other cultural pastimes, followed the wider pattern of division into high and low, with pugilism at the bottom. Yet boxing drew Upper Tendom as powerfully as it did the middle and immigrant working classes, and, in tandem with the entertainment industry in general, gradually grew more and more into a standardized commercial product, moving upward from its barroom and dockside origins. Nothing illustrates this better than the 1879 opening of William Kissam Vanderbilt's first Madison Square Garden. The great indoor arena of the antebellum era, Castle Garden (where Jenny Lind made her American debut in 1850), had been turned into a portal for arriving immigrants. Vanderbilt hoped to fill the gap it left. He already owned an appropriate site on the east side of Madison Avenue between 26th and 27th Streets, a disused depot for milk and produce coming into the city on night trains, and a stable for the horses that pulled railroad cars south of 32nd Street, where steam engines were banned. But when William Vanderbilt's grandfather Cornelius opened the first Grand Central Terminal in 1871, the Harlem railroad stopped running altogether south of 42nd Street, and in 1873 William rented the Madison Square property out to P. T. Barnum.

Barnum built a 28-foot-high wall around the lot, making an outdoor arena that could be roofed over with canvas, and dubbed it the "Great Roman Hippodrome." It was big enough—200 feet by 425—for circuses and sporting events, but it fizzled. Barnum gave up the lease in 1875, and Patrick Gilmore, a popular bandmaster,* turned it into Gilmore's Concert Garden, and filled it with music, temperance rallies, religious revivals, and beauty contests. These too failed to draw crowds, and in June 1879 William K. Vanderbilt reclaimed the site, renamed it Madison Square Garden, installed an electric arc lighting system powered by a generator, and eventually turned the place into a nighttime sports arena.

Walking races had become quite popular and yet were almost comically civilized—Edward Weston, America's most famous pedestrian, wore a white ruffled shirt and black velvet knee breeches when he competed. The sport had first been popularized in England by Sir John Dugdale Astley, who donated a trophy made of solid gold and silver and supposedly worth £100, the "Astley Belt." Racers were allowed breaks and could either walk or run as they preferred: whoever had covered the greatest distance in six days won the belt. Spectators came and went all day and all night, and were free to stay as long as the contest—listlessly accumulating rather than blazing—held their interest. Vanderbilt had charged the Astley Belt promoters $10,000 in rent, and tickets sold for 50 cents each. But crowds were elusive and at subsequent footraces the gate was disappointing. Nor was the building particularly satisfactory, especially when it was being used on a 24-hour basis. The electric arc lighting apparently didn't work out, and the Garden went back to gaslights, which steeped both the competitors and spectators in noxious fumes. And the heating was erratic—one frigid November night in 1888 left the athletes at a track event so cold they could barely move.

Vanderbilt soon concluded that prizefights would prove a better draw, and neither the adrenaline-stoked fans nor the bruisers who fought were likely to wither from gas fumes or a chill. Thus the sport that had become darkly great with working-class brawlers like Butcher Bill Poole and John Morrissey entered the sphere of a Vanderbilt yachtsman (William was devoted to his boats). And a pillar of the New York business aristocracy found himself sponsoring slugfests that drew vulgar crowds and were always an eyelash shy of a raid: from the outset the business of sports made for unlikely alliances.

---

* Now best remembered as the composer of "When Johnny Comes Marching Home Again."

Monday, January 19, 1885, saw a feverishly anticipated contest at the Garden between John L. Sullivan and Paddy Ryan (another Troy-bred fighter in the Morrissey mold). To calm the authorities, it had been billed as a sparring match, but the fans had cranked themselves up in anticipation of blood. Along with scalpers and onlookers, they were mobbing the street outside by six in the evening. By nine o'clock a crowd of 10,000 jostled each other under the cigar smoke that hovered above them like mist over a whirlpool. From Troy, Paddy Ryan had brought 600 supporters, who shared the hall with a contingent of sporting men, more urbane in looks but of even more dubious reputation—like 35-year-old "Vicar General" Billy McGlory (as the *Herald* archly titled him).

McGlory was in fact a gangster, described by Police Chief George Washington Walling (1823–1891) as "slim, . . . with dark sunken eyes and thin lips," and also as "a man out of whom forty devils might be cast were it possible to get at him." Rubbing shoulders with McGlory were cops, politicians, and a cross section of the sporting aristocracy, like William L. Travers, a horse racing enthusiast, who arrived with a contingent of friends from the blue-blooded Union Club. There was also a crowd of small boys who had sneaked in and were now dangling perilously from the rafters above the ring.

At a quarter to ten, Sullivan strode in wearing white pants and blue stockings, followed by Paddy Ryan. The police inspector supervising, Thomas W. Thorne, a club in hand and a wad of chewing tobacco wedged in his left cheek, signaled the start. Then, all of 30 seconds later, when the boxers briefly clinched, Thorne stamped into the ring, seized Ryan by the feet, and ended the match. The crowd hissed, but unavailingly: the mayor, William R. Grace (1831–1904), had bullied the police into promising they would stop the fight at the slightest sign of violence. Grace was, as the first Irish Catholic to hold the mayoralty, determined to explode the nativist slander that branded his fellow Irish-Americans as loutish. He was a moral reformer, and a staunch ally of the anti-vice crusade, no matter that Irish cops made up a good part of the audience.

Meanwhile, down at the Academy of Music on 14th Street, the Cercle Français de l'Harmonie was hosting its annual shindig. By eleven the party had flown off its never very stout hinges. "The social cake," the *Herald* observed, was thoroughly represented, "from the frosted crust to the soggy bottom. . . . The best and the worst, the highest and the lowest, the most respected and the least regarded, danced, flirted, ate, drank, hurrahed together." Chief Walling also offered juicy recollections of the Cercle Français, including a scene in which one man carried an obese lady up some stairs while another yelled, "Drop that mountain of loveliness!" Here too the neighborhood police captain, William Clinchy, was supposed to intervene if the party got out of control, but he was, as his later career will soon illustrate, very much a hands-off type. Some of the frustrated stragglers from Madison Square Garden, heading south, no doubt joined in the fun at the Academy.

"DEPRAVITY OF A DEPTH UNKNOWN": THE TURN-OF-THE-CENTURY UNDERWORLD

Anti-vice crusaders—then as now—insisted that though sin is old, it is forever growing and creating new monsters of threat to civil society. Powerful though this conviction was, it was far from universal, and it wasn't just the criminal classes or pleasure-starved laborers who resisted it. For the cops to break up an impromptu slugfest in a bar or along the waterfront was one thing; it was another to brave the hisses of 10,000 at Madison Square Garden—a civic landmark owned by one of the city's great names. Vanderbilt, unlike the Livingstons (who made real estate money from prostitution back in the 1830s but kept quiet about it), was not to be intimidated by the threat of publicity.

When under attack, carousing, commercial sex, and violence could often count on at least some protection. One highly desirable source of such aid was the good favor of the rich, who were capable of declaring anything respectable by the fiat of wealth and influence. The other was to pay off the police, square the local Tammany ward-heeler, and keep a low profile. Underworld shows got into the public record only when raided or when a newspaper or vigilante group embarked on a crusade (though such exposés—by now almost ritualistically demanding how it could be that everyone in New York knew about the place in question yet nobody did anything about it—undercut their own professions of astonishment).

In a 1932 memoir, the writer and historian Frederick Van Wyck nostalgically recalled a livery stable run by Tommy Norris on 8th Street between Fifth and Sixth Avenues. At night Norris put on a sort of vaudeville of violence, which Van Wyck attended as a rapt teenager in 1870. The performances usually started with a dogfight, followed by a cockfight, then rat-baiting. The latter called for a dog and ten or fifteen rats, with onlookers placing bets on how many the dog could kill in a stated interval. It was not an entirely uneven contest, because Norris chose "big husky rats, some of them of a dark type such as we never hear of any more; they had long gray whiskers and were very vicious."* After rat-baiting came a human prizefight, followed by "a battle of billy goats, and then a boxing match between two ladies, with nothing but trunks on." These, however, were the only parts of the show Van Wyck felt he could describe in print. "The later performances I am afraid I shall have to skip. Your imagination can run riot, as far as you can let it! Certainly, for a lad of seventeen, such as I was, a night with Tommy Norris and his attractions was quite a night."

Places like Norris's stable were off the public map, but they were also patronized by respectable men like Van Wyck. Nor were they invariably dead ends or gates to the gutter; they could serve as platforms for the launching of a brilliant career. John Morrissey's heroism in the ring gained him a reputation outsized enough to neutralize, even romanticize, a string of indictments for robbery, assault, and murder that stretched back to his Troy childhood. In 1859 he fought a well-publicized charity exhibition match for a destitute widow. The afterglow lent cachet to his gambling house for the rich on Barclay Street, which, beyond fat profits, won him cronies among the city's wealthiest and most influential men.

Morrissey also worked his way into Tammany politics. In 1866 he ran for the U.S. House of Representatives and gained the Fourth District seat (the west side of Manhattan south of Houston Street). In 1868 he won a second congressional race in the Lower East Side Fifth District by a 69 percent majority. He turned reformer, battling Tammany and testifying against Boss Tweed during the investigations that in the end led this don of all machine politicians to his mortal agony in the Ludlow Street jail. Later in life Morrissey cultivated his sporting side, helping to found (along with the gold-plated William L. Travers) the tony Saratoga Race Track, about twenty miles north of Troy in upstate New York. Morrissey died a millionaire in 1878 at the young age of 47.

Organized moral reform had, at least since Anthony Comstock and his revived Society for the Suppression of Vice, always insisted that pornographers and sex merchants were not just a fly-by-night rabble, but rather an

---

* These, probably, were New York's original black rats, of the species *Rattus rattus,* increasingly outnumbered during the 1800s by the Norway or brown rat. Evidence does corroborate Van Wyck's memory: black rats, especially the females, outclass their brown cousins as fighters.

organized conspiracy that, countenanced by the authorities, had attained the stability and power of a big business, in grotesque (or was it merely faithful?) imitation of the new corporations now coming to dominate the economic scene. By 1890 clear evidence that the reformers knew what they were talking about had taken on human shape in Billy McGlory—the "Vicar General" whose presence the *Herald* had noted among the notables at the Sullivan-Ryan fight.

McGlory had first gained fame for his concert saloon, the Armory Hall at 156–60 Hester Street, a haunt so infamous that it had been condemned (and thus incidentally publicized) from as far away as Cincinnati. Like many similar places, Armory Hall featured a cancan (though here, Chief Walling observed, "the women throw their legs a little higher, and display a larger extent of nether garments.") But the balcony, typically in concert saloons a retreat for lewd semipublic behavior, here had been turned into private assignation rooms. And Armory Hall may have been most notorious for the men in makeup and dresses whom McGlory hired to circulate through the crowd, offering the customers private shows in the upstairs booths.

Authorities tried to close Armory Hall in 1889, though not with much initial success. In a February meeting with Mayor Hugh Grant, McGlory insisted he'd been trying to rent his hall out for use as a church, but hadn't found any takers; in March the police visited and reported blandly that they'd seen nothing improper there, not even a cancan. Finally the place did shut down: McGlory sold it to a furniture manufacturer late in March, and in June auctioned off the bar, piano, iceboxes, and stage scenery.

But he wasn't out of business for long. He branched out uptown in the spring of 1891, muscling his way into the Hotel Irving, a hitherto nondescript restaurant and lodging house at the conspicuous corner of 14th Street and Irving Place. McGlory turned it into a large-scale all-night bar, dance hall, and hot-sheet hotel. It was a bold act: the Irving was just across the street from the Academy of Music, a few steps from Tammany Hall and Tony Pastor's theater. Nor was it long before the shouts and shrieks, the swearing, the barrelhouse music, the fights, and the disheveled men and women staggering in and out at all hours aroused the neighbors. Yet all that summer Clinchy and his patrolmen did nothing. Only in late fall, when the *Herald* raised hell, did the district attorney—the hitherto blithe DeLancey Nicoll—finally secure an arrest.

In December 1891 McGlory went on trial at the Court of General Sessions for keeping a disorderly house. The court stenographer's transcript, which has survived, is a graphic picture of the goings-on in a vice emporium just before the turn of the century. McGlory's trade was, of course, nothing new. But the casual arrogance and calculated violence with which he ran it was distinctive: it was, compared to the low-profile female-owned brothels of the 1830s, a brazen operation, and McGlory treated it as a business enterprise open to full public view; it was no different, or so he insisted, from any legitimate hotel or restaurant.

According to the testimony of Frederick Krause, the Irving's manager and a star witness at the trial, the hotel had once been legitimate, owing most of its business to a comfortably carpeted and gaslit bar and lunchroom on the ground floor. An extra room upstairs accommodated overflow after-theater crowds from the Amberg Theatre next door (then it was the city's leading German-language playhouse; now it's the site of a rock venue, Irving Plaza). The 25 hotel rooms, Krause insisted, had been open only to families and respectable singles—that is, until McGlory began making appearances at the bar downstairs in the early months of 1891.

Since his Armory Hall days, McGlory (if the drawings of him in the *Herald* are accurate) had added poundage to his once wolfish frame and become intimidatingly burly. At first it seemed as if he had just adopted the Irving as a hangout. But soon he began acting more or less as if he owned it, standing behind the bar, even counting the money in the till. But no one seems to have taken this amiss until March, when Krause saw him loudly berating a man named Edward Corey, whom McGlory threatened to kill if he ever dared show his face in the Irving again. This struck Krause as strange, since McGlory had no particular business in the place, whereas Corey had recently bought a financial stake in it. It doesn't seem so strange in hindsight, however; rather, it seems like a classic gang turf war. Corey, remember, was also the proprietor of the Haymarket saloon, the "prostitutes' market" in the Tenderloin.*

To the incongruous sight of an interloper kicking a proprietor out of his own bar Krause's response was to scuttle out and make himself scarce for a week. When he finally summoned up the courage to return, he met an unmarried-looking man and woman going up the stairs, and appealed

---

* Corey did not appear at the trial and was not identified in the transcript as the owner of the Haymarket, but although the name is common, it seems unlikely that two Edward Coreys would have been involved in New York prostitution rackets at the same time.

to McGlory, once again placidly installed in the bar. Krause objected to the couple.

"What do you mean, you Dutch son of a bitch?" McGlory snarled. "I am running this place"—a statement whose factuality he confirmed by knocking Krause down, kicking him in the face, and putting him on crutches for six weeks. Once Krause had recuperated and wrestled his nerves into submission, he hobbled back, this time to find a lady cashier at the till; he seems not to have remonstrated with McGlory. By June, the Irving had lost its liquor license. But McGlory merely scoffed and kept on selling drinks, even after his bartender, Edward Kelly, got caught in the act and was arrested.

Liquor law violations were the least of it. The Irving's bar and restaurant had become a clearinghouse for assignations, the overflow lounge a dance hall, the bedrooms a resort for horny couples and a place of business for prostitutes like Nellie Martin, who testified that she'd taken clients there at all hours. She added that, until the robbery that finally goaded the police into closing it down, the hotel countenanced 24-hour dancing, drunkenness, and fights. The bookkeeper, Samuel Guggenheim, said that McGlory charged $1.50 or $2 for rooms, but that men and women rarely spent the night in them; they were in fact being rented by the hour.

Benno Brauner, a waiter who handled room service, admitted that when he arrived bearing drinks, he had sometimes been asked to join in on whatever was underway:

Q. Do you ever remember being called up to room 4 . . . to serve drinks? . . . And did you see a man named, "Sam," and a man named, "Kopp," in there?

A. Yes, sir.

Q. Did you see a naked woman on the bed there?

A. Yes, sir; that's so.

Q. Now what did Kopp or Sam say to you, when you got into this room?

A. The small gentleman—Kopp—or whatever his name is—locked the door, and he said, "Come nearer." He gave me a comb, and he asked something, and I didn't want to do it.

Q. What did he ask you to do?

A. He gave me a small comb, and said I should comb with it the abdomen of the lady.

A neighbor, Henry Hanf, whose bedroom wall abutted the Irving's second-floor dance hall, complained he'd been kept awake as late as five in the morning by "singing and dancing and yelling and shouting and playing piano and everything of that sort, and also swearing and profane language." On the stand the local beat cop, Officer Charles Dooley, testified—with an apparently straight face—that he had, in many surprise visits at all hours of the night, never been able to catch the Irving's unlicensed drinking and all-night orgies in a violation. "I have called for liquor," he protested, "and have been refused. They told me they were selling nothing but temperance drinks" (he seems never to have asked to sniff or sample any).

It certainly looked as if the local precinct—commanded by the same William Clinchy who had been treating the Cercle Français balls with such a gentle touch—was undermotivated, even when McGlory's racket had begun to rile the neighbors. But nothing happened until the *Herald* began a crusade and demanded a shutdown. An indictment was lodged against it as a disorderly house on December 2. But the police stalled until the night of December 6, when two streetwalkers, Annie McCoy and Mamie Thompson, robbed a Brooklyn electrotyper named Alexander Walsh in the dance hall.

McGlory, according to the testimony of a black waiter and musician, Charles Payton, had charged up the stairs and grabbed Annie McCoy, subjecting her to a public body search. Nellie Martin witnessed the scene.

Q. And you saw McGlory do something then, didn't you?

A. Yes sir. I saw him search one of the girls.

Q. What?

A. I saw him search one of the girls.

Q. And held her until the police arrived—didn't he?

A. He said he wanted to make a parable of her to square himself in the eye of the public.

Q. To make a parable of himself?

A. No sir; of her—to square himself in the eyes of the public.

Martin's testimony ended with a wrenching surprise: Mamie Thompson, she said, was her sister, and it appeared that it was Martin who had called in the force and got McGlory arrested along with the women (thinking, perhaps, that Mamie would be safer in police custody than in

McGlory's hands). In the end, everybody wound up at the precinct house. According to Officer Dooley, McGlory was outraged, claiming he himself had been behind the call to the police. "If the bloody bitch had turned up the leather [i.e., given back the pocketbook], I wouldn't be in this trouble," McGlory fumed. "It is the first time I ever called a copper in my house on a squeal, and I get it in the neck for trying to do what's right. I have been trying to run or keep a dead square joint, and I get it in the neck."

Police reluctance to shutter McGlory's "dead square" premises was evident throughout the trial, but never became a real issue. The assistant district attorneys tiptoed away from suggesting that there might have been payoffs (though they did ask both Dooley and Clinchy how it was that they'd never detected any lawbreaking). Their lack of curiosity in this respect suggests the district attorney's office may well have been part of the corruption loop. Instead the testimony got entangled in the question of who actually owned the Irving and who therefore was legally responsible for what went on in it. No clear answer ever emerged, but it took the jury just seven minutes to convict McGlory of keeping a disorderly house. Uncowed, he tossed his coat to the floor, dug both hands into his pants pockets, and strode up to the bar to glower at them. Krause got off. McGlory went to the Tombs, from which, in January 1892, he was sentenced to a $300 fine and a year in prison, but he was soon on the streets again, and was in trouble as late as 1903, when he was arrested for selling liquor without a license at a saloon he owned in the Bronx.

McGlory, however studiously the trial avoided the issue, clearly depended on a culture of profitable mutual back-rubbing among racketeers, the police, even the district attorney's office and the courts. It was a corrupt rogues' orchestra conducted by Tammany Hall, long since grown from the feather-topped fraternal drinking society of 1790 to the political juggernaut of William Tweed and his successor, Richard Croker. Tammany's mascot was the tiger, but by the number and reach of its tentacles it was more like an octopus. Prizefighting, legally sanctioned or otherwise, had become inextricably mixed with Tammany politics, but so had almost every other questionable activity in New York. The anti-vice movement increasingly blamed Tammany as the bane of virtuous city life, the creator of an inextricable Gordian tangle between public power and private sin.

In the 1890s, perhaps the most indignant of Tammany's detractors was the Reverend Charles Parkhurst (1842–1933), pastor of the Madison

Square Presbyterian Church, ardent admirer of Anthony Comstock, and eventually president of his own reform group, the Society for the Prevention of Crime. Parkhurst's church, on the southeast corner of Madison Avenue and 24th Street, served a large congregation of single young men. For Parkhurst they were innocents, defenseless before the lures of vice. Full of New England rectitude and an Amherst education, he set himself the mission of molding them into an army of virtue.

Parkhurst found himself especially galled by the McGlory case; the Hotel Irving was, after all, only a ten-minute walk from his pulpit. He, like the *Herald*, blamed not only the police but politics and city government, from the mayor down "a lying, perjured rum-soaked, and libidinous lot." Nicoll, "our guileless District Attorney, with the down of unsuspecting innocence upon his blushing cheek," Parkhurst acidly remarked, refused to act on calls for a crackdown. "The fact of it is that they all stand in with each other. It is simply one solid gang of rascals, half of the gang in office and the other half out, and the two halves catering to each other across the official line."

Determined to prove that the law was not just ignoring but actively encouraging vice, Parkhurst hired Charles Gardner, a Broadway detective familiar with New York's underworld. Together with Parkhurst's assistant, John Erving (a purse-lipped young man with blond hair parted in the middle), they ventured out on a tour in the spring of 1892. Gardner was a mixed asset: slick Virgil to Parkhurst's bumbling Dante, but also a student of humanity who relished every nuance of ridiculousness in the pastor's adventure, and compiled an anthology of choice examples in a self-published 1894 book, *The Doctor and the Devil: or, Midnight Adventures of Dr. Parkhurst.*

On the evening of their first foray, Gardner realized Parkhurst radiated a clerical aura so dense it would have clung to him stark naked, and tried to hide it for the sake of the mission. He began by forcing the diminutive cleric into a castoff pair of outsized black-and-white checked pants, cinching the waistband just beneath Parkhurst's shoulder blades. To these Gardner added a tie (fashioned by ripping apart the remains of an old red flannel shirt), a slouch hat, and a reefer jacket. This ensemble didn't, however, quite dissipate the odor of sanctity, so as a final touch Gardner liberally sudsed Parkhurst's softly curling hair, equipping him with Mose-style soap-locks.

McGlory was in jail by now, so the Hotel Irving wasn't on the itinerary. They headed first to the Lower East Side and Tom Summers's saloon at 33 Cherry Street, where Parkhurst downed a stiff "Manhattan Reserve Club" whiskey, and then to a dance hall. Here Erving tried to order a ginger ale (which the bartender indignantly refused to serve), women were seen smoking cigars, and a leering nineteen-year-old girl came up to Parkhurst and demanded, "Hey, whiskers, . . . going to ball me off?" Then a Salvation Army detachment stormed in, bearing tracts that they tried to distribute among the unreceptive customers.

After that Gardner led his charges through a 5-cent flophouse on Park Row (where men bedded down on canvas cots under the infernal heat flooding out from two sheet-iron stoves), a brothel patronized by cops, an opium den on Doyers Street in Chinatown, and the one place that terrified rather than transfixed the minister: the Golden Rule Pleasure Club on West 3rd Street, a gay brothel run by a woman known as Scotch Ann. The party walked in through a basement door; a buzzer sounded to announce them, and they filed past a succession of cubicles, in "each of which," Gardner wrote, "sat a youth whose face was painted, eye-brows blackened, and whose airs were those of a young girl. Each person talked in a high falsetto voice and called the others by women's names." This, alone in the cavalcade of enormities, so shocked Parkhurst that he balked and bolted back outdoors, exclaiming, "I wouldn't stay in that house . . . for all the money in the world."

Straight brothels proved less traumatizing. Parkhurst and Erving saw a number of skin shows at various sites, in which the women, clad in Mother Hubbard gowns, displayed themselves to the customers, who then decided which girls would join the performance. Maria Andrea's house at 42 West 4th Street had a baton-twirling cop on the front steps (for protection, possibly); inside, Andrea offered a $5 "French circus." But the show fated for notoriety was at 29–31 East 27th Street in a brothel belonging to Hattie Adams—according to Gardner "a scraggy, thin, little woman, with hay-colored hair and colorless light eyes." She was a nearby neighbor both of the Madison Square Presbyterian Church and Parkhurst, who then lived on East 35th Street. Adams's show, billed as a "dance of nature," cost $15, and the women, once they'd shed their Mother Hubbards, topped their act with a game of nude leapfrog (customers invited to join) with Gardner dutifully playing frog as Parkhurst and Erving looked on.

Adams, who somehow smelled out the agenda behind this visit, was infuriated and tipped off the police, whom she had been paying off. Thus she made the incident public and a laughingstock of Parkhurst. But he didn't care: his point had been to expose the city's shame. He insisted that his targets had never been the women or men involved in the trade but rather the city authorities who tolerated vice and indeed worked hand in glove with it. He called this "The Social Evil," and its heart of darkness, Parkhurst believed, was a corrupt police force. "Social vice," he wrote, "has been so protected and encouraged by the filthy officials who control the department, that the number of abandoned women and disorderly houses now existing in the city is no measure of what it would be if we had a police force, from top down, who conceived of sexual crime as an evil to be suppressed, not as capital to draw dividend from."

Parkhurst's church tried to outmanuever sin by sponsoring evening socials for its young male parishioners—an illustrated lecture on ancient Athens, a smorgasbord supper given by the Young Men's Society "to the ladies of the church who had assisted them in receiving their guests at former meetings," and a party for the Young Men's Bible Class. Delightful these all may have been, but they clearly weren't putting saloons and disorderly houses out of business, as evidenced by a list of prices for police protection compiled by Gardner. The going rate for a pool hall was $250 a month; it was $5 a month for saloons and $100 for disorderly houses. These were steep fees indeed, but income apparently covered them with profit to spare.

There was nothing new in this détente between authorities and the city's permanent corps of lawless entrepreneurs. But it had become far better organized, almost a shadow government. Bars, brothels, prizefights, concert saloons, and dance halls enjoyed a constituency among the city's poor, whom reformers thus stirred into boiling resentment. Tammany's cohabitation with vice bought it an influential presence in working-class neighborhoods, a gold mine in payoffs, and camaraderie with a massive population of low-income male voters (women didn't count, since they couldn't yet vote).

Still, poverty was far from universal among the crowds seeking low-down pleasure. The 1885 Sullivan-Ryan bout drew rich men as well as slum dwellers; there were at least two police court justices in the audience; and the off-duty cops who'd crowded in to watch the fight outnumbered those sent to shut it down. At night theoretically incompatible human strata mixed again. Society women prided themselves on furnishing sometimes imperious settlement house charity to their less fortunate sisters, but the men, at least sometimes, fraternized equitably with their working-class counterparts in a comradely, toxic miasma of cigar smoke.

More or less contemporaneously with its exposé of McGlory and the Hotel Irving, the *Herald* also renewed attack on another favorite target, the Slide at 157 Bleecker Street, just west of Sullivan. It was a gay bar, a scene, the *Herald* screamed, putrid with "Depravity of a Depth Unknown in the Lowest Slums of London or Paris" (by the late 1800s, slums and moral decay had been made to seem synonymous in the public mind). The *Herald* adopted the schizophrenic rhetoric pioneered by the sporting press of the 1840s—shrill denunciation mixed with exact details about how to find the place and what to expect when you got there.

In the *Herald*'s crude line drawing, several customers, including a limp-wristed, knock-kneed man (the era's standard icon of homosexuality), stand in the barroom. As the reporter orders a drink, "one of the gaudily bedecked young men minced up to me and lisped:—'Aren't you going to buy me something?'" In the background the illustration shows a dance floor with two men, locked in a clinch and kiss, one fluttering a fan at the other's waist. The *Herald,* with McGlory's antlers now high above its mantle, had attacked the Slide as a further challenge to DeLancey Nicoll: "the conviction of McGlory has so encouraged me that I have determined to keep up the crusade," the reporter wrote, and the headline read, "HERE, MR. NICOLL, IS A PLACE TO PROSECUTE," observing that the owner was Frank Stevenson, "gambler, sport, fosterer of prizefights and stakeholder." The reporter quoted a customer at the Slide to the effect that the scene was rather quiet at the moment owing to the *Herald*-generated heat. A waiter, however, seemed unworried. "Come in again in a week," he said, "and . . . we'll show you something worth seeing."

More or less untouched, the old Slide remains in existence today as Kenny's Castaways, a well-known rock and blues nightclub, and much of it is still recognizable from the 1891 drawing and description in the *Herald*: a high barroom in the front with a stamped tin ceiling and a dance floor and orchestra platform at the back, flanked by two staircases to the right and left that lead up to a gallery. The ceiling, woodwork, and ceramic tile floor are all 19th-century, and the room, in spite of its rock-era role, probably looks and feels much as it did when it was the Slide; it's certainly still alive at night.

Kenny's opens directly onto the street; the *Herald* said customers had to descend a staircase to get in. Though it's now used only for deliveries, a staircase leads down to the basement from a street door, and the current proprietor, Roger Probert, recalls that during some construction in the basement—a warren of cellars and cubicles with old, possibly original, plasterwork and doors—the carpenter discovered traces of a second vanished stairway that led up again into the bar. This was most likely a security precaution, hiding the Slide from the street. The gauntlet of two staircases and an underground passage would have been a way to spot and eject potential troublemakers: many 19th-century dives seem to have made more or less this same arrangement, and it survived into the 20th century to become standard in Prohibition speakeasies.

This time of spirited engagement between repression and unashamed license made for an era of odd couples indeed: louche Charles Gardner and rectilinear Charles Parkhurst, William Travers and Old Smoke Morrissey, William K. Vanderbilt and Paddy Ryan, Hattie Adams and her allies in the precincts and even the district attorney's office. Who sided with whom changed constantly as new threats or advantages loomed. But the networking principle prevailed everywhere. Like good and evil twins whose lives uncannily mirror each other, both vice and vigilantism were becoming not merely institutionalized but existentially intertwined: especially the latter, which depended on the former for its very existence.

In the end both libertinism and crusading conscience became standardized and commercialized. What had been backroom grifts or personal ministries were becoming brand names, even citywide and national chains. Vaudeville circuits promised and delivered family diversion, but ran like Tammany Hall or any organized urban gang—rewarding the faithfully obedient, strong-arming any interlopers, crushing attempts by actors to form unions. By the 1890s, the commercial sex trade had become so widespread that, in the teeth of the anti-vice movement, significant parts of it had become virtual and in some respects literal corporations. Among the biggest, the Lower East Side–based International Benevolent Association (its eerily logo-like street name was "IBA," its business was brothels, and it belonged to a consortium of McGlory types) offered a formal benefits plan to members, including insurance and free burial plots.

A trail had been blazed to fame, wealth, and success for once obscure impresarios of the night. By the 1920s, that path would fork even more sharply, leading in one direction toward the world of Prohibition-era gangsters like Dutch Schultz and Legs Diamond, in another to theater and vaudeville magnificos like Florenz Ziegfeld (1867–1932). And there would be, of course, a gray world between, made up of nightclub queens like Texas Guinan (1884–1933) and kings like Sherman Billingsley (1896–1966) of the Stork Club, fated to become the legendary venue of the 1930s and after.

CENTURY'S END

In the twenty years between 1870 and 1890, a half a million more people had flooded into Manhattan. The multitudinous poor crowded the streets, rumbling els, and tenements. The far fewer rich overwhelmed the landscape not with numbers but block-gobbling mansions, which transformed once ragged Fifth Avenue into a ruler-straight cordon of palaces. The public city also became more imposing, as Central Park came into its own and a government and commercial construction binge overpowered the streets with soaring railway stations, grand hotels, cathedral-sized theaters, and palace restaurants, each outdoing the last in opulence. The history of New York grandeur is a story of insatiable expectation, generating ever bolder redefinitions of what makes a tower tall, a hall or lobby imposing, or decoration lavish.

This skyward reach was a product of many forces: increases in population, rising real estate prices, advances in structural engineering, the invention of the elevator. And yet none of these by itself could have raised the skyline to the heights to which it had begun to aspire: rather it was the vaulting commercial ambition that, however otherwise ill-matched they might have been, united the Astors with the Vanderbilts, with John Morrissey, even Edward Corey and Billy McGlory. Until the 1880s, such ambition fulfilled itself chiefly along the horizontal plane. But then the skyline began to climb, because new construction techniques allowed it and hubris demanded it. In 1875 the 230-foot-tall Western Union Building rose on Broadway. Then, in 1876, came the towers of the Brooklyn Bridge (271 feet), followed by the 260-foot Tribune Tower on Park Row in 1882, and the Statue of Liberty (265 feet) in 1886. Through all this the Trinity steeple remained the tallest structure in the city—until 1890, when Joseph Pulitzer overtopped it with his 309-foot *World* building. Then a new Madison Square Garden opened at 26th and Madison, eclipsing Pulitzer's headquarters with a 341-foot spire, modeled on the Giralda tower in Seville (but 66 feet taller). The new Madison Square

Garden raised, in more than one way, the New York night of the 19th century to its pinnacle.

In 1887 William K. Vanderbilt had finally sold the old and unprofitable Garden to (yes) a syndicate, the Madison Square Amusement Company, which demolished it in the summer of 1889. The new Garden, designed by Stanford White, opened in June 1890, with a main hall, 200 feet by 350, that could hold over 10,000 people. In daytime sunlight filtered in through a moving skylight. At night, rows of electric bulbs blazed along the curved iron trusses that held up the roof. Once all its finishing touches were in place, by the fall of 1891, Madison Square Garden was most spectacular seen at night—especially that November, when White introduced the outdoor lighting with an extravaganza. Two searchlights crossed and recrossed the sky; 6,600 bulbs seared their way along the outline of the sprawling Mediterranean-looking auditorium block, with 1,400 more picking out the spire—which White had crowned with a rotating and electrically illuminated eighteen-foot statue of Diana. It was an odd choice of goddess, given the priapic exploits for which White was famous and to which he devoted his private apartment in the tower. And even he came to agree that she looked a little vulgar; by 1893 a smaller, less Barnumesque Diana had replaced the glowing and twirling original.

The new Madison Square Garden was a fiercely inflated and electrified remake of modest old pleasure gardens like Ranelagh and Vauxhall, scaled to the gluttonous epicureanism of the 1890s (and also to White's own appetite for luxury, which outdid even the exuberant decade he epitomized). Apart from the main hall and tower, the complex included a 1,200-seat playhouse, a 1,500-seat concert hall, and a 300-table roof garden stretching nearly 300 feet along Madison Avenue. The complex was a bazaar of pleasures from the *raffiné* to the neo-pagan (though prizefights remained a prime attraction). White presided, an imperial Bacchus, and made the new Garden a magnet for New York nightlife that endured into the next century.

White's reign finally ended on the night of June 25, 1906, when Harry K. Thaw, a jealous Pittsburgh husband, shot him dead at a table in the roof garden during the premiere of a new musical, *Mamzelle Champagne*. The Gilded Age had been sputtering well before that, however: another depression struck in the early 1890s, culminating in another financial panic in the spring and summer of 1893, which led in turn to a plague of bank and railroad failures. Still, bad times didn't kill the craving for ever-grander grandeur. In 1893 the Waldorf Hotel opened on Fifth Avenue at 34th Street; anyone impressed by the old Astor House of the 1830s would have been floored by this thirteen-story pseudo-Renaissance behemoth, with its instantly famous Palm Garden and its Empire Dining Room, modeled on the grand hall of the Residenz Palace in Munich. In 1897 the hotel expanded to become the Waldorf-Astoria, seventeen stories tall and with more than 1,000 rooms. Theaters kept pace: Hammerstein's 5,200-seat Victoria opened at Seventh Avenue and 42nd Street in 1893. Skyscrapers accelerated their competition, especially on the blocks surrounding City Hall Park. Commerce had overtaken religion as the city's reigning belief system, and the brick and stone towers of business now dwarfed the Trinity spire. In 1899 the 29-story, 386-foot Park Row Building became the tallest in the world, a title it would retain well into the next century.

In 1897, after decades of discord among feuding planners, Manhattan itself joined a syndicate, merging with Brooklyn, Queens, Staten Island, and the Bronx. By fiat New York thus flooded across the section map like a tidal wave, becoming an instant megalopolis. Its population was now nearly three and a half million—a million more than Paris and on a bigger tract of land (though greater London, with six-million-plus souls, still dwarfed its transatlantic rival). The five boroughs wed formally at midnight on December 31, 1898, and the celebration took place in City Hall Park, which had been the place to congregate on New Year's Eve since the early decades of the 1800s (the party was a fiasco: an afternoon downpour of rain turned into snow after dark; the mood was dismal and the crowd thinned out into a few chilled, wet, and crestfallen celebrants).

The boroughs had been economically and socially interdependent since the 17th century, so at first unification did more to streamline the management of infrastructure than to generate a new sense of metropolitan wholeness. And Manhattan would remain the center of commerce, wealth, and nightlife throughout the 20th century. But perceptions— which shouldn't be undervalued—did slowly begin to aggrandize the city's vision of itself after dark. No longer was this a perspective of Stygian streets and alleys in dim gaslight. Rather, with tall public structures now everywhere, from the Brooklyn Bridge and the Statue of Liberty to the ever-higher apartment and office buildings, people could visualize a city alight, reaching across a distance below like a view seen from the sky. One could now imagine New York at night as a panorama, unrolling from the skyscrapers of Manhattan, outward across the cable-strung bridges and tunnels, and washed by vast, invisible tides of people, eddying back and forth from the theaters and bars and clubs into the far-flung new city limits—Wakefield, Sheepshead Bay, Little Neck, Tottenville—to name a few remote country villages now reborn as nodes of the urban commonwealth.

Brooklyn, the Bronx, Queens, and Staten Island kept their own identities, but New Yorkers gradually found themselves both exhilarated and intimidated by the idea of their city as unknowably huge, owing its collective identity mainly to newspapers, each of which claimed to be the true voice of New York. They bulleted off the presses and sped into the boroughs by the million—the *Times,* the *Sun,* the *World,* the *Herald,* the *Tribune,* the *Commercial Advertiser,* the *Wall Street Journal,* the *Mail and Express,* the *Brooklyn Daily Times,* and many more. Reporting took on a big-city hardness: the florid and fussy rhetoric of the 1800s began shattering into a new, mean-edged prose, smoky with menace, mystery, and lost-soul cynicism. Stories no longer described crimes and astonishments as our-town anomalies. Instead, they were the cold secrets of an anonymous metropolis: ruthless bunco scams, strange disappearances, haunted houses, crimes of Aeschylean passion in the drab lower middle-class streets of the outer boroughs, strangers slipping into town on sinister missions, then vanishing forever.

In the late fall of 1899 a female gangster, 22-year-old Chicago Mabel (her real name was either Mabel Ray, Molly McClure, Mrs. May Bell, Norah Jones, or Mrs. J. W. Crouch), moved east. Mabel and three accomplices, wholesome-looking types from Chicago, Little Rock, and Memphis, shared a room in a boardinghouse at 212 East 32nd Street, and could be seen strolling along Madison and Lexington Avenues at night, well dressed and behaving with demure expectancy, as if looking for someone they'd previously arranged to meet. The police caught wind of them, smelled a criminal plot, and quietly investigated.

No victim came forward, but the cops deduced that the scheme was to flirt, pick a man up, and lure him to the room on 32nd Street. Then the gang either served him a Mickey Finn or sapped him off to dreamland with a set of brass knuckles ("my knucks," Mabel called them; the cops found a set in her room, along with the knockout drops and a pearl-handled baby revolver). They then relieved the victim of his valuables, dumped him in an alley or vacant lot before he could come to, and hocked the spoils: the cops confiscated a sheaf of pawn tickets for items like diamond rings, gold, and watches.

Though a long-distance phone line had linked Chicago with New York in 1892, the *Herald* investigated by telegraph, and discovered Mabel had a reputation as one of the "'shrewdest operators' in the West," with a long rap sheet for similar grifts in both Chicago and Sioux City. But, probably thanks to the same embarrassment that had kept anybody from complaining in New York, she had managed to avoid conviction: "there are men in Chicago who could give evidence, but they do not care to."

The breakup of Chicago Mabel's Murray Hill gang was only one piece of flotsam on the urban Styx that week, competing with a dozen others for ink. A ghost, for example, haunting a run-down house on Bathgate Avenue near 174th Street in the Bronx. The new tenants, not knowing it was the scene of two recent deaths and an attempted double suicide, heard rustling papers, footsteps crossing the vacant floor above them at night, and finally a disembodied scream—which propelled them and their scared dog posthaste to new quarters on Webster Avenue. Or, about a week earlier, the Reverend William Hart Dexter, a Nyack minister, who disembarked from a night steamer at Peck Slip and vanished, leaving only a Masonic charm and a stateroom key, found on Water Street the next morning. A man named Thomas Daw accidentally met a grotesque end when his folding bed suddenly sprang haywire and broke his neck. A baby, taken for dead and brought to the city morgue, woke up wailing on a stone slab. The staff tried to save it, but it had taken a fatal chill and soon died.

Night became a theater of sudden appearances and quick escapes, lonely crowds, wanderers, strollers, and predators—spinoffs of a burgeoning and diversifying population, the proliferation of new things to do after dark and the technologies that invented them, lit them up, and transported their patrons. Once the old custom of noon dinner had finally migrated into evening, it left day as an uninterrupted round of business and night as the reserve of pleasure. Evening was, if it ever had been, no longer just a diurnal measure identified by the clock or starlight. It had acquired a mystique.

As 1899 wound down toward the start of the new century, New Yorkers felt on the whole more gloomy than celebratory, despite a victory in the three-month-long Spanish-American War. It had been another bad year on Wall Street. And though the Boer War was Britain's catastrophe, the pall from it hung over Americans, who could follow the bad news with a new immediacy over the transatlantic cable (in service since 1866), and in battlefield photographs, which were just now starting to appear regularly in newspapers. Even the Metropolitan Opera's December opening suffered a blow to its dignity: a dog show held in the house a few weeks earlier had left a major infestation of fleas in the auditorium's plush seats and hangings, leading *Town Topics* to advise sardonically that "décolleté patrons will have to equip themselves with back-scratchers and even air-tight lingerie."

But the pace of change accelerated nonetheless. Overhead wires, dense as jungle vines in Madame Restell's day, began disappearing underground in the 1890s, and sky, both by day and night, returned to the streetscape. Electric bulbs, glaring, racing, popping on and off in sequence like Chinese firecrackers, soon overshadowed the modest brilliance of old-fashioned gaslit signage. A five-story-high plaster and wood arch over Fifth Avenue at Madison Square, built to commemorate the Spanish-American War, featured a garland of electric lights. But it looked stodgy beside a 45-foot-long Heinz pickle blazing out across the square, outlined in rapidly blinking green bulbs and with "57 GOOD THINGS FOR THE TABLE" flashing beneath it in a riot of color (boxes with motor-driven rolling drums activated switches and rheostats, creating fade-ins, dissolves, and animations even in the earliest days of electric illumination).

Transport had evolved far beyond the els. Horse-drawn streetcars, the reliable if uncomfortable backbone of urban transit since William Dunlap's day, were in their last throes. By 1899 electricity powered 750 miles of street railway, leaving only 150 miles to the horses. Automobiles were common now, a passionate hobby among the well-to-do: the upmarket *Commercial Advertiser* carried a regular "Automobilism" column, and in the fall of 1899 a debate broke out about whether or not cars should be allowed to use the roads in Central Park. In 1892 William Steinway began digging two trolley tunnels between 42nd Street and Queens; they still carry traffic today on the Number 7 subway line. At the same time 2,000 feet of tunnel under the Hudson River from Hoboken were also driving their way toward Morton Street in Greenwich Village (work on this project, however, wasn't to be finished until 1909, when it became part of what's now the PATH system).

Finally, in the fall of 1899, bidding opened for the construction of the city's first full-scale subway line—a transport technology that reached the city 40 years after London's pioneering underground, but which has become the world's largest, its endless 24-hour-a-day rhythm synonymous with the pulse of New York. The first segment to open took a route shaped like an elongated S: it ran up from South Ferry along the current East Side line, turned left under 42nd Street, followed the present-day Shuttle route to Times Square, then turned north and headed under Broadway up to 96th Street. Digging began just as the new century did, in 1900.

More prophetic in their way than even the proliferating tunnels were new leaps into the air, predating and foreshadowing aviation and wireless communication. As the 1899 elections neared, the *Herald* announced, "residents of New York City and of the country around will be able to read in the skies the result of the battle of the ballots to-morrow." A searchlight, placed atop the Madison Square Garden Tower, beamed out the results as soon as they came in, pointing southward to announce that Boss Croker's Tammany Hall Democrats won all the offices it had run for by at least 50,000 votes each.

Wires, in 1899, still carried the buzz of most gossip and most news (the superintendent of elections complained that his phone was tapped when he heard somebody say "Cheese it" on the line). Messages could pass through the air only via unwieldy means like the *Herald*'s searchlight and the lantern slide projections used by other papers to post breaking news to pedestrians. But on September 21, 1899, Guglielmo Marconi arrived in New York aboard the Cunard liner *Aurania,* invited by the U.S. War and Navy Departments: they were interested in his experiments with wireless telegraphy. And on Thursday, October 26, two navy warships, the *New York* and the *Massachusetts,* could be seen riding at anchor in the Hudson between 34th and 38th Streets, about a quarter of a mile apart.

To most observers, nothing about them looked unusual, though the sharp-eyed could have discerned a brass globe atop the mast of each ship. But Marconi, tapping an old-fashioned-looking telegraph key, unleashed something remarkable from one to the other: bursts of invisible energy, tearing at the speed of light through the air between, and delivering a 100-word newspaper paragraph, strings of words, random numbers, a message in naval code. Speech and music had yet to fly in electromagnetic waves. Only in 1902 did Marconi discover that radio signals traveled much further in the dark of night, enabling the first wireless signal to flash across the Atlantic; the first American radio broadcast occurred in 1906. But the earliest harbingers of the future flood had arrived: by the early

1920s mass broadcasting had come to wield a power over entertainment that dwarfed even the film industry's.

In November, Marconi left the United States to work on radio communications in the Boer War. For the time being the airwaves vanished. In the next century they would spring back to life, and in the long run transform night once again—and when it happened, New York would become America's broadcasting capital, with fateful consequences for the experience of night not only in Manhattan but for the nation at large.

CHAPTER EIGHT

MR. DIETER VANISHES, NOVEMBER 1923

The Volstead Act, Jazz, and Earl Carroll's Vanities

AMONG THE ICONS OF Jazz Age New York, F. Scott and Zelda Fitzgerald seem as potent now as they did in their own day. Like many New York legends, they'd grown up in the provinces, he in St. Paul and Buffalo, she in Alabama. They'd wed in the spring of 1920, and, flush with the success of *This Side of Paradise,* thrown themselves head-long into a lightheaded and incandescent New York honeymoon. It was a short fling—by the early 1920s the Fitzgeralds were spending much of their time in Connecticut, Europe, Minnesota, and Long Island—but while it lasted they flew, addled with youth and fame, through Manhattan's theaters, nightclubs, speakeasies, a world to which Prohibition had now lent a seductive perfume of lawlessness.

Zelda and Scott were—or at least were believed to be—beautiful, bright, leaders of the post–World War I vanguard, and not merely libertine but splendidly heedless even of the possibility of repression. Fitzgerald, according to *Hearst's International* magazine, believed that Zelda had "started the flapper movement in this country." And he played up to the role of flapper's madcap escort: when the girls peeled off their costumes at George White's *Scandals,* Scott, in the audience, started stripping in accompaniment, and got down to his undershirt before the ushers threw him out. At another show, *Enter Madame,* the Fitzgeralds and their entourage made themselves so loud and obnoxious (at one point Zelda fell off her seat) that the manager issued them a stern warning; they both stormed out. And the famous fountain plunges (Scott in front of the Plaza Hotel, Zelda in either Union or Washington Square, nobody knows which) became symbols of a gloriously unhinged era of nightlife, signal events of the 1920s and benchmarks for the pixilated self-indulgence ever after demanded of celebrities.

For the Fitzgeralds the binge ended sourly. "Within a few months after our embarkation on the Metropolitan venture," Fitzgerald wrote, "we scarcely knew any more who we were and we hadn't a notion what we were." This could be an exhilarating sensation as well as a sobering one; it was certainly a common thread among stories from the period that marks, at least thus far, the apotheosis of the New York night. World War I finally ended; gradually, prosperity and optimism returned; technology and commercial innovation continued apace; Prohibition gave an unintended boost to the spirit of nonconformity; and a war-ravaged generation of young adults broke away from what they saw as the prison of 19th-century hypocrisy.

But perhaps the determining innovation of the 1920s night was its return to the spirit of democracy (if not to economic equality). Social and economic class survived, but a rise in income brought once exclusive pleasures like motorcars within reach of ever less wealthy people. Flourishing mass entertainment like radio seemed to be making leisure into everybody's property, and thus ameliorating the war of cultural castes that had been underway ever since the 1840s. Now, Broadway, Harlem, and Greenwich Village became, in the public consciousness at least, universal playgrounds; beginning in 1920, Prohibition made gangsters the friends of socialites; the clash and blend of high and low, always the engine of nightlife but once its secret, now became its boast.

Anybody, living no matter where in Brooklyn or Queens, might suddenly be transfixed in the limelight. Dissipation leading to disaster—in antivice tracts the favorite subject of dire warnings—could, in a new climate where risk was itself a form of entertainment, now seem even more romantic, more chic, than success. Difficult to say which was the more striking feature of this new ethos, the rejection of old-fashioned narrow-mindedness or its modern-age hardness. Celebrities and the rich had not lost their place in gossip. But newspapers and their readers increasingly craved stories of extraordinary moments in otherwise ordinary (and not necessarily pleasant) lives—a common theme of the era, filling the tabloids week by week and a staple of 1920s fiction like Fitzgerald's own *The Great Gatsby* (1925).

Richard Dieter was the protagonist of one such tale. In the summer of 1923 he was a struggling young man, living with his wife and two young children near downtown Brooklyn, in a small flat in Boerum Hill. He was 29 years old and clinging—unlike the Fitzgeralds but like many others his age—to the fringes of the civilized city. He worked nights, earning $21.25 a week as a switchboard operator at the Brooklyn Heights headquarters of the posh Crescent Athletic Club, to which, every afternoon at around 5:30, he made his way from his rented apartment at 52 Bergen Street.*

Dieter and his 28-year-old wife, Catherine, had two children, Richard Jr., six, and Catherine, eight. Their apartment, probably on the second floor, was meager: a bedroom for the children and a combined living-dining room where the parents also slept. When Dieter wasn't working at the club the couple sat in their flat stringing beads for extra income. "Dick was a homebody," Catherine said of him. "Nearly always he came on time straight from work. If he was late he found some way to let me know so I wouldn't worry." A photo shows him, grinning—proud and bashful—in the driver's seat of his car. A male friend on the passenger side puts an arm around him. His smiling wife and two chubby children are in the back seat. The *Brooklyn Daily Eagle* described him as "a very small man and somewhat timorous."

New York had already perfected its own heady version of the national binge unleashed by Prohibition; only 24 years after the close of the old century, nighttime had evolved into a glorious debauch on which millions wanted to stake a claim. For the first time, Manhattan and the outer boroughs after dark seem familiar to us now—the movie and stage stars, the hoodlums, the music, and the speakeasies still haven't lost hold of the American imagination. On the evening of November 3, when Dieter's life skidded from invisibility into fame, Fanny Brice was playing in the 1923 *Ziegfeld Follies* at the New Amsterdam Theatre. The girls in George White's *Scandals* paraded to the rhythms of a score by George Gershwin. Ann Nichols's *Abie's Irish Rose* was running, as was Irving Berlin's third annual *Music Box Revue,* at the theater named after it and still operating today.

Silent movies, no longer novelties, had become an industry with stars and theaters of their own: Mary Pickford was in *Rosita* at the Capitol on Broadway at 51st Street. Radio had become a popular form of home entertainment: on November 3, WEAF (now WNBC) broadcast two sets of songs by Warren Proctor, a tenor, followed at 11 p.m. by Vincent Lopez's

---

* Dieter's house is still standing, upgraded in a recent residential revival. But the block retains some of the deserted, vacant character its stables, garages and small workshops gave it in 1923. The ground floor seems to have been a workshop. A wooden gate, still in place, opened onto a driveway and back yard where Dieter kept the family's prize possession, a touring car. Behind that there was and is an old, small-scale factory building.

orchestra live from the Hotel Pennsylvania. WJZ featured the Hotel Commodore Dance Orchestra. It was, in other words, a night world with a distinctive 20th-century energy and attitude, with which the stretched and hardworking Dieter family, more worried about survival than fun, offered a sobering contrast. But this was 1923, the era of Gatsby and innumerable other nobodies who rocketed overnight into wealth or notoriety, in myth if not in fact. And tonight, Dieter's number came up in this lottery of fame, when, at 5:30 in the afternoon, following his usual habit, he left for the Crescent Athletic Club.

He never got there, and never came back home to Bergen Street. Early Sunday morning, on a routine patrol, a beat cop walking across the Manhattan Bridge found Dieter's coat and cap, a few photos, and Dieter's name and address. Catherine Dieter, abandoned and scared, appealed to the police and the district attorney, but when Monday dawned he was still missing. The *Eagle* visited Catherine at home and found her distraught, her terrorized children weeping in the bedroom. "'They are crying for their daddy,' she explained, herself beginning to sob hysterically. 'They are crying also because they haven't anything to eat, and I have no money. When Dick left home Saturday to go to work at the Crescent Club he had just 15 cents. I broke my last dollar the same day.'"

She knew, she told the reporter, why her husband had disappeared, though not where: he'd been either kidnapped or murdered by a club member. Working as a phone operator at the Crescent Club didn't pay much, but it required diplomacy, since the club served, if not the richest and most powerful men in the borough, at least those with enough money and self-regard to demand VIP treatment. Some joined, no doubt, for the athletic facilities, or to smoke cigars, drink discreetly, and rub comradely elbows with other males. Others used it as a headquarters for the hard partying and extramarital affairs that had now become a badge of urban attainment. The man at the telephone desk thus heard more than orders for soda water, and saw things more provocative than pudgy executives on their way to a splash in the basement swimming pool.

A few months before Dieter's disappearance, a member named Ephraim F. Jeffe had begun receiving mysterious letters and phone calls at the club from a woman in Philadelphia. Jeffe was a thirty-something electric power salesman for the Brooklyn Edison Company, unpopular with the club staff because, as the bell captain put it, they disliked "his manner in addressing them and his failure to recompense them for their services."

Such as the service Dieter rendered early one morning, when Jeffe ordered him to place a long-distance call to Bala Cynwyd, on the Philadelphia Main Line, but to hang up if a man answered. Dieter, eavesdropping, overheard Jeffe say, "My God, Lola, my wife knows everything!"

Jeffe's wife, Pearl, described by the *Daily News* as "an extremely good-looking young woman," was also a jealous one; guessing that Dieter might have been tapping phone calls and reading letters, she had been pestering him. Somehow Jeffe got wind of this, and began showing up at the Dieters' apartment at all hours, uttering threats while the children cowered behind the half-portiere that separated their bedroom from the rest of the flat. "Jeffe said he was going to hound me," Dieter later recalled. "He was going to get my job at the club. He was going to keep after me wherever I went until he brought my wife and little ones to starvation unless I gave him the letters written to him by the Philadelphia woman and which he said I had."

As a last warning, Jeffe had come to Bergen Street at about one o'clock Saturday afternoon (just as WEAF was broadcasting the Yale-Army football game from New Haven), and herded the couple to a drugstore at the corner of Court and Amity Streets, where he placed a call to a mysterious woman who insisted to both Dieter and his wife that she'd seen him with the letters. Jeffe ended by drawing a pistol on the petrified couple and brandishing it at them as he stepped onto a streetcar.

That, for Richard Dieter, was the last straw—as he explained when, after no corpse surfaced in the East River and a manhunt ensued, the police ran him to earth near Woonsocket, Rhode Island, three days after his disappearance. "I was almost in nervous collapse and didn't know what to do," he said. "I shaved and got ready to go to work at 5:30. But I didn't go there." Instead, he took an extra coat and cap, left them on the Manhattan Bridge to suggest a suicide, and made his way to Grand Central Terminal—not the helter-skelter building of the late 1800s, but the glorious Warren and Wetmore structure we still use today.

Once he got there, a milling crowd swallowed him up. Two fires had broken out near Times Square during the pre-theater rush: the traffic was pandemonium and 15,000 rubbernecks had gathered in front of the Public Library to gape at one of the blazes, in a building on the corner of Fifth Avenue and 42nd Street. In the confusion Dieter escaped notice (not that he was conspicuous to begin with). He boarded a train for Hartford, switched for another to Worcester, slept in the station through Sunday morning, then took a final train to Woonsocket. He ended up hiding out with two friends who lived in the nearby village of Blackstone, Massachusetts, where the police finally located him. His panic dissipated, he was escorted back to Grand Central by Brooklyn detective Jimmy Powers (a photo shows the detective with a stony-faced glare, but Dieter with a grin in equal measures sheepish and pleased). "He seemed to relish the commotion his arrival caused," the *Eagle* reported, and "walked jauntily" through the Grand Central crowds. It was an instant of flash-in-the-pan media fame that would have been inconceivable in the 1800s, and for the moment at least, he was delighted.

Back in Brooklyn Dieter first enjoyed a reunion with his wife and children on Bergen Street. According to the *Daily News,* young Catherine and little Richard "shrieked in delight and leapt into his arms," but Mrs. Dieter "lay in a coma." Her two sisters, on hand to help out, both fainted; Catherine herself revived briefly but then fell unconscious once again in her sobbing husband's arms. But then, over the next few days the newspapers, battling each other for exclusives, began to shed a pitiless light on the whole intrigue, which reached far beyond the Jeffes. It wasn't a triangle or quadrangle, but at least a pentagram and maybe a hexagon. Richard Dieter was being hounded not just by the Jeffes, but also by another riled-up Brooklyn woman, Marguerite White. She was married to a doll manufacturer, Frederick W. White, and living just east of Prospect Park, on Clarkson Avenue in then posh Flatbush (today it's a thriving Caribbean neighborhood). The *News* described her as a "youthful matron and mother of two children," and "a comely brunette."

As it turned out, Marguerite White had been, back in October, the first person to contact Dieter about the letters and phone logs that incriminated Ephraim Jeffe and the Philadelphia matron (who had in the meantime been identified as Mrs. Lola Robinson of Bala Cynwyd, Pennsylvania). White claimed to reporters that she had only been trying to help the suspicious Pearl Jeffe. But then another character appeared on the scene—a young bachelor named C. Edwin Butz, Marguerite White's "personal attorney," a friend of Jeffe, and also a Crescent Club member. Butz worked in the Woolworth Building in Manhattan (at this time the tallest in the world). But he lived with the Whites in Brooklyn. As the press scrutiny intensified, Marguerite White insisted with increasing shrillness that he was a mere boarder and family friend, denying to the *Daily News* "the insinuations broadcast through Mrs. Jeffe in an attempt to injure my good name."

In fact Jeffe and Butz were cronies, both using the Crescent Club as a base of operations. The club, founded in 1884 by William H. Ford (a Yale graduate and football enthusiast), had grown to 2,650 members by 1912 and branched out into boating, hockey, and lacrosse. The Pierrepont Street building was impressive, with a swimming pool, rifle range, and bowling alley in the basement, a gym on the top floor, and squash courts. It was also a pied-à-terre hotel, with bedrooms and a dining hall. By the 1920s these, if the Dieter case is typical, were attracting men like Jeffe and Butz, who were using it as a refuge from home life. Eventually Jeffe had become friendly with Lola Robinson, Butz with a woman from Los Angeles, never named, who had "recently obtained a divorce in Reno, remarried, and who came to New York to 'have a good time.'"

Both Pearl Jeffe and Marguerite White had been trying to dig evidence out of Dieter, who had certainly seen and apparently saved both telephone logs and letters. On Sunday, October 7, Ephraim Jeffe had thrown a letter into a wastebasket at the club. Dieter and the bell captain, Ralph Hande, differed as to whether they retrieved it intact, or painstakingly reassembled it from torn-up pieces. They also disagreed about who had read it first and then asked the other to take a look. But they both remembered the greeting: "My darling, blue-eyed boy . . ." (Jeffe, pointing to his eyes for the benefit of an *Eagle* reporter, noted that they were brown).

On Monday, October 15, Marguerite White telephoned Dieter at work to ask if he knew anything about letters and phone calls to Jeffe from a woman in Philadelphia. Though she was supposedly acting on behalf of Pearl Jeffe, White showed a lively interest in Butz's whereabouts as well as Ephraim Jeffe's. Then, the following week, Jeffe told Pearl he had to make a weekend business trip to Boston. But somehow she had gotten wind of a party Jeffe and Butz had planned for Saturday night in a mysterious apartment on West 90th Street in Manhattan. The other guests were supposedly to be Lola Robinson and the woman from Los Angeles. Both Pearl Jeffe and Marguerite White formed (along with Pearl's irate mother) a posse.

On Saturday morning, October 27, Marguerite White called the club and talked to Dieter, who told her that Butz and Jeffe had just left separately, five minutes apart. White relayed the bulletin to Pearl; she and her mother stormed into Manhattan that evening and descended on the apartment, only to find it empty. Then, on Sunday evening, she showed up at the Crescent Club ladies' entrance to ask Dieter if he had any letters. Later, at about ten o'clock, Marguerite White motored in from Clarkson

Avenue to Brooklyn Heights for a tête-à-tête with Dieter. As she drove him around the streets, then parked on Columbia Heights, Dieter showed her (she later claimed) five letters and two phone logs that, he said, Pearl Jeffe was planning to use as evidence in a $100,000 alienation-of-affection suit against Lola Robinson. Jeffe, he added, had promised him $10,000 as a reward. Dieter later vehemently denied showing anything to anybody, but this meeting and Pearl's raid on Manhattan triggered a nerve-wracking week for everybody. Pearl Jeffe demanded another meeting Tuesday night; increasingly scared of losing his job, Dieter sent in his place a cabdriver friend, Edward Emmett, who met her a block away from the club in a teeming rain, and heard her renewed plea for letters and phone logs.

By this time Ephraim Jeffe had been alerted, probably by his wife's accusations, and instantly suspected Dieter. He stormed into the Bergen Street flat, accompanied by a friend, Edward Johnson, a moonlighting detective from the Poplar Street police station in Brooklyn Heights. At midnight the two of them dragged Richard off to the precinct house and grilled him there until four in the morning (with no official sanction, which later caused trouble for Johnson). At about two they put in a phone call to the White residence: Edwin Butz and Marguerite White were awake and both spoke (nobody mentioned Frederick White). Again, Marguerite insisted she'd seen the letters; again, Dieter insisted he had none. But when Jeffe got home at dawn on November 1, he'd apparently secured at least a phone log from Dieter: Pearl, as he crawled into bed, faked a fainting spell and managed to lift it from the pocket of his pajama coat.

There were more confrontations: for example, a meeting Thursday night in the club's basement swimming pool between Jeffe and Emmett, in which the former threatened the latter with prosecution on a grand larceny charge if he couldn't get Dieter to give back the letters. The drama finally reached its climax Saturday afternoon with the drugstore call to Marguerite White (for she was the mysterious woman at the other end of the line), followed by the gun-wielding episode that pushed Dieter over the edge and precipitated his flight.

In the end, the press tumbrel flattened everybody. A veiled woman swept into the district attorney's office with a story, never followed up, of a blackmail ring victimizing Brooklyn husbands. Both Dieter and Jeffe were fired from their jobs; Pearl Jeffe decided that a box of candied fruit sent her from Atlantic City, suspiciously close to Philadelphia, had been poisoned to silence her forever (lab tests declared the fruit harmless, and

Jeffe continued to speak out freely). In its wrap-up of the case, the *Brooklyn Daily Eagle* noted that the story had come to three ends: two men were jobless, "there are domestic difficulties in various households," and "the public has seen a fancy tragedy dwindle to a tawdry intrigue."

It was a story tailor-made for a week-long sensation in the 1920s. In 1899 public scandal had gravitated toward ostentatious wealth, with the handy excuse that satire put pretense and foolish money in their places. But by the Jazz Age and Prohibition everybody's dirty linen had acquired street value. Entertainment, commercialized and mass-marketed through national booking circuits for theater and vaudeville, made actors and actresses into commodities. The rise of the film industry magnified this, and stars' private lives became irresistible copy. And eventually the postwar boom spread money outward and downward, scattering it far enough that unprivileged families like the Dieters could afford luxuries—like their car—once available only to the upper middle classes and beyond. Further, Prohibition gave the majority of New Yorkers who flouted it the thrill of joining the stars, the smart set, and (once James J. Walker took office in 1925) even the mayor as outlaws in a small but gratifying way. Average people reached up for glamour, and glamour's publicity machine sometimes reached down to touch average people with its magic spark—occasionally burning them to a crisp in the process.

Indeed in its class dynamics, the Crescent Club scandal duplicates the story of George and Myrtle Wilson—the Queens gas station owner and his wife caught up in and destroyed by the narcissistic intrigues of the rich and the climbing in Fitzgerald's *The Great Gatsby*. The Dieters were a real-life version of the Wilsons: hardworking, timid, slow-witted, and sucked over their heads into the whirling, reckless hedonism of the era.

You Cannot Make Your Shimmy Shake on Tea: Prohibition Unleashed

What accounted for this democratization of pleasure? The early years of the new century had not, overall, been easy ones, either for the United States or for New York: both remained in the doldrums through the early 1920s. Financial panics recurred in 1900, 1901, and again in 1907. Statistics show a gradual rise in poverty from 1900 to 1910, then a sharp upsurge around 1915, just as the war in Europe was wrapping the country in a new shroud of pessimism. At the National Storage Company plant on

Black Tom Island in Jersey City, at 2:08 in the morning on July 31, 1916, two million pounds of explosives awaiting shipment to Europe blew up. The shockwave broke windows in Brooklyn and in Manhattan as far as 42nd Street; tremors of it could be felt as far as Pennsylvania, Maryland, and Connecticut.

Though the cause never came to light, New York was already in the throes of anti-German passion, and the blast aroused even more suspicion of a group that had traditionally been the city's most sober, comfortably settled, and admired immigrants. When the U.S. entered the war in 1917, New York became the chief port for both cargo and troops—1,656,000 soldiers passed through the city on their way to France, and fear understandably persisted: German submarines mined Sandy Hook (though the mines were detonated safely), and a series of mysterious fires broke out along the Brooklyn waterfront.

Nor, in the immediate aftermath of the Armistice, did morale improve much. The influenza epidemic struck in 1918, killing 12,562 New Yorkers. Between 1914 and 1919 the cost of living in the city soared by 79 percent. The specter of the Bolshevik revolution had begun haunting the city's capitalists, and there was still another unexplained explosion, this one on Wall Street at the stroke of noon on August 16, 1920. It killed 35 people and caused $3 million in property damage, but the perpetrators were never identified or caught, and the fear of bomb-throwing terrorists and anarchists spread. Only after a prolonged downturn in 1920 and 1921 did the economy take a turn for the better. Things were looking up by 1923, but in the early years of the Jazz Age, New York still harbored a large population ground down by the war and long-term economic malaise. Modest wage-earners like the Dieters remained anxious onlookers rather than participants in the boom.

Nor was all this postwar unhappiness financial in origin. Anti-liquor agitation had been gathering strength for years, an outgrowth of the anti-vice crusades of the 1800s. World War I austerity had led to restrictions on liquor sales, and transformed the temperance movement into a juggernaut. And though, when Prohibition went into effect in 1920, it did spur some rebellion, the governessy spirit embodied in the Volstead Act was not unpopular at first, and it pleased or at least cowed many Americans. The Dieters, for example: Catherine insisted that Richard was a teetotaler.

But New York on the whole welcomed Prohibition with scorn. When the Volstead Act took effect on the frigid night of January 16, 1920, the waiters at Maxim's wore pallbearer costumes, but the mock funeral they enacted was premature. Stanley Walker, city editor of the *Herald Tribune,* writing an epitaph on the dry decade, began his book *The Night Club Era* (1933) with a friend he called Filthy Phil, who stumbled into an upstairs bar on Nassau Street just before midnight on the 16th. "There was a bar, a bartender, and glasses and red liquor," Walker wrote. "Outside was the blizzard; inside, Phil was at home. Always, he said, there would be places like this. He became very drunk."

Filthy Phil was right about the survival of the bar. In 1919 the *Ziegfeld Follies* opened with a funeral march for an enormous whiskey bottle, and climaxed with an Irving Berlin song, "You Cannot Make Your Shimmy Shake on Tea," sung by Bert Williams (1874–1922), the *Follies'* star comic. The song predicted that the vanishing of whiskey and cognac would torpedo the era's signature sexy dance, the shimmy, with its lascivious shoulder- and torso-shaking (the name probably came from "shaking your chemise"). The shimmy, however, survived, and so did heavy drinking. New York, along with other big cities in the East and the Midwest, became a center of bootlegging, distilling, and imbibing, while blasé magazines like *The New Yorker, Vanity Fair,* and *Smart Set* heaped ridicule on bumbling government enforcers.

Disagreement among historians about the actual effect of Prohibition continues even now. Temperance advocates insisted drinking had fallen sharply after 1920, particularly among the lower classes, and the most reliable figures on alcohol consumption, compiled by W. J. Rorabaugh for his classic *The Alcoholic Republic* (1979), bear them out to some extent. Absolute consumption of alcohol in the U.S. stood at 2.4 gallons per capita in 1915, just before World War I anti-drinking laws took effect. Figures for Prohibition itself are of course unavailable (making something illegal also has the effect of making it officially invisible and therefore impossible to track and freer to operate on its own terms). Yet in 1935, after repeal, the per capita alcohol consumption had shrunk to 1.5 gallons.

To, say, Ella Boole, in 1923 president of the Women's Christian Temperance Union, Dieter would have been a typical heartening example of Prohibition's triumph: a low-paid worker now unable and thus no longer tempted to squander money on drink, instead taking advantage of rising prosperity to splurge on a family car. And though historians of alcohol use have increasingly accepted the view that Prohibition was a qualified success, the matter remains debatable.* The low alcohol consumption figure for 1935 comes only from legal suppliers, many of whom weren't yet up to full production; bootleggers were still operating to fill the void. And in any case the decline was nationwide, when compliance varied enormously by region, with the Midwest and rural America obedient, but the ethnically diverse big cities—notably Chicago, Detroit, Philadelphia, and New York—defiant.

Anti-Prohibitionists insisted drinking had actually increased in the wake of the Volstead Act; that the rise of bootlegging precipitated a mob crime wave, a galloping contempt for law, and a glamorization of antisocial behavior; that the new nightclubs and speakcasies, replacing the saloons of the pre–World War I era and operating outside the law, were far friendlier to vice than the old working-class haunts; and that higher liquor prices, by making alcohol into an emblem of sophistication, had encouraged once abstemious women to drink. Speakeasy chic reverberated in the amiable drunks of Hollywood (a 1930 study of 115 films noted that more than three quarters of them either showed or referred to alcohol, and that heroes were shown drinking more than three times as often as villains). In New York neither the governor, Al Smith, nor Congressman Fiorello La Guardia (1882–1947), nor the mayor, Jimmy Walker (who served until 1932), was sympathetic to the dry cause. "A reformer," Walker once said, "is a guy who rides through a sewer in a glass-bottomed boat."

By 1928 whiskey cost about one and a half times, gin five times, and beer six times what they had in 1916. With beer so expensive (and difficult to bootleg because of its bulk), by the 1930s hard liquor accounted for 75 percent of liquor sales. The beer drought does seem to have helped kill off the male working-class bars that so enraged the reformers. In 1915 there had been 10,058 licensed saloons in the city. All of them officially evaporated at midnight on January 16, 1920. But by the last years of Prohibition, somewhere between 9,000 and 32,000 speakeasies had replaced them.

---

* In a 1923 report, for example, the National Temperance Council took an optimistic line, but conceded that arrests in New York for intoxication had gone from 5,936 in 1920 to 6,237 in 1921, and to 8,578 in 1922. Admissions for alcoholism at Bellevue rose from 2,779 to 4,861 during the same two-year period. A 1991 study by Jeffrey Miron and Jeffrey Zwiebel questions claims that drinking either fell or rose sharply after 1920, contending that nationally alcohol consumption at first dropped by about a third, but then rose again toward pre-Prohibition levels over the course of the 1920s.

Rising prices also helped transform public drinking from a working-class vice into a middle- and upper-class pleasure. Because speakeasies, at least posh ones like the Mansion (at 27 West 51st Street) with its domed, circular, chandelier-hung bar, breathed an urbanity no saloon ever aspired to, they drew tyro lady drinkers, newly empowered by the vote and a dawning era of sexual liberation. As Alice-Leone Moats observed in her 1933 etiquette guide, *No Nice Girl Swears,* "once a woman has felt a brass rail under her instep, there can be no more needlepoint footstools for her." Proscription, rendering speakeasies officially invisible to the paid-off police, helped encourage the toppling of other taboos as well: gay male urban culture, for example, which, according to the historian George Chauncey, gained a strong foothold in theater-district bars during this period.

As Prohibition groaned toward demise, speakeasies got bolder and more various. In his 1935 novel *BUtterfield 8,* John O'Hara described, with an anatomist's precision, the places haunted by Gloria Wandrous, his Jazz Age heroine, and her adulterous businessman lover, Weston Liggett:

> They went to a lot of speakeasies, especially to the then new kind, as it was the beginning of the elaborate era. From serving furtive drinks of bad liquor disguised as demi-tasse the speakeasy had progressed to whole town houses, with uniformed pages and cigarette girls, a string orchestra and a four- or five-piece Negro band for dancing, free hors d'oeuvres, four and five bartenders, silver-plated keys and other souvenir-admittance tokens to regular patrons, expensive entertainment, Cordon Bleu chefs, engraved announcements in pretty good taste, intricate accounting systems and business machinery—all a very good, and because of the competition, necessary front for the picturesque and deadly business of supplying liquor at a huge financial profit.

Supper Clubs:
Benzine and White Rock at 3 a.m.

Indeed the 1920s constituted a high-water mark in New York history. The classic speakeasy may have been underwhelming—a door with a peephole on a back street, a goon who gave customers the once-over, a dim barroom serving God knew what. But illegality lent romance even to a grimy cellar, and O'Hara's description in *BUtterfield 8* wasn't fictional. The

Colony on 63rd Street did indeed serve its drinks in demitasse coffee cups (and stored the liquor in an elevator, which the owner sent up to the top floor of the building when any suspicious-looking customer appeared). At the Bath Club, in a three-story mansion at 35 West 53rd Street, the doorman wore a uniform with braided shoulders instead of a scowl; the dining room had a chamber orchestra, and the cellar stocked wines that actually were what their labels said they were. On Park Avenue the Kinvara employed a man in a gigantic overcoat stuffed with bottles, which he handed across to the bartender as orders came in; in the event of a raid he simply buttoned up the coat and walked out with the customers.

At times even club entrepreneurs sometimes wondered why their speakeasies, nightclubs, and dives (the terms were semi-synonymous) kept drawing customers in spite of mediocre food, high prices, and often sub-par alcohol. Barney Gallant (1884–1968), a Greenwich Village club owner, had an explanation. "Exclusiveness is the night club's great and only stock in trade," he once said. "Take this away and the glamour and romance and mystery are gone. The night club manager realizes that he must pander to the hidden and unconscious snobbery of the great majorities. It is because they make it so difficult of access that everybody is fighting to get into them." Thus the doorman (or in some cases woman) had a double function, protecting against raids but also pleasing customers who felt chic if they were let in. Even the criminal element, if it didn't get out of hand, added star power: bootlegging gangsters became part of the color of nightclub life, treated as famous, eccentric, and even lovable big-city characters.*

Nightclubs, despite their novelty, had ancestors, tracing back to the 1700s at least. Though the 18th-century Tammany Wigwam is mostly remembered as the nursery of the city's Tammany Hall political machine, its meetings, with their drinking rituals, music, getups, and licensed whoopee, anticipated the nightclub era, as did the concert saloons of the mid-1800s. And the lobster palaces of the 1890s—Shanley's, Rector's, Bustanoby's, and Murray's Roman Gardens—were in effect supper clubs, reaching their apogee after the theaters closed, when moneyed men showed up with young women (often chorus girls) for late-night orgies of champagne and

---

* Bootleggers weren't always thugs; they weren't even always male. In 1922, for example, when a biplane crashed in New York State, investigators crawling through the abandoned wreck found 150 unbroken bottles of whiskey from Canada and a powder puff, suggesting a woman pilot.

gluttony. Some of them—Bustanoby's and Rector's at least—even had doormen and silk ropes barring their entrances. Prohibition finished them off, though their spirit lives on today in theatrically decorated theme clubs and restaurants: their ropes are velvet instead of silk but the doormen are still formidable.

Prohibition-era clubs in part modeled themselves on a slightly earlier Manhattan venue, the roof gardens,* which featured broader and riskier acts than were typical of indoor stages at the time. Such fare blended easily with a modern Parisian import, cabaret (often traced back to the 1880s and the Chat Noir in Montmartre), with its distinctively naughty, topical, off-color character. The Volstead Act helped blend these and other elements into the 1920s boîte, from the beginning a fluid concept that could result in any number of arrangements. At theaters the customers watched a performance; at dance halls they danced; at bare-bones speakeasies they drank. They usually did all of these and little more at nightclubs, yet somehow the clubs acquired an aura, a mystique, a buzz of their own, became a permanent part of American memory, and survive today, though without the importance they had in the 1920s.

Clubs were often transient, run by gangsters and subject to serial shutdowns by police and federal Prohibition agents; they lacked the grandeur of places like Rector's. But they made up for it with personalities—most notably Mary Louise Cecelia Guinan (1884–1933), better known as "Tex" or "Texas," still remembered for her two favorite taglines, "Hello, suckers!" and "Give the little girl a big hand!" Born in Waco, she claimed she'd learned to ride horses and handle a six-shooter on a 50,000-acre ranch belonging to her family (her biographer, Louise Berliner, established that Tex's father, Mike Guinan, was a wholesale grocer, that the family lived in town, and that Texas got her education not in a corral but the Convent School of the Sacred Heart). She did know something about horses and guns, however: she scored her first big success in the silent movies as a girl gunslinger and rider in westerns: *The Gun Woman, South of Santa Fe, Little Miss Deputy*. Eventually she formed her own company and produced movies with eponymous titles like *Texas of the Mounted*.

---

* Late 19th- and early 20th-century roof gardens were high-rise versions of the old pleasure grounds like Vauxhall, well suited to warm-weather entertainment before the advent of air conditioning. Madison Square Garden's was the most famous, but there were many others, notably the Casino roof garden, which opened in 1833 across from the Metropolitan Opera House at Broadway and 39th Street.

In 1922 Guinan was in New York, just as bars and restaurants were either closing up or trying, within the law or outside, to swallow the pill of Prohibition. An established French restaurant, the Café des Beaux Arts, had just opened its new Gold Room at 80 West 40th Street (the studio building where the married William Randolph Hearst kept his bachelor apartment). Guinan, an opening night guest, got up to sing, dragged the composer Sigmund Romberg out of the audience to play the piano for her, then dragooned other celebrities into impromptu performances. The Gold Room was supposed to close at 1 a.m., but Guinan's manic energy kept the place open until 5:30. The management took her on as hostess, and she quickly perfected the strategy she stuck to for the rest of her career and the succession of popular nightclubs she either worked for or operated.

Her act wasn't one in any normal sense of the word. She sang a little; she managed and introduced the girls in the chorus line. But her real genius lay in an uncanny ability to hornswoggle customers into good humor, in part by telling them, over and over again, what a great time they were all having. Often a Guinan club would begin to fill up after ten, with a pall of bored glumness draping the tables, the customers sullenly draining their hip flasks (most nightclubs sold liquor, but allowed customers to bring their own supply because the biggest profits came from cover charges and extortionate prices* for setups).

Then, around one o'clock in the morning, Guinan would make her entrance, bellowing "Hello, suckers!" and distributing her trademark free noisemakers: red wooden clappers. She would summon the chorus girls to pass out cherries from a basket and kiss the men customers' blushing bald heads, deliver a few one-liners, then spot celebrities in the room and coax them to the stage or the dance floor for banter and an unrehearsed, sometimes humiliating, performance. Another stratagem was to invite displays of talent from the audience—amateur composers singing their songs, birdcall imitators, and, in a tribute to Charles Parkhurst's most famous moment, customers playing leapfrog with the dancers. She wisecracked freely about her outrageous prices, yet this seemed never to offend anyone, and indeed put the crowd in better humor.

Gangsters were everywhere in the nightclub industry, and Guinan became involved with them (though she avoided entanglement in the dark

* In 1928 at Guinan's Club Intime the cover charges started at $20, more than Richard Dieter's weekly salary in 1923; in typical 1920s clubs a bottle of White Rock seltzer sold for $1, and a pitcher of plain tap water for $2.

and violent side of their business). Larry Fay, hitherto a taxi racketeer and wanting a ticket to the high-hat world, hired Guinan as hostess for his El Fey Club, up a narrow stairway, then past a peephole and doorman, at 105 West 45th Street. The only sign on the front door was a swastika (Fay's good luck talisman, already being used as a Nazi symbol), but the place quickly drew crowds. El Fey served food; there were showgirls and drinks—passed bottle by bottle through a hole in the wall from the building next door, so liquor wouldn't be stored on the premises. But none of these made the club in any way distinctive. Guinan was El Fey's magnet, and it was here that she perfected the art that somehow transfigured Larry Fay, his lousy food, and horrible $25-a-bottle champagne (actually a blend of hard cider and raw alcohol) into ecstasy. In any case, gangsters like Fay were an asset as long as they kept their tempers—their presence made even tremble-chinned customers feel daring without exposing them to real danger.

But perhaps Guinan's shrewdest move was the canny marketing of her own fame. Walter Winchell (1897–1972), a columnist for the *New York Evening Graphic* beginning in 1924 and in 1929 for Hearst's tabloid *New York Mirror,* was an early habitué of Guinan's nightclubs, where he held court, depending on Guinan—who chattered to everyone and got many earfuls in return—for the gossip that eventually became his mainstay and turned him into the poison-tongued egomaniac he soon became. "She 'invented' the gossip column," he wrote, characteristically adding, "I mean the one for which I am best known."

Along with his crony and rival Mark Hellinger (1903–1947), who wrote for the *Daily News,* he became a Guinan regular: she reeled in the celebrities, the celebrities attracted more columnists, and the columnists drew still more celebrities. And all of these scheming careerists, flocking together in El Fey or the Club Intime or the Salon Royale (all Guinan sites), attracted a public eager to meet, overhear, or at least be seen in public among the famous, beautiful, and witty. Thus anyone who could scrape together the cover charge might rub elbows with celebrity and buy a chance for secondhand fame, should Winchell describe the scene in his column the next morning.

New Yorkers like the Dieters were too poor and too scared to reach for the vicarious celebrity of a hot club. But the echelon just above them—Ephraim Jeffe, C. Edwin Butz, Lola Robinson from Bala Cynwyd, and the nameless woman from Los Angeles with the Reno divorce—typified the bedrock clientele of the nightclubs. Young, flush, bored with their humdrum jobs, and hell-bent on high life or at least a facsimile, they may or may not have been as befuddled and joyless at their tables as cynics sometimes said most nightclubbers were. But the urge that propelled them past the doormen and reconciled them to the astronomical checks was powerful enough to overcome any small-hours second thoughts. If you were still carousing in a club at three, five, or seven in the morning, they seemed to think, it proved to everyone's satisfaction that you were enjoying yourself hugely.

Cocktails, the specialty of clubs and speakeasies that catered to the high-flying, were a pleasure rooted in necessity. While mixed drinks had a long history in the United States, dating back to the South's pre-bellum mint juleps, they'd typically been consumed as tonics or mixed up in preparation for travel; they weren't common in saloons. But bootleggers who bought up or stole industrial alcohol were often careless about removing the additives like iodine, benzine, and sulfuric acid, required by law to make it nauseating and in quantity poisonous. Gin, often homemade, could be a crude blend of juniper syrup, raw alcohol brewed in widely available one-gallon stills, and water from the bathtub (bottles were too tall to fill in a kitchen sink).

Sweet, thick, spicy, cold, hot, sometimes fatty, spiked with strong aromatic flavorings, cocktails masked the strange chemical tastes, and every bartender, at least at the more modish places, served a signature drink. Some, like the Old Fashioned and the Manhattan, survived their era and remain in recipe books, but others passed away with bootleg alcohol. Roma, the bartender at the 163 Club, specialized in something he called the Leroi, made of a raw egg yolk, curaçao, sloe gin, raspberry syrup, cream, and lemon juice. It is hard to imagine this drink as tastier than whatever varnish or solvent lurked in the sloe gin and curaçao, but there were many other recipes like it. They faded only in the 1930s, as good-quality distilled liquor reappeared, and cocktails worked at accentuating taste rather than concealing it.

Cocktails soon migrated from the nightclubs to the home, since they made for a relatively inexpensive and bother-free evening. The ice and the shaker, the lemons and the cherries and the bar sugar and the bitters, all lent a cocktail party more panache than could have come from simply handing the guest a glass of gin or scotch. It was also less time-consuming than the preparation of a full dinner, and didn't demand servants. According to Alice-Leone Moats, writing in 1933, "Cocktail parties have become the line of least resistance in entertaining," adding that "all you need is a case of synthetic gin and a tin of anchovy paste. The greater the number of the guests, the smaller and more airless the room, the stronger the gin, the more successful the party." Thus Prohibition, at least among the nightclub set, helped turn drinking from something one did in a bar or supper club to a mainstay—often a nightly one—of domestic ritual.

Jazz and the Jazz Age Night

Jazz was from the beginning night music—and at least a hint of its African ancestry was probably audible in New York as early as the 1700s, in the dirges sung by Africans bringing their dead to the Burial Ground at midnight. But black music made its definitive entry into American culture at the turn of the 20th century, and found its most congenial early home in the clubs and speakeasies of the 1920s, particularly (though not only) in Harlem. Jazz was a popular music of a power, vigor, and complexity unknown in the concert saloons, the minstrel shows, or the quavering comic ballad operas of the 18th century.

Even before World War I jazz was beginning to invigorate American popular music. Nothing illustrates this better than the Castle craze. Public dancing, thanks in part to the concert saloons, had suffered a bad reputation for decades. But then, in 1913, Vernon Castle (a reassuringly aristocratic-looking Englishman), and his even more reassuring all-American wife, Irene, put together an act that made ballroom dancing into a national craze. On the face of it, Vernon and Irene Castle were impeccable. "Our aim," they wrote, "is to uplift dancing, purify it, and place it before the public in its proper light. When this has been done we feel convinced that no objection can possibly be urged against it on the grounds of impropriety." And as dance instructors, they added a list of don'ts, prescient in that it forbade every hallmark of popular 1920s dances like the shimmy and the Charleston.

> Do not wriggle the shoulders.
> Do not shake the hips.
> Do not twist the body.
> Do not bounce the elbows.
> Do not pump the arms.

But in fact from the very beginning the Castles were steeped in jazz, and so were their dances. They owed—and gratefully attributed—much of their success to James Reese Europe (1881–1919), their black orchestra conductor and composer. In 1914, with his collaborator Ford Dabney, Europe wrote the "Dance Which Made Mr. & Mrs. Vernon Castle Famous," the "Castle Walk," a rhythmically complex number, with ragtime's felicitous blend of simple, formal bass lines and jazzy syncopation. Europe and the Castles formed an interracial collaboration, conducted so tactfully that it passed under the nation's fine-tuned race radar, and it marked a significant step up from the blackface and minstrel modes.

Jazz is a complex subject, and its American history a matter of controversy, but its basics aren't difficult to grasp. Jazz traces back in part to the African tradition of a strong beat that emerged boldly, from a drum, handclaps, sharp footfalls in dance, or (in work music) ax or hammer blows. Powerful beats served as anchors for complex cross rhythms, permitted any accompanying tune to move freely away from the beat without confusing the composition, and encouraged a looser, more flexible fit between rhythm and melody than was traditional in Western music. In classic early ragtime piano pieces by composers like Scott Joplin, rhythmic innovation took the form of syncopations so carefully composed that they sound measured, indeed stately. But by the 1920s, syncopation opened still further into full-fledged solo improvisation, which in the end became among the dominant hallmarks of jazz. Here Louis Armstrong (1901–1971) was a pioneer: he'd begun playing in New Orleans, moved to Chicago, and first reached New York in 1924.

Then too there was the blues. The blues is a technical thing (if one passes over its thematic link with grief and lament), characterized by its tendency to lower three notes in the scale: the third, the seventh, and sometimes the fifth (in practice jazz allows a wide variety of dipping, reaching, and sliding to achieve the effect). Blues also became associated with a particular song form, twelve measures long, in which the tune fills four bars, then cycles through a series of modulations before finally returning to its home key. These are technicalities, but in practice they helped transform the sound and feel of American popular music. Jazz and blues, infused into the simple popular song forms of the 1890s and 1910s, created a feeling of movement, of propulsion, and of inventiveness popular music had never had before.

Jazz has become so subsumed in American popular music that we've in many cases lost our awareness of it. Classic jazz was a craze in the 1920s and early 1930s: in his first breakthrough performance in New York, Louis Armstrong sang from the orchestra pit in Fats Waller's hit musical *Hot Chocolates* (1929), and was so popular that he moved up onto the stage and became part of the show. But in filtered form jazz was even more pervasive, in the Tin Pan Alley tunes that were playing everywhere, and it remains the bedrock of American popular music, whether swing, the more or less acoustic rock of the 1950s, or the electronically processed popular music that began arriving in the 1960s and has tended to blur the distinctions between pop genres. Under everything now heard lies the complex rhythm of jazz, and its free-form cohabitation between voice and accompaniment.

For wild partying, the Gilded Age's Cercle Français de l'Harmonie could hold its own with any later supper club or speakeasy. Yet it's hard to imagine such carousings accompanied, as they must often have been, by the popular music of the 1880s and 1890s, with its pristine harmonies, delicately shaped tunes, and sedate rhythms. It was equivalent to using Mendelssohn to accompany a demolition derby. The aspect of night that gloried in overturning taboos had to wait until jazz for a soundtrack that supported the loosened-up dancing and energized atmosphere that fit the democratic and polycentric abandon of 1920s nightlife.

WAY DOWNTOWN, WAY UPTOWN: GREENWICH VILLAGE AND HARLEM

Until the 1920s, the uptown drive of Broadway had given the city's nightlife its most consistent momentum. The first subway line, opened in 1904, ran up the East Side, then crossed 42nd Street to Long Acre (soon to be renamed Times) Square before turning northward up Broadway: its route thus confirmed and reinforced an established pattern, and theatrical activity did indeed surge into Times Square and the neighborhoods just above it. Curiously, though, the theaters—instead of continuing northward with the subway—stopped, planting themselves more or less permanently south of Columbus Circle. Upper Broadway's boom was fated to be largely residential.

With theatrical and nightclub Broadway more or less fixed in midtown, two nocturnal outposts rose to prominence in the 1920s: Harlem uptown and Greenwich Village downtown. Transport technology also played a part in these developments: both districts benefited from an expanding subway network. The first route to open joined Harlem to the rest of Manhattan, and in 1913, Seventh Avenue, which had ended at 11th Street, was extended southward to accommodate a subway tunnel for the new Lower West Side line that went into service in 1918 and still carries number 1 trains downtown to South Ferry.

But the rise of Harlem and Greenwich Village owed as much to their distinctive characters as their new accessibility. In the 1920s, rebellion went beyond the liquor laws, and spurred discontent not just with imposed standards, but the very idea of standardization itself. The spreading commercial consolidation of theater, the inherently homogenized mass-market character of movies, and a recording industry slowly turning music into a product buyable in every town of any size—all spurred a search for the new, the exotic, the edgy. Harlem and the Village appealed powerfully to anyone on the lookout for whatever the masses hadn't seen or couldn't abide.

In her classic 1935 study of Greenwich Village, Caroline Ware observed that in the late 1800s the neighborhood had, after a period of industrialization, seen some deterioration in its housing: a few tenement buildings had gone up in the Village by the 1890s. But many old brick row houses, still intact, had begun to fill with newly prosperous Italian and Irish Catholics, who left the East Side to join the few old American families who had held on in the neighborhood. They, along with the arrival of artists, writers, and intellectuals looking for affordable housing within reach of the rest of Manhattan, stabilized the market. And then the new subway drew developers, who cut up old three-story houses into moderately priced apartments.

Gerald W. McFarland, in his recent history *Inside Greenwich Village* (2001), gives a highly nuanced picture of the pre-nonconformist Village, when it was a neighborhood of multiple classes and mixed ethnicities, defined by black and immigrant churches like Zion A.M.E. (since torn down), St. Joseph's, and Our Lady of Pompeii (both still standing and active). Greenwich Village wasn't yet "America's Bohemia," the name awarded it by the national press and still deeply embedded in American lore. By most calculations that happened around 1913, when Buffalo-born Mabel Dodge, having acquired a rich husband, bought an apartment at 23 Fifth Avenue, painted it white, and started a salon that quickly became famous and engendered what McFarland calls the "selling-of-bohemia or 'faux bohemia' period that solidified the Village's popular reputation as a playground for unconventional spirits."

Dodge, thanks to what Lincoln Steffens called her "centralizing, magnetic social faculty," attracted virtually every major name in early 20th-century radicalism: Steffens himself, Gertrude Stein, John Reed, Carl Van Vechten, Max Weber, Walter Lippmann, Freud's American acolyte J. J. Brill, and dozens more. Her partner in building the salon was Hutchins Hapgood, still working for the Steffens-edited *Commercial Advertiser*. But Hapgood was no longer the curious city wanderer fascinated by hidden worlds like the Lower East Side ghetto and Yiddish theater. He had met another *Advertiser* writer, Neith Boyce (1872–1951); they fell in love while they were both living in separate digs near Washington Square. He bullied Boyce into an open marriage, about which both spent much of their later careers agonizing in print, with Hapgood's contributions often pompous compared to his earlier work.

But in the Village ethos achievement wasn't mandatory, and many who contributed to its aura are now remembered for nothing else—like the six otherwise obscure bohemians, who on a January night in 1917 sneaked into the innards of the Washington Square Arch, got drunk on wine, climbed out onto the roof, shot off a battery of cap pistols, and (uttering a proclamation that read, "Whereas, whereas, whereas, whereas, whereas . . .") declared Greenwich Village a free and independent republic. Sexual rebels—gay men and women, for instance—were a visible presence by the mid-1920s; they added atmosphere, and helped attract the tourist buses already nosing along the streets. But not all the residents were cultural insurgents: dwindling but still visible Irish and Italian settlements remained, and there was a continuing influx of newcomers with nine-to-five jobs but a thirst for liberty after hours.

Greenwich Village theaters were small in scale and avant-garde in mission: the Provincetown Playhouse, just off Washington Square, premiered pathbreaking plays like Edna St. Vincent Millay's *Aria da Capo* (1919) and Eugene O'Neill's *The Emperor Jones* (1920). But the tearooms were the distinctive Village social rendezvous. They'd appeared in the early bohemian years as cheap, informal hangouts, serving food, drinks, and social interaction to people who lived in kitchenless rooms or dank apartments. By the 1920s, tearooms were flourishing—Ware estimated there were typically forty at any given time, though they tended to be transient. Candles

were the trademark furnishing; artists, writers, and oddballs the most no-
ticeable customers, sometimes because they'd been paid or served free by
proprietors to create atmosphere.

Caroline Ware described a typical Prohibition-era tearoom, which she
called "Jo's." It was a crowded room in a tenement basement, crammed
with tables, chairs, and a piano. The customers included burned-out writers and artists, cadgers waylaying the unwary for handouts, young adult
drinkers (Jo's didn't serve alcohol but allowed people to bring it themselves), and those preferring ambidextrous sex—though they got poetry
readings, lectures, and scheduled discussions as a bonus. Among the regulars, Ware noted two rich southern girls who always got drunk and ended
up dancing with each other, a gay man who performed a burlesque pansy
act, and a contingent of women who either were or were trying to be lesbians (one woman became a joke because as soon as she'd had a few
drinks she'd begin dancing with men). An outsider at Jo's seeking a taste
of the American Left Bank (or was it Montmartre?) could also hope to be
invited to an impromptu "studio party" at somebody's apartment, another
Village tradition that over the course of the 1920s became iconic and fostered a "wild party" fad that spread nationwide.

By the mid-1920s, business entrepreneurs, sensing a market, had
begun to open Village cabarets aimed mainly at tourists, distinguished
from uptown nightclubs by the absence of seminude showgirls and the
presence of gimmicks. Don Dickerman, a promoter, made a specialty of
these. At his Pirate's Den on Christopher Street, customers descended a
gangplank into the club, where they were greeted by the six-foot, six-inch
Dickerman in buccaneer costume and entertained by a live parrot who
shrieked "Hello!" for hours on end. At his County Fair club on East 9th
Street the dance floor was surrounded by a picket fence. Customers unin-
terested in dancing could zoom around in an amusement-park-style kid-
die car concession that stayed open till 3 a.m.

Tourists gradually became the mainstay of Village nightlife, and historians have tried to trace the evolution of the neighborhood from quiet
backwater to countercultural ghetto to theme park. But disentangling
these stages is difficult. Village artists predated the 20th century: William
Dunlap—writer, painter, theater manager—settled in Greenwich Village
in search of cheap housing in the 1830s; New York University opened on
Washington Square in 1831. Even today, a significant population of
artists, writers, and media professionals remains there; the Irish and Ital-

ians are a diminished but still visible presence. What does seem permanent in Village life is this split personality, half garden of the soul, half tourist trap, with everything from delicatessens and restaurants to bars and apartment buildings constantly on the swing between invisibility (either chic or anti-chic) and the dread article in *Time Out* or the real estate page of the *New York Observer* that unleashes a shopping, munching, or nesting horde.

Prohibition too had its own character south of 14th Street. The sizable Irish population had always supported saloons, the Italians were adept winemakers, and by the mid-1920s, when enforcement grew lax, the neighborhood became not just a liquor emporium but a factory. Ware's research team of Columbia graduate students conducted a survey of 44 well-known liquor establishments in 1930, and found several types, with Italian restaurants the most stable and numerous. Restaurants evaded raids either by operating behind locked and unmarked doors, or serving wine and liquor only to known customers. The bars, also mostly neighborhood-owned, tended to cater to males and to retain the strong ethnic affinities traditional in the pre-Prohibition saloons. But in the mid-1920s heyday of Prohibition-flouting, almost every business in the neighborhood sold alcohol—groceries, cigar stores, barber shops, even shoeshine parlors.

Harlem, the northern nighttown of the 1920s, shared with Greenwich Village a transforming population influx in the decade before World War I. Developers had flooded the neighborhood with a plethora of new apartments in anticipation of the subway line under Lenox Avenue; then the economy shrank, making them hard to rent. In *When Harlem Was in Vogue* (1979), David Levering Lewis identifies Philip A. Payton as the black businessman who first filled up the vacancies with tenants willing to pay a $5 rent premium. By the 1920s East Harlem, from Eighth Avenue to the East River, had become predominantly black, and seemed filled with the fresh air of a new world—an unprecedented gathering of people with a common culture and shared aspirations, but denied a voice since the days of slavery.

Like Greenwich Village, Harlem soon formed an intellectual elite. It had a salon in the 1920s, run by A'Lelia Walker (1885–1931), the statuesque daughter of Madame C. J. Walker (1867–1919), who had become a millionaire manufacturing cosmetics in Indiana. But Harlem's leading, indeed dominant figure was W. E. B. Du Bois (1868–1963), who proposed the mission that inaugurated what's now called the Harlem Renaissance: the education of a "Talented Tenth" who would serve as the vanguard of a distinctive African-American culture. This was a departure from Booker T. Washington's assimilationist philosophy, and it fostered a remarkable generation of writers and intellectuals—Langston Hughes, James Weldon Johnson, Jean Toomer, Countee Cullen, Zora Neale Hurston. But it also opened a significant rift: many among the Talented Tenth were suspicious of "low" culture—particularly jazz. It was inseparable from Harlem nightlife, but it still bore a lowbrow reputation, and suggested embarrassing links to minstrel and blackface performance.

There were exceptions to this climate of suspicion, notably in James Weldon Johnson (1871–1938), who, despite credentials as a lawyer and newspaper publisher in Florida, won his earliest New York success as a popular composer (his best remembered song is "Under the Bamboo Tree"). Among Harlem's intellectual leaders, James Weldon Johnson was the most sympathetic to the vitality of its popular musical culture. Although in his 1930 history of Harlem's rise, *Black Manhattan*, Johnson emphasized its highbrow achievements, he also offered cautious praise of its nightlife. "To many, especially among colored people," Johnson wrote, "a Harlem night-club is a den of iniquity, where the Devil holds high revel. The fact is that the average night-club is as orderly as many a Sunday-school picnic." And his reading of the nightclub experience was, on balance, more benign than Barney Gallant's; he saw the Harlem clubs as harmless places where people "laugh and talk and they dance to the most exhilarating music. And they watch a first-rate revue. Certainly, there are infractions of the Volstead Act; but they also take place in the best-regulated houses. The larger clubs maintain permanent companies of performers and such clubs as Connie's Inn, the Cotton Club, and Small's Paradise put on revues that are often better than what may be seen in the theaters downtown." Johnson noted that the clubs had served as a training ground for performers in black Broadway shows like Eubie Blake's *Shuffle Along* (1921) or mixed-cast productions like the Jerome Kern and Oscar Hammerstein *Show Boat* (1927).

Hindsight, however, doesn't make the Harlem nightclub scene of the 1920s and 30s seem quite so benign. Charles Shaw's 1931 *Nightlife:* Vanity Fair*'s Guide to New York After Dark,* was an offshoot of the city's most chic magazine, but its section on Harlem will strike most modern readers with discomfort. Shaw dubbed the conglomeration of clubs on 133rd Street as

"Jungle Alley," and the entry on Connie's Inn (just around the corner on Seventh Avenue) describes it as "rambling, subterranean, and black as an African coal mine. Its clientele is wholly white and, for the most part, dressy; its decor pleasing; its ceiling low; its tables happily spaced." The even more famous Cotton Club, on Lenox Avenue, also kept black patrons out, but Shaw called it the "toniest" of the Harlem clubs, noted that Cab Calloway and Duke Ellington "serve up the syncopation," and praised the decor: "à la old plantation with log cabin overtones."

In reality, the Cotton Club was owned and run by a white mobster, Owney Madden; it had begun as the Club Deluxe, which seated almost 500 and was too big to succeed. Madden took it over because he wanted a Harlem base from which to sell his own brand of beer, Madden's No. 1, to white people. Black customers, unless they were light enough to pass, got no further than the sidewalk, from which they could watch the limousines of enthralled patrons like Lady Mountbatten. When Cab Calloway, one of the Cotton Club's headliners, decided to defect to the Plantation Club on Lenox Avenue at 126th Street, Madden's gang wrecked the place, throwing the bar out onto the sidewalk; Calloway stayed at the Cotton Club.

Midtown Manhattan also had a few clubs designed to give Harlem-style entertainment to a whites-only audience, and their ambience verged on the grotesque. In his 1925 restaurant guide, for example, George Chappell described the Plantation on Broadway at 52nd Street: "Lights gleam from a huge half watermelon and near the entrance a black Mammy cooks waffles in her log cabin. Across the dance floor runs a white picket fence. The performers are grade A, café-au-lait 'browns,' the darker hues not being favored." The tone in such descriptions offers more than a whiff of 19th-century writing about minstrel and blackface performance, yet wavers into respectful praise for musicians like Ellington and Calloway.

It was an uneasy stage in the long journey from the unreflective racism of the past toward the still nervous and incomplete tolerance of the present. *Vanity Fair*, at least, was aware enough to include some reference to interracial and even mainly black clubs, like the Savoy on Lenox Avenue, a third-floor ballroom open until two in the morning; most of the dancing couples were black. The 10 percent of the customers who were white were thus seeing part of the real rather than the packaged-for-visitors Harlem. Cecil Beaton, the English photographer, stage designer, and adoptive New Yorker, captured the ambivalence of this phenomenon. "The white man," he wrote in 1938, "visits Harlem with a sense of adventure, as if he is violating something undefinable, like a workman entering to demolish an ancient church."

Most of these were racial tourists, just as the customers of ersatz Greenwich Village hangouts like the County Fair were cultural tourists. But were they sneering at the foreign element they thought they'd plunged into? Conquering their fears of it? Or perhaps—as an optimistic mind might conclude—they were beginning to dismantle the barriers so steadily built up between races, classes, and modes of life from the earliest days of New Amsterdam.

NUDE AND STEWED:
THE STORY OF THE BATHTUB GIRL

Richard and Catherine Dieter were not the only people caught up unawares in the roar of the early 1920s, pinned like entomological exhibits to the smudged pages of the tabloids, then discarded. It was close to becoming a hackneyed theme, and there were three tabloids in New York to make headlines of it: the *Daily News,* Hearst's *Daily Mirror,* and Bernarr Macfadden's short-lived but accurately named *Evening Graphic.* In 1924 Walter Winchell had worked his way up from being a Texas Guinan groupie to a column in the *Graphic*; he moved on to the *Mirror* in 1929, having in essence invented celebrity gossip, a form that could suck in everybody, from the famous to the obscure. With a twist of bad or good luck, anybody might swerve into the celebrity maelstrom and end up in Winchell's column.

Maurine Watkins's *Chicago,** which first opened on Broadway at the end of 1926, was based on the life of a real woman named Beulah Annan, who, like the play's Roxie Hart, shot her lover in a Chicago flat, sweet-talked her husband, Albert, into paying for a high-priced lawyer, and became momentarily famous when she won acquittal. *Chicago's* satirical picture—of a revolving door of notoriety once reserved for the rich but now swallowing and spitting out everybody—seems to have struck a nerve newly sensitized in the 1920s.

---

* *Chicago* enjoyed an enduring afterlife as a 1927 silent film, a 1942 Ginger Rogers movie, *Roxie Hart,* and John Kander and Fred Ebb's 1975 musical version, revived first on Broadway in 1997 and then as an Academy Award–winning movie in 2002.

For the Dieters, fame was an accident and a disaster. But there were real-life Roxie Harts besides Beulah Annan. Some, like Peggy Hopkins Joyce (1893–1957), the doyenne of 1920s sex-bombs, worked their way into long-lived success. She was a half-educated and semiliterate barber's daughter from Berkley, Virginia. But by 1917, thanks to hard calculation and easy virtue, she'd married two wealthy men (one a millionaire) and had become a featured performer in the *Ziegfeld Follies*—this despite a cadaverous horse face and an apparently complete lack of talent except at roping gullible tycoons into wedlock.

Joyce was rumored to be the model for Lorelei Lee in Anita Loos's *Gentlemen Prefer Blondes* (1925), and her own memoirs, published five years afterward as *Men, Marriage, and Me,* sound too uncannily like Lorelei not to have been modeled in turn on her, with entries like "I have married Everett Archer and my name is no longer Margaret Upton it is Mrs. Everett Archer, wife of the Borax King's son, and I am so excited," or, "I lie awake sometimes in the morning or early afternoon because we do not rise generally before two and I look at Stanley in the other bed and, 'My God,' I think, 'whatever made me marry that?' Men look awful without a shave."

Joyce embroidered blithely in these memoirs (Constance Rosenblum, her biographer, discovered that the Borax King's son was actually Everette Archibald Jr., a traveling salesman for a Utah grocery wholesaler). But the fibs were in the end outdone by reality; by the mid-1920s Peggy Joyce's claylike face with its habitual expression—which suggests a seven-year-old trying to impersonate Marilyn Monroe—was everywhere. It was in the papers (often in connection with the reported $1.5 million in jewels she wore in theatrical performances) or in drugstore windows, plastered on ad placards for Korell night gloves and bleaching creams.

In July of 1923, she reached a pinnacle by starring in the first edition of *Earl Carroll's Vanities.* This was essentially a showgirl extravaganza in the Ziegfeld mold, but edgier and with much more exposed flesh than had yet been seen on Broadway. "When the Carroll cunning is rampant," the *World's* drama critic leeringly raved in 1925, the girls "conceal no assets." The high point of the 1923 *Vanities* was a "Furs" number, in which girls paraded in pelts of vast expense, with Peggy Hopkins Joyce appearing at the climax, dripping chinchilla. And Carroll's Theatre, at the corner of Seventh Avenue and 50th Street, was also a part of the performance: an Art Deco masterpiece. The lounge, with its swooping curves, molded surfaces, and sleek furnishings, has often been identified as the room that in-spired Hollywood's rendering of glamorous Manhattan nightlife.

The show proved a hit, still running in the fall when the Dieter case had its moment of fame, but the most dramatic event of the opening night happened after the curtain had fallen. Joyce returned to her dressing room to find a gift from a French ex-lover—a monkey named Bo Bo ("so adorable," Joyce cooed). Earl Carroll, however, soon joined the party. His interest in women was not merely businesslike; he was sexually insatiable, a corrupt-looking satyr with a long vulpine countenance whose chin, eyes, and nose seemed assembled from different faces, his hair receding from a domed forehead and drooping in a lank queue at the back of his neck. First the monkey jumped up onto Joyce's lap and ripped her negligée open. "Then Earl turned to me, his eyes casually undressing me further." Carroll fell on her ("Relax, Peggy, it's good for you") and they were soon entangled ("Oh God it was wonderful").

This enraged the monkey, which began screeching and caroming around the dressing room. He broke Joyce's cosmetic bottles, smashed a flowerpot, and hurled fruit from a gift basket at the lovers: an orange sailed narrowly past Carroll's head, thudded against the wall, and ex-ploded. Oblivious to the juice running down his face, Carroll labored on, stopping only when the monkey swung from a chandelier, ripped it from the ceiling, and landed on Carroll's back. That, at least, was Joyce's version of the story, and, true or not, it was a tale matched to the expectations of the period. The public adored feral cavortings in high places, so the stars complied in story if not always in reality. It made the city seem like a wild party that with luck anybody might crash.

Peggy Hopkins Joyce did become Earl Carroll's on-again, off-again mistress. And she was a survivor: neither the publicity nor the rigors of her life destroyed her, and though she eventually vanished from the pa-pers, she kept enough of her spoils to live well and survive until 1957. But even little-known chorus girls could, at least for a time, live in precarious luxury without necessarily descending to prostitution. They might attract a moneyed admirer and command—as had been the case even back in the 1890s at Rector's or Shanley's—an expensive after-theater supper. A small industry of all-night shoe, jewelry, and millinery stores grew up around Times Square, catering to momentarily flush chorus girls: their most prof-itable hours were just after the theaters let out and again after 3 a.m., when the nightclubs began to shut down. A girl would come on the arm of a date and ask if the earrings or hat she'd ordered were ready. The knowing shopkeeper would reply that it was, and the fawning escort would usually pay for it; this was more likely the later the visit and thus the drunker and/or more eager the boyfriend.

But not every new girl in nighttown enjoyed such modest luck; Theresa Daugelas was particularly unfortunate. Her story played itself out in 1926, a few months before the original *Chicago* opened on Broadway, and it echoes Roxie Hart's in atmosphere if not detail. Theresa Daugelas had been born on the West Side of Chicago on March 3, 1909, finished high school, and spent a year in a convent. But she, the convent, and her parents couldn't see eye to eye. She left home in her mid-teens and began a marginal existence in $3-a-night Chicago hotel rooms; she made her living as an artist's model, earning $1.50 to $2.50 a day under a series of made-up names.

She moved to New York in the late summer of 1925, lived for a while at the 44th Street Hotel, then boarded with a nurse and the nurse's husband. She began calling herself Joyce Hawley, and resumed her career, which went nowhere in particular until she met a man named Juan Tomadelli. He became, she said, her "closest friend," and he must indeed have seemed a glamorous prospect. He was Italian, sometimes called himself "Count" Tomadelli, and had invented—he claimed—a new kind of electric lightbulb that would burn for years on current stored within the bulb itself (he called it "Bottled Sunshine").

Tomadelli had impressive friends, and counted Earl Carroll among them. He got Hawley a one-time job as a lingerie mannequin in an Astor Hotel fashion show Carroll produced for a convention of silk manufacturers, and she netted $20 for modeling the lingerie over tights and a chemise. In 1925 the *Vanities* had overtaken its rivals, Ziegfeld's *Follies* and George White's *Scandals,* to become the most successful revue of its kind, and Hawley must have thought she'd met with a big break when Tomadelli and Carroll hired her once more, this time to appear at a party on the stage of the theater after a performance. Her job was to loll stark naked in a bathtub full of champagne into which the guests, male and female, were to dip their glasses. The pay was supposed to be $1,000 (about what Richard Dieter had earned at the Crescent Athletic Club in a year). She was only seventeen years old, but this fazed neither her nor Carroll.

The party was a publicity event, starting just after the Monday evening performance, at midnight on Tuesday, February 23, 1926. More than 500 people showed up, and the lobby, auditorium, and stage were soon crawling with celebrities: Peggy Hopkins Joyce, Walter Winchell, Condé Nast, and Vera, Countess of Cathcart, the most controversial noblewoman Britain could supply at short notice (she'd nearly been turned back at Ellis Island because of a recent divorce scandal). At 2 a.m., Harry K. Thaw arrived, still celebrating his 1924 release from the insane asylum to which he'd been sent after murdering Stanford White in 1906. Every guest had to sign a mock contract, promising to "forever discharge the Earl Carroll *Vanities* and the beauties contained therein from any and all claims . . . arising out of any injury or death, that might occur by reason of the said revel irrespective of how much injury or death may occur." The form also asked that guests "please remember this phone number—*TRafalgar 8200*"—the listing for the Frank Campbell Funeral Home.

The *Vanities* girls had removed their show costumes and were now circulating through the crowd in filmy chemises. There were two open bars, waiters distributing canapés, a Charleston contest, and a bathing suit competition. The event didn't even clearly violate Prohibition law, since the serving of alcohol gratis at private parties wasn't illegal, and an unwritten tabloid press code forbade reporters from publishing anything they'd seen as guests at a private function. Except for a mention of notable attendees, the *Vanities* party might have passed without comment, if it hadn't been for Hawley.

At four in the morning somebody wheeled a bathtub on a platform onto stage center, filled it with something that looked and tasted like champagne (Carroll insisted it was ginger ale), and placed a chair next to it. Joyce Hawley was by her own account so drunk at this point that she hardly knew what she was doing, but she stepped up to the tub clad in an orange chemise and shoes. She climbed the chair. Carroll asked someone to lend him a coat (some witnesses remembered it as green, but others insisted Peggy Hopkins Joyce had donated her sables). While Carroll held the coat up, Hawley stepped out of the shoes and chemise. In captions accompanying its cartoon rendering of the scene the *Daily Mirror* slavered that despite the sable camouflage "her bare limbs are visible to the gasping audience under the wrap [*sic*]" and then, "completely nude, the laughing Joyce is placed in the tub brimming with wine. She splashes gleefully about in the forbidden fluid under the bulging eyes of Harry Thaw, whose jaded nerves are given a new thrill."

The bottom-feeding *Evening Graphic* outdid even the *Mirror,* with its lurid specialty, a "Composograph" of the scene, showing Joyce in the tub, a chemise-clad Dorothy Knapp (a startlingly beautiful *Vanities* star and Carroll's current girlfriend) dancing a Charleston, Carroll and Thaw looking on in dirty delight. A Composograph was a collage of drawings and cropped photos assembled to re-create a scene, with head shots of the principals pasted in, usually at angles so freakish they suggested Grand Guignol horror, no matter how absurd or mundane the event. The bathtub Composograph shows a tub filled to the brim with wine spilling out over the lip and a Joyce Hawley posing languidly with head thrown back and four fingers just brushing her chin.

When Philip Payne, the managing editor of the *Daily Mirror* and a guest at the party, broke the traditional embargo and published a lurid front-page story in his paper, he created an uproar. Prohibition authorities, now in effect central headquarters for anti-vice prosecutions, hauled Earl Carroll before two federal grand juries. He testified that he'd served no alcohol at the party, and that the supposed champagne was in fact Canada Dry ginger ale. A technicality in the Volstead Act prohibited lying about the presence or absence of alcohol at a gathering, and the grand jury indicted Carroll for perjury. His trial opened on Thursday, May 20, 1926. Hawley appeared as a witness on the 25th, and she was mercurial under questioning: with Memorial Day approaching, she'd brought a cloth veterans' poppy with her, and as she alternately wept, flared out in anger, and begged that some remnant of her privacy be protected, she picked it to tatters.

She said she'd had a few drinks and then gone to the party with Tomadelli, whose elder-brotherly caution was not to switch drinks in mid-carouse. She retreated behind a curtain and instantly began to ignore his advice, downing four or five glasses of wine and accepting several more mixed drinks from Carroll's staff. She first put on a bathing suit, then the orange chemise. By 4 a.m., when Carroll intoned, "All right, baby," and led her onstage, she was completely drunk, though at that point everything still seemed jolly: "I was feeling good. I had to feel very good to do a thing like that." She remembered somebody pouring about an inch and a half of champagne into the tub. But at the very moment she slipped out of the orange chemise and sat in the puddle of cold, alcohol-fuming wine ("NUDE AND STEWED," said the *Daily News* headline), the reality of what she was doing hit her, and instantly the happy buzz locked into panic. She started sobbing. Carroll, unmoved, turned to the guests. "He told them to come up and have a drink of the beautiful liquor, or something like that. Men did come up. Carroll drank and so did lots of others. And then I cried some more."

It was never clear whether the guests were filling their glasses from whatever had been poured into the tub, or, less grossly, from a spigot that had been fitted onto a pipe coming up through the drain. Finally, they wheeled the tub offstage. Earl Carroll brusquely handed her two towels, "and bawled me out. He told me to keep my head or get out of the damn place." After that the story becomes confused. Hawley got none of her promised thousand dollars, though at some point over the next couple of days Carroll dangled a part in the *Vanities* in front of her. He seemed eager to get her out of town, ordering her off on a trip to Pittsburgh with Tomadelli.

Back in the 1800s Hawley's story, in the unlikely event it was told at all, would have been framed as the tragedy of a waif, swallowed up by the evils of the metropolis. Underneath this anxiety about the fate of innocence in the great city, the historian Alan Trachtenberg detected the huge influence on English-speaking Protestant culture of John Bunyan's *The Pilgrim's Progress*—and particularly of its city of peril and temptation, Vanity Fair:

> At this fair are all such merchandise sold as houses, lands, trades, places, honors, preferments, titles, countries, kingdoms, lusts, pleasures, and delights of all sorts, as whores, bawds, wives, husbands, children, masters, servants, lives, blood, bodies, souls, silver, gold, pearls, precious stones, and what not. And moreover, at this fair there is at all times to be seen jugglings, cheats, games, plays, fools, apes, knaves, and rogues, and that of all sorts. Here are to be seen too, and that for nothing, thefts, murders, adulteries, false-swearers, and that of a blood-red color.

The city as real-life Vanity Fair was a frequent theme in late 19th- and early 20th-century fiction with a New York center: Horatio Alger's *Ragged Dick,* Crane's *Maggie,* Lily Bart in Edith Wharton's *The House of Mirth,* Dreiser's *Sister Carrie,* Constance Fenimore Woolson's *Anne,* all told versions of the story against a New York background, though their characters set out for the city with very different kinds and degrees of innocence, and varied as to the social level from which their temptations came.

But by the 1920s Vanity Fair had undergone a revolution. It was now the name of perhaps the most urbane and morally adventurous magazine of the era; Condé Nast's *Vanity Fair* was the province of iconoclasts like Dorothy Parker, and used its name with conscious irony in the celebration of speakeasies, nightlife, jazz, and the modern impatience with the palpitating rhetoric of Victorian sensibility. No matter how salacious the *Herald* or the *Sun* or the *World* got in the 1800s, their prose still read like a page from Bulwer-Lytton. But by the 1920s, this style had been replaced by the leering and sneering slang of newspapermen like Walter Winchell at the *Daily Mirror,* or his counterpart at the *Daily News,* Mark Hellinger (who wrote of Joyce Hawley's appearance at the Earl Carroll trial that "she was a vision of blonde loveliness, all dressed up in a loose gown with a very short skirt. Many a juror will have a stiff neck this morning").

It was language whose very nastiness gave the night world of the revues, the supper clubs, and the speakeasies their louche allure. Histrionic sympathy for hapless types like Hawley had long since given way in the press to cold cynicism. Peggy Hopkins Joyce, the Fitzgeralds, and all the other amply publicized high livers of the 1920s embraced Vanity Fair and gloried in it, inspiring the belief that, if only you kept your composure, publicity was a goddess more likely to crown than kill you. The famous and unknown, rich and poor, black and white had always coursed through New York at night, but once the listened-to urban authorities had persuaded many of them it was a place of mortal peril. Now it was the stage for everybody's hoped-for apotheosis. The upright, hardworking country striver who wins millions in the city by truthfulness and hard work had been the model urban myth of the 19th century. But Peggy Hopkins Joyce was more famous than Ragged Dick had ever been, and real besides.

Joyce Hawley caught a brief glimpse of such possibilities. On the strength of her notoriety as the "Bathtub Girl" ("MODEL TAKES BATH IN WINE, CELEBRITIES DRINK TUB DRY" was the *Mirror's* story-breaking headline), she landed a job in the *Greenwich Village Follies,* hired a series of lawyers in a vain attempt to extract money from Carroll, and set off on a disastrous tour. She'd gamely admitted she couldn't act, sing, or dance but, after all, Peggy Hopkins Joyce couldn't either, and yet she'd triumphed in the *Vanities* and bagged millionaires anyway. Hawley had no such luck; her bookings were too small-time to be lucrative but just risqué enough to arouse the wrath of the provinces. The rakehells of the Pittsfield, Massachusetts, Boat Club invited her to dance for them, but the conservative members demanded and got a cancellation. She went on to Cincinnati, which quickly shut her act down. By the summer of 1926 she'd drifted back to Illinois, and was working in a cabaret in Morton Grove, just outside Chicago.

But trouble always seemed to follow her, and she whistled for it when it didn't. She got caught driving through traffic signals and smart-mouthed the police who arrested her. The town protested to the club owner, who fired her in July. On July 24, when a man outside her hotel hurled an insult at her, she rushed back to her room, took an overdose of sleeping powder, and instead of passing out or dying became hysterical and ended up in the hospital. Her father, Anthony Daugelas, said he thought the overdose was just "another advertising stunt"; she said she was "flat broke" and "scared to die."

She may have been a self-promoter, as her father charged, or a wayward innocent: her rough ride through fact-challenged tabloid exploitation makes it difficult to judge. She was, after all, also only seventeen, with an adolescent's mercurial temper and labile character. Maria and Harriet Trumbull, visiting from Connecticut in 1800, were on a broadly similar mission, but they'd been protected by an upper-middle-class security shield, impregnable even when they were far away from their Connecticut home. But throughout the 19th century other young women, poor and adrift, not content to sew or do factory work for a living, had been drawn into careers as performers, waiter girls, or prostitutes. As in the celebrated case of Helen Jewett, their lives became synonymous with poverty, disease, and horrible death.

But the 20th century was more case-hardened, and treated Hawley first with its tongue hanging out and finally with derision and dismissal. We don't know what happened to her; the suicide attempt in Morton Grove was the last New York heard of her. Like the Dieters and any number of others, she had stumbled or stridden into the urban dynamo, then vanished forever.

CHAPTER NINE

FROM POORHOUSE TO PENTHOUSE AND BACK

At Home, Homeless, and On the Town in the Mid-1930s

Times were terrible in the early fall of 1933, with the Great Depression at its worst and once irrepressible New York sagging under the weight. But at least one ray of hope emanated, though from an unlikely source: a gaping pit on Park Avenue between 40th and 41st Streets, left after the demolition of the old Belmont Hotel. Prohibition was finally in its death throes: 3.2 percent beer (though not wine and hard liquor) had become legal, and contractors were now replacing the Belmont debris with the city's first big post-Volstead beer garden. A rustic cedar fence surrounded the excavation; small tables and bright umbrellas filled most of the bottom; it opened in mid-September as the Belmont Bar.

Though its hayseed air sorted oddly with the urbane Grand Central neighborhood, customers instantly mobbed the Belmont, intoxicated as much by the novelty of drinking in full view of the street as by the alcohol. Once wine and distilled beverages became legal, a boom blessed the bars, if little else. By the summer of 1934, more than 5,000 liquor licenses had been issued to the city's hotels, clubs, and restaurants. Speakeasies clambered from their basements, descended from their old upper floors, and emerged from their back rooms. Boards and blackout curtains disappeared from windows, which had turned from a liability in dry New York to a legal requirement: post-Prohibition law demanded that places serving alcohol be visible from the street.

Moral reform, it seemed, had yielded to the grim times, and conceded the necessity of heel kicking. In early 1933, Rev. Charles Parkhurst was still alive,* but had abandoned his crusader's zeal, opposing Prohibition because it interfered with individual rights. He had concluded that anti-vice campaigns were fruitless: "You cannot legislate the human race into heaven," he told an interviewer, and reality bore him out. In the darkest days of the collapse there still were thousands of people in the theaters, bars, and nightclubs, throwing their money away either confidently or as a gesture of defiance.

But hardship inevitably darkened the night for those at the edge of the cliff or already off it. One such was an alcoholic out-of-work fireman named Michael Malloy, who became the protagonist in a series of bizarre but quintessentially Depression-era events that riveted New York during the winter of 1933 and unfolded in Anthony Marino's bar at 3804 Third Avenue (near 171st Street) in the Bronx. Malloy's story began when four other scrounging Marino's barflies took out an insurance policy on his life.

Mike Malloy had seemed to be teetering at the edge of a rummy's grave, but he held on interminably and indomitably (he was an ex-fireman, after all). The beneficiaries' patience wore thin, and they decided to stage a quick rubout. But when they undertook it, instead of a cheap funeral fol-lowed by a fat check, they found themselves embarked on a nightmare marathon. Their first stratagem seemed a sure thing: they lured Malloy into Marino's and fed him oysters pickled in denatured alcohol and poi-soned sardines. But without effect; Mike relished them and partied on. Then they tried to machine-gun him, but he escaped. They drugged him, doused him with water, stripped him to the waist and left him for dead on a bench in a Bronx park in the depth of winter; he woke up and returned to the bar. They ran over him three times with a car, but he walked away. Finally, in desperation, on the night of February 22, 1933, they plied him with drink until he passed out and then finished him off in a rented room with a dose of lighting gas.

But the insurance company launched an investigation as soon as the murderers filed their patently fishy claim (one of them, a 24-year-old un-

---

* Not for long, however. Parkhurst had, after the death of his wife two years before, grown frail and moved into his nephew's house outside Atlantic City. About three o'clock in the morning of September 8, 1933, the nephew's wife heard Parkhurst get up to go to the bathroom. The old man had taken to sleepwalking, and when she heard nothing further, she got up to investigate. But the bathroom was empty: Parkhurst had apparently crawled from the window onto a porch roof, ambled across it, and fallen sixteen feet to the sidewalk below, where she found him in a heap. He died in Atlantic City Hospital at 4:15 a.m.

dertaker named Anthony Pasqua, had overreached, demanding $600 for Malloy's funeral); the conspirators were quickly caught and condemned to die. On the evening of June 7, 1934, the rituals of American-style execution commenced. Two of the men kowtowed to the sadism of the last meal: Joseph Murphy had chicken, French fries, and fruit salad, while Daniel Kriesberger ate frogs' legs and a veal cutlet; they finished off with ice cream and coffee. But Anthony Pasqua had merely pushed the menu away, and because he was the most terrified of the prisoners (Sing Sing's doctor had been called in to determine this), he was killed first.

A sign over the death chamber door read "Silence." Shortly after 11 p.m., Pasqua, wearing slippers, a gray sweater, and rumpled flannel pants, shuffled in. Staring, he sat down in the electric chair and kissed a crucifix held for him by the prison's Catholic chaplain. The executioner, Robert Elliott, a bent and dwarfish figure, strapped him in, dipped the headpiece into a wooden bucket full of brine beside the chair, and placed it on the prisoner's head. Elliott walked out; Pasqua gripped the armrests so tightly his knuckles turned white, clinging to the last thing left to him of the human world. The warden, Lewis E. Lawes, opposed capital punishment, and though forced to witness the death, protested by turning his face to the wall. Elliott threw a switch in the adjoining room, and the equipment squealed an audible "kwe-e-e-" sound as it discharged three 2,000-volt, ten-ampere shocks through the prisoner's frame. Three minutes later—a short time to the observers, nobody knows how long to Anthony Pasqua—the undertaker was a small open-eyed corpse, dropped on a gurney and being wheeled out of the death chamber to his autopsy.

Everyone in this grim story was Depression flotsam (or, to be more morally exact, jetsam), from Malloy himself to Dr. Frank Manzella, the physician Pasqua bribed to issue a death certificate attesting that Malloy had died of pneumonia, to Marino's retarded bartender. New York murderers had been dying in the electric chair since 1890, and that horror was no novelty. But in the desperation of 1933, the lives of the small-time chiselers immured in the Death House seem like an allegory of the Depression, with thousands driven to self-destructive folly in the panic to survive, and ground down mercilessly in punishment for the consequences of their schemes.

In the end the only real beneficiary of Mike Malloy's death was an unemployed drifter on whom luck briefly smiled—Joseph Patrick Murray, a 31-year-old plasterer's helper who lived in a shantytown along the Hudson River near Twelfth Avenue and 133rd Street. On the night of February 7, 1933, he got drunk in a bar on East 127th Street, and remembered sloshing into a taxicab afterward. Everything else was blank until, at the corner of 145th Street and Austin Place in the Bronx, he somehow got run over by the cab he'd been riding in. Murray spent nearly two months in Lincoln Hospital with internal injuries, broken ribs, and a fractured shoulder. But a bystander at the accident took down the license number of the cab, and it turned out to belong to one of the gang who were trying to finish off Mike Malloy. At some desperate midpoint in their series of botched murder attempts, evidently, they'd decided to waylay another drunk, dispatch him, and pass the corpse off as Malloy's.

Joseph Murray, however, had been living so miserably that his ordeal seemed to him like a bonanza. Detained as a material witness in the Malloy case, he was remanded to the Bronx County jail, where he said he was overjoyed by the regular meals, the improvement in his general living conditions, and the $3 a day he earned while the case was pending. Murray was an even more saddening victim of the times: that he saw the grim Bronx jailhouse as a refuge shows how the lure of home gained more psychic power with every slip downward into a more precarious and marginal existence. Place didn't matter—the windy ledge in a corner of Central Park, a seedy bar in the Bronx or East Harlem, a shack made of billboards in a vacant lot or at the water's edge.

Both the homeless and those who tracked their lives saw all these alternatives as preferable to the city's shelters. Publicity photos of the places show neat rows of beds with blankets, immaculate linen, and feather pillows; the kitchens served oatmeal and coffee for breakfast and, for supper, ample bowls of beef stew with tomatoes, onions, carrots, turnips, and potatoes. But homeless men and women saw the reality—bullied as they were into line, herded into the dining hall to wolf down the stale bread and stringy, nearly meatless stew, then deloused and hosed down in a mass shower. A man's night in these shelters ended in a room with nearly 2,000 snoring, coughing, and yelling roommates, all in fumigated nightshirts with open sides. The air was thick with disinfectant and body odor.

Small wonder that the desire for a place of one's own had become so powerful. Whether one was homeless, dining at the Waldorf, or sitting at home in a modest Bronx apartment, a warm room, light, a program on the radio, or a Monopoly game on the parlor table seemed more desirable than perhaps domestic evenings ever had. Those who could afford to still went out. Those who walked the streets, jobless and out of contact with friends and families, dreamed of going home. And home they often found, in the unlikeliest of places.

HOOVERVILLE LULLABY

Even as economic conditions worsened by the week, the city began refurbishing Central Park to accommodate increasingly heavy usage, and to offer more recreation to the immigrant populations in the nearby neighborhoods. In the winter of 1930 workers began draining the old reservoir behind the Metropolitan Museum, between 81st and 84th Streets. Urban legend said it was full of fish, including a giant trout, and on night duty in February, with the reservoir nearly empty and the remaining water sheeted with ice, a park patrolman said he saw a colossal, snarling fish with whiskers lunging toward him. The police, firemen, and experts from the aquarium who converged on the scene, however, dredged up only four dead clams and a five-inch-long perch, which they transported upstate and released. By June, the reservoir's stone walls were being dismantled and a convoy of 400 dump trucks was filling it with dirt.

Plans were afoot for a lagoon, a wading pool for children, a bowling green, croquet courts, and gardens (eventually, the area became the Great Lawn). But more and more breadwinners—by no means always poor or working-class—were sputtering to the end of their resources and losing their homes. The unluckiest spent their days wandering, sitting glassy-eyed in libraries or railroad stations, gaping in despair at the few jobs posted in employment agency windows, begging at newsstands for a free look at the Help Wanted pages of the *Times*. At night they scrounged for cast-off vegetables in the Washington Market; at bedtime they might head for a Bowery flophouse if they had some money, or the public shelters (by 1931 the original lodging house and an annex, both on East 25th Street, had been swamped, and the city opened emergency quarters in the Municipal Ferry Terminal on Whitehall Street). In 1934 alone New York's shelters racked up a total of 2,230,086 overnight stays. Compared to these unappetizing choices, a shack began to seem desirable. In all the nation's great cities, shantytowns* sprang up along

---

* Of these the first and biggest was in St. Louis. By 1931 about 400 men and women had built several colonies of shacks alongside the Mississippi, defiantly christening them "Happyland," "Merryland," "Hoover Heights," and "Hooverville" (the name that stuck most durably to squatter encampments). They even appointed a mayor, Gus Smith.

river edges or in vacant tracts and brownfields. Hoovervilles, as they were often called, went nationwide. In New York there were many, but the best known and probably the most elaborate was in Central Park, on the site of the filled-in reservoir.

A disused tunnel ran underneath it, and six "hoboes," as virtually everyone called the homeless in the Depression, were living there by December 1930. They wandered by day, but returned faithfully every night to the old reservoir's abandoned caretaker cottage, from which a long flight of stairs led downward. The tunnel was narrow, but ten feet high, 150 feet long, and deep enough underground to stay warm all winter. A homeless man named John Broderick, the "Kingpin," ran the place, and the men had brought in chairs and tables and hung chintz curtains along the walls. Every evening, they pooled whatever they'd earned, found, or been given during the day to make up a communal meal.

Afterward they played cards to while away the time. The papers called the tunnel the "Park Club" or the "Little Casino" (the hoboes used red lanterns whose soft light did indeed resemble the nightclub glow, though this was probably unintentional; they took their furniture as they found it). While it wasn't clear from the newspaper accounts that the men living there had themselves coined such names, they certainly ran it as a club. Applicants had to be proposed by the members or introduced by the Kingpin, and went through a Saturday night initiation ritual, which— apparently on the analogy of the old Tammany Wigwam and the later Elks and the Moose—ended in an all-night binge.

In mid-December of 1930, however, the members got into an argument over the day's take and wound up brawling in the park. This attracted the police, who quickly discovered the tunnel. The next day—just in time for the holiday season—the police turned the group out and took axes to all their belongings. A photo in the *Mirror* belied the breezy rhetoric of the news reports: the furnishings were junk and the tunnel itself a dismal catacomb, funereal and claustrophobic.

But poverty was more powerful than the police. Almost as soon as the tunnel had been blocked, the homeless returned to the filled-in reservoir above. By the fall of 1932 they'd built seventeen structures there. Some were by any definition shacks, but others were far more. Three bricklayers, for example, had erected a twenty-foot-tall house with an inlaid tile roof; it was in front of a boulder, so they called it the Rockside Inn. Another place, made of egg and fruit crates, had an American flag and a sign that read "Radio City." The owner had a working radio, around which residents gathered every night: even in destitution, isolation, and homelessness, the lost held on to a 1930s version of home by the hearthside as an evening refuge.

At first the Parks Department allowed the settlement to remain and even gave it an official name—Hoover Valley. But permanent structures like the Rockside Inn challenged official tolerance until, on the night of September 21, 1932, the police—albeit professing reluctance—mounted a raid. They said the lack of sanitation and a water supply constituted a health hazard, and arrested 25 of the residents for vagrancy. They were quickly released, however, and came back to Hoover Valley for a sandwich party as soon as night court let out. New York had come to accept the squatter settlements; the press treated them with a blend of condescension and conscience-stricken sympathy.

Six hundred people lived in Brooklyn's Hoover City, near present-day Cadman Plaza in Brooklyn Heights. They drew water from a fire hydrant on nearby Columbia Street, matched Hoover Valley's ingenuity (one house consisted of two abandoned truck bodies), and also shared its yearning for domesticity, furnishing their shacks with tables, chairs, linoleum, carpets, and overstuffed sofas. Though predominantly male like most shantytowns, Hoover City even had a baby at one point, born there in the winter of 1933. Such settlements gave residents courage for the next day's struggle, even a place from which to bounce back: a few residents got jobs, moved out, and sold their digs for as much as $50.

Once, the importance of a stable home had been obscured in New York by the abundance of its nightlife, and perhaps even more by its long established and heady Mayday tradition of picking up and moving to a new apartment every year. But values changed with the Depression, and squatter settlements aroused so much sympathy that they became—rather unsettlingly—tourist sites. Edward Newhouse (1911–2002), in *You Can't Sleep Here,* his 1934 novel about squatter life based on firsthand experience, reports Sunday as the prime day for people and their children to gawk, as if the encampments were a zoo or circus* (the men of Newhouse's settlement retaliated by peering through the windows of apartment buildings across the street to watch women undress).

---

* A few residents profited by Hooverville tourism. A tightrope walker named Ralph Redfield, unable to make his living on the fading vaudeville circuits, set up a high wire in Hoover Valley and gave public performances.

Movies like *My Man Godfrey* (1936) and *Sullivan's Travels* (1941) sometimes sentimentalized Hooverville life, but the prevailing attitude was not always unreservedly compassionate. As Joan Crouse remarks in *The Homeless Transient in the Great Depression* (1986), Americans made careful distinctions in the newly aware 1930s. "Hobo" was supposed to be nonpejorative, denoting an involuntarily jobless man who would work whenever he could—as opposed to a "tramp" (who moved from place to place but avoided work), or a "bum" (a down-and-out alcoholic, waiting for death on the Bowery or other skid rows). But the distinctions blurred in practice; newspaper accounts vacillated between sympathy and condescension, and in popular usage a "hobo" seemed more often happy-go-lucky, winsome, and fundamentally irresponsible than an unwilling and struggling casualty of the national catastrophe.

Forgotten lives became a Depression theme, with writers, photographers, and filmmakers determined to ensure that the suffering and endurance of plain men and women would not pass unrecorded. As the historian William Stott has observed, this led to an upsurge of interest in documentaries of all genres; even novelists, though their points of view might be tendentious, found themselves drawn to fact.

In *You Can't Sleep Here,* Edward Newhouse does see his fictional Hooverville through a left-wing lens, and does evince fellow feeling with the dispossessed, but that doesn't weaken his credentials as an experienced observer; to some extent he had lived the life he wrote about. Newhouse first saw New York as a twelve-year-old Hungarian immigrant named Ede Ujhazi, arriving on the steamship *Berengaria* in November 1923, just as Richard Dieter's life splattered like a broken egg across the front pages of the tabloids. After school and a semester at City College, Newhouse set out to live as a hobo, drifting south to Galveston, then to Los Angeles and Seattle, finally returning to New York, where he wrote for the *New Masses* and became a sports columnist for the communist *Daily Worker.* "I guess I must have done about twenty thousand miles," he later recalled, "on the usual assortment of empties, tankers, and refrigerator cars. For a long time I was very proud of that."

As research for *You Can't Sleep Here,* he spent three weeks living in a Queens Hooverville. The result was a proletarian novel typical of its genre: the hero suffers joblessness, poverty, and homelessness, then undergoes a leftward conversion to become an organizer and leader of the dispossessed. Newhouse's vision thus may have erred on the side of attributing more insight to his homeless characters than the reality of poverty always allowed them. But he had seen firsthand lives whose desperation scared most people, and the voice of his hero, describing his first homeless night in the bushes on a high ledge in southwest Central Park, rings true.

> As darkness came on the signs of the Park Central, Fisk Tires and General Motors lit up, and the vapors glowed white over Broadway. Beside the attraction that New York's customs held for me, . . . natural grandeur . . . faded rapidly. I took pride in the great evenly spaced heaps of stone and my eyes roved affectionately over the throbbing avenues.
>
> When a light goes out its image continues to show before you and it was on a like principle that I enjoyed this sight of New York around me.

The Fisk sign was a poignant touch: it rose high above the West 50s, seeming to float alone in the sky; in it a boy in a nightshirt is carrying a Fisk tire over his shoulder and a lit candle in his hand. The caption read, "Time to Re-Tire."

Lost people were coming into their own as part of the urban picture, as they never had before, even in the 1920s. It was an irreversible 20th-century trend: lives that had once passed and ended in shadow, written about sentimentally or bombastically if at all, now began to emerge in realistic (if not always real) detail. Whether the portraiture was accurate or not, it had made its way into the national imagination.

SKYSCRAPER NOCTURNE

Yet life on the skids was only one exhibit in the Depression's cluttered museum of images.

True, in 1933, according to the U.S. census, about a million and a half of the country's more than 125 million people were homeless. In New York in 1934 about 6,100 showed up at the municipal shelters every day, and no one knew how many more turned to private charity, shantytowns, or the parks, alleys, and vacant lots. Tens of thousands, surely. Yet however they troubled the conscience, they were a small minority: in 1930 New York had 6,930,446 people, double the number in 1900. Most still had roofs over their heads. Seventeenth-century housing had almost vanished from the scene,* but the housed could choose from an anthology of architectural history: 18th-century and Federal-era row houses, tenements built during every epoch of low-cost housing reform, even a few surviving Fifth Avenue mansions. But now the cynosure of Manhattan living was the apartment in the sky, an inevitable product of New York's skyscraper frenzy. By the late 1920s, apartment towers were common on the West and East Sides, and had appeared even among the narrow streets and row houses of Greenwich Village.

With the Depression filling these buildings became a struggle, but for anyone able to afford the rent, they offered a night-centered vision of city life unimaginable even as recently as a decade before. A view, for example. A high apartment with a commanding vista of Manhattan, the rivers, or Central Park, meant independence, power, and sophistication. In a glassed-in penthouse or out on the terrace, one became part of the view oneself, seen and envied from the streets or other skyscrapers (ideally with the watchers a little too far away for satisfying voyeurism). And in deluxe buildings some of this cachet rubbed off even on viewless low-floor or air-shaft units.

Initially, at least, such buildings were planned to attract the rich, like the Dakota, built in 1884 by Edward Severin Clark. During the 1920s and 30s, Emery Roth (1871–1948) was perhaps the best-known figure in a remarkably talented group of high-rise hotel and apartment architects. One of his masterpieces, the Beresford (built in 1929 on Central Park West), is sumptuous from the turrets crowning it to the immense duplex apartments below. The D line units, for example, typically consist of an entry vestibule, a 30-foot-long gallery, a 19-by-30-foot living room with fireplace, three bedrooms, a library, a kitchen huge by Manhattan standards (21 feet long), three maids' bedrooms, and three baths.

As Elizabeth Hawes remarks in her 1993 book, *New York, New York: How the Apartment House Transformed the Life of the City (1869–1930)*, the earliest luxury builders—determined to distinguish their projects from the tenements that had formerly dominated apartment life—at first de-

---

* The Wyckoff house on Clarendon Road in Brooklyn is probably the city's earliest surviving house, dating from 1652 and now a museum. In 1934 the John Schenck house, probably built between 1675 and 1677, was still standing at the corner of Avenue U and East 63rd Street in Brooklyn, and you could take a Flatbush Avenue streetcar to see it. In 1953 it was dismantled, then reassembled at the Brooklyn Museum in 1964, where it's still on view today.

signed lavish and massive islands of self-sufficiency reminiscent of mansion life: the spacious rooms, the accommodations for many servants and large-scale food preparation, all suggest they were meant not as trim temporary lodgings but compact palaces, joined together in a fortress of permanency and wealth.

Later buildings, while imitating the Beresford and its ilk and promoting themselves as luxury dwellings, really aimed to attract the upper middle class and its junior division: moneyless young people beginning their first jobs in the city, who doubled and tripled up to afford the rents. In the best of these buildings, apartments marked a high point in American domestic architecture. Their designs reflected a new concept of what home was supposed to be—neither a retreat for a family shutting out the world nor a fully staffed stackable mansion, but a pied-à-terre, a place to make forays from and come back to at all hours of the day and night. Such apartments weren't castles; rather, they were quiet corners in one's real home, the city. It was among the keener ironies of the Depression that having a secure apartment lured the occupant into nights out while having none made one long to curl up in whatever shelter one had.

By 1900 about half of middle-class New Yorkers lived in apartments, and that ushered in a future of towers scaled to fit moderate budgets. By 1930, dozens had appeared on the Upper East and West Sides. To their tenants they spelled success and luxury, but a 1928 survey of recent apartment constructions aptly described them as "intended for low rental tenants of good class." Emery Roth and his firm designed many such apartments, adapting some of the inspiration he'd brought to landmarks like the Beresford to a series of more modest high-rises he and his firm designed for Bing & Bing, one of the leading large-scale residential developers of the era.

By the late 1920s such projects already dotted midtown and were making a beachhead in Greenwich Village: Bing & Bing, prompted by the building of the Eighth Avenue subway line, quietly assembled 75 small properties in the neighborhood to erect a series of apartment towers. In 1930, another architect, Henry Mandel, followed a similar strategy in building London Terrace—at the time the largest residential complex ever built, sprawling across the city block between Ninth and Tenth Avenues from 23rd Street to 24th Street. Mandel's plan was remarkably inventive in creating small-apartment amenities, both obvious and subtle.

A one-bedroom unit in the E line, for example, is a compact 900 square feet. The main rooms are spacious—the living room is fourteen by twenty feet with a working fireplace; the bedroom thirteen by seventeen. Short but cleverly arranged branching corridors suggest the apartment is larger than it is. Adopting a device characteristic of Emery Roth, Mandel also added an ample entrance foyer to create an impression of spaciousness. Economy shows only where it's least obvious, in the tiny kitchen, the absence of spare rooms, and the lack of a separate dining room or alcove.

Such apartments were rich in cozy detail that hinted luxury, often with Tudor and Georgian accents—beamed ceilings, fireplaces, spacious closets with mirrors in their doors. Yet the details were restrained enough to permit a tenant to create his or her own decorative look. In the end, the effect not just of the best but even of the good prewar luxury apartment was to set up a pleasing contrast between one's twentieth-story nest and the pulse of nightlife quickening in the streets, restaurants, theaters, and bars. Hence the galley kitchens (better suited to breakfast, lunch, snacks, and light entertaining than dinner) and the high level of service usually included in one's lease. Such buildings catered to tenants who expected to spend most of their time out, working during the day and entertaining themselves at night.

This trend flowered in the so-called apartment hotel, designed to combine the privacy of a flat with hotel-style service. The *Architectural Record* opined that the merger of apartment and hotel was "a hybrid forged in the hothouse of New York demand," and traced it to a growing tendency for the well-off to spend summers in the country, returning to New York only seasonally, and also to a large population of renters who wanted to be relieved of housekeeping: single men and women, and businesspeople who wanted a permanent base in New York but didn't live there all the time.*

An illustration of the concept can be seen in a 57-story apartment tower proposed in 1929 (though never built) by Fred French (1883–1936). It was to go up in French's Tudor City development, near the East River, and it was to be the tallest residential structure in the world. But otherwise it resembled many similar buildings already in service both in Tudor City and across Manhattan—a collection of one- and two-room

---

* A more cynical reason has been advanced for the popularity of apartment hotels. Because they were treated for legal purposes as apartment buildings, they were exempt from the much more stringent building and safety codes that applied to hotels, thus allowing a developer to put up a building that could attract the profitable transient trade while cutting construction costs.

apartments, "each provided with serving pantries and electrical refrigeration." Refrigerators were a new attraction, clearly intended—given the absence of full kitchens—for snack storage, ice, and (both before and after Prohibition) mixers. Meals were catered: French's new tower was to have a main dining room and seven banquet rooms for parties. The serving pantries, also typical in apartment hotels, were staging areas for meals ordered up from the central kitchen. The plan also called for a "gymnasium, billiard rooms, bowling alleys, beauty shops, a swimming pool 150 feet long and thirty feet wide, and indoor handball and squash courts."

Life in a residential tower or apartment hotel was supposed to be a celebration of glittering and self-confident transience, carried on almost as if to ward off the specter of homelessness. In the late 1920s, and even more in the straitened 1930s, housing was plentiful. During this period *The New Yorker* ran a regular "New Apartments" feature every April, and it was as much a heady celebration of high-rise life as a real estate service feature. In 1928 the writer, Marcia Davenport, praised the views from high-floor terraces at then far-uptown 21 East 90th Street. "The Central Park Reservoir lies just to the west of this site, and the vista of swan-decked water, green grass and trees, hazy skyline, and the red-roofed stucco bungalow atop the Kahn mansion, is too extraordinary for words. . . . They tell me the view of the reservoir by moonlight from one of these Cozy Roofs for Two is . . . well, after all, this is solely about new apartments" (by 1932 the reservoir had been drained and the view was dominated by Hoover Valley's Rockside Inn).

Other buildings featured in the April 1928 *New Yorker* columns included budget Park Avenue apartments with fake fireplaces "for those whose desire for a Park Avenue address is only exceeded by their inability to pay Park Avenue prices" (they rented for as little as $175 a month). An apartment hotel for women at 18 Gramercy Park South had maple-furnished rooms, a roof garden, a restaurant, and an economical rent of $15 a week, though it was a ladies-only hotel, and—as Davenport put it—you couldn't "squabble in it behind your own closed door, with your brother." The Alrae, at 37 East 64th Street, had a lobby fountain and a restaurant with stained glass windows; the apartments had serving pantries with electric refrigerators, and could be leased with or without furniture: "all that is necessary for a happy life is to move in and start non-housekeeping."

The sheer self-indulgence of life in an apartment hotel became part of

Manhattan lore. But the footloose life of the hotel dweller was not always fancy-free, and a dark James Thurber short story, "One Is a Wanderer," first published in *The New Yorker* on March 2, 1935, describes a lost middle-aged Manhattanite prowling the streets on a slushy winter evening:

> The dark was coming quickly down, the dark of a February Sunday evening, and that vaguely perturbed him. He didn't want to go "home," though, and get out of it. It would be gloomy and close in his hotel room, and his soiled shirts would be piled on the floor of the closet where he had been flinging them for weeks. . . .

The main character sits in the lobby, drinking brandy and asking if he's received any messages (he hasn't). Restless, he wanders out again, wondering whether to drop in on his few married and housekeeping friends (he decides not to). Finally after moping from bar to bar, he shuffles, drunk and maudlin, back to his hotel. It's three o'clock Monday morning; nothing awaits him but the night clerk and an absence of messages.

Gloria Wandrous, the doomed demimondaine of John O'Hara's *BUtterfield 8,* is a female and more graphic version of Thurber's wanderer. Her story begins in a posh but empty apartment in which she wakes up stark naked after a night of drunken sex and from which she escapes clad only in a stolen fur coat. In a befogged marathon that takes her through a succession of bars, nightclubs, and half-occupied apartments (some luxurious, some seedy), she stumbles her way to death on the Boston-bound steamer in which she's escaping from Manhattan. In *BUtterfield 8,* apartments are the corridors through which reckless hedonists rush toward oblivion. As the book's leading betrayed wife puts it, "Wasn't it a good thing New York meant living in an apartment? How awful if it had been a house, a real home? Ah, but if it had been anywhere else he wouldn't have brought that girl here, to an apartment. No, it wasn't so good that New York meant living in an apartment."

DECO DEFIANCE:
GOOD TIMES IN HARD TIMES

They may have been going to hell while they did it, but real-life Gloria Wandrouses still went out, Depression or not. Despite all the dislocations, the city remained dynamic. Police sirens first wailed on the streets in December 1929. Planes flew overhead, dragging electric advertising signs through the sky. In Times Square and the surrounding blocks, the sputtering of incandescent bulbs had been joined by a new technology that enriched the visual mix: the swooping, multicolored radiance of neon. The first neon sign in the square—a speeding Willys-Overland automobile—had gone up in 1924. And by the 1930s the new liquid light was everywhere.

Going to a speakeasy had always been a paradoxically self-publicizing act: knowing where the bars were and how to get past the doorman into a good one placed you among the cognoscenti, and visible as such at least to the other patrons. But in the Depression clubbing and bar-hopping were routine activities, as unremarkable as shopping or museum-going. Whiskey and gin had to wait on the state-by-state voting needed to reverse the Prohibition amendment, but Utah finally made up the magic number when it voted for repeal on December 5, 1933. The triumphant homecoming of the hard stuff helped lighten the darkest years of the Depression. The quality of alcohol improved markedly,* but the more visible consequence was a major improvement in the look and feel of new night resorts. Desperate for work in the wake of the collapsing apartment, hotel, and office building markets, architects and decorators turned to a rising demand for entertainment spaces, and the 1930s saw a remarkable series of clubs, restaurants, cocktail lounges, and theaters.

These often were, despite the economic conditions, more suave, dashing, and brilliant than anything to be seen in the prosperous days of Prohibition. The neon in the streets—at the time it seemed to thrill with modernity, like radio—also made its way into the new interiors in the indirect cove lighting beloved by Deco architectural designers, casting a subdued yet emphatic glow across ceilings, walls, and mirrors, accenting the bold curves and planes beloved of the style. Radio City Music Hall was the epitome of Art Deco, a Depression-modern reinvention of the movie palace, and a sharp turn away from the fairy castles and faux Alhambras of the late 1920s. The Music Hall's marquee, with its forthright neon block lettering, signaled the even more revolutionary interior, freed from the heavy bric-a-brac of old-style opulence, and a confident celebration of futurity. The auditorium was a composition of clean lines, with concentric arches that seemed to leap upward like a sunrise over—

---

* High liquor taxes, however, kept some bootleggers in business after repeal.

while warmly covering—the declivity of the orchestra rake. It was a celebration of space that fought the constant straitening and shrinking of everything else.

Helen Morgan, the singer and nightclub diva who had nearly as many brushes with Prohibition enforcement as Texas Guinan, moved in 1936 into a new club, the House of Morgan on Madison Avenue and 54th Street. It featured a circular bar, deep banquettes, chrome trim, and walls of faceted mirrors, white leather, and burgundy plush. The Persian Room at the Plaza, the Rainbow Room on the 65th floor of the RCA Building in Rockefeller Center, and the huge International Casino at the corner of Broadway and 44th Street, all offered comparable modernist grandeur. The Casino was—much like the lounge in the Earl Carroll Theatre—a Hollywood fantasy of nightlife, with its levitating staircases, curved balcony, revolving dance floor, and moving bandstand. Both its roof and plate glass windows could be retracted for dancing under the stars.

Other destinations, though less visually stunning than the Persian or Rainbow Rooms, became famous less for their decor than for their celebrities, like Charles Berns and Jack Kriendler's "21" Club, El Morocco (known as Elmo's to regulars, with its trademark blue and white zebra-striped banquettes), and Sherman Billingsley's Stork Club, perhaps the best known nightclub in New York history. Like his mentor, Tex Guinan (who had died in 1933), Billingsley danced with the mob, but where Guinan's was a careful gavotte, Billingsley's was a steamy tango. He'd opened his first speakeasy on West 58th Street in 1929, kept it going with the aid of one gangster, Frank Costello, and prospered under another, Owney Madden (also impresario of the Cotton Club) and his associates Big Bill Dwyer and Frenchy De Mange. Guinan—eager to boost Billingsley because he too was a westerner by birth—persuaded Walter Winchell to plug the Stork Club, which in a *Daily Mirror* column he dubbed "New York's New Yorkiest place on W. 58th." In the late 1930s and 1940s the Stork became Winchell's professional home, the drinking club and war room from which he consolidated his power.

In contrast with the expendable clubs of the 1920s, the leading destinations of the 1930s were survivors. The Stork Club lasted until 1965; El Morocco into the 1990s; "21" and the Rainbow Room remain in business today. To keep such places going in bad times, the proprietors relied on publicity and "Café Society." The latter was an endlessly malleable concept, current since the 1920s, and impossible to fix to any particular group, though it vaguely suggested money (or at least a show of it), leisure, and conspicuousness; it was also synonymous with rootless apartment dwellers in the Gloria Wandrous mold. To Billingsley and El Morocco's John Perona, Café Society meant celebrities, the surviving rich, and wannabes drawn by unrelenting plugs from Broadway columnists like Winchell.

Robert Sylvester, in his first-person retrospective of 1930s nightlife, *No Cover Charge* (1956), recalled that both Billingsley and Perona admitted and served college kids for free, because their attractiveness drew paying customers. "Nobody wants anything from you, these kids were assured. Why, the house photographer will even take your picture, sitting there with your girl in your nice dinner jacket, and we'll even have your picture printed in the newspapers. No charge for that, either." The owners also hoped that after fledging from their Ivy-League suburbs in New Haven or Princeton they'd return as free-spending youthful tycoons.

There were cheaper thrills for those who couldn't afford the top clubs or get in for free. One could visit "The Spanish Inquisition" at 1670 Broadway, an exhibit of nineteen oil paintings of torture by Franz Vinck: it stayed open till one in the morning. Or—also open till one—a midtown night court at 316 West 54th Street. The Chrysler Building observatory, 1,046 feet above Grand Central Station, stayed open until ten, and the Empire State Building (as it does today) until midnight, its swift elevators speeding tourists up into the midst of a skyline alive with light and so endless one could see it bending away over the curvature of the earth.

Eighty-five cents bought a ticket to Roseland, the soft-drinks-only dance hall. Once in you could find another customer to dance with, or hire someone: there were men for women and women for men. The spectacle, excitement, and affordability of Roseland pleased people who worked for a living, though Café Society types sneered. Cecil Beaton described it in the mid-1930s as "a low ceilinged inferno of noise," with dark amber lighting, a loud swing band, and a clientele whom he described as "salesgirls, typists, telephone operators, manicurists and models. . . . The smell of double-mint gum permeates the atmosphere of this monstrous paradise of black, orange and pink."

Or, one could dilute depression, personal or general, by a quick escape from the city. In 1934 the Hudson Night Line steamer sailed every evening for Albany and Troy from the foot of Christopher Street in the Village. The line was in receivership at the time, but it was a bargain—

$2.25 round-trip, with an outside-facing stateroom for as little as an additional dollar. The night line had acquired a raunchy reputation—it became the butt of one-liners in the routines of burlesque comedians—as an economical way to conduct a quickie affair; failing that, the bar offered a safe all-night binge that could be slept off on the return sail. If, however you were after truly all-American night entertainment, on whose wholesomeness even the Bible Belt could agree, you were out of luck until June 15, 1939, when Brooklyn played New York's first night baseball game under the lights at Ebbets Field (the Dodgers lost 6–0, perhaps because the opposing team, Cincinnati, had played the first night baseball game back in 1935).

MRS. MURPHY'S PARLOR:
RADIO NIGHTS AND EVENINGS AT
HOME IN THE DEPRESSION

Whether home was an East Side aerie or a few nailed-together signboards, there were some evening experiences that drew together people whom the extremities of the Depression had sundered. Listening to the radio, for instance, formed at least an imagined bond among those who survived unscathed, those who economized out of fear or necessity, and the lost, down even to the hoboes gathered at "Radio City" in Central Park's Hoover Valley.

Broadcasting permeated the nights of the 1930s, both the herald and the engine of a general return of nightlife from the streets and city lights to the home. Even poverty didn't exclude one: the average price of a radio receiver had shrunk from $90 in 1930 to $47 in 1932, when, despite rocketing unemployment, four million sets were sold. Programming had grown into a profitable national industry based on advertising. WEAF had originally been set up in lower Manhattan as an experiment by AT&T, with studios on Walker Street and a transmitter on West Street. But in 1926, the Radio Corporation of America—a descendant of Guglielmo Marconi's American Marconi Company—had bought WEAF (and also WJZ, a Westinghouse station that had first gone on the air in 1921), in order to form the first broadcast network, with programming to be distributed nationally over AT&T's landlines.

Soon the business grew from a speculative oddity to a booming entertainment medium with a multiplying audience and profits. The National

Broadcasting Company went on the air with a radio gala on November 15, 1926. It began at 8 p.m., lasted till midnight, and may have reached as many as twelve million listeners. By early 1927 the new company had split into two divisions: the "Red" network, which evolved into today's NBC, and the "Blue" web, later ABC. Soon money was flowing in from advertiser-sponsored programs like the *Maxwell House Hour*, the *Palmolive Hour*, and the *General Motors Family Party*. And by the 1930s the radio was as much the center of a family evening as television would be in the 1950s.

Thanks to the advent of nighttime photography, we can see not only the home cocoon of the 1930s and the metropolis beyond, but the invisible threads that joined them. *Metropolis: An American City in Photographs*, a 1934 book by Agnes Rogers, Frederick Lewis Allen, and Edward M. Weyer,* was a montage of text photographs that froze—as wouldn't have been technologically possible only a few years before—a parade of spontaneous moments, indoors or on the street, by day or night, capturing 24 hours of the city's life. Particularly evocative is the book's rendering of its 1934 winter nightfall. As the darkness closes in, photographs show the sun setting over Manhattan, commuters on the 5:27 from Grand Central, cocktail hour first on a penthouse terrace, then in a Washington Square restaurant where the most expensive meals are $1.25, and finally in a cocktail-less tenement kitchen on Henry Street, where a family socializes between the stove and the bathtub, with dinner already underway.

In *Metropolis*, the evening finds its center not in a nightclub or theater but in a modest apartment in the Fordham section of the Bronx, somewhere off the Grand Concourse. In the photograph two women sit side by side in matching armchairs. Mrs. Murphy—the ample, matronly looking woman in a print dress who dominates the picture—sits half-smiling, her head resting on her hand, in an attitude of placid contemplation. The light from a floor lamp behind her chair falls onto the unregarded newspaper in her lap. Her sister, a few feet to her right, rests her feet on an ottoman and hunches forward, pince-nez in place, concentrating on a tatting project.

In the dead center of the room, against the wall and behind the work basket, is a console radio. Both women are listening; the dial indicates

---

* Weyer took most of the photographs; Rogers and Allen (an historian of 20th-century America and later the editor of *Harper's* magazine) supplied them with linking text.

they're tuned to WEAF, now the flagship station of the national NBC network. The program tonight is a concert broadcast from a sweeping new Art Deco studio auditorium in Rockefeller Center's 70-story RCA building, opened in 1933. Thanks to the ranging photographers of *Metropolis,* there is also a companion photo of the studio at Radio City, with an orchestra and singer on the stage, and a live audience, seated in sleek arcs of raked seats. Most network radio originated in New York, and the most carefully produced and expensive programs went on at night, when the audience was at its biggest and therefore attractive to sponsors.

If you were listening from the Bronx like Mrs. Murphy, the aura of instant long-distance travel dissipated: the shows weren't sparking through a thousand miles of darkness, but merely vaulting across the Harlem River from a Manhattan midtown whose towers could be seen from any number of midrise apartments. But in the hinterlands, the mere announcement that a program was originating from Rockefeller Plaza conjured up a visual fantasy of urbanity and modernity that surely added to the impact of a live broadcast: the excitement of the studio in mid-Manhattan, with its artists, its buzzing audience, its imagined dozens of alert but silent technicians, and the arcane humming equipment that levitated it and sped the dazzle of theater into the air. For someone sitting at home, whether in the Bronx or Biloxi, it was an imaginary flight into the heart of Manhattan, a chance to feel its pulse in real time.

NBC and CBS, the two major networks, both forbade recorded programming till well into the 1940s: the thrill of radio, after all, was that listeners were hearing the words or music the very second they were spoken or sung (radio performers, expected to give duplicate broadcasts hours later for West Coast audiences, often passed the time between shows in a cluster of midtown bars that grew up to cater to them). Nothing like evening radio entertainment had been known before—a virtual night, which offered a version of a nightclub's immediacy, a sense of live nationwide communion joining stars with strangers, linking a vibrant audience in a Manhattan skyscraper to quiet homes and apartments like Mrs. Murphy's.

Nevertheless, the programs weren't quite as edgy as the technology or Radio City's architecture. In fact they were distinctly middlebrow and domestic, and would be instantly recognizable to anyone familiar with TV fare in the 1950s or 1960s. One week in February 1934 was typical. There were fifteen-minute situation comedies, like Gertrude Berg's *The Goldbergs,* about a family of Jewish immigrants in New York, and a peren-

nial favorite that survived into the television era. Its competitor on WOR
was the syndicated *Detectives Black and Blue*. Its heroes, Jim Black and
Frank Blue, were bumbling correspondence school sleuths from Duluth.
Music was a mainstay of the hours from 8 p.m. onward, and ranged from
serious (NBC aired Serge Koussevitzky leading the Boston Symphony on
Friday evening) to Paul Whiteman at 11:30 on Tuesday, followed by
Rudy Vallee at midnight, and a half hour of "Hillbilly Music" on Wednes-
day. Eddie Cantor, Ed Wynn, Jack Benny, and Fred Allen did comic skits;
Maude Adams acted on Friday in a half-hour version of *Peter Pan*. Public
service programming included *A Republican Looks at the New Deal*, with
Senator David Reed of Pennsylvania.

Most of these performers remain familiar names, many of their programs still available as recordings avidly traded by nostalgic radio buffs.
Others, though, have been largely forgotten, like the darling of 1930s
radio, NBC's Jessica Dragonette (1905–1980). Her shrieking soprano,
preserved in recordings, suggests what an average, less-than-classic evening
of 1930s radio probably sounded like. Dragonette specialized in showy
pieces that gave a soupçon of the concert hall and sugar shocks by the
ladleful. Schubert's setting of the "Ave Maria" was one of her most popular
renditions. The fans who loved it ignored a lack of vocal control that
turns her singing into an avalanche of squeals and rasps, disconcertingly
punctuated by an occasional tone of bloodless purity, like a note struck on
a tuning fork. Her voice may have been erratic, but her appearance (she
was beautiful, yet diminutive and rabbity enough to look unthreatening),
combined with her reputation (she was a devout Catholic), carried her
through. A listener poll conducted by *Radio Guide* magazine crowned her
as the "Queen of Radio for 1935."

Only the voice, of course, came over the radio, but the medium's virtue,
as has endlessly been remarked, was its effect on the imagination. Listeners
seemed to feel by instinct that Dragonette's pure being had materialized in
their living rooms along with her voice, and what came out of the console
felt wholesome, uplifting, and comforting. Bing Crosby—though endowed,
unlike Dragonette, with an extraordinary voice and impeccable musician-
ship—also exuded an air of calming approachability that lulled listeners as
much as his singing did. The best radio performers created a species of vocal
apparition that affected listeners even more viscerally than a face-to-face
performance.

Thus even well-educated radio listeners, when they came to New York and sat in a studio audience to watch their favorite programs being broadcast, repeatedly expressed dismay at the shattering of their illusions. Of course many of them knew that sound effects were faked, that the pirate was growling threats in a cardigan and loafers, and that the wailing baby was a full-grown woman who floated from studio to studio and did the sound as a profitable specialty. Yet they were taken aback, even angered, when they saw it firsthand. "To me the studio visit was a revelation; a disappointment," an upstate photographer told the *Times* in 1934, "for it robbed me of the pleasures my imagination had given me. Broadcasting is wonderful, I admit, but for me I prefer broadcasting fortified by imagination, as it carries me into the delightful realm of mentally pictured scenes that are most enjoyable."

Imagination bore a high value during the Depression; it was, after all, a cost-free way to fill up the vacant time left by vanishing work. Even in the earliest days following the crash, hard-hit employers had begun giving their employees two-day weekends to soften the blow of lower pay and less work. By 1933 and 1934, the National Recovery Administration institutionalized this as social policy, and the changes stuck even after the abolition of the NRA at the end of 1935. By 1937, according to a survey by the National Industrial Conference Board, about half the American working population had won two-day weekends; in New York businesses had been particularly quick to give office workers a Saturday holiday. And finally, in 1938, with the passage after much debate of the national Wage and Hour Act, the forty-hour workweek became the national norm (until, that is, the reemergence of sweatshop hours in the 1980s and 1990s).

With money scarce, cheap home diversions loomed large, and radio wasn't the only choice. Bridge became a craze, and among the pictures in *Metropolis* is a middle-class foursome rapt in a game. Then too there was Monopoly. Supposedly it was the invention of an out-of-work engineer, Charles Darrow; Parker Brothers, after some hesitation, put it on the market in 1935. It was soon selling at the rate of 200,000 every week, and Darrow became a Depression millionaire who spent the rest of his life taking photographs and tending orchids. In truth, Monopoly was based on The Landlord's Game, invented in 1904 by a Maryland woman named Lizzie Magie, and meant not to glorify greed but rather to show how pernicious it was. Still, few Americans needed a lesson on the perils of too much money in the mid-1930s, and wealth was a pleasure all the more tasty because it could so often be enjoyed only vicariously.

While homebodies' minds gloated over game board riches or spun in the gale coming out of their radio speakers, the city kept up its crowds and traffic and noise—without them the radio studios would have conveyed no metropolitan illusion to fortify their music or drama. While Mrs. Murphy and her sister sat at home, a *Metropolis* photograph showed Times Square crowded that night in spite of a winter rain. Electric bulbs and neon tubes flow, bubble, and fizz everywhere (in life they were now flashing faster than ever before, so they could be digested by people in speeding cars). Three flaring billboards at the northern end of the square advertised Chevrolet, Squibb, and Coca-Cola. *Forgotten Men,* a documentary of battle films from World War I, was playing at the Criterion Theatre (where it made a considerable success, running from February 5 to April 1, 1934). The Palace Theatre on the north end of the square was still playing vaudeville.

Once the evening radio programs were over, and Mrs. Murphy probably in bed, the book's pictures moved toward—and finally past—midnight, as the hours see a succession of pleasures and burnt-out ends. A married couple on the Astoria subway line, heading home from a movie as their baby sucks its evening bottle. A gathering at a commodious Manhattan apartment. Dancers onstage in Harlem. And, at four in the morning, in the shadows of a near-empty nightclub, a dark-haired man at a table with a nearly naked hostess hovering nearby. In the photo it doesn't look much like a relationship, but it was the kind of live encounter that television and radio would never replace. If you walk after midnight into a topless bar near Times Square you can see the same tableau today, will surely be able to see it ten years from today, and quite probably in a hundred as well.

HARLEM ONCE MORE:
FLOOR SHOW AT THE CLUB BARRON, 1937

In 1933 the Independent Subway's A Train went into service, running nonstop from 59th Street to 125th Street. The new line put Harlem a mere five minutes' ride from Columbus Circle (and inspired "Take the A Train," the Billy Strayhorn tune made famous by Duke Ellington). Uptown clubs were a bargain, even by Roseland standards: the Savoy Ballroom at 140th Street and Lenox Avenue hired perhaps the best bands in the city and charged only 65 cents on weekdays. But the halcyon days of Harlem were over. Robberies and knifings began getting enough publicity to frighten customers away, and in 1932, when a mob war erupted between Vincent "Mad Dog" Coll and Dutch Schultz, Harlem became embroiled in it. March of that year saw a Chicago-style gangland shooting in front of Connie's Inn, run by Conrad "Connie" Immerman and his brother George—whom the gangsters kidnapped in an attempt to extort money from Connie's own mob backers, the Owney Madden gang.

Nineteen thirty-five marked a crisis, with a major March race riot that resulted in one death and hundreds of arrests and injuries; whatever the trigger, its root causes seem to have been poverty, hunger, and long-simmering anger at race discrimination, especially envenomed by the white invasions into the economy and culture of Harlem that had begun by the mid-1920s, if not earlier. Connie's Inn decamped downtown to Broadway and 48th Street and soon folded; the Cotton Club, fleeing in its footsteps, took over Connie's midtown premises in 1936, but managed to linger on only until 1940.

Still, Harlem hadn't died. Many clubs remained, including Small's Paradise, which survived into the 1960s. And we can snatch an intimate glimpse of this post-golden-age Harlem from 1937 in the Club Barron, in a basement on West 134th Street near Seventh Avenue. It had been one of the first Harlem nightspots, opened in 1915 as the Exclusive Club by Barron Wilkins, a black entrepreneur who kept the place popular by opening it only to paid members, many of whom were rich, white, and politically connected friends of Wilkins himself. Barron's was one of the earliest great jazz venues (Duke Ellington played there in the early 1920s and remembered it fondly), and was also integrated from the beginning, with a reputation as a club for black and white rich men, where hundred-dollar bills flew freely. From the beginning strip acts were part of its allure.

For Barron Wilkins, the fame ended in May 1925, when a man named Julius Miller (nicknamed "Yellow Charleston" Miller) shot him dead on the sidewalk outside the club in a gambling argument; Miller died in the Sing Sing electric chair on September 17, 1925. The Club Barron lost its fame after that, but it was still apparently open in the late 1930s as a small strip venue—about twenty feet wide, with a one-table-deep balcony—a layout identical to the typical concert saloon of the 19th century.

Aaron Siskind (1903–1991) captured an evening in this unpromising space in 1937. Siskind, a grammar school teacher in the New York City public schools from 1926 until 1947, took up photography during the Depression and became an active member of the New York Workers' Film and Photo League, as well as its successor group, the New York Photo League. During his association with the Photo League, Siskind took, between 1932 and 1940, a remarkable collection of pictures now known as the Harlem Document, in which he caught Harlem streetscapes, children and adults, apartments both comfortable and threadbare, and—in one series taken at Barron's in 1937—a Harlem floor show.

Siskind was driven by an omnivorous interest in New York as he saw it. Unlike many Photo League members, Siskind shied away from using photography mainly as a political tool or a personalized vision.* The Barron's series shows this passion for objectivity. Siskind took most of the pictures from one side of the balcony about eight feet above the hardwood dance floor stage, and probably from underneath a photographer's veil using a heavy stationary camera on a tripod, with the stage lighting providing enough illumination for his exposures. It was a cumbersome process, but he could take a new exposure every minute or so, which allowed him to capture the continuity of the scene.

In 1937 Club Barron looks shoddy. Vaguely Moorish stepped arches crown the bays between the columns that support the balcony, with decorative moldings that never quite meet up; a naked lightbulb hangs over the musicians; wires droop from spotlights mounted in each corner of the room. The beat-up upright piano wheeled in for solos has been daubed with paint; crude bas-relief faces and stencils with Art-Deco-cum-Sahara motifs decorate the walls. Siskind's photographs show the dark-skinned musicians on the band platform, the café-au-lait entertainers in front of them, and a ringside table around which four restless white customers fidget. As one shot follows another, their beverage glasses fill, empty, and change places on the checkered tablecloth, which scrunches up and then unwrinkles again. Behind this foursome, and barely discernible, are another table in the shadows (at which a woman is sometimes sitting), a staircase to the balcony, and a narrow gangway from which the singer and dancers make their entrances or watch each other's acts.

In several photographs a light-skinned and heavily made-up boy soloist—

* This distinguished him from photographers like Arthur Fellig (1899–1968), better known as Weegee. His images of slain gangsters, society dames grotesque in evening plumage, street drifters, and accident victims have influenced the vision of nighttime New York in the popular mind from the latter years of the Depression through World War II and into the 1950s.

about six feet tall, with huge wide-set eyes, long lashes, and wavy hair, wearing high-rise pleated trousers and a bolero jacket—sings at a microphone. His arms spread in a wide gesture, he dangles a handkerchief from his right hand, then crushes it in his fist while his left hand brushes the studio piano. In other shots he reappears in a bikini bottom with a grass skirt whisking around his waist, more streamers whirling at his calves just above the knee. Two nearly naked girls dance with him, then all three take a bow. Mouth half smiling, eyes luminous but vacant, the man looks off to the right. One woman, topless, has her right hand on his chest; the other circles his waist.

A third woman—actually a seventeen-year-old girl, as Siskind later remembered—undulates back and forth in a striptease, while the customers watch intently. She casts her eyes down, languorously posing or slinking along in sidewise, knee-dipping strides. Her face is remote and her body disengaged, as if she were a pull toy being yanked along by the ostrich-plume fan and cape, which seem to move with a power of their own. Then the dress, cape, and fan disappear, leaving a G-string and a Salomé veil that she caresses and leans into as if it were alive. Her mother, Siskind also remembered, came to the club every night, forbade her to talk with anyone, and draped her with a blanket as soon as she walked off the stage. And indeed she may be the woman who can be made out, sitting in the shadows just offstage in several shots.

At the ringside table, the customers seem to have ants in their pants. The heavyset man keeps shifting his chair into different positions, turning backward to watch people come and go through the gangway, listening (or not) to the song with a faraway smile, hunching himself up to within reaching distance of the stripper, who draws from him an expression half like a parent beaming at a toddler, half like the toddler itself about to burst into tears. Both men are wearing suits, in which they look pleased with themselves but not at home. The two women sit nearer the dance floor, both wearing the top-heavy hats popular in the 1930s. One leans back against a column, her face mostly turned away from the show. Only once—when the hula-skirted dancer bends his partner backward in a tango clinch—does she grin and hunch forward, cigarette in hand.

The second woman, closer to the stage, is restless in a somber dress and matching flowered hat. She pitches in mood from seeming catatonia to rage. Her body is heavy but her face witchlike—sharpening into a chin whose point seems to aim inward at her dark dress. Listening to the song she stares at the floor, abstracted. During the striptease, she turns her body away, but twists her head back to glower, not at the dancer's face or body but her feet. Once, staring upward toward the balcony, she nails Siskind (or at least his camera) with a threatening glare. When the three dancers embrace for what looks like a curtain call, she's seen in profile, slumped backward, chin resting on her arm, staring at them as if she were working out a theorem.

Everyone in the picture, watcher or performer, seems distracted, looking out on the club with the fractured attention of an alien, mind still mostly taken up by the world just abandoned. Only once is there a visible human interchange, and it's in the background—two musicians on the band platform, crouching together to talk while the soloist and his accompanist perform on the dance floor. Are all the pole-axed looks a trace of 1937—a hard year in which to have fun? Do they illuminate the momentary fugue state both performers and audiences enter in the midst of entertainment, a suspension between reality and playacting, a dark wood between real life and a rescuing vision?

Night photography, an invaluable tool for recovering the history of the era, raises such questions yet doesn't answer them, even in pictures as seemingly transparent as Siskind's. Flashbulbs, perfected in 1929, were first sold in the United States in 1930 (where they were apparently first used to photograph Herbert Hoover signing the Unemployment Relief Bill). Large-aperture lenses, flooding the camera with light, further shortened exposure times. Such breakthroughs circumvented the trade tricks once necessary to photograph urban night scenes. In the old-fashioned long exposures anything that moved simply disappeared—pedestrians, vehicles, horses. The 1911 *Cassell's Cyclopaedia of Photography* advised that exposure time could be cut by a third if the pavement was covered with rainwater, but even so the lens had to be left open so long to register an image that movement slipped through the frame invisibly.

Thus William A. Fraser's night photograph of Columbus Circle, *A Wet Night* (taken in 1897 or 1898), may owe its moody atmosphere as much to technological necessity as to the photographer's vision. Is the rain-glazed street there because Fraser fell in love with its mystery, or just because he needed it to make a picture at all? And when progress in night photography rendered such stratagems unnecessary, why did photographs in the Weegee vein continue to dwell on the stark contrast of murky black, wet pavement, blurring streetlights, and the harsh rectangles of lit windows? Is this a real modernist vision, or only the repetition of a useful photographer's trick?

So the photographic record creates as much mystery as it dissolves. In one respect photography is by nature ill-suited to night: it needs light, hence has to destroy darkness in order to represent it. Yet at the same time the momentary materialization of figures and faces from shadow into fleeting illumination is the night in its essence. Technology has over the course of modern history transformed, even to some extent created the possibility of life at night, and has repeatedly reinvented our perceptions of it. The 1930s, though historians are prone to fasten on its economic dislocations, also extended the reach of human perception. Both had been revolutionized by technology, from photographic advances that could illuminate the secrets of an ink-black alley at midnight, to the electromagnetic radiation that had been harnessed to capture any event anytime, and instantly transmit it to anyone.

Even bigger changes were on the way and all of them were at least initially enemies to city nightlife. World War II loomed; one didn't have to be prescient to see it coming by the mid-1930s. And though radio was already keeping people at home by the millions, television, its even more irresistible successor, had risen above the horizon. In 1931 experimental signals were already beaming out from the top of the newly completed (and practically vacant) Empire State Building. And real TV broadcasting began in 1939 with the opening of the New York World's Fair. On Sunday, April 30, beginning at 12:30 in the afternoon, the first boxy and elephantine TV cameras panned across the sunlit Trylon and Perisphere, then over crowds gathering at the Court of Peace for an inaugural address by Franklin Roosevelt. The signal flashed from a mobile unit to the transmitter, again atop the Empire State Building, then out to a 50-mile perimeter, within which about 1,000 people with access to television sets saw the broadcast.

The new medium generated instant interest. A mob of 6,000 thronged Macy's to look at a display of TV sets (they sold for between $199.50 and $600). Bloomingdale's and Harvey Radio also drew crowds when NBC beamed out a sample program of films, newsreels, and fashion parades. The first live television shows, broadcast between 8 and 9 p.m. on Wednesdays and Fridays, originated in Studio 3H at Radio City. By the 1940s the CBS and DuMont television networks had joined NBC, and there were 23 stations across the country. War temporarily broke the momentum of commercial television: the defense effort diverted materials and expertise from the new medium into critical military technologies like radar. But in later decades, the suburbs would begin vacuuming people by the hundreds of thousands from the urban core, and planting them night after night in front of their TV sets. In the process the New York night wouldn't die, but it would be forced to—and in the end did—reinvent itself, in part by gradually rediscovering the forgotten neighborhoods where it had first begun.

CHAPTER TEN

WHEN THE LIGHTS WENT OUT
World War II, the 1950s, and the Suburbanization of Night

AT 7:53 A.M. ON the morning of Sunday, December 7, 1941, the first Japanese bomb fell on Pearl Harbor. In Washington, D.C., it was early afternoon; the news flashed out across the nation at 2:22 p.m. New York's state and city officials were stunned: no possible course of action seemed adequate to the magnitude of the shock. Toward sunset, as Manhattan lit up, cannonading an even greater Niagara of wattage out into the air than it had in the 1930s, authorities came up with an earnest but feeble response: they stopped twenty Japanese who were about to leave the city by plane. Then, as darkness fell, the police fanned out to the city's Japanese eateries, waited till the patrons finished their meals, closed the restaurants down, and escorted the cooks and waiters home.

But paralysis didn't last. Within a week of December 7, 1941, the governor, Herbert Lehman, and Mayor La Guardia had ordered practice blackouts and drills as a precaution against air raids.* But these never happened, and within weeks, defense officials realized that the true threat lay in New York's signs, streetlamps, and more than ten million lit windows, whose radiance spilled out 50 miles over the sea, silhouetting the ships and convoys that glided against the dark waters of the harbor and beyond, and turning them into visible targets for the German U-boats now lurking offshore.

---

* On March 31 the South Bronx blacked itself out between 9 and 9:15 p.m. It was a clear, moonlit night, and from above the view was ghostly: streets empty, windows black, severe moonlight throwing the shadows of tenements and factories across pavements; one warden even ordered people smoking on the streets to put out their cigarettes. Only the Third and Jerome Avenues els, as well as a few trains passing in and out of the Mott Haven rail yards, occasionally plowed through the darkness, headlights glaring, windows and taillights bouncing behind. A week later the North Bronx tried a twenty-minute blackout, this time including the transit system.

Against such a threat, dimouts were the best and most easily achieved defense: New York's began on May 18, 1942, and lasted until 1945. All illuminated advertising signs had to be shut off permanently. Theaters were allowed faint outside lights, but only on the undersides of their marquees to guide patrons leaving and entering. At home any lamp visible from outdoors had to beam downward. Anyone living above the fifteenth floor of a skyscraper with lights visible from the sea had to douse them or hide them behind blackout curtains. Streetlights had earlier been fitted with individual switches so that wardens could turn them off if needed; now crews began daubing the globes with black paint to block any light radiating toward the ocean or the sky.

In Times Square the effect was drastic. The swimming fish in the Wrigley sign, the peanuts that endlessly tumbled from a Planters bag, and the glowing Sunkist sunburst all froze into stillness and went dark. The *Times* tower news ribbon, which had been chasing itself around the 360-foot circumference of the building since 1928, clattered to a halt on May 18, and the three electricians who ran it were disconsolate as the conveyor belt of troughs—in which the individual letters had been speeding for fourteen years—stopped moving and the lights sputtered off. The Camel billboard on the east side of the square had appeared in 1941; its handsome smoker, now unlit, nevertheless still puffed out his five-foot smoke rings (actually heating steam), which floated out over the darkened square. Indoors, the hotels and theaters remained bright. Outside, the hulking buildings shouldered themselves broodingly into a space once made airy and ebullient by moving lights.

Meyer Berger (1898–1959), perhaps the greatest chronicler of under-the-radar New York between the 1930s and the 50s, reporting for the Sunday *New York Times Magazine* a week into the dimout, wrote that at least one night-duty cop in Times Square believed that energy had subtly but noticeably drained away from the evening crowds. "People don't realize it," he said, "but when they move around in the dark their speech is softer." The roar of traffic had dulled: a third of the city's cabs were off the streets, grounded when their drivers volunteered or were drafted, and gas rationing had discouraged everyone else from making unnecessary trips. There were compensations: one cabdriver noted the dimout had helped couples, who could now neck on a ride through a once glaring crossroads that had now become as shadowy as a lovers' lane. In 1942, New York put up its traditional Christmas tree in Madison Square, a 35-foot Douglas fir, but it was bereft of its usual 3,500 lights, and the carolers sang out beneath it in a forestlike darkness.

Yet even as the noise and glare of Times Square sank, the crowds began to thicken. New York was full of soldiers and sailors, crowding into the Stage Door Canteen on 44th Street, where Broadway's best known stars volunteered to entertain them: the hugely theatrical Katharine Cornell poured coffee; Alfred Lunt (of Lunt and Fontanne, the famed and hammy husband-wife acting team) worked garbage detail in the kitchen. Male New Yorkers had disappeared into the services, but out-of-town soldiers and sailors took their place, passing through on their way to the battlefields and desperate for entertainment. For the thousands of young men awaiting an uncertain future in the European theater of war, a 24-hours' leave in the city became the last chance for a night of wonders with an undertow of sadness, a few hours to soak up the after-dark urban glamour made mythical in movies, over the radio, and in print. That was the story of *On the Town,* the 1944 musical comedy by Leonard Bernstein, Betty Comden, and Adolph Green: three sailors free for a day and a night in the city, eager to live and also shadowed by the war. The show opens with a burst of energy as they clamber joyously off the ship and ends sadly, as they return the next dawn, heading into an unknown future.

War, especially at the beginning, brought with it inevitable economic and demographic dislocations. Populations fluctuated from night to night and week to week as the servicemen tided through on their way abroad, and residents churned in and out* as the demands of the home front war effort evolved. In the earlier years of the war the city economy remained sluggish; by the dimout summer of 1942 the city had 75,000 vacant apartments and 400,000 unemployed. Mayor La Guardia petitioned the federal government to bring defense contracts to the city, and the campaign bore fruit: by 1943 the *Herald Tribune* reported three-quarters of the 3,500 adaptable New York area factories had converted to weapons manufacture. Elevator plants were now building gun carriages, and a toymaker was turning out hand grenades. By 1944 the city was second only to Los Angeles in the number of defense workers it employed.

---

* In fact despite such fluctuations an underlying out-migration from the city had already begun, with Manhattan reaching a population peak in 1910 that it has yet to equal. Growth in the outer boroughs compensated for Manhattan's shrinkage, and an influx of Hispanics and African-Americans masked a white urban flight already underway.

Minsky Agonistes:
Times Square at War

Dimout or no, Times Square, at least, was booming: a 1943 survey claimed that every week the 53 nightclubs in the vicinity were reporting an average of 225,540 customers (a higher level of patronage than even Prohibition had managed to generate). The 200 restaurants were dishing out five million meals, and over a million and three-quarters people were filling the movie and legitimate theaters—25 percent above previous records. Every week 93,700 servicemen passed through the neighborhood. Radio City Music Hall, the Paramount, and the Criterion reported record crowds during Easter Week of 1942. Gasoline rationing had thinned the traffic, but had also discouraged long out-of-town trips, which boosted urban entertainment districts well served by subways and buses.

Still, bustling though it was, chunks were falling off Times Square's facade, and the neighborhood was fraying, both at its edges and in the center. Capital and energy were pouring chiefly into the war effort, and not all of the servicemen were after the arch-thespianism of Katharine Cornell and the Lunts. By the 1940s, as James Traub notes in *The Devil's Playground: A Century of Pleasure and Profit in Times Square* (2004), pinball parlors and cafeterias had appeared alongside the theaters; Ripley's Believe-It-or-Not Wax Museum had opened on Broadway between 43rd and 44th Streets. And 42nd Street had been invaded by crooked auction parlors, where barkers and planted bidders swindled the naive sailor or soldier into paying outrageous prices for worthless junk.

In all this the anti-vice movement saw a new opportunity: protecting the innocent serviceman from the clutches of bunco operators, venereal disease, and bad women. A national panic erupted in the early 1940s over "victory girls"—women who were supposed to have gathered in military towns like New York or Norfolk, offering sex to servicemen, free and with no strings attached, but presenting the same moral and medical dangers as prostitutes. Maine's Margaret Chase Smith (1897–1995), in 1944 a young Republican congresswoman, gained a reputation as the nation's "Vice Admiral" for her investigations of this phenomenon. In New York, the mania to save military men from vice found an excitable ally in Fiorello La Guardia, the mayor since 1934. Both populist and a progressive, a man of boundless sympathy for working New Yorkers, he also had an irascible streak of prudishness and some of the wild-eyed intensity of the vice hunter. Along with his attack-dog of a license commissioner, Paul Moss (who once tried to close down the Ringling Brothers circus), La Guardia encouraged a vendetta against a long-established working-class entertainment industry and a powerful draw for servicemen: burlesque.

After nearly a century in the hinterlands, the outer boroughs, and the Lower East Side, burlesque arrived—around the same time as the auction parlors and pinball arcades—on 42nd Street in the early 1930s, when the Depression's box office slump left theaters empty and their owners desperate. The Minsky brothers, who had been running a successful burlesque house at Houston Street and Second Avenue since 1913, were the pioneers. Ann Nichols's *Abie's Irish Rose* finally came to the end of its marathon six-year run at the Republic Theatre in 1927; in February 1931 Billy Minsky moved in, and a month later Max Rudnick turned the Eltinge Theatre across the street into a competing venue. Almost from the moment Rudnick and Minsky opened, they raised an outcry, not just from government but also among Times Square businessmen and theater owners. Howard Lindsay and Russell Crouse (authors of the ponderously wholesome *Life with Father*) even shrieked that the girlie shows posed a threat comparable to Nazism: "burlesque is the Czechoslovakia of the stage and the legitimate theater might soon be its Poland," they warned.

Lindsay and Crouse had staked their careers on middle-class morality, but the chorus of outrage also included Earl Carroll and George White, the leading flesh peddlers of the 1930s and 40s. Their complaint, predictably, was that burlesque was obscene and immoral. And it was certainly true that the high point of a burlesque show was the striptease, performed on a runway that projected from the stage into the audience, breaking the invisible proscenium wall between the stripper and her ogling, howling audience. The Minskys had put up their first runway in 1917, claiming to have imported the idea from the *Folies Bergères,* but for practical rather than aesthetic reasons: the old Lower East Side Minsky house was a converted movie theater with poor stage illumination, and it was cheaper to build a runway than install new lighting.

Burlesque impresarios insisted the women in their shows were no more (and were perhaps less) exposed than the models in Carroll's *Vanities,* White's *Scandals,* or Ziegfeld's *Follies,* all of which occasioned protests but never faced a complete shutdown. What, then, was the real offense? The dudgeon certainly included a mercenary motive: George White's *Scandals* charged a top admission price of $5.50; the Republic offered approximately as much flesh for as little as 25 cents and put on four shows a day (at noon, 2 p.m., 8 p.m., 10 p.m., plus midnight on Fridays). This drew an audience of layabouts and working people, and threatened to scare off the middle-class patrons of shows like *Life with Father*.

Minsky's and Rudnick's burlesque was part of a tradition that traced back nearly a hundred years, at least to the pink tights of *The Black Crook, Ixion, The White Fawn,* and before. Though historians have disagreed about whether they were direct progenitors of burlesque, they were certainly related to it. Nineteenth-century commentators from the aging George Templeton Strong onward insisted that dancers were in a state of virtual nudity, even though every inch of leg was covered. Systematic stripping down to bare flesh didn't become an invariable burlesque feature until the 1920s, but contemporary accounts, even photographs, are ambiguous about what one actually saw on the runways.

Gypsy Rose Lee and Sally Rand worked audiences into a lather of anticipation, which they satisfied at most with a fleeting glimpse of the top of a hip or breast. Many strippers, swathed at first in fans, flowers, and veils, peeled down only to pasties and G-strings. Some seem to have worn panties with painted-on pubic hair, with quick movements and flying veils to fool the eye. Even chorus members or strippers who bared it all (common in the nude tableaux that dated back to the early 1800s and also to be seen in both expensive shows like the *Follies* and cheap ones like burlesque) weren't, strictly speaking, naked, since they wore a body makeup called Stage White. Slathered on with a sponge, according to Morton Minsky, it "made the girl's skin look like satin under the spotlight"—which in Minsky shows was usually a trademark magenta. A surviving handbill from a 1920s burlesque show in the Midwest advertised "Red-Hot Dancers," and promised, "You'll See What You Expect To See"—a line that may have been more penetrating than intended in its implication that nudity and eros reside more in the psyche of the gazer than the skin being ogled.

Perhaps burlesque also rankled because of its derisive attitude toward all things snooty and artful, especially self-satisfied bourgeois offerings like the *Vanities,* the *Scandals,* and *Life with Father.* Originally, "burlesque" denoted broad parody, a Bronx cheer aimed at high art. Tony Pastor's slapstick Shakespeare travesties were close in spirit to Minsky's baggy-pants comic sketches, with their self-parodying double-entendres and titles like "Desire Under the El" or "Anatomy and Cleopatra." The strippers and chorus girls wore cheap send-ups of costumes from the high-priced shows, and reveled in the tatty gimmicks immortalized in *Gypsy* (the 1958 Arthur Laurents–Stephen Sondheim–Jule Styne musical commemoration of burlesque). The effect was sometimes—even usually—intentionally mocking, and it's difficult to decide whether laughter was a way to incite lust or short-circuit it. How did a typical audience of soldiers, sailors, and nondescript men—who made up the audience crowded under the marquee of Minsky's in a photograph dating from the period—react? Did they catch the satirical hints, or were they just at home in a theater where neither the actors, the material, nor the audience was incomprehensible or condescending?

Broadway producers, whose franchise was supposed to be both urbane and urban, may also have been annoyed that burlesque smelled so of the circuses, carnivals, and freak shows that traveled the boondocks. Together with the bargain prices, this may have formed part of the attraction for servicemen from small hometowns and low-income people from the outer boroughs. During Minsky intermissions a candy butcher plied the aisles, hawking chocolates:

> I'm holding up a box. You all see it? In each and every box that I'm holding up is an exotic assortment of genuine, imported chocolate bonbons especially made for this exacting Minsky audience at this famous theater. . . .

The boxes were supposed to (though they usually didn't) contain valuable prizes like Elgin watches, but complaints seem to have been rare: the chicanery was part of the entertainment, as it had been when Texas Guinan greeted her customers with, "Hello, sucker!" Gullibility in the audience was essential to the spirit of the show.

Until the 1930s, burlesque had been a phenomenon of the hinterlands. Burlesque "wheels"—humble versions of the national vaudeville circuits—sent their shows to places like Toledo, booking a complete crazy salad of acts, from girls to leering skits to opera arias to serious playlets (during the World War I era, Minsky's Lower East Side burlesque pro-

gram often included a mini-melodrama in which the vices of the city ruined an innocent young man). An all-purpose flouting of logical consis-
tency was a staple of burlesque, and the arty touches served as fig leaves
when they were solemn and raspberries when they weren't.

Burlesque may have passed without reproach in western Ohio, but
New York was more prudish. La Guardia's Commissioner Moss cracked
down in 1942, shuttering Minsky's, the Eltinge, and the Gaiety (a third
burlesque house on Broadway at 46th Street); they never reopened. Apart
from its famous alumni—strippers like Lee and Ann Corio, comedians
like W. C. Fields, Lou Costello, and Ed Wynn, and singers like Sophie
Tucker, few traces of typical burlesque performance survived its collapse
in the 1940s, and reconstructing its ambience is a challenge.

But there are clues. Among the most valuable is a collection of skits
and memorabilia left to the Hampden-Booth Theatre Library by the family of Chuck Callahan (1891–1964). Callahan's story seems to typify life
in the burlesque business—blue-collar, itinerant, always on the verge of
poverty, sometimes nearly destitute. Callahan grew up in Ohio, and
began working locally as a dancer in 1909. By the 1920s he was appearing
as "Toledo's Rotund Jester" at the Empire Burlesk Theatre, a seedy hall
that also sponsored Monday night boxing matches and Wednesday
wrestling bouts.

Callahan was broad-faced and stocky. In comedy skits he wore outsized shoes, a porkpie hat, wire-rimmed glasses with huge, three-inch
lenses, and a dark Dutch Boy wig with low-hanging bangs and a cowlick.
Eventually he came to New York, landing parts in a 1924 Shubert revue,
The Passing Show, and performing at Reisenweber's restaurant on Columbus Circle. He moved to California and wrote comedy for Universal Studios (he was, he said, responsible for all 24 episodes of the Andy Gump
comedies—rudimentary two-reel movies starring Slim Summerville). His
most successful burlesque sketch, about a society chump who gives clue-
less answers to riddles, featured the line "Atta-Boy-Petey-Old-Boy," which
caught on as a short-lived catchphrase.

Between such fleeting successes Callahan drifted along the frontier between modest prominence and anonymity. His unpretentious life and
happily rowdy theatrical taste seems, like burlesque itself and its audiences, essentially harmless. It's hard to see why such innocuous entertainment aroused La Guardia's and Moss's crusading ire. It can't have been
fears of a real crime wave: between 1941 and 1946 the city's homicide rate

fell to an all-time low for the 20th century: 3.5 murders per 100,000 people. Yet somehow an undercurrent was rising in the midst of the improving economy and the crowds out at night, eager to forget grief or fear. In the darkness above the marquees, in the scabby businesses now an unavoidable part of the neighborhood texture, there was an inkling of pessimism, and a sense that the great Times Square moment of the 1920s and 30s was beginning to fade. The Rainbow Room at Rockefeller Center had closed in 1943 in order to comply with the dimout; other high-end nightclubs had already begun shifting north and east, away from the increasingly proletarian atmosphere of west midtown.

UNEASY SUMMER:
1948, DRUGS, AND THE SOURING OF POSTWAR NEW YORK

Among the images with which wartime New York engraved itself on the American imagination, the most famous, probably, is Alfred Eisenstaedt's *Life* magazine photograph of a sailor and nurse, kissing in front of the Times Square Walgreen's on V-J Day, August 15, 1945. It was a delirious moment in a euphoric summer that would soon give way to routine. By 1948 most of the servicemen were home, their postwar marriages had become assembly lines, and the mass-produced toddlers of the baby boom were prattling and tottering in crowded city flats.* The war was receding into memory. The economy remained essentially robust: inflation was a problem (subway fares had risen from 5 to 10 cents in March, the first hike in the system's history), but the average unemployment rate for the year was a low 3.8 percent. Toward the end of June, the summer's heat waves began to stifle a city whose windows didn't yet rumble with the air conditioners that would later sag in front of them like open drawers. It was almost a last glimpse of summer in the city as it had been for 50 and 100 years before, and as it would never be again.

One tropical blast struck at the end of June; another, one of the fiercest in New York history, came toward the end of August. During the worst of it, on Thursday, August 26, with a high pressure system stalled over Virginia and a hurricane building in the South Atlantic, the temperature rose to 100.8 degrees Fahrenheit, the third highest ever recorded (the all-time

---

* Levittown had opened in 1947, and by July of 1948 its first 2,000 houses had been built and occupied on the potato fields of Long Island. But the suburban exodus was not yet the full-fledged rout it would later become.

high had been 102.3 in July of 1936). Evening brought no relief; it was still 99. Wilted crowds trudged along the streets, in torpid flight from their stifling apartments. The Times Square barkers whose usual job was to stand under the marquees of the Capitol, Strand, and Paramount, pitching movies to passersby, now shoved away mobs gathered in the cold breeze that surged out from the air-conditioned lobby every time someone opened a door. The doorman at the Astor Hotel said he kept himself at least notionally cool by staring up at the cascading waterfall of the Bond Clothing sign across the square. The heat stretched on through the weekend. Sunday night, people walking the streets for relief read news headlines in the sky: the *Sunday Mirror* had hired the Goodyear Blimp, outfitted with an eighteen-foot-high news crawl and floating above the city after dark.

At nine o'clock it was still 93 degrees, and so many people had filled their tubs to soak in cold water, or opened the hydrants on the streets for a public dousing, that the water supply dwindled to a trickle, and the police switchboards lit up with complaints. Coney Island sank under an onslaught of an estimated 700,000 people fleeing the heat, and the police let more than 1,000 people sleep all night on the beach. Forty-five air passengers from Iceland (where it had been a chilly 52 degrees when they boarded) disembarked at Idlewild Airport and began frantically stripping off overcoats and even wool underwear as the ovenlike heat pressed dully up from the tarmac.

Late night brought no relief; it was still 92. Everyone who had a car and a place to drive it to fled the cement, brick, and glass that magnified the temperatures all day and then exuded heat all night. Roofs and fire escapes filled with apartment dwellers trying to sleep, praying for a hint of movement in the air (which wouldn't come for four more days). City parks, which normally closed at midnight, stayed open and police allowed anyone in search of a breeze to sleep in them. The best the department stores could offer in the way of relief was an eight-inch electric fan that Gimbels advertised for $3.98: the first window air conditioners had gone on sale in 1938, but they were still expensive and rare. Life was immobilized; fresh fruits and vegetables rotted on their stands; even ice-cream vendors reported a drop in business—people were so overcome, one of them complained, that they didn't have the energy to stop for a cone.

But if this was a smothering interval, it was also a lulling one. The economy remained in good shape, simmering anti-communism hadn't reached the full boil of the McCarthy years. But trouble was in the offing: a postwar recession would begin that November; Alger Hiss and Whittaker Chambers were trading the accusations that led up to the Pumpkin Papers scandal. But perhaps the most nagging concern, later to grow into a national preoccupation, was a perceived rise in the illegal drug trade.

Drugs weren't new to New York, but suddenly they seemed to be proliferating: that, at least, was what a drumbeat of headlines insisted. During the June hot spell a dozen customs inspectors, acting on a tip, descended on the Department of Sanitation's Garbage Scow No. 11, docked on the Hudson at the foot of 57th Street. It was put under surveillance, towed first to 52nd Street in Brooklyn, and finally, as the heat ripened its stench, to Fresh Kills Creek near the Staten Island landfill. For five days, in tropical temperatures that steamed and prickled like warm, wet felt, a dozen workers, stripped to the waist, pawed through the garbage as a crane bit clumps of it out of the barge and served it up by dipperfuls. Finally, on Monday, June 28, they found a stash of heroin and morphine worth, by different estimates, between $800,000 and $2 million on the street. The drugs, in ten metal-topped jars first wrapped in sodden burlap then stuffed into a carton, had come into port from Italy on June 19, concealed in a ship, the *Marine Perch*. The smugglers' plan, apparently, had been to sneak the shipment into the city by disguising it as waste, and unloading it under the noses of inspectors onto a garbage truck. But somehow the contraband drugs ended up with the wrong driver: he refused to let three members of the drug ring go through his garbage, even when they offered him $200; he carted it off and dumped it into Scow No. 11.

Just two hours after customs workers had found what they were after in the scow at Fresh Kills, an Air France plane landed at La Guardia Airport, and inspectors, searching the tail section at two o'clock Tuesday morning, found a sealed green can; opened, it disgorged eight pounds of heroin, worth $500,000 at retail. A month later federal officers tracked the drugs to Lucien Ignaro, a 45-year-old French sailor, living illegally in the U.S. on West 82nd Street. They charged him with being the country's biggest dealer in heroin, asserting he'd netted $1.5 million dollars in four months by buying the drug wholesale at $50 an ounce and selling it to street dealers all over the U.S. for $200. Addiction, with supply lines disrupted by the war and a huge population of susceptible young men diverted to military service, had ebbed in the early 1940s. But now it seemed to be making a comeback.

Opium had been known in the Western world since the Middle Ages; by the 1600s it had become commonplace to dissolve it in alcohol, add flavorings to give it either a pleasant or at least medicinal taste, and call the result laudanum, which became a standard medication for pain and sleeplessness by 1700. By 1805 Friedrich Sertürner, a German pharmacist, had discovered a method for isolating and concentrating opium's chief narcotic compound, morphine; the medical syringe, which came into widespread use around the time of the Civil War, allowed users to deliver the narcotic effect with a quick and potent stab of the needle.

Narcotics abuse had become common by the mid-1800s: the historian David Courtwright has suggested that the repeated epidemics of cholera and dysentery that struck the U.S. between 1830 and 1860 may have spurred physicians, trying to relieve suffering from diseases they couldn't otherwise cope with, to prescribe opium and morphine indiscriminately. Yet addiction was nearly invisible because drugs were legal and socially acceptable, sold openly by doctors and druggists, whose advice constituted the only brake on the quantities anyone consumed. Americans thought of narcotics as medicine, and the people using them as invalids. But over time opium addiction did become a recognized if not scandalous phenomenon, rising from less than one addict per thousand Americans in 1842 to nearly five per thousand in the 1890s. Courtwright estimates that between 1900 and 1914 America had perhaps 313,000 opiate addicts (that same year 7,464 people registered at New York's narcotics clinic).

Yet for all their familiarity narcotics hadn't become omnipresent accessories to nightlife: their preferred arena wasn't a vacant lot or tenement stoop, but rather the parlors and boudoirs of the middle- or upper-class home. Women formed a significant majority of addicts well into the early 1900s—housewives, actresses, teachers, servants, prostitutes, nurses, and doctors' wives were especially prone. Doctors themselves were a risk group, and (gender aside) addicts were predominantly white, middle-class, urban, and southern. The stereotypical addict drew sympathy and even admiration as a victim, racked by sickness, pain, or some crisis of the spirit. The iconic drug user was the polar opposite of the modern club druggie, gyrating wild-eyed in a disco, copulating in an after-hours club, lying in the filth of a crack den, or stalking victims on the street.

Still, physicians, reformers, and civic leaders had become alarmed about drug use in the late 1800s, and a new picture of it began to take shape. By the 1870s, New York–by–night books, still a popular genre, had begun to include obligatory stops at a new urban horror: the Chinese opium den, an early appearance of the shadowy recreational drug culture that would both drive and blight much of the city's nightlife after the Second World War. James McCabe's 1872 *Lights and Shadows of New York Life*, in a chapter called "The 'Heathen Chinee,'" claims that in 1870 there were (officially at least) only 23 Chinese in New York. But already, McCabe reports, an opium den for Chinese sailors had opened in a Baxter Street boardinghouse. It was a room with "a series of beds or berths, one above another, extending around it. At almost any time one may find several Chinese lying in these berths smoking opium." McCabe describes an opium pipe and tells how it's used, but the scene is presented as a curiosity rather than an abomination; the Chinese, he says, are on the whole "very innocent and well-behaved."

But as the Chinese population increased, the opium dens multiplied, and native New Yorkers could increasingly be spied in the oblivion of the berths. Only a few years later, in a November 1883 *Harper's* magazine article, Police Chief George Walling described a deluxe hashish den whose clients included upper- and middle-class women. As the century drew to a close, the menu of available drugs lengthened. Marijuana, familiar in China as early as 4,000 B.C.E., gained its first major American foothold in the Southwest between 1900 and 1930 with a million-strong influx of Mexican laborers. By the 1920s the drug had become popular in Harlem and was already well on its way to becoming nearly universal among jazz musicians. Heroin, a purified form of morphine, had come on the market in 1898 as a treatment for respiratory diseases; cocaine had become popular in the West toward the end of the 1800s. By 1906 Americans were devouring eleven tons of it every year; it was, famously, the active ingredient in the early recipe for Coca-Cola and the more bluntly named Dope Cola.

Alarm about this caused a break in America's once insouciant attitude toward drug use. After years of debate, anti-drug reformers came to an uneasy but fateful consensus that the medical prescription of narcotics should be strictly controlled, and all other uses outlawed (though marijuana had never spurred as much panic as narcotics, and wasn't effectively banned until 1937). But illegalization, just as had happened with alcohol, didn't erase demand and it turned the business of supply over to criminals. It stripped the cover of medical need away from addiction, but at the cost of making it into a secret pleasure that gradually joined the smoking and drinking that had accompanied every night out at the tavern and its successors since the 17th century. New Yorkers had been coping with alcohol from the beginning of the republic and before, but narcotics gave intoxication strange new paraphernalia (water pipes, syringes, bent spoons, and ultimately crack vials) and queasy accompaniments like the sickish aroma of opium or the bittersweet woodiness of burning marijuana.

Organized crime, exploiting forbidden desire for profit since the days of McGlory and the Hotel Irving, muscled its way into narcotics in the aftermath of World War I. It was Arnold Rothstein (1882–1928) who first led the mobs into the drug trade. Rothstein was a highly untypical gangster, with polished manners and a successful cotton-merchant father, in whose firm he worked as a young man. But gambling was his true forte, and he was soon running a silk-stocking casino, which made him an intimate of his famous and semifamous clientele. In the 1920s, wholesale opium was selling for only $1,000 a pound but fetched $150,000 at retail and Rothstein, seeing opportunity, became the first major organized crime boss to exploit the market. After he was murdered in a room at the Park Central Hotel, federal agents combed his files to track down $9 million worth of drugs stashed along the waterfront, in a 42nd Street hotel, and even on the New York Central's *20th Century Limited* as it thundered its way toward New York from Chicago.

In the 1920s drugs were beginning to make their debut in Harlem. Marijuana—still legal in New York, though under attack—was an ingrained if secretive local custom, easily available in secluded and tastefully decorated "tearooms." One could also buy it on the street, from (among others) Milton "Mezz" Mezzrow (1899–1972), a white jazz clarinetist so smitten with Harlem and black culture that he learned jive talk and made it his mission to sell happiness to his adopted neighborhood in the form of reefers, which in the 1930s he peddled on a block he called "The Stroll," along Lexington Avenue between 131st and 132nd Streets. Mezzrow would, he later recalled, wake up at about four in the afternoon, pay a social call on Louis Armstrong (usually catching him in the shower), and then as the night began in earnest take up his station on the Stroll under what he called "The Tree of Hope."

The vipers [Harlem's then current word for pot smokers] come up, one by one.

FIRST CAT: Hey there Poppa Mezz, is you anywhere?
ME: Man I'm down with it, stickin' like a honky.
FIRST CAT: Lay a trey on me, ole man.
ME: Got to do it, slot.

Harlem street slang, Mezzrow plausibly said, was the language of people
who "don't want to be spied on, resent eavesdroppers; when they're jeal-
ously guarding their private lives, which are lived under great pressure,
and don't want details known to outsiders."

When Meyer Berger decided to attend a Harlem marijuana party in
1938 for a *New Yorker* piece, it took weeks before, at eleven o'clock one
Saturday night, he finally wangled an invitation to a dark tenement apartment on 140th Street, lit in pipe-dream blue and with a jukebox that
played "special recordings of viper, or weed, songs with weird ritualistic
themes." The vipers themselves presented a scene that modeled all future
zonked-out pot parties, complete with giggles and blissful vapidities,
though Berger was clearly on edge because federal drug agents had told
him that "vipers are always dangerous; that an overdose of marijuana gen-
erates savage and sadistic traits likely to reach a climax in axe and icepick
murders."

After its wartime lull, the drug trade revived. In 1949 Harry Anslinger,
the headline-hungry U.S. commissioner of narcotics, announced that
seizures of cocaine, heroin, and marijuana had returned to prewar levels.
The battle between smugglers and the law became a constant source of
headlines, with intrepid investigators, huge drug hauls, and gang turf wars
appearing weekly if not daily. In 1949 a city detective, the matronly Margaret Leonard, got headlines when she posed as a maid in an apartment
building on West 85th Street and ferreted out a nest of three distributors
who'd amassed a stash of cocaine with a street value of nearly $2 million.
Two other undercover operatives, Katherine Barry and Patrick Murphy,
drew a stakeout in which they spent their nights necking, apparently be-
sotted, on a park bench at the corner of East Houston Street and the
Bowery. At 8:45 p.m. on September 21, 1949, they spied a suspected
drug dealer in mid-trade, nabbed him, and netted $100,000 worth of
opium, heroin, and paraphernalia.

A scan of news stories on drugs in the 1940s reveals that most were
celebrations of enforcement triumphs, prominently featuring the huge
street value of the seized opium or cocaine or heroin or marijuana. But if

the captured narcotics were destroyed as they were supposed to be, who cared what they were worth to buyers; was this simply a way to justify the growing resources devoted to drug enforcement? By contrast, stories about drug users—who they were, how they behaved, what drew them to illegal drugs, what damage they sustained by or what pleasure they got from their habits—were rare until the 1950s, when marijuana and even hard drugs were beginning to infiltrate the white middle class.

As Berger had noted in his *New Yorker* piece, the marijuana habit was particularly well established among jazz musicians by the late 1930s, almost universal in the 1940s. This tradition persisted into the postwar years. Billie Holiday (1915–1959) is now a figure venerated beyond celebrity as perhaps the greatest of jazz and popular vocalists, her life as famous for its long battle with drugs as for Holiday's voice. Yet there was nothing unusual for a musician in her habits except, perhaps, the gusto with which she was enjoying them. The little-known clubs along 141st Street were where Harlem threw off the commercial slickness of the Cotton Club or Small's Paradise, and Holiday haunted them in the late 1930s—particularly fond, according to one friend, of a sex club called the Daisy Chain (between Lenox and Seventh Avenues), where a woman evocatively named Sewing Machine Bertha specialized in woman-to-woman oral sex. An admirer, later a friend, spotted Holiday one night, standing upright in an open-roofed taxicab parked in front of the Alhambra Grill at the corner of 126th Street and Seventh Avenue, casually smoking a reefer.

Before Holiday began injecting heroin in the early years of World War II, a friend and fellow entertainer, Ruby Helena, recalled that both of them puffed marijuana day and night while Holiday was working in the landmark row of jazz clubs on 52nd Street. "When we got off at night, we'd walk down the block to Fifth Avenue and have smoked a joint, and then stop off at the White Rose and have a drink at 51st and then go back to work." Holiday was never off drugs of one kind or another. "If she wasn't asleep, she was getting high."

No one thought it strange when she lived in a building that had sustained a drug raid (though apparently not one aimed at her), and had a white cop standing guard outside. Even in 1942 or 1943, when she began mainlining heroin, nothing seemed disturbingly out of place—at first. John Simmons, a bassist who met her when she was performing at Minton's Playhouse on West 118th Street, knew her once the floodgates had opened. "She would smoke opium when we got home from work at night, and she'd light up a joint, and she had a ten-pound candy box full of pills—she'd grab a fistful of them—all kinds of pills—and chase it with a big tumbler of ale. And she would drink scotch behind that. And she would go in the bathroom and fix." Gradually, her habit became known on 52nd Street; club doormen would take her heroin deliveries and bring them to the dressing room; fans would hold her supply to keep it safe while she was performing; she seems even to have shot up her dog, a beloved boxer named Mister.

She remained physically strong: in one famous war-era incident she decked two sailors who had wandered into a club where she was singing and burned her coat with cigarettes. But her behavior became more and more erratic, and by the end of the war or shortly after she'd begun to attract the notice of narcotics agents. In 1947 she was arrested and sent to the federal women's reformatory at Alderson, West Virginia, not to be released until March 1948.

POSTWAR BLUES:
LOST IN BEAT MANHATTAN, 1950–1960

In almost every account of Holiday's life, her prison sentence figures as a crisis and a catastrophe, the event that damaged her voice, sent her personal life into a tailspin—and made one of the great 20th-century myths of American popular culture, enshrined in Holiday's 1956 autobiography, *Lady Sings the Blues,* the 1972 Diana Ross movie based on it, and numerous biographies and appreciations since. Yet when the arrest happened, it passed almost without notice in the mainstream press. The *New York Times,* for example, ignored the story; only *Downbeat* published a full account in an interview with Holiday. Some of the silence may have traced to Holiday's race, or the fact that she hadn't achieved the broad popularity of an Ella Fitzgerald or Jo Stafford. Sensational accounts of investigations and busts had become routine, as had wild anti-drug propaganda, but there seems at the same time to have been a tacit embargo on details of real-life drug use. The venerated saxophone giant, Charlie Parker (1920–1955), as deep into drugs as Holiday, was fated for an even shorter life. He too attracted federal drug investigators, and when they questioned him in 1948 at the Dewey Square Hotel on West 117th Street, they found, lying on a table in his room, a glassine envelope with some heroin in it along with a spoon, two syringes, and three hypodermic needles. They arrested him; but again, no story appeared in the *Times*.

The established newspapers, the mass-circulation magazines, and the readers whose opinions they shaped seemed unaware that the ground beneath was shifting. They hadn't realized that stories like Parker's and Holiday's were destined to become hallmarks of the 1950s and afterward. Nor was it only the advent of narcotics that marked a crisis; so did the changing population, and so too did a shift in popular fascination away from the sophisticated metropolises of the East to the music and lore of the rural South and West. New stars, new shows, new styles, new music, new fears, new tragedies, and new crimes—all were on the way, and many weren't invented in Manhattan. Cumulatively they amounted to a slow earthquake for a city that had dominated American urban culture since the 18th century.

After the war Chuck Callahan, back in Toledo and at loose ends with the fading of burlesque, took a job in the Libbey-Owens-Ford glass plant in nearby Rossford, Ohio; he and his wife, Virginia, seemed to be disappearing forever into the anonymity of mid-America's postwar industrial economy. But eventually Callahan rebelled, and in 1950—against the general grain—he moved back to New York, and stayed there until he died fourteen years later, living first in hotels in the West 40s and finally at 564 Ninth Avenue. He'd come with a sheaf of his old burlesque skits, and fell in with a public relations man on West 45th Street, Julian Agart Martin, who was trying to produce a half-hour weekly TV series on film, to be titled *Burlesque Hall of Fame,* featuring such acts from the great days as could be safely broadcast. The project failed, though, and Callahan eked out a living on the outermost edges of show business. He took bit parts on network television, tried out a nightclub act, entertained wounded veterans at army hospitals, and worked as a security guard for a detective agency; Virginia Callahan took a job as a secretary. Callahan suffered a stroke in 1955, and gradually deteriorated after that, dying in obscurity in 1964. He had come back, an alien and a wanderer, to a New York transformed. It had never quite been his home, and the show business world he thought he was returning to was gone.

Callahan was adrift, but far from alone. Michael Todd (remembered now as the producer of *Around the World in 80 Days*) had tried to revive burlesque at the Winter Garden Theatre on Broadway in 1950, with an extravaganza called *Peep Show*. It featured strippers (though they worked only in silhouette), a cast of veteran burlesque comedians that included Bozo Snyder, Red Marshall, and Peanuts Mann, and a score by various hands, including a Thai prince (who contributed a song called "Blue Night"). But the current license commissioner, Edward T. McCaffrey, showed up on opening night and summoned Todd to his office to complain about the suggestive dancing of Lilly Christine (the "Cat Girl"), the striptease (objectionable even behind a scrim), and some tassel-twirling by another dancer, June Allen. "We won't stand for more bumps and grinds than we have in past years," he warned. Todd complied, altering six scenes in the show to remove the bumps, the grinds, and the striptease. In bowdlerized form the show was moderately successful, running through February 1951.

Peep Show was a nostalgic throwback to a vigorous and raucous era of city entertainment, now gone or going. Fifty-second Street, an emporium of different jazz styles into the 1940s, began to deteriorate in the 1950s, edged out by low-rent cabarets. In any case jazz, at its more progressive edges, had begun pulling away from the popular music it had been energizing since the 1920s, with musicians like Parker pushing it toward a cerebral complexity too demanding for a mass audience. Slowly jazz moved uptown, downtown, or out of town, while spotless Rodgers and Hammerstein musicals became the dominant dress of popular Broadway.*

Meanwhile annual statistics emanating from the city police seemed, slowly at first, to warn of impending trouble. In 1946 the city's murder rate had plunged to its 20th-century low point, and as late as 1950, the police department logged only 244 murders. By 1952 there were 308, with 350 the year after: crime, dormant in the war years, had begun to stir and rouse itself. Felony complaints for prostitution and commercialized vice also were on the rise, from fourteen in 1949 to 60 in 1956. Of all these it was narcotics violations that rose most sharply, from 1,100 misdemeanors and felonies in 1948 to 5,988 in 1958—a fivefold-plus increase. Such statistics can't be taken completely at face value: rather than the actual number of incidents on the street, they may convey the crimes cops were most determined to hunt down, whether on their own initiative or goaded by public and government panics. But the crimes reported did happen, and the numbers are a barometer of perceived threats to the equanimity of city life.

* The real-life prince of Thailand who wrote a song for Michael Todd's exhumation of burlesque had far less impact on the American imagination than his romanticized ancestor, the blustering hero of *The King and I* (which opened in 1951, a month after *Peep Show* closed).

As the 1950s approached, popular magazines like *Life* were already doing features about nighttime New York as a jungle in which drug- and sex-crazed minorities committed mayhem on one another and on the innocents who strayed among them. In a 1948 *Life* feature, "A Night on the Beat," the writer, Joe McCarthy, accompanied James W. Murphy and Peter Fitzpatrick in their dark green radio car as they worked their 4 p.m.-to-midnight shift on the streets of the still rough far Upper East Side and East Harlem. Both were World War II vets, toughened by the armed services, the article implies, for East Harlem, "a mixture of Puerto Ricans, Negroes, Italians, and hard-boiled Irish." Drugs are a shadowy presence—Murphy stops to confer with a friend from the Narcotics Squad, also patrolling the area—but mostly, as dusk falls, the cops break up stickball games or deal with household agonies of varying seriousness: a family fight on East 89th Street, a woman on 98th Street who orders a shrugging Murphy to change a blown fuse. Later, beneath a Ferris wheel at a Puerto Rican street carnival, they find a blood-covered man lying on the ground, his mouth slashed from lip to ear and his teeth showing through the cut.

Within minutes after they've arrested the slasher and sent the victim for medical care, another blood-soaked Puerto Rican grabs the patrol car's door handle as it waits for a traffic light to turn. "I'm stabbed. . . . Get me to a hospital." The man's wife, screaming hysterically, tries to push into the car; by the time they've shoved her away and reached the emergency room on East 106th Street, the man, Ramón Soler, is dead. Around a quarter to midnight, Murphy's shift is over, and he stands gaping at Soler's father, who has just arrived, heard the news, and is leaning, stunned and speechless, against a corridor wall.

Stark portraiture of the brutality of slum life was a staple for newspapers and picture magazines like *Life*. In the mid–1950s, writers, striving to give life to rising crime statistics, battened again and again on juveniles run amok, drugs, and the Hispanic population of East Harlem. It took little time for all three to migrate into literature and popular culture as surefire themes. *West Side Story,* the 1957 musical by Leonard Bernstein, Arthur Laurents, and Stephen Sondheim, mythologized troubled Hispanic (and other) teens. Drug addiction surfaced in two notable autobiographies, both of which appeared in 1953. The more notorious of the two, *Junky,* formed the basis of William Burroughs's fame, though he first published it under a pseudonym, William Lee. Burroughs's experience showed the romance of drug use as it passed from the secretive, black-centered world of jazz into the vanguard of the Beat Generation's white high priests. In the late 1940s, as James Traub notes in *The Devil's Playground*, Burroughs, Jack Kerouac, Allen Ginsberg, and others were already all-night haunters of the Bickford's Cafeteria in Times Square, making forays out onto 42nd Street and the Pokerino, a pinball parlor. All of them, Beats and pinball addicts alike, buzzed on amphetamines or Benzedrine like high-voltage wires.

The less-well-known memoir, *I Was a Drug Addict*, by the pseudonymous "Leroy Street," reached back to 1910, when Street, fifteen years old, was living with his family on then working-class Bank Street in Greenwich Village. Lured into inhaling heroin by a local pusher whose money-eyed and worldly mien is a magnet for local teenage boys, he describes his first high, his first ecstatic walk home along Bank Street at two o'clock in the morning, and his misery the next day. Soon, mainlining heroin, and having progressed as well to opium ("hop") and cocaine ("snow") sold in a local drug parlor, he's become part of a band of addicted kids scrounging for cash, shooting up on stoops and in vacant lots, and embarking on a series of harrowing quack cures, the first in St. Vincent's Hospital, the second in Metropolitan Hospital on Blackwell's Island. Street had overcome his habit by the early 1920s, but his memoir found its natural home in the 1950s, as addiction narratives were breaking into public consciousness.

The Beats were younger than Street: typically Depression-era children who had come of age during World War II and found a natural home among the epic dislocations of New York. Their manifesto, if they could be said to have had one, was to embrace the sense of helplessness the last twenty years had left as a legacy. In 1952 John Clellon Holmes, in a widely quoted article for the *New York Times Magazine,* credited the word "beat" to Jack Kerouac. "More than mere weariness," Holmes wrote, the term implied,

the feeling of having been used, of being raw. It involves a sort of nakedness of mind, and ultimately, of soul; a feeling of being reduced to the bedrock of consciousness. In short, it means being undramatically pushed up against the wall of oneself. A man is beat whenever he goes for broke and wagers the sum of his resources on a single number.

The Beats, Holmes insisted, weren't beset by grief, like the Lost Generation mourning the wreckage of World War I. Rather, "they were brought
up in these ruins and no longer notice them. They drink to 'come down'
or to 'get high,' not to illustrate anything. Their excursions into drugs or
promiscuity come out of curiosity, not disillusionment."

But their detachment, Holmes and other Beats claimed, wasn't detached: it was the one thing necessary for anyone embarking on the rough
passage from illusion to reality. Thus Beat New York was, in theory, not a
warren of alleys and apartments to brood or shoot up in, but a harbor
from which to see the world as it was. One cold night in October of
1951, advised by a friend to think of himself as a painter with words, Kerouac rushed out to stand in front of a bakery window, intently sketching
its contents into his notebook. He regarded this as a breakthrough, the
beginning of a newfound power to capture what was before him, whether
it was profound or trivial.

Postwar Greenwich Village thus invented a new kind of bohemian:
the young veteran, demobilized in New York and reluctant to be reabsorbed into a faceless America, yet not necessarily bent on starving for
art. At least in Holmes's formulation, the Beat Generation reached far beyond the nonconformists surrounding Kerouac, Ginsberg, and Burroughs. It might include anyone, from the novelist, the poet, and the
drug-scrambled genius to the truck driver and the junior executive. Rebellion and unenthusiastic conformity could be equally Beat: both subverted loyalty to a group or an abstract ideology, one actively and the
other passively. "For in the wildest hipster," Holmes wrote, "making a
mystique of bop, drugs and the night life, there is no desire to shatter the
'square' society in which he lives, only to elude it."

A mass population of ex-servicemen did return to the city after the
war, either to work, go to college, or simply find themselves, with the
Village a natural destination for anyone who wanted to live in a place
unlikely to press conventionality on its residents. They weren't quite a
cross section of the country: a 1948 study claimed 95 percent of all veterans in the New York area had lived here before their induction. But
they, and everyone else, male or female, drawn to nonconformist New
York in the 1950s, were a critical mass, an audience for musicians like
Parker and writers like Kerouac, and a population willing to experiment
and sometimes step over boundaries—yet without making a lifelong
commitment.

Joe Gould, a quintessential Village figure, was an example of the classic bohemian who made a life out of intellectual posturing. He became almost famous for his habit of scribbling furiously and ostentatiously in coffeehouses and restaurants from 1916 to 1952 (when alcoholism and a raft of other illnesses took him to Pilgrim State Hospital on Long Island). Supposedly he was engaged on a Proustian masterpiece, *An Oral History of Our Time*. But when he died in 1957, a friend—*New Yorker* writer Joseph Mitchell—had given up trying to piece the *Oral History* together from the piles of composition books Gould had supposedly deposited with various friends, and concluded the book never existed at all, except in a few incoherent fragments, many of them repeated obsessively over and over.

But one didn't have either to achieve or fake an artist's life: you were also part of the Beat Generation's silent majority if, in the long run, you slipped from hand-to-mouth existence into a corporate job, and then drifted into marriage, children, and the Westchester or Connecticut suburbs. This, of course, was the fictional territory of John Cheever, but found perhaps its best chronicler in Richard Yates, who captured it in his 1961 novel, *Revolutionary Road*. The hero is a veteran and former Greenwich Villager, Frank Wheeler, who somehow finds himself stranded in a ranch house in Connecticut with a distraught wife and two small children.

Wheeler's nights are empty except for droning conversations about real estate, parties of willed conviviality with other, equally lost suburbanites (who often chat about the emptiness and smugness of suburban life), and a disastrous amateur theater production of *The Petrified Forest*, which begins his gradual descent into tragedy. *Revolutionary Road* is a book set primarily in the suburbs, but it—and its characters—are haunted by a New York past, now abandoned except as the destination of their morning commute (and as the place from which to miss trains homeward if they're trying to manage an affair or drinking after hours in a midtown bar).

For Wheeler, his claustrophobic house and the front path he tries to build but never finishes constantly betray him to memories of the postwar years during which he'd gone to college and moved to Bethune Street in the West Village, "wearing the proud mantles of 'veteran' and 'intellectual' as bravely as he wore his carefully aged tweed jacket and washed-out khakis." As a young veteran, he proudly takes on odd jobs as a longshoreman and night cashier in a cafeteria (the Depression tendency to romanticize hard masculine work had kept its power).

Eventually he meets his future wife, April. But her ambitions as a drama student and his as an intellectual both atrophy, and thus they end up in Connecticut, she cold, confused, and resentful, he holding down a vacuous job at a Manhattan business machine company. His only sources of hope are a chimerical plan to move to France, a blowhard business entrepreneur who courts him for a new job, and an affair with a secretary, conducted in and around the Village as if to revisit his few years of postwar hopefulness, but curdled by the fear that April's old friends might spot them in Washington Square.

Of course countless husbands happily fled the city every evening, eager for darkening lawns, whispering trees, wives, children, martinis, and Milton Berle on television. But a shadow had fallen on both the country and city nights, a malaise that kept reasserting itself in fiction and nonfiction alike. New York began figuring in the public imagination as a jungle of tourists, dissolute beatniks, philandering husbands, battling youth gangs, raving drug addicts, and knife-happy minorities. But the suburbs, for all their attraction to families, somehow failed to benefit from the contrast: they were already being labeled as dispiriting and sterile.

NIGHTCLUB REQUIEM: MODERNITY, CRIME, AND THE NERVOUS STREETS OF THE LATE 1950S

As Manhattan's last elevated line began coming down in 1955, Third Avenue emerged from beneath its tracks and girders like a hungover drunk waking up in the sunlight: it was disheveled, grimy, unsure where it had been or where it was going. The el had been running overhead 24 hours a day since 1878, depressing real estate values but also offering cover to seedy bars and a vital if shady street life. When the rows of dingy brick tenements, their begrimed windows, and their aged storefronts emerged into the harsh Manhattan light, for a time they remained a mocking contrast to the new, clean, and spare International Style skyscrapers that were beginning to rise in midtown. Third Avenue, especially in the blocks near 50th Street, had become a mecca for gay cruising, called "Bird Alley" because of a cluster of bars with avian names, like the Blue Parrot on 53rd Street, the Golden Pheasant on 48th, and the Swan on 54th.

In recollections of the 1950s, in films, and in photographs, perhaps the most striking feature of Manhattan that emerges again and again is its emptiness—the abandoned look of even its most important arteries. Third and Sixth Avenues had the excuse of sudden exposure after decades under the shadow, soot, and screech of their elevated lines. But much of the rest of New York looked similar—beaten up and exhausted by hard use. This comes out most poignantly in photographic records of Greenwich Village. The streets are void of traffic, both vehicular and pedestrian; parking spaces abound; the signs are handmade and amateurish (the creepy-crawly lettering on the banner of Rick Allmen's famed Café Bizarre on West 3rd Street looks like a high school effort). Café and restaurant interiors resemble grammar school classrooms, a clutter of junk and a creativity more childish than avant-garde. Exteriors seem forgotten, embalmed: in a 1960 photo the White Horse Tavern on Hudson Street, now a sidewalk café overrun by models and stockbrokers, looks like what it then really was: a seedy bar on a corner of fire escapes and walkup apartments. Its literary clientele, like Dylan Thomas and Delmore Schwartz, drank in a dankness that was a result of neglect rather than artful image preservation.

Even triumphs of modernism could look bewildered or bereft against the backdrop of early postwar New York. On Park Avenue in midtown, Lever House (1952) and the Seagram Building (1959), photographed before they've aged into the streetscape, seem wet behind the ears, just blocks away from a Third Avenue still holding on to the grubbiness it would soon lose under high-rise development. The whole atmosphere of the city in the 1950s was a blend of energy and enervation. In retrospect it looks—and the culture that surrounded it seems—incomplete, either half-built or half-decayed, with energy seeping away even where it seemed abundant.

Television particularly fed on the city night scene, and sold its allure to Americans everywhere, yet sapped it in the long run. As a medium New York had invented and in the early 1950s still largely controlled, it grew so robustly after World War II that it panicked both the radio and film industries. And, in its early years, TV seemed, perhaps even more than radio, a direct emanation from a Manhattan of nightclubs, theaters, restaurateurs, and newspapermen, flashed out over the nation in a burst of urban energy. One of the earliest television hits was Ed Sullivan's *Toast of the Town,* which premiered in 1948 as a CBS broadcast and emanated from an old legitimate theater, the Manhattan, built in 1927.* It was eminently New Yorky. Sullivan had an equine face and corpselike demeanor, but he was a *Daily News* columnist, in close contact with the city's entertainment industry. The sprinkling of celebrities usually found in the audience, called up by Sullivan for a bow, gave the program a glaze of excitement and urbanity, although the performers ranged from Metropolitan Opera stars to Elvis Presley to jugglers and puppets.

Sullivan's archrival, Walter Winchell, had been hosting a popular radio program since 1930, and in 1952 brought his gossip and manic persona to television on ABC, with a program broadcast at 6:45 every Sunday evening. Viewers who tuned in for Winchell's first show, and who switched to CBS at 8 for Ed Sullivan (who that night was featuring Lauritz Melchior from the Met and blues pioneer W. C. Handy), saw not only a sharp contrast in personal styles, but the protagonists in a feud: Sullivan and Winchell cordially hated each other. And they were only part of a large and fractious group of New York media hustlers, all busy parlaying themselves into national celebrity and cementing nighttime New York's position as a transcontinental powerhouse of popular entertainment. Milton Berle, whose Tuesday night *Texaco Star Theater* had begun airing from Radio City only a few months after Sullivan's 1948 premiere, had become a national phenomenon. Quintessential Gothamites like Bennett Cerf, Arlene Francis, and Dorothy Kilgallen chatted with mystery celebrities on CBS's *What's My Line.* (Kilgallen, in a feathery blindfold, would tap her head and say, "Let me see—who's in town? Who's in town?") Between 1950 and 1955 Sherman Billingsley hosted a celebrity-driven weekly CBS interview show, live from the Stork Club.

In September 1954, NBC extended the reach of TV past midnight with Steve Allen in *Tonight.* In advance newspaper ads drumming up sponsors for the new show, NBC touted the romance of nighttime New York as the program's chief draw. "TONIGHT takes America to Broadway during its most glamorous hours. It will go backstage and out front on glittering opening nights. . . . [It] brings world-famous stars, critics and nightclub entertainers to the hearthsides of the nation." *Tonight* became a major hit when Jack Paar took over from Allen in 1957 and by the 1960s

---

* The theater became Billy Rose's Music Hall in 1933 and CBS had refitted it as a radio studio in 1936. It was well adapted to the vaudevillesque roster of acts that characterized Sullivan's show; the building is still used by David Letterman today.

it was opening with airborne views of the Manhattan skyline—supposedly sophisticated metropolitan champagne for a pajama-clad and curler-wearing nation as it drowsed in bed.

Despite Lauritz Melchior on *Ed Sullivan* and high-hat dramatic programs like *Playhouse 90,* New York television was as often lowbrow as otherwise: many of Berle's comedy turns were essentially burlesque. Thus Chuck Callahan's attempt to retrofit his old skits was not quixotic in inspiration, even though it failed to make him a living. And despite Paar's reputation for intelligence and literate wit, his premiere program began with Helen O'Connell singing "Let's Get Away from It All" in the company of Kokomo Jr., a baby chimpanzee in overalls who had become a network mascot and last-ditch crowd pleaser (in a surviving tape of the show, O'Connell comes as close to gritting her teeth as it's possible to do while still singing).

But even by the mid-1950s, changes in the television industry—and in the nation at large—were unmistakably pulling the center of gravity away from New York. The sentiment behind McCarthy-era witch hunts and *Red Channels* (1950), the rabid book that made an exposé of supposed communist influence on radio and television, was anti-urban, beneath that anti-Semitic, and thus inherently anti–New York. Movie studios, at first contemptuous of television, had become so afraid it would make dinosaurs of them, that they leapt at the opportunity when ABC, an upstart network contending with the dominance of NBC and CBS, turned to Hollywood for new programs. In 1954 Disney came up with *Disneyland*; Warner Brothers agreed to a deal for several new series, including *Cheyenne,* a hit that lasted seven seasons. This marked the beginning of television's exodus to the West Coast. News, soap operas, and a few other kinds of programming remained, but New York had begun relinquishing its grip on the taste and texture of the American evening.

Newspapers were also losing their vitality, and that too was ominous for New York. Since the 1700s they'd been interpreting the city night, sensationalizing it, making of it a reverberator of the desires and fears of readers. But television began looking for bland leading men like Ronald Reagan to serve as hosts; hawk-faced and hatchet-minded big-town newsmen didn't fit the Hollywood paradigm. Ed Sullivan's Sunday evening show stayed on the air until 1971, but Winchell's career had sunk into a prolonged and agonizing decline. He got into a feud with Sherman Billingsley, lost his radio program and last television show in 1959, then mired himself in yet another quarrel, this time with Jack Paar. He finally lost the column that had made him famous when Hearst's *New York Mirror* folded in 1963. Mellowed, Winchell and Sullivan patched up their old enmity, but they did so as old elephants expiring in their graveyard—a spirit Winchell conveyed in a speech prepared for delivery at the Friars Club. "As we both grew older," it read, "we found that we were citizens of a kingdom more beautiful than Camelot, . . . a very real and magic place called Broadway." It was mawkish, but there was truth in it. Both men were survivals of a nightclub era that had peaked in the 1920s and 1930s and was now, like them, in its dotage. Winchell died in 1972, Sullivan in 1974.

All the prevailing cultural winds blew away from the fraying Northeast, and particularly New York. Increasingly it was rural America that soothed movie, popular music, and television audiences. ABC's early success with Warner Brothers' *Cheyenne* was prophetic, spawning a long line of successor westerns. Mass-market music, especially early rock and roll, drew many of its singers and much of its energy from the South. Elvis Presley famously appeared on *The Ed Sullivan Show* in 1956, and set off a national shockwave, an eruption of redneck energy in the ancestral Broadway of vaudeville, Florenz Ziegfeld, and *My Fair Lady*. It was as if a Southland raree show had invaded and conquered both Manhattans—the sophisticated island of penthouses and the brawling metropolis of factories, tenements, and saloons.

By 1960, New York was not so much eclipsed as fractured between the cool, modernist, Kennedy-era elegance that still made it a magnet for the elite, and the bloody urban jungle it had increasingly become, while the popular imagination drifted toward Mayberry and Disneyland. Of course declining popular appeal had a hidden benefit: New York once again became attractive to the misfit, the inspired malcontent, and other swimmers against the current whose energy promised an eventual revival. But in spite of them the energy of the city seemed endangered as never before. Nineteen-fifty-nine and 1960 were a hinge, with the new chic and the new anomie both visible, in jarring proximity, and abundantly publicized.

An abiding vitality showed in two new landmark restaurants, just opened: they marked the earliest dawn of New York's latest, most durable, and still roaring restaurant mania. The Forum of the Twelve Caesars opened in 1957 at 57 West 48th Street, and the Four Seasons in 1959 in the Seagram Building at 52nd Street and Park Avenue. Both were brain-children of Restaurant Associates, headed by Jerome Brody and Joe Baum. Both were designed to be celebrations of luxury on an imperial scale, like Rector's and Murray's Roman Gardens, the theatrical lobster palaces of the Gilded Age. Brody and Baum wanted even more luxury, yet they were also determined to score it in a modern key. Both the Forum and the Four Seasons were meant to, and both did, become topics of national discussion. More important, both served to lure suburbanites back to the city for an evening that promised something unattainable in their homes and shopping centers.

Of the two, the Four Seasons was the more expensive, the more strikingly designed, and the longer-lived. But the Forum of the Twelve Caesars was the trailblazer. In photographs and descriptions, it looks like a furniture store catering to the Mafia—garish red-flocked wallpaper (albeit imported from Venice), wood paneling, marble tabletops, a pseudo-Roman mosaic, and vaguely classical-looking settees in place of banquettes—a tipsy blend of austere modernism and the rococo urge that was just beginning to assert itself as the 1960s neared. The designer, William Pahlmann, had discovered a dozen paintings of the Caesars in an antique shop, and worked them into a concept. The paintings were mirrored by twelve mini-busts mounted on 1950s-modern hexagonal panels. A massive bronze chandelier hung over the bar, and the bartenders, clad in leather jerkins, stirred martinis.

The food was dressed up as if for a toga party—Fiddler Crab à la Nero, Young Chicken Roasted in Clay (brought to the table complete with attached blue ribbon and waxen seal), and Nubian Chocolate Roll (essentially the flourless chocolate cake still standard in pricey restaurants). A full dinner ran about $22, including a bottle of Château Carbonnieux, 1953. The Four Seasons was more ambitious than the Forum—it cost a then unprecedented $4.5 million; its Philip Johnson interior, its restrained setting in the Seagram Building, and its serious approach to its food gave it a staying power that has yet to fade.

In the postwar boom there was more than enough money in Manhattan for the Restaurant Associates theme to become a trend, and the city was full of places suitable as backdrops for Jackie Kennedy, the Duke and Duchess of Windsor, or aspirants to their international style. But the rest of the picture was ragged. Broadway was holding on, although it hadn't regained its prewar vitality, and—as with jazz—the center of theatrical vitality had begun shifting downtown to off-Broadway venues. The 1950s wasn't a boom era for nightclubs—the Stork was fading (it closed for good in 1965). El Morocco relocated into elaborate new quarters on East 54th Street and flourished for a while, but shut down in 1961 (later, in a prolonged twilight, it reopened and closed several times; it was still in business as late as 1991).

For tourists the Latin Quarter was the chief nightclub mecca; in 1958 it was producing a somewhat chastened Eisenhower-era version of the *Ziegfeld Follies*. The dancers came onstage in baby buggies and gondolas, dressed, according to a *Life* magazine story, as "angels, temptresses and caged birds." One swooped out over the audience on a flying rig, trailing an eight-foot-long train of feathers. An "island beauty" took a topless onstage shower under a wooden tub, though with her back to the viewers. The girls glided out into the audience and, *Life* promised, "sometimes do their shaking and swirling so close to the tables that their skirts knock over the customers' drinks."

But it was a short walk from the Four Seasons, the new El Morocco, or even the Latin Quarter, to a darker New York. In the early summer of 1959 Billie Holiday died in New York Hospital after another drug arrest. On the West Side, Lincoln Center was under construction, but as it went up the poverty and violence of the surrounding neighborhood remained. On Saturday evening, August 29, a gang murder was brewing. It wasn't more senseless and grotesque than the usual: two innocent sixteen-year-old boys, on their way home from a movie at midnight, took a shortcut through the playground on 47th Street between Ninth and Tenth Avenues, ran into a ragtag gang—the Vampires—and were stabbed to death with a seven-inch Mexican dagger.

Salvador Agron (1943–1986), the sixteen-year-old killer, became famous first as "Dracula," and eventually as "the Capeman"—because when he and a friend murdered the teens, Agron was wearing a blue nurse's cape with a red lining. We know his story because Agron had been visited in prison and later befriended by Richard Jacoby, a graduate student working on a thesis about the death penalty; they later collaborated on a book, *Conversations with the Capeman,* which Jacoby published in 2000. Asked by veteran New York reporter Gabe Pressman whether he'd kill again if he could, Agron snapped back, "I feel like killing you, that's what I feel like." He'd told the cops who arrested him, "I don't care if I burn, my mother can watch." The murder was a stupid, drugged-out mistake: Agron and his accomplice, Tony Hernández, both Puerto Rican, thought they were avenging an anti-Hispanic attack by a rival gang of Anglos, the Norsemen (in fact no such attack had taken place).

After his arrest Agron swore that he had no memory of the killing. He did recall, though, the light rain that had been falling on the early evening of August 29. He was living on West 77th Street, hustling to make his rent, and he had gone out walking. "Saturday night," Agron later wrote,

> the night life was taking its usual course. Young Puerto Ricans . . . would congregate earlier in the evening, drink the cheap wine, and share it with different gangs that were considered "brother clubs." . . . Some liked to dance. Some liked to smoke Marijuana. And others like to fight. There is not much good to be found in cities such as New York, and even more so during the 1950s.

At 9:30 the pay phone on the corner of 73rd Street rang (this was how gangs communicated before pagers and cell phones), and a member of a "brother club" told the Vampires that the Norsemen had just attacked and beaten some Puerto Ricans; Agron and his friend Tony Hernández made their way to the playground and stabbed two victims, Anthony Krezinski and Robert Young, who staggered off and died separately, in two nearby tenement buildings where they'd gone for help.

Puerto Ricans were still the minority that most scared the city, and the reaction was hysterical: Agron was convicted on two counts of murder and sentenced to die, the youngest New Yorker ever to be so condemned. By the summer of 1960, he was in the death house at Sing Sing—listening, twice every week, to a whining sound somewhere in the building, as the staff tested the generator that powered the electric chair. Sometimes, both the inmates and guards would hear an odd noise from the Dance Hall, the corridor that led to the execution chamber, as if chains were being dragged along the concrete floor. The guards heard it too, and investigated, but could find no cause. New York's governor, Nelson Rockefeller, commuted Agron's death sentence, and he left Sing Sing to spend the next twenty years shuttling through the New York State penal system, doing time at Attica, Dannemora, Auburn, and Greenhaven, finally winning parole in 1979. He worked as a porter, but within a year he was on crack, and had begun a final downward spiral: he died of pneumonia in North Central Bronx Hospital on April 22, 1986.

Agron continued to insist he couldn't remember the actual stabbings, even after years of mulling over his past and trying incessantly to recall the night of the crime. Born in Puerto Rico, he'd come to New York at the age of about ten, quickly gotten into trouble on the streets, and spent time in reform schools and rehabilitation programs. There was only one memory he could call up to presage the Capeman episode. As an eleven-year-old, playing Superman on the fire escape, he'd slipped or jumped (he couldn't remember which), plunged five stories into the yard, and been taken to Bellevue Hospital with, luckily, only a broken arm. But from that point to his death, he was rarely out of trouble, with the playground crime the nemesis that would govern the rest of his life.

The Night They Busted Sophie Tucker

By 1960 Robert Moses (1888–1981), the imperious czar of urban renewal, had been imposing his will on the map of New York since the Depression. Superhighways now ringed Manhattan and were preparing to rip into it. The Major Deegan Expressway had plowed down from Westchester along the Harlem River; by the 1960s the Brooklyn-Queens and Cross-Bronx Expressways had devoured block upon block of once vital neighborhoods in their boroughs. Slum houses had been bulldozed by the hundreds and thousands, to be replaced by barren tower-in-the-park housing projects, privately financed (like Stuyvesant Town) for middle-class tenants, or publicly funded for the poor. The former were comfortable if uniform; the latter turned into warehouses of ugliness and misery; both killed street life wherever they appeared. Moses was a confident advocate of parks and playgrounds, and built hundreds—many of which turned into sordid gathering places for low life and crime, like the Capeman murders.

Thus it wasn't surprising that his favored solution to the rapid deterioration of the West Side (which seemed to be turning into a black and Hispanic ghetto to rival Harlem in size) was a grand monumental plaza—Lincoln Center, which did, over time, transform the neighborhood. But increasingly, his plow-it-under mentality was giving pause to urbanists like Jane Jacobs (whose watershed book, *The Death and Life of Great American Cities*, came out in 1961). Vast public works, Jacobs argued, drained life from the crowded streets, prevented unplannable neighborhood serendipities, and torpedoed the random encounters that generate the vitality of the urban night.

Moses never succeeded in his scheme to blast an expressway across midtown Manhattan at 30th Street. But he did epitomize an era of urban planning suspicious of population density and spontaneous street life. His superhighways, even his vast recreational utopias like Jones Beach State Park, drew people out of the city. Where he left off developers like William Levitt took over, with housing tracts and shopping centers that kept them there. Manhattan was still powerful, but more and more as a work and entertainment destination, less and less as a self-sustaining environment. The Times Square signs were still lit and still kinetic, and Broadway still drawing crowds. Yet the ever longer runs of smashes like *My Fair Lady* were turning theater into a planned and expensive excursion for a guaranteed good time at a pre-certified hit. Broadway was no longer a crowded habitat one haunted on a nightly basis, and whose interest lay in variety and opportunity rather than predictability.

There was a tiredness in the air, a sinking sense that reacted to crime and mayhem already on the rise and destined shortly to explode. In spite of it, however, Sophie Tucker (1884–1966) was still performing. Her career as the Last of the Red-Hot Mamas had begun in the Gilded Age, passed through burlesque, theater, the *Ziegfeld Follies,* vaudeville (she debuted at Tony Pastor's last theater just before it closed), nightclubs, movies, and television. She had been a frequent Ed Sullivan guest, and played at the Latin Quarter well into the 1960s. Tucker herself attributed her longevity in the business to three sources: "spangled sentimentality; noisy vulgarity; and brassy nostalgia."

Raunch was also a venerable part of her act, and though television restricted her, her conspiratorial leer nonetheless preserved the spirit of her signature song lyrics, like "When I kiss men, they feel they've had their tonsils taken out." By 1960 she was an institution, presumably untouchable, and when she opened on October 26 at Jack Silverman's International Theatre Restaurant, a basement venue at the corner of Broadway and 54th Street, it would have seemed absurd to expect trouble: the only new elements in her show were a cowgirl routine and a parade of dresses she'd acquired for a stint in Las Vegas.

But the New York police department still had on its books a system of cabaret licenses dating back to 1941—the protect-our-boys-in-uniform era. Everyone working in a bar, a nightclub, or even a bowling alley that sold liquor had to carry a license card: these cost $2 and had to be renewed every two years, which meant a trip downtown to Worth Street for fingerprinting, photographing, and a background check. The police could shut down the entertainment at any club if even one employee lacked a valid card. Raids had been rare, but suddenly the police commissioner, Stephen Kennedy, ordered a sweep, and beginning Saturday, November 19, a thousand cops fanned out across the city and descended on nearly 2,500 clubs looking for violators. For whatever reason, they were particularly hard on some of the best-known places, including the Copacabana, the Stork (where Sherman Billingsley turned out not to have a card), Birdland, and Silverman's International, which took a particularly hard hit. Sophie Tucker's card had expired, her accompanist Ted Shapiro had none at all, and Bea Kalmus, who originated a radio show on WMGM from the club, also got a citation. The International lost its club license for four days, including Thanksgiving.

Variety smelled a rat, hinting that the licensing law had been functioning largely as a shakedown opportunity for corrupt cops, and that this was a move against clubs that had stiffed them. Cabdrivers, *Variety* said, remarked on "'regular' visits by some cops to certain niteries and eateries who are 'seen coming out nightly loaded down with groceries and sometimes booze.'" The same article added that while Tucker—76 years old, sick, and grieving over the recent death of her sister Anna—had been booted off the stage, far raunchier clubs escaped persecution. "Certain Greenwich Village spots," the grammatically challenged reporter said, "with their known 'third sex' (both genders) shows and clientele, not to mention open 'mixing' by nitery entertainers (hostesses) with the male trade, was generally believed to have had local precinct okay, else it would not have been tolerated."

Eventually the mayor, Robert Wagner, intervened, and the heat, whatever its source, subsided. But it was a revealing episode—a throwback to an era of cheeky entertainers and walrus-mustached vice crusaders, which at least now appears quaint against a background of rising violence and insidious decay. Perhaps New York's time might be running out, the energy that had never failed it before now seeping into the suburbs and beyond. From today's vantage point, the suburbs of the 1950s seem, despite their bold forms and primary colors, washed-out, stranded along barren highways that led to emptiness. But in 1960, the suburbs and largely virgin exurbs still looked full of promise. It was New York that seemed exhausted, moribund, waiting vacantly for the next wrecking ball.

In the summer of 1960, apocalypse struck the Roxy Theatre, a 50th Street landmark since 1927. It had closed in March, and by July the Lehigh Salvaging Company had been commissioned to demolish it. By the middle of that fall the outer walls were still standing, but the interior was a wreck, its roof shattered, the stage and proscenium a pile of concrete, plaster, and wood chunks. It was a photo opportunity, and on October 14, Gloria Swanson (1897–1983), the silent movie actress, picked her way through the rubble with a photographer, Eliot Elisofon. In a black evening gown, black elbow-length gloves, and a huge red feather boa that gashed like a welt of blood across the brown and gray ruins, she posed with her head thrown back and arms skyward. Behind her, sunlight filtered into the auditorium, projecting the outlines of dangling girders onto the broken columns and wrecked loges. The picture appeared in the November 7 issue of *Life* and it became—it remains—famous. Swanson's pose was more or less defiant, but the photograph looked like a vision of a New York in ruins as well as an elegy for the Roxy.

Something, it seemed, had ended with a final crash. So, at least, it looked in *Life*. A boom in massive office buildings was squeezing the vitality out of midtown after dark. The Lower East Side seemed doomed to desertion, Greenwich Village forlorn, Chelsea tattered. Battery Park was a dusty patch of green, gasping while commerce sucked the air out of what had once been a rowdy seaport, a home to the extravaganzas of P. T. Barnum, and a resort of theaters, brothels, all-night markets, and bars. Whole stretches of Brooklyn were sinking into poverty and dereliction.

Yet in 1960, in the midst of all this, demographers remarked a new, apparently minor, apparently anomalous fact—an odd blip in recent demographic surveys of New York. A trickle of people had begun returning to the city. Many of them had moved to the suburbs in the great waves of the 1940s and 50s and raised their children. Now, apparently, they were looking hard at their lawns, shrubbery, and recreation rooms, finding themselves increasingly discontent with what they saw, and heading back to New York. They often were, as untiring conservative jeremiads against the abominated 1960s have painted them, malcontents, rebels, troublemakers, misfits, and narcissists. But they were also the future of the city night.

CHAPTER ELEVEN

FULL MOON OVER THE STONEWALL
The Gay Epiphany, Discomania,
and the Surfacing of Hidden Night

B ETWEEN 1950 AND 1980 New York shrank from nearly
eight million people to just under seven. Manhattan and Brooklyn each went down by nearly 500,000, the Bronx by 300,000.
Only Queens and Staten Island grew at all, with their front and back
yards, garages, and TV antennas—two low-density boroughs that most
nearly resembled the close-by suburbs. Despite the excitement and
anticipation spurred by John F. Kennedy's inauguration, despite the
1964–1965 World's Fair (Robert Moses's farewell imperial extravaganza), loss and anxiety were the constant companions of a period
marked by an economic boom and a blaze of cultural experimentation.

Crime had begun a meteoric climb that would carry it to unprecedented heights in the 1970s: murders and nonnegligent manslaughters
nearly tripled within the decade, from 390 in 1960 to 634 in 1965 to
over 1,000 in 1969. Felonious assaults went from about 11,000 in 1960
to nearly 25,000 in 1967. Interracial tension mounted. Blacks, growing
increasingly discontented, vocal, and rebellious, began to replace Hispanics as the city's most feared minority, while traditional African-American
neighborhoods like Harlem and Bedford-Stuyvesant, increasingly violent,
acquired reputations as armed camps of hellish disorder—war zones cut
off from an increasingly alarmed and beleaguered city.

During the summer of 1966 riots broke out in East New York. A year
later violence erupted again, this time in East Harlem, when police shot a
man at the corner of 111th Street and Third Avenue on Sunday, July 23.
Nostrand Avenue in Brooklyn flared up later that month, then Browns-
ville in September. Riots, as always, were at their worst after dark and particularly after midnight. Television and the newspapers amplified them,

and they kept breaking out at intervals regular enough to make natives and tourists alike picture the nighttime streets as hostile jungles, teeming with predators and regressing into barbarism. And while the unrest in New York never approached the devastation wrought by the cataclysmic Los Angeles, Detroit, or Newark riots, it nonetheless contaminated the city's communal atmosphere.

Midtown, since shortly after 1900 the city's nighttime center, looked more threadbare and tired every year, with decades-old institutions like the Stork Club, Lindy's, or Toots Shor's aging and moribund. Yet by the 1960s the suburbs were beginning to show unmistakable hints of senescence as well. Levittown and similar developments, dream housing in the after-war years, had come to figure as cheaply built cattleyards, full of passive human livestock who lumbered unseeingly through mindless workdays, then sat out their evenings, faces gaping and gray-blue in the light from television sets. Their baby boom sons and daughters, restless even as children, entering adolescence and early adulthood, were showing signs of discontent. To them, dangerous or not, New York started to seem desirable, even its decrepitude romantic and alive with opportunity.

Younger entrepreneurs quickly caught on to such yearnings, and responded with the discothèque, which began generating Manhattan buzz around 1963 and became an early harbinger of revival. As suggested by its accent grave, always carefully preserved in early publicity, disco was a French import, already a plus at a time when Americans were looking toward Europe for pointers on sophistication and well-spent leisure. The *New York Times* instantly put its imprimatur on disco by publicizing two private, in fact frankly exclusionary, venues—Le Club on East 55th Street and a nearby neighbor, L'Interdit, in the basement of the Gotham Hotel on 55th at the corner of Fifth Avenue. John S. Wilson, the *Times* reporter, anatomized them with an anthropologist's tone of sober discovery. "One attraction of the discothèque," he wrote,

> is continuous recorded dance music. Primarily geared to the twist, the Madison and allied steps, the records are played through a stereo system and programmed by a concealed disk jockey in response to the moods and requests of the dancers themselves who are drawn from what used to be known as Café Society and frequently include people of some prominence.

Of course everyone who had tried to define Café Society, from Emily Post onward (she struggled with the term in the 1940s), found it elusive. But it seemed to include celebrities of whatever stripe, their friends, and whoever else had the money, the looks, the clothes, or sometimes just the yearning to be seen among the rich and famous. This might bother a taxonomist, but retailers were delighted, since Café Society radiated cachet and anybody who wanted to be fashionable could aspire to it. By 1964, Saks's mid-priced 34th Street outlet was selling disco dresses for as little as $17.98—obligatorily black, figure-hugging, and with a tight circular ruffle just above the knees. "The swingiest, zingiest of dancing Disco dresses," Saks called one, "a skirt that ends in double flounces of the hemline for the perpetual motion of the lively new dances. The neckline dips provocatively in back. In soft clinging acetate and rayon black crepe, fully lined."

Disco energized the languishing nightclub world. The Village Vanguard, whose jazz programs were faltering (the club was often empty and shuttered by 1:30 a.m.), introduced disco dancing between jazz sets in 1964, and the mix was an immediate success, keeping the Vanguard open until three or four in the morning. Shepheard's, in the basement of the Drake Hotel on East 56th Street, was small, with a dance floor only twelve feet square, but unlike L'Interdit and Il Mio (another new disco, at Delmonico's on Park Avenue), it wasn't private, admitted all comers, and was promptly mobbed. By late 1964 even the floundering El Morocco, in a new location at 307 East 54th Street, had opened an on-premises disco called Garrison, with an orange and red decor and fake plants hanging from the ceiling. The next month the Stork Club, gasping and even closer to demise than El Morocco, opened a disco in its Shermaine suite, in a bid to supplement its wheezy clientele with young people dancing the frug, the twist, and the watusi.

But the most successful early discos were more shrewdly planned. Sybil Burton was the entrepreneur behind the wildly successful Arthur,* which opened in 1965 on the site of the original El Morocco at 154 East 54th Street. Arthur was a late night place (it didn't open until 10:30). It was proudly British (a live band, the Wild Ones, performed between recorded sets, and all its members were dressed like Rex Harrison). And from the

---

* Burton chose this name to ride the current Beatles craze: supposedly when someone asked what he called his haircut, John Lennon answered, "Arthur."

outset Burton crammed it with celebrities: Rudolf Nureyev, clad in a Beatles suit, danced the frug with Burton on the club's opening night, and the crowd included Senator Jacob Javits, Tennessee Williams, Truman Capote, Liza Minnelli, and the dauntless Sophie Tucker, now 81 and only a few months away from death.

By 1966 another disco, Cheetah, financed by Borden Stevenson (Adlai's son), had opened on Broadway at 53rd Street. It was immense: the dance floor could handle a thousand couples. Soon, in a sign of nighttime activity's quickening migration to lower Manhattan, two clubs—the Electric Circus and Dom—appeared in the old Polish National Hall building on St. Mark's Place. Electric Circus specialized in brain-scrambling light effects and a suburban crowd eager for East Village edge; Dom was a more traditional dance club with a jukebox and mostly black customers. As discos proliferated, however, the jukeboxes disappeared and the disc jockey, once a nonentity crouched in a booth, mixing tracks on turntables, became an immured celebrity, lauded for his skill at capturing the mood on the dance floor and maneuvering it toward ecstasy (Slim Hyatt of Le Club and later Shepheard's was an early example).

But why the disco, and why has it survived a half century later? In part at least, because its formula was in fact old and tested: the music, dancing, drinking, noise, and moral adventurousness are also the distinguishing traits of the 19th-century concert saloon; the disco's glamour and conspicuous partying also linked it with the speakeasies and nightclubs of the 1920s and 30s. Its only real innovation was the introduction of postwar sound and lighting technology. But that had a profound effect: live musicians disappeared and paying customers, gyrating under the lights, became the entertainment. Go-Go dancers were an appurtenance; live performers occasionally appeared, but only as novelties. The energy and the allure of a successful disco came from its dance floor brushes with celebrities, the electricity of writhing bodies, and the knowledge that in the mob and the thunder of the music, everyone was both the center of all attention and safely anonymous. The barrier between star and audience seemed to dissolve; even dancing celebrities, like the nobodies, were wrapped up as if in cellophane by exuberant motion and the pounding musical surf.

Discos were an industrial version of the home sound system to which, by the 1960s, almost every discontented high school and college student was addicted. Also, at the heart of any disco—commanding the bacchic

dance, the behemoth amplifiers, leviathan speakers, turntables, and vinyl—
a techie wizard crouches in his exalted isolation booth, not unlike the
brooding, megalomaniac adolescent in his Baldwin, Long Island, bedroom.
Still, clubs like Electric Circus and Cheetah promised a breakout from that
very suburban isolation. Once again the city was making itself an attrac-
tant, this time by reurbanizing the very electronic miasma of radio, TV,
and recorded music that had helped support suburban sprawl.

By 1965, disco had thrust out a branch, destined to be influential in
later Manhattan nightlife—the catered disco party, held at regular intervals for an invited clientele. These were pioneered by David Mancuso in
the Loft at 647 Broadway, near Houston Street. His earliest parties were
bimonthly and served no alcohol. Aside from the music, their attraction
came from the dancers themselves and whatever stimulants they might
have brought with them. Mancuso carefully made the place homey, in
1960s fashion, by equipping it with a yoga shrine; he was also fond of bal-
loons, and his aim, he said, was to regenerate the lost atmosphere of a
child's birthday party: "It was a childlike experience, not childish, . . . a
very safe environment. You could let yourself go."

Of course its hominess to the select group invited lent the disco party
an irresistible air of exclusivity.

REVOLUTION IN SHERIDAN SQUARE:
THE STONEWALL RIOTS, JUNE 27–28, 1969

In New York, discos were also safety zones—havens where those normally
excluded from the city's visible life could meet and mix with the prominent. Sybil Burton wanted celebrities at Arthur, but her business depended, as Tim Lawrence phrases it in his disco history, *Love Saves the
Day* (2004), on "the new urban class of hairdressers, models, and shop assistants." This new class—and its occupations, of course, stretched well
beyond these three representative jobs—included a heavy cohort of gay
men. And from the very beginning of the trend, disco entrepreneurs had
drawn a gay clientele even when (as often happened) they officially discouraged it.

Arthur, Shepheard's, L'Interdit, and Il Mio were all in the East 50s,
near Bird Alley, the cluster of bars and the gay cruising strip along Third
Avenue. The dancers at David Mancuso's Loft were a polyglot crowd,
black and white, female and male (though with males predominating),

and heavily gay. But this was rarely even whispered in the mainstream media: despite its reputation as the fount of all things permissive, the 1960s began as a decade of pronounced hostility toward gay men, particularly in New York. Except for a respite in the 1920s, little had changed since 19th-century spasms of intolerance like the sporting press attack on Captain Collins and the Star House in 1842, or the *Herald*'s 1892 crusade against the Slide on Bleecker Street.

In the 1960s homophobia often took on a tone of academic pseudo-impartiality, in which the writer is pained to contemplate the sad depravity of the man who desires other men. Such was a pharisaical 1963 piece by Robert Doty in the *New York Times,* "Growth of Overt Homosexuality in City Provokes Wide Concern." As Charles Kaiser observes in *The Gay Metropolis: 1940–1996,* the piece was replete with sententious and seemingly authoritative pronouncements: "The old idea, assiduously propagated by homosexuals," Doty wrote, "that homosexuality is an inborn, incurable disease, has been exploded by modern psychiatry, in the opinion of many experts." Clearly the animating principle of the article was to intimidate, perhaps because of an inkling that gay men were beginning to emerge too bravely from their proper back alleys: Doty carefully identifies the neighborhoods that gay men seemed to be overrunning in the early 1960s—Greenwich Village, the Upper East Side from the 40s through the 70s, the West 70s, and the "dregs of the invert world" on Eighth Avenue and 42nd Street.

However threatening it was to have their haunts pointedly identified by the city's leading newspaper, gay men nonetheless found a sense of safety in discos, and a group bond that may have been passing or wholly illusory but which was powerful nonetheless. The hideaway that allows something forgotten or forbidden to remember itself and come to life had always been a specialty of nightlife. The disco dance floors, loud, dark, and crowded, veiled as much as revealed by the mirrored balls and rapid-fire lights, were a reassuring place to dance with other men. There were women on the floor as well, and the dancing was frenetic, as much a solo as a pair activity: it often wasn't clear who was dancing with whom. Both the gay or the straight "club kids," as they were beginning to be known, could both be themselves and not themselves.

This new, hesitant visibility irked even supposedly tolerant cultural organs like the *Village Voice.* Its tone in the mid-1960s wasn't Olympian, like the *Times*; rather, it was often cold and dismissive. Greenwich Village remained a bastion of the Old Left, whose passion for racial equality didn't always extend to sexual preference. Much as the Village of the 1950s and early 1960s might revere Marx or welcome Timothy Leary, it was decidedly nervous about the Mattachine Society, it seemed. In a 1965 piece, "MacDougal at Midnight: A Street Under Pressure," Jack Newfield describes a police department crackdown on a street the cops, and apparently the *Voice,* perceived as too shameless even for the Village.

"MacDougal Street at midnight," Newfield wrote. "Homosexuals cruising, pill-buyers waiting, transvestites parading, and tourists watching. Aging Kerouac heroes picking up Lolitas. Black-leather-jacketed motorcyclists gunning their growling motors. High-school kids looking for a party; drunks looking for a fight." While Newfield himself remained objective about the denizens of MacDougal Street, the piece isn't sympathetic, devoting considerable space to the complaints of merchants and traditional intellectuals against the marauding lowlifes and trashy teenagers.

The bars on MacDougal, a coffeehouse owner complains, "serve drinks to minors. They let queers and whores hang out. They have belly dancers. They get people drunk." Bob Dylan's "The Times They Are A-Changin'" blares from a loudspeaker in one place, while in a coffeehouse nearby an NYU junior opines that "the bad characters who come down here are drawn by the really criminal things—drugs, prostitution, perversion." In 1965 gay venues were largely invisible in the *Voice*'s display ads, and not the subject of much attention in its editorial pages. Gay men and women were famous components of Village eccentricity, and had been since the 1920s, yet the neighborhood itself, even its most famously progressive weekly, were at best indifferent and at worst actively hostile to a population that had by now come to define it.

Within a few years, however, the ice had begun to thaw. Mart Crowley's *The Boys in the Band,* a breakthrough play about a gay birthday party, opened in 1968 at the Theatre Four on 55th Street, and the *Voice* praised it as "an earnest, compassionate effort to speak honestly about homosexual experience." *Hair,* the musical that opened on April 28 at the Biltmore Theatre and ran until 1972, made an even more widely visible breakthrough. In its earliest version, it had played at Joseph Papp's Public Theater in 1967, then moved to Cheetah, the disco on Broadway at 53rd Street, where it performed before the dance floor opened. *Hair*'s plot made no sense whatever, but its spirit was clear, reducing the Vietnam

War to dark absurdity while celebrating sex (interracial, straight, and gay), and, famously, nudity, when the cast stripped for the first-act finale. Perhaps for the first time in history, there was no question that Broadway nudity *was* nudity—not an illusion of pink tights or burlesque teases or the *Ziegfeld Follies'* peekaboo staging. *Oh! Calcutta!* followed a couple of months later with more nudity and more sex, but couldn't compete as a cultural phenomenon.

Hair ran into trouble on tour—Boston and Chattanooga closed it down—but in New York, Chicago, and Los Angeles, it struck a chord. It was too giddy to seem confrontational, and that allowed it to insinuate once forbidden thoughts into the mass-audience mind. If *The Boys in the Band* was a harbinger of a new seriousness soon to be accorded to the lives of gay men, *Hair* marked an early stage in the emergence of what had once seemed to be dark perversions into whimsies, causes for public celebration rather than private guilt. And the line between the stage and the auditorium blurred: the Broadway version of *Hair* began with the cast mingling with the audience before gathering onstage for the opening number, "The Age of Aquarius."

Yet there was something tentative about such events; in retrospect they were only a prelude to real enactment, which came a little over a year later, striking with a surprise and a violence that unmistakably mark it as a watershed. The revolution began imperceptibly on a Friday evening, June 27, at the Stonewall Inn, a Christopher Street bar even its regulars admitted to be tough and sleazy. Like a majority of gay bars at the time, it was owned and run by the Mafia, who paid off the police to leave it alone.

This wasn't exactly a live-and-let-live arrangement: the gangsters on the whole despised their customers, and even the gay mobsters who sometimes patronized the place were nervous about being seen there. The cops, though handsomely bribed, gave up none of their contempt for the people paying them off: they still staged frequent raids, if only to swagger and remind both the customers and owners who really held the strings of power. The Stonewall itself served the customers as if they were livestock: the bar had no running water, and the bartenders cleaned used glasses by dunking them in tubs of standing water that grew filthier by the hour.

According to Martin Duberman's 1993 account of the riots in *Stonewall,* the men (and relatively few women) who frequented the Stonewall seemed eminently likely to crumble under intimidation. There was a contingent of drag queens among the Stonewall's regulars, including Sonia (born Ray or Rey) Rivera, whom Duberman interviewed extensively for his book, as well as a mixed crowd of younger gay men, ranging in age from their teens through their thirties, and a few lesbians. Among the Stonewall's chief attractions were its tolerance for drugs, its dance floor (at the time the only one in any New York gay bar), and a Go-Go boy in a cage. It was a refuge of sorts, but not a comfortable one, given its mob ownership, the police periodically dropping in to intimidate and humiliate the customers, and the vocal contempt of the mostly male, two-fisted, by-God macho literary set that patronized the Lion's Head Bar next door.

June 27 began as an otherwise uneventful Friday evening at the Stonewall, with no warning that the gears of routine were complaining, no inkling that a subterranean fault line had been pressured beyond endurance and that an earthquake was about to strike. Accounts of eyewitnesses differ widely about what actually happened that night and over the few days following.* Everyone, though, agrees on the immediate cause: an unexpected raid on the bar, spearheaded by Deputy Inspector Seymour Pine from the First Division police headquarters on East 21st Street.

The riot broke out after midnight, on the morning of Saturday, June 28. The local police unit—the Sixth Precinct, long on the bar's payroll—wasn't part of the raid, and had even tipped off the Stonewall management that trouble was imminent. According to David Carter, Pine's operation was part of a larger attack on gay bars in the Village, motivated not by homophobia, but rather by an attempt to break up a mob-run international money swindle that involved the blackmailing of gay financiers and seemed to be headquartered in the Village bars.

But the customers didn't know that at 1:20 a.m., when the white raid warning lights suddenly flashed on over the dance floor and the grim plainclothes cops strode in through the bar. At first it seemed just one more ritual humiliation. According to local law, transvestites could be arrested if they weren't wearing at least three garments appropriate to their actual gender; drag queens thus had either to convince the cops they were women or face arrest. As usual, the managers of the place had vanished, leaving the consequences to the staff and customers.

* David Carter's 2004 *Stonewall*—the most recent, detailed, and thoroughly researched history of the riots—is the source I generally follow here in cases where accounts differ from or contradict each other.

But tonight some mysterious power seemed to have changed the lines of force. It was subtly evident from the moment Pine and his entourage barged in and disappeared behind the black plywood that backed the plate glass windows fronting Christopher Street. Instead of scuttling off into the tangle of streets that branch off from Sheridan Square in various directions—the usual routine in raids—the crowd stayed put, assembling watchfully in the vest-pocket park across from the bar, as if expecting something. Then, as the cops moved heavily through the bar, some psychic switch seemed to trip. Roy Rivera recalled: "You could feel the electricity going through people. You could actually feel it."

Inside the bar the customers who hadn't fled, and who according to established raid protocol were supposed to produce identification, began to balk. Those who showed IDs were allowed to leave, but instead of skulking away, they joined the crowd. The triangular park opposite the Stonewall and the streets bordering it are a small space; merely by not dispersing the assembly reached critical mass faster than would have been the case in a more open area. It was also an easy territory to defend, and the angled streets and short blocks made for easy escape. It was a clear night, just a week past midsummer's eve, an ancient occasion for carnival; a full moon hung over the scene. When Pine came out of the bar and set about herding the arrestees into the van, he felt a sudden spasm of panic. "The crowd had grown to ten times the size," he remembered; "it was really frightening."

Gradually at first, a small train of scuffles flashed like sparks along a fuse. A drag queen, shoved by a cop into the van, hit him over the head with her purse. When he clubbed her in response the crowd began first shouting, then beating the sides of the paddy wagon. A hail of pennies began flying out of the crowd, clinking off the van and falling at the cops' feet, a silent but contemptuous reminder of the payoffs they'd been pocketing for years.

Then the bomb went off. A lesbian—never afterward identified, either by herself or by anyone else—balked when the police locked her in handcuffs and tried to push her into the van. At one point four cops at once were clawing at her as they tried to force her, flailing and screaming, toward a patrol car, but she burst out and fought them all the way back to the bar entrance; at one point, according to one witness, she pleaded with the crowd: "Why don't you guys do something?" Suddenly, a man pried a cobblestone from the pavement and heaved it across Christopher Street, where it clunked onto the trunk of a police car. This was the first of a volley of bricks and cobblestones with which the mob prosecuted its attack—a ghost memory of the loose cobbles that had served as window-smashing weapons during the 1849 Astor Place riot.

The shouting picked up in volume, and the crowd kept growing, joined by more and more passersby. Someone slashed the tires on a patrol car. The arrestees began clambering out of the now unguarded paddy wagon. The mob got angrier by the moment, and by now the police, under a derisive hail of pennies, nickels, quarters, beer cans, glass bottles, and sundry trash, realized the situation was swerving out of control. Pine decided that his five policemen were in danger of their lives and, with the mob shrieking "Pigs" and "Faggot cops!" ordered them all inside the now wrecked and empty bar, where they slammed the doors shut behind them and frantically shoved tables, two-by-fours, and anything else they could lay their hands on against them as barricades.

Now the crowd seemed to scent the cops' fear and to realize, with mounting excitement, that the tide had shifted in its favor. They assaulted the Stonewall Inn itself, pelting it with bricks, more cobblestones, garbage cans, and finally a battering ram—a parking meter ripped from its cement moorings and smashed repeatedly into the doors. The plate glass windows shattered, and the parking meter began thudding into and eventually breaking through the plywood behind it. Then someone in the crowd squirted jets of lighter fluid through the cracks. Lit matches started sailing in and landing on the lighter fluid.

Then came Molotov cocktails, which luckily sputtered out. The cops tried frantically to close the breaches opening up everywhere, but they were trapped, outnumbered, and facing a volcano of wrath powered by decades of pent-up fury. As Carter slyly notes, Detective Pine had seen heavy action at the Battle of the Bulge in World War II and had in fact written the army's manual for hand-to-hand combat. But Stonewall, he later said, was at least the equal of anything he'd seen in the war. "There was never any time that I felt more scared than I felt that night."

To their considerable credit, the police, who were armed, never fired on the crowd. This took nerve, particularly with Molotov cocktails landing everywhere, and—finally—a flaming wire-mesh trash can hurtling in: the Stonewall had little firefighting equipment. Eventually Pine discovered a vent hole just big enough to accommodate the smaller of the two policewomen who were part of the raiding party. She climbed out onto the roof, made her way to the firehouse and summoned help. When it finally arrived on the scene, it included two busloads of riot police, armored in the Darth Vader–ish helmets and shields whose design seemed meant as much to instill terror as to protect the wearer. But as they bore down on the Stonewall crowd, these threatening figures met an opposing formation: a line of men, arms linked, and advancing on them in a chorus-girl kick line and singing,

> We are the Stonewall girls!
> We wear our hair in curls.
> We wear no underwear;
> We show our pubic hair!

As the nonplussed riot troops hesitated before one kick line, another would suddenly appear behind them, mockery dissipating the symbolism of force. The shock of this reversal was, though at first unacknowledged, palpable in the stock reaction both of the police and the city's still largely unsympathetic press, which shied away from admitting the unprecedented nature of the scene. They gave it a raised-eyebrow treatment, suggested by the breezy title of the *Village Voice* report, "Full Moon Over the Stonewall." The *Times*—in one column on page 33 in the June 29 issue—presented the incident as an anomaly, and mentioned nothing about the police having been trapped in the bar at the mercy of the crowd, nothing about the fires, nothing about the kick lines.

But something had changed, and in retrospect the dismissive early accounts seem more like denials than expressions of settled contempt. Aftershock disturbances followed over the next few days, the worst on Wednesday, July 3. But their import hadn't yet sunk in, certainly not in the city at large, not even in the West Village. One man I interviewed, who had been at the International Stud, a bar on the corner of Bank and Washington Streets, only a few blocks from Sheridan Square, remembers walking home during what in retrospect was the height of the riot, but had no special recollection of the night other than that the streets seemed more crowded than usual.

Other interviewees, not caught up in the riot, and not, thanks to its back-page treatment in the press, even aware of it, recall it as marginal in their lives at the time. They were simply men, abroad at night, looking for companionship or entertainment or sex. It was only later, in the 1970s, that Stonewall achieved a significant impact. At Stonewall itself more protesters than police suffered injury, and in its immediate aftermath the harassment of gay bars went on as it had before.

But in fact a momentous transformation was underway. It's still being worked out on the city nightscape, and its theme is the emergence, even the triumph, of the outsider. For the time being the daylight New York of government and business remained in the establishment hands that had always gripped it, although a few shifts in ethnicity (and fewer still in race) had begun to occur. But what was once the outlaw night was now on its way to becoming the normal—even the normative—night.

The Return of Monsieur Daguerre: Postmodern Night, 1970–2004

Stonewall marked the beginning of a generation during which gays emerged into the national consciousness, then passed beyond mere acceptance and began to set trends. Officially, the early discos had discouraged gay patrons, while at the same time sensing that their presence made a club feel more daring, more cool. Arthur and Cheetah, for example, seem to have wanted some gay men on their dance floors but strictly limited them in both numbers and visibility by imposing a tacit quota on the number of gays to be admitted nightly. But however grudging the acceptance, the discos were a godsend: for the first time they allowed homosexuality a public forum. Within a few years drag would become a staple of American entertainment, making more or less mainstream New York stars of Charles Busch, Charles Ludlam, even the obese Divine, with her fright makeup and hoarse baritone.*

This was a break with a discriminatory past that went back as far as the sporting press attacks of the 1840s. But the disco went back even past the concert saloons of that era. Indeed they represented the curious, perhaps the last, return of Monsieur Daguerre to New York nightlife, for they were subtle heirs of his 1822 diorama near the Place de la République. Discos adapted to their own purposes the old Daguerre

---

* By 1973, so acceptable to the cultural elite had gay men become that Eleanor Steber, the revered Metropolitan Opera soprano, gave a "black towel" concert at what amounted to a gay sex club—the Continental Baths—in the basement of the Ansonia Hotel.

principle: trapping light in a three-dimensional prison of darkness, then, with lenses, mirrors, scenery, and illumination, creating an environment that thrilled and freed the suggestible imagination of an audience shut up in disorienting gloom.

Discos were at best a greenhouse in which the seeds of change could germinate: the root causes lay in history and social evolution. But the shift was unmistakable by 1970, when the Sanctuary, a disco in a converted Catholic church on West 43rd Street, began to turn itself into a primarily gay venue—though it had to cope with a law that specified that at least a quarter of the customers at a disco had to be women. Gay men first won tacit tolerance in such mixed nightclubs, then inevitably demanded and got nightclubs of their own, which then began in turn to attract adventurous straights. Homosexual lives began to seem independent, bold, and witty rather than ridiculous, and, when they led to trouble, tragic rather than sordid.

Historians differ as to whether Stonewall fomented the revolution or simply served as a watershed emblem of a change already underway. But the riots, even more than the proliferation of bars, discos, and bathhouses that both preceded and followed them, was a deep reverberation in the old ground bass of nightlife. It was one of the most remarkable episodes ever in New York's centuries-long drama of insider, outsider, and the clashes in which they meet and merge, from the 17th-century Indian massacre to slave revolts of the pre-Revolutionary period to the Astor Place riots in 1849. All were peripeties on a scale to match Greek drama. But Stonewall, while not so violent as its predecessors, introduced a new element, challenging an old scenario in which a burly male figure, embodying boulderlike American virtue, hulks over a degenerate, who cowers in the fierce light of just indignation before being swept up and tossed out of the public sight.

It was not only gays who had suffered under such treatment; almost every new wave of immigrants had undergone something similar. In the 20th- and 21st-century transformation of nightlife, Stonewall was a signal event, but only one among many. An old spell, under which New York had responded only slowly and grudgingly to the impact of new populations, had broken, allowing alien cultures to flow more easily into the life of the city, carried by ever more affordable world travel and a glut of new channels of communication eager for novel content. In the 1980s and 90s an enrichment of the city's nightlife took place as a polyglot new inflow began to repopulate the city—Dominicans, Haitians, Koreans, Chinese, Russians, Albanians, Jamaicans, few as yet with footholds in political power, but all bringing new food to the restaurants, new strains to the music, new dance and performance styles to the clubs and theaters.

Allen Ginsberg visited the Stonewall Inn after the riots; later, strolling around the Village, he remarked, "the guys there were so beautiful—they've lost that wounded look that fags all had ten years ago." In the decades after Stonewall, what was hidden became visible; what was taboo became first permissible and eventually even admirable; lives once stamped into oblivion whenever they came to light became, at least in arbiters of opinion like the now homophilic *New York Times,* measuring rods for independence, bravery, taste.

Like all revolutions this one took a toll on its beneficiaries. First there was HIV—surely already in hidden circulation in the clubs and discos ten years before the sickenings and deaths began. But there was another dimension of loss as well, inevitable where any minority assimilates itself in a broader culture. Gay life had been a secret—and thus a source not only of terror, but also excitement. It was an invisible republic with a shared language of code words, facial expressions, and gestures. Even the threat of persecution, as long as it didn't actually materialize, aroused a certain sense of adventure and exhilaration—not an uncommon thing among proscribed minorities, who respond by strengthening their bonds and devising subtler forms of communication.

Living as you would not be permitted to in cold daylight, making a nightly foray into the strange, unknown, and forbidden—these went well beyond homosexuals; they were the addictive thrills of night as western metropolises invented it. To make nighttime existence wholly visible, to declare it normal and acceptable, may be an act of generous inclusion, but also potentially deprives it of an essential alienness. Nonetheless, the 1970s and 1980s saw a considerable revival in the availability if not the adventurousness of nightlife. New places opened—Maxwell's Plum, Max's Kansas City. The news continued to register the meanness of New York's streets, its rampant crime (the murder rate kept rising until 1990), and urban flight (the population, both of Manhattan and the city at large, didn't bottom out until the 1980 census). But once dismal neighborhoods were already showing signs of renewal. By the 1970s SoHo's empty factory lofts began to fill with homesteading urban pioneers, and when Leo Castelli's gallery, long a presence on the Upper East Side, opened a SoHo branch in 1971, it precipitated a trend that turned the neighborhood first into an art center and ultimately into a tourist shopping mecca. If the typical suburban heart didn't yet burn for the pulse of Manhattan, people in flight from the average felt differently.

Nighttime New York still figured in television and in films as a nightmare—Martin Scorsese's 1976 *Taxi Driver* was an instance. But there had been a shift; Scorsese's film, with its brooding, jazzy Bernard Herrmann score, exuded a violent glamour missing from John Schlesinger's 1969 *Midnight Cowboy*, whose Manhattan was scrofulous, decrepit, fatigued, and sick. The same evolution appears in two comedies of similar date: in *The Out-of-Towners* (1970), New York turns two apple-cheeked Ohioans, Sandy Dennis and Jack Lemmon, into victims of every imaginable urban outrage. But in Woody Allen's 1977 *Annie Hall*, Manhattan was improbably romantic, a modern and at least sometimes convincing revival of the Hollywood-glamorous metropolis of the 1930s.

In the real New York of the mid-1970s, it was the second-generation discos that most visibly embodied the awakening. Ian Schrager and Steve Rubell's Studio 54 opened at 254 West 54th Street in 1977. Though many of its patrons were gay, mobs of every composition tried to pass its velvet ropes. Like some of its predecessors and many of its imitators, it was a product of recycling: an old opera house, redecorated but with the lineaments of its old existence everywhere visible. The famished appetite of trend was beginning to glut itself not on the new, but on a return to the ghost-haunted places of the city's past. History became an ingredient in the manufacture of novelties, and pastiche was the technique of choice.

Transformed into Studio 54, the 1927 theater, built by an over-hopeful opera entrepreneur named Fortune Gallo, remained more than spectrally visible, even though it had been taken over by CBS in the 1940s and used ever since as a radio and television studio. As Anthony Haden-Guest describes it in his 1997 memoir, *The Last Party*, Studio 54 was planned not to hide the theater but to celebrate it: the dance floor was the stage, complete with movable sets, and surrounded by banquettes, intended to make patrons feel both like performers and an audience. The bar was under the balcony. The theater's old dress circle, now furnished with bleachers, was a sex lounge: "You would look around and you'd see somebody's back," one habitué recalled. "And then you'd see little toes twinkling behind their ears." The basement was a VIP room. But the real secret of the club's success, apparently, was its aura of exclusivity: hopeful crowds formed every night outside the entrance; Rubell emerged to admit a chosen few and banish everyone else.

Even the serially rejected often showed up night after night, mesmerized either by the celebrities or their own masochism. But the vogue of the place—indeed of the 1970s disco phenomenon—was transient. As Haden-Guest pictures it, Studio 54's star-mobbed opening on April 26, 1977, was an unpredicted and apparently accidental fluke, the beneficiary of some arcane exchange of celebrity smoke signals. Rivals quickly sprang up, like Xenon (in Henry Miller's Theatre on West 43rd Street), and the black and gay Paradise Garage, which opened in early 1978. The reign of Schrager and Rubell ended abruptly in 1979 when they were indicted for income tax evasion: federal agents found hundreds of thousands of dollars stashed in the club, apparently in an effort to keep it off the books. Studio 54 survived the scandal, but Schrager and Rubell were sentenced to prison in 1980 and ceded control of the club to others.

By the late 1970s discos were already beginning to fade, thrashing for novelty as the vogue petered out. Discos for roller-skaters started appearing as early as 1977; determinedly seedy downtown venues like the Mudd Club opened in reaction against the bland monotony of disco music, the preening celebrities, and the club addicts. But transience was not unique to discos; it's a constant in theaters, restaurants, bars, and clubs. Both their dedication to illusion and the devotion of their patrons make them seem momentarily eternal, but the decor is characteristically gimcrack and the customers fickle. The Saint (the fabled gay disco that opened at the Old Fillmore East site on Second Avenue at 6th Street in 1980) went for Andrew Lloyd Webber–ish spectacle, with a huge suspended dome against which a planetarium projector threw light shows—most famously a panorama of stars, moving by the hundreds over a dark night sky. Xenon had a $100,000 contraption dubbed the Mothership. It was supposed to swoop down over the dancers' heads, but it broke more often than a Canal Street wristwatch.

While such places sent columnists and flaks into overdrive, and the publicity culminated in the 1977 smash hit movie *Saturday Night Fever,* discos were little more than latter-day concert saloons with recorded rather than live music and the patrons themselves supplying the entertainment. Like the John Street Theatre at the 1787 premiere of *The Contrast,* like Hanington's Panorama at the City Hotel in 1835, like the Park and Bowery Theatres, like all the saloons and movie palaces and nightclubs, the disco was in essence a black box, big enough and neutral enough to generate a self-accelerating whirlpool of people, lights, and illusion.

Despite technology, the living presence of other humans remained (and remains) a permanent magnet. Haden-Guest estimates that by 1980 perhaps 60,000 people formed the core population of New York club-goers, faithful even when the euphoria broke and one suddenly saw the dangling wires, blobbed paint, soiled fabrics, and bedraggled dancers. Of course the buzz was never wholly spontaneous; it depended on two universal stimulants, in the 1970s appearing in more extreme forms than they'd ever before assumed: sex and intoxicants. There was, of course, nothing new and everything ancient about both. Prostitutes appeared outside 17th-century Fort Amsterdam almost as soon as men took up their duties inside it. Sex clubs too had a long lineage, as Charles Dickens might have attested on the basis of his 1842 visit to Frank McCabe's Anthony Street dive. But by the end of the 1970s they were run more or less openly, like Plato's Retreat, a club that in 1975 succeeded the gay Continental Baths in the basement of the Ansonia Hotel.* A cluster of places in the meatpacking district on the western edge of Greenwich Village were early ancestors of the neighborhood's current hotel and nightclub explosion, but were much more louche, as their names explicitly suggest: the Hellfire Club (straight), or the Toilet, the Sewer, the International Stud, and the Mineshaft (gay).

Drugs were often inseparable from both the discos and the sex clubs. Like alcohol, they flouted any law or civic crusade designed to control them. But thanks to the anti-drug legislation of the World War I era, the recreational drugs of the 1970s, the 1980s, and afterward were wholly illegal and thus wholly beyond regulation, except through arrest, trial, and the draconian punishments meted out by the 1973 Rockefeller drug laws in New York. This failed to get them out of the clubs, however, and may even have sharpened their appeal to a night culture in which outlawry, to the extent that it didn't seem immediately perilous, was an attraction. By the early 1980s, moreover, the menu of fashionable drugs had expanded beyond marijuana and heroin. LSD and the hallucinogens, popularized in the 1960s by media-friendly gurus like Timothy Leary and Allen Ginsberg, had become common; cocaine had, after a period of eclipse, come back into fashion, particularly among the ambitious and striving Manhat-

* Plato's Retreat later moved to West 34th Street and closed in 1985.

tanites of the early Reagan era, who binged with equal ferocity on both work and partying. Jay McInerney's 1984 *Bright Lights, Big City* gave the phenomenon its most widely known fictional form.

While sex is surely its own catalyst, drugs, particularly in a club whose every cubic inch seems packed with sound, light, and people so close they can feel each other's body heat, no doubt helped weaken inhibitions. Promiscuity, however liberating it may have been (and in the late 1970s and early 1980s gay men were particularly likely to define their identities as primarily sexual), laid down a superhighway for sexually transmitted diseases, particularly HIV. So did the cycling fads for club drugs like PCP, methamphetamines, or poppers.

Sex and drugs were available in the suburbs, but without the excitement aroused by a crowd of exotic strangers, the absurd conviction of one's own remarkableness that comes from being in a famous place in what feels like the company of the famous, and also the occasional hint of danger. To a veteran of the 1920s or 1930s, the ricocheting lights, the booming loudspeakers, and the man spinning records in a booth might have seemed synthetic and artificial, but this merely reflected the electronic ambience of postwar American life, particularly for the baby boom.

There was a hangover; the rampant drugs and the careless sex (with its pre-AIDS faith in the omnipotence of penicillin) guaranteed one. And the churning novelties of which nightlife is built itself generate what might be called avant-garde fatigue—an instant jadedness that mocks the self-congratulatory rapture that accompanies the crossing of aesthetic or moral frontiers, and the rapidity with which this year's enfant terrible suddenly shrivels into next year's bore. And almost as soon as gentrification got underway in once raw neighborhoods like the East Village, it generated a backlash, culminating in the August 1988 Tompkins Square riots, in which squatters, driven out of their apartments by real-estate-grabbing yuppies, pelted the cops with beer bottles, rocks, and fireworks.

Yet the club scene reeled on with drugs and sex in spite of the ravages of HIV: the Saint lasted until 1988. And to a surprising degree, a remnant of much earlier nightspots soldiered on as well: vintage dance halls like the Roseland ballroom, movie palaces like Radio City Music Hall, pre-Depression supper clubs like "21," and 1930s palaces like the Rainbow Room. The highbrow culture that had begun defining itself before the Civil War remained strong, now ensconced at Carnegie Hall, Lincoln Center, and elsewhere. A few Prohibition speakeasies survive even now, still drawing crowds, like two downtown mainstays, Pete's on Irving Place and Chumley's on Bedford Street (the latter is particularly evocative, sign-free and with a cleverly placed stairway at the entrance that makes it invisible from the street).

Perhaps the chief beneficiary of the slack left in the 1980s by the ebbing of the discos was a revival of the restaurant industry. Restaurant Associates' Forum of the Twelve Caesars and Four Seasons inspired a raft of imitators: the allure of a spectacular setting reaffirmed itself when Windows on the World opened in 1976 on the 107th floor of the World Trade Center's North Tower. The luxury restaurant trade accelerated in the post-disco lull, gained momentum as the stock market boomed under first Reagan, then Clinton, and retains its energy today, with celebrity chefs like Rocco DiSpirito, Anthony Bourdain, and Jean-Georges Vongerichten inheriting much of the aura (and occasionally the inflated egotism) of movie stars, and food critics acquiring the sort of fame and power once accorded figures like Walter Winchell or the *Times's* revered drama critic, Brooks Atkinson. In the process New York, which in the beginning won its fame in food from its fields, woods, and fishing grounds, then from its mix of ethnic cuisines, became a city of gourmands to rival Paris, with chefs and restaurants striving to outdo themselves and one another with a manic energy that owes as much to Barnum and Tony Pastor as it does to Carême.

NAKED BROADWAY AND THE NEW MILLENNIUM

Times Square, at its nadir in the 1970s and 80s, famously revived in the 1990s,* driven—like almost every other change in New York's landscape—by real estate speculation. The revival was carefully planned to preserve the area's tradition of vivid streetlife, eliminating or at least hiding its sleazier elements so as to make it more attractive to theatergoers, tourists, and office workers. And indeed the New Times Square has become as much a national legend as the decline in crime rates; Disney is now more visible on Broadway than in Hollywood.

But at some cost: Times Square today has been brand-named from the

* Apart from James Traub's *The Devil's Playground,* previously mentioned, two other recent books document the Times Square revival, Alexander J. Reichl's *Reconstructing Times Square: Politics and Culture in Urban Development* (1999), and Lynne B. Sagalyn's *Times Square Roulette: Remaking the City Icon* (2001).

statue of Father Duffy at its north end to the bunkerlike cement stump of the old Times Tower at the south, and this has prompted sharp criticism from some urbanists, who see in it a theme-park blandness. Even the crowds and tour buses make it feel like an artifice conjured as if by Daguerre, an image of nightlife rather than the reality. The preponderance of tourists in the streets, armored by the innocence of their gazes, their chatter, and their rampart of coats, kids, shopping bags, home video cameras, and strollers, seem to ward off the incursions of the square's old seediness.

To some extent, however, the cleanliness is deceptive. Beneath its Disney jingles, the old guttural Times Square rasp still sounds, more insistent as the hours laten. Once the crowds thin out, especially after curtain time, one stops noticing the new office towers and the distracted morphing of the LCD billboards. Instead one starts to see the ramshackle businesses on the side streets, the mad-eyed evangelists and raree performers, crowds of tough outer borough teenagers crowding in and around the multiplex movies, and even—a survival of long gone but unforgotten burlesque— the strip clubs, reformed only to the extent that they've cut back the amount and garishness of their signage, and now appear to the street as oak-paneled doorways of the mass-produced kind that bar and steakhouse chains use to suggest upscale solidity.

Such is Flash Dancers, "A Gentlemen's Club" at 1674 Broadway, between 52nd and 53rd Streets. Once the premises was Charlie Parker's Birdland, which stopped presenting jazz in 1964 and closed in 1965; it's also just a block north of the old International Casino, the basement club where Sophie Tucker got caught in the 1960 nightclub raids. Flash Dancers sports an optimistic velvet rope in front of the entrance, a glass door rather than an oaken one, and a red-uniformed doorman, but none of the busty, leering photos that used to clutter the entrances of burlesque houses. Nonetheless it's a topless (and close to but not quite bottomless) strip club. Past the doorway, a flight of stairs leads down to a counter where you pay a cover charge, then walk into a slice of nightlife that, despite its flashing lights and disco mirror-ball, has existed in one form or another in New York since the concert saloons of the 1850s and long before.

It's not a huge place: the barroom and stage are perhaps 50 feet square, and as is true with most popular entertainment venues, commercial efficiency is the dominant design feature. Aesthetics appear to be an afterthought. The entrance seems to vanish the moment you walk through it, and the place is, like a Las Vegas or Atlantic City casino, an involutional labyrinth designed to make you circulate in a daze: the thing most visible from every corner of the room is a neon-lit cash machine bearing the legend "ATM FLASH CASH"; if you spend any time at the club, you'll need it. To the left of the ATM is the bar, to the right the stage—actually a T-shaped runway lined with chairs for patrons. A balcony with tables rises about two feet above the main floor.

At first, the women are almost invisible: the room's clutter and arrhythmically flashing lights are disorienting, and this has the effect of making flesh look less bare. When I went there, on a Monday night in the fall of 2004, the crowd was still thin. Instantly a hostess materialized and took me to a table. She was dressed in a white, synthetic-fiber gown, designed to look both demure and slinky—a recognizable latter-day evolution, even to the liquid folds and ruffles, of the Mother Hubbard gown that women always wore in the Victorian strip shows at places like Hattie Adams's near Madison Square. This could have been her first night at work. She was palpably uncomfortable, her English almost nonexistent: when she brought the $25 worth of drinks—a small diet cola and a micro-martini—and hovered by the table, she kept painfully trying to say something, which turned out, when she finally resorted to a shout, to be "I WORK ON THE TIP!" uttered with both shame and determination.

The hour was still early evening; the crowd, all male, was beginning to grow. A few sat in the chairs that line the front of the runways and make them look like sushi bars, a few others at tables in the shadows of the balcony. Flash Dancers is the antithesis of downtown, to which the quest for edginess and novelty has long since decamped. The men here seemed immobile, their faces unreadable. Two Asian businessmen sat, staring impassively toward the stage as if waiting to witness some natural event like a solar eclipse. Another, an older man in a leather jacket, was stony-faced and immobile, backed up against a column, planted on a chair, and glowering balefully toward the stage, as if he were a new Reverend Parkhurst, about to rush home and write a sermon against it.

The music is loud, jumping abruptly from track to track; the DJ seemed to be trying to spark a not otherwise evident enthusiasm for the dancers, one behind the bar and two more on the stage, as they arrived in filmy gowns, and stripped down, languidly rather than teasingly, to thongs. The women range from their mid-20s to very early 30s; as at Minsky's they wear body makeup, and the club's lighting is a flashy modesty device, with the traveling footlights that line the runway stage, the disco ball, and the colored spots that flash on and off confusing the eye and making the flesh look slightly unreal. Both behind the bar and on the runway the women's energies seem erratic; occasionally they stand absently, as if they were waiting for a bus, then they suddenly undulate around the two brass poles that serve as stage anchors, butts rotating 360 degrees and beamed like searchlights toward the audience.

One man, sitting shyly by the stage, suddenly stands up, and with rapture on his face, like an angel at a nativity scene, approaches a red-wigged dancer, and slips a $5 bill into the bikini strap that rides along the top of her hip. He seems awestruck, while she looks both remote and a little goose-bumpy, reaching down to caress his neck. They don't exchange glances, but a few minutes later he comes back, then again, and then again. Under the black lights that back all the disco spots, the money—all paper, as a matter of fact—nearly disappears, and certainly loses its business aura: the effect is as courtly and formal as masquers dancing at a Renaissance ball.

Meanwhile other women circulate from table to table. Do I want another drink? What (a modest hand kneading my shoulder) about a back rub? Would I like to dance? By this time I'd have thought it would have become obvious to everybody that I'm gay and thus a clear deadbeat, but apparently not. What about a tête-à-tête in the champagne room? "Just pick one of our elegant ladies of your choice," the club's website says, "to enjoy some private time in one of our exclusive champagne rooms sipping on only the finest of champagnes." This too is an old feature of New York clubs and concert saloons, like Billy McGlory's Armory Hall, on the way to which champagne was the first pay-as-you-go step (though not with anything in particular guaranteed as an end point).

Here too, everything is commercial, and nobody pretends otherwise. At a singles bar, gay or straight, there would be more noise, more nerve, more anxiety, and fewer tourists; at any downtown club reserved for the cool there would be more attitude, more serious attention to display—not to speak of much more interesting music, whether live or recorded. But Flash Dancers is—with no air of condescension intended—somehow more universal, more reflective of the ancient continuity beneath the city's nightly reinvention. The scene here, to someone fortuitously removed from it by sexual preference, looks neither like the victimizing of women nor the cheating of gullible men.

New York has never, for all its reputation, been quite as wide open as, at different times during their histories, New Orleans, San Francisco, Chicago, and Kansas City all have. Every push from the bars, brothels, concert saloons, dance halls, and burlesque houses met with a return shove from the churches, government, and an alarmed citizenry. Under La Guardia, New York shut burlesque down, but it soldiered on in the supposedly staid Midwest. It was Richard Rodgers and Lorenz Hart, the epitome of wit and Manhattan sophistication, after all, who wrote the lugubrious and essentially moralistic "Ten Cents a Dance." We have our fleshpots, but a long history of alternately tolerating and harassing them has produced the management skills that keep things from going too far, and with that a kind of dignity.

Apparently, Flash Dancers affords customers neither mad heights of ecstasy nor the depths of whatever they imagine to be hell. It seems neither a palace of license in which to throw off your inhibitions, nor a barn of rutting lust against which to swing your reformer's ax. From a detached viewpoint, the most surprising thing about it is its gravity. Its sound system, disco lights, and ATM appear as transient decorations on something rarely made visible to history but nevertheless ancient; more important, it is something that seems to have a clearer future ahead of it than the publishing, media, and financial bastions that rise to the south in their New Times Square skyscrapers.

Both the women and the men here seem formal, anxious—whatever may or may not happen in the champagne rooms—to make the right gestures, the right movements, which are not exactly those of lust (though they might prepare the way for it). Though the owners may be making big profits, and the dancers make no bones about wanting their tips, in the main room and at the edge of the stage this seems almost irrelevant, almost as if paying too much for so little is as much a sign of contempt for money as the buyer's disadvantage in a seller's market.

Flash Dancers looked, to me at least, about as romantic as a used car lot, its sex disengaged, eye contact always virtual rather than real, gazes welling with lust but slamming up against an invisible wall just before they reach the recipient's eyes. The movements of the girls and the customers are slow, hypnotic, like some pantomime long buried in a ruin, and returning slowly, under a magic spell, to reenact the ancient spectacle. It's a mechanical scene like Bridges's Microcosm with its painted landscapes and jerking clockwork figures, seeming to depend on a driving spirit nowhere to be seen in the figures themselves.

Ever since what's now prissily called the "adult entertainment" industry began, many forces, probably, have propelled men and women either to work in or patronize it—sexual exploitation, the freezing of spontaneous life into the soulless rituals of commerce, the monomaniacal pressure of inborn desire that drives us on through life and never relents. And we do not live in an auspicious time. In the 1960s, science seemed to be the guarantor of joy, ready to alleviate the consequences of all excess with limitless cures, from penicillin to tranquilizers and painkillers to methadone. But by the 1990s, with HIV and other cure-proof plagues abroad, medicine seemed to be declining from the miracle that saves us from ourselves into an exhausted scold that can only reiterate the iron law of cause and effect: sex brings disease, disease prompts the discovery of cures, cures bring more sex, more sex brings worse, more devious diseases, and death is the end of all.

Greenwich Village's famed Halloween Parade, in the years following Stonewall, grew bigger and bigger, a gay extravaganza, a nocturnal masque slowly subjugating the streets to its stately and grotesque procession. Behind the masks were mostly ordinary men and women releasing themselves into the costumes that loose private desires from their many prisons, and send them gliding, stalking, preening, or staggering through the avenues and streets. And by the 1990s, the Halloween Parade had become a tourist phenomenon, one of the city's major holiday events. It now draws big and slightly unnerving crowds, light-headed with the spectacle and the beer they drink while watching it, yet also bearing an edge of angst and threat appropriate to the original meaning of Halloween—a celebration of death by the living.

Yet night's endless formal dance of desire, melancholy, and release is far more than a spectacle of sinister futility; it's also an enchantment. Not, of course, in the Disney sense: instead it seems rapt by ancient, irresistible spells deeper than the gods—a chthonic pageant beyond the human and older than time, bursting through the gates of the underworld, and rolling every creature and every desire it meets into a parade for good or ill. All the masquers, male and female, customer and performer, lawbreaker and punisher, seem to walk, gesture, even dance with glacial slowness, with the stony faces and ratcheted movements of mechanical figures driven by ponderous clockwork or a silent water engine, powered by a river in a cavern.

From a detached distance, all the real life of a modern urban night might seem to reside in the flashing lights, the thudding rock soundtracks, and the stimulants and sedatives glinting on trays and tables or squirting out of hypodermics into skin, muscle, and blood. The people, by contrast, are frozen allegories, whether of lust or yearning or temptation or aspiration—whatever passion has infiltrated the brain, seized the life, appropriated the identity. Everyone in any topless bar or strip club seems moonstruck, transfixed, from the dancers executing their measured spirals or draping seemingly boneless arms over a customer's shoulders, to the men sliding dollars with solemn gravity into their G-strings.

But nobody can escape his or her place in the pageant. It reaches, surely, back long before Dutch and Indian Manhattan, indeed long before the coming of the human race, to the prehistoric forest nights where animals rutted, prowled, killed, saw the glare of strange fires they couldn't light, and looked up uncomprehendingly at the stars. Here, in the subterranean cave of the Flash Dancers Gentleman's Club in 2004, we were all—like the customers in the Wooden Horse tavern and all humans before them—taking our turn in the pageant.

Epilogue

Spring 2004
Back to the Wooden Horse

ON THE EVENING OF Wednesday, March 31, 2004, I stood at the corner of Fifth Avenue and 52nd Street. The weather was raw and cloudy, with drizzle and intermittent rain—much as it had been 126 years before, when, just across the street, Madame Caroline Restell paced, and wept, and cried out through her last night in the world, her heavy mansion weighing down on her like a sarcophagus lid. Fifty years before her, this was all open country; the Kissing Bridge—the quiet lovers' lane where Maria Trumbull may have enjoyed a chaste make-out session in the winter of 1800—just a short green walk downhill toward the East River. Fifty years after Restell's agony, 52nd had become Swing Street, hard-edged and urban, a hotbed of late-1920s and 1930s jazz, a place where, late at night, you might run into Billie Holiday between sets, out for a stroll with a friend and smoking a joint.

But tonight the corner was dully prosperous, a high-rise intersection dominated by offices, stores, and tourists, all sagging in an early-evening lull. Still, as a neighborhood from which to start a retrospective tour, it was as good as any, I thought—near midtown, where the three-centuries-long northward trek of Manhattan nightlife reached a terminus in the 1940s (for all their vitality, Harlem and Greenwich Village were always, and still remain, outposts). Thus, to walk south from here is to go back in time through the New York night, down to its origins in New Amsterdam, by the old fort, in the neighborhood of Philip Geraerdy's Wooden Horse, where this history began.

When, just at 6:12, I came up from the subway station at Fifth Avenue and 53rd Street, the sidewalks were crowded with office workers on their way home. Restell's house had long since been replaced by a blocky office building. On its ground floor, at the corner of 52nd, there was now a Ferragamo shoe store, with a sign in its window, "A LOVE AFFAIR WITH SHOES," just about where the outdoor staircase led clients down to Restell's basement consulting room. Across the way, where the Catholic orphan asylum once rose on its hill, the sidewalk tonight was all business and pleasure, with a 24-hour Kinko's, a sushi bar, an entrance to the Olympic Tower, and Cartier on the corner of Fifth. The neighborhood was noisy with traffic, the twilight pierced by columns of headlights. The Ferragamo building's third-floor corner (about at the level of Restell's bedroom) was vacant and potentially ghostly, but it was still quite a reach to imagine Restell peering out over this impersonal glare and rush. William Kissam Vanderbilt's mansion, baptized in 1883 with the imperial party that challenged Mrs. Astor's iron hegemony over social New York, was—like Restell's—long torn down, and was now an NBA basketball store.

Tonight the sun set at 6:21. At the corner of 51st Street, a lingering whiff of cigar smoke floated in the damp air, startling in the tobacco-hating New York of the new millennium, a relic of an already fading 1990s fad, but also a reminder of an aroma that hung everywhere in the 1870s and 80s. This was a transitional hour, when the office buildings gape, suspended between day and night. At 50th Street, the promenade at Rockefeller Plaza, a few skaters gliding listlessly around the wet rink, was nearly unoccupied in a momentary drought of tourists and commuters.

From Fifth Avenue, 44th Street leads west into Times Square, with the Algonquin Hotel still serving the cocktails that oiled the wits of the *New Yorker* Round Table—but no longer the homey Chicken à la King and sirloin tips they ate. Tonight, as I passed the entrance, a group of tourists emerged gingerly onto the sidewalk. A few steps past them, Sixth Avenue, a sterile vista both earlier in the day and later at night, looks its best now, with all its office towers still lit, like a city in faraway perspective.

Times Square, a block ahead, is already pouring its light into the side streets, along with straggling sightseers, some excited and babbling, others with a preoccupied look that could either mean vacuity or the shock of release from everyday life. The smoking Camel billboard is gone, but Wrigley's still flashes from the same perch it occupied 50 years ago. Tonight most of the signage appeared desperate to confer urban excitement on the brand names of middle America and the buildings to advertise their inner workings to the street—like the second-floor MTV studios where rock stars are interviewed while teenagers shriek from the sidewalk, the hyperkinetic ABC news crawl and glassed-in news set, a Toys R Us outlet with a mostly stationary Ferris wheel rising from the basement to the roof. Flash Dancers and a few dauntless strip clubs hang on nearby along Seventh and Eighth Avenues, but they're out of the center; the crowds are elsewhere, and they have a jilted look. Now, it seems, you come to Times Square at night in hopes of recovering a real-life night overshadowed by TV and mall shopping; once arrived, you find TV and mall shopping, though in outsized form. Children dawdle or shriek, teenagers are rowdy bridge-and-tunnel types or improbably wholesome, adults either gawk or—in an agony of self-consciousness—refuse to look at anything.

This Times Square, now in so many respects a mid-American encampment in alien urban terrain, nonetheless remains secretly linked to the highs and lows of the native city by the subways that rush underground, their damp garbage-and-carbon smell and intermittent whoosh coming up through the sidewalk grates to puzzle newcomers. Uptown the lines head to the Upper West Side and Queens; two more radiate downtown, one along Seventh Avenue and the other down Broadway.

The moment you walk south of 42nd Street, while the trains still speed below, the surface Broadway puts a quick end to the artificial energy of Times Square, nearly all traces of which have vanished by 40th Street. The 1883 Metropolitan Opera House at 39th, and the Casino Theatre with its roof garden, are both gone, the former a mute office tower with red factory sash windows, the latter a cluttered Duane Reade drugstore and a sparsely peopled Bead World outlet. It was raining now, and the loudest noise was a wet and plaintive newspaper vendor shouting, "Hurry up and buy my 25-cent papers. I have 77 left." The few blocks between Times Square and the Korean business district to the south have for now settled into the relaxing seediness that's become an endangered ambience, at least in Manhattan and Brooklyn—nondescript blocks of orphaned commercial spaces, shabby offices, even an occasional vacant lot.

From here southward, Broadway seems to be a street mulling over its past and waiting for something. At 34th Street, Gimbels, Orbachs, and Saks 34th Street are lost to history. Macy's is a holdout; at seven o'clock, in the twilight, it looked dispirited—at loose ends before the opening of its annual spring flower show, and as bemused as the tourists standing

around on the ground floor. In the late 1800s this neighborhood was the
Tenderloin. At the turn of the 20th century it went over to commerce: the
Herald moved here in 1893 and gave its name to Herald Square. Later,
the district turned seedy once again: the Martinique at the corner of 33rd
Street, a luxury hotel built in 1897 and a block from the first Waldorf at
Fifth Avenue, spent much of the mid-20th century as an SRO and has
now been kitschily refurbished as a Holiday Inn.

Below the Martinique, Broadway becomes Asian, chiefly Korean, still
alive after dusk, but with business—fluorescent-lit and low-priced—featuring polyglot store names and specializing in T-shirts, socks, ribbons,
perfume, and costume jewelry. Edward Corey's Haymarket concert saloon ("the prostitutes' market") had stood a short block away at Sixth Avenue and 30th Street, but the building was sold in 1911 and eventually
torn down. The area hasn't recovered its 24-hour vitality: the stores are
nearly empty and the last open sidewalk vendor is closing down his beef,
chicken, and rice pita stand.

At 29th Street, the booming Flatiron District begins to make its influence felt. An old hotel, the Gilsey House, an airy white masterpiece built
in 1841, is under careful restoration, and seems to be turning into luxury
apartments. In recent years literary agents, photographers, and other
media types have begun to move in, retooling old high-rise loft buildings
as office and studio space. At Madison Square the Flatiron Building
comes into view in a halo of mist, its dignity a presiding presence in the
area. On the east side of the square, somewhat obscured by greenery in
the newly refurbished park, the New York Life and Metropolitan Life
Buildings rise: the floodlit MetLife tower, built in 1909, still bears on its
peak "The Light That Never Fails" (a beacon meant to signal the company's solidity).

This neighborhood now has a prosperous, almost European look, as if
forgetting its tempestuous turn-of-the-20th-century past. Back then the
site of the New York Life headquarters was first Vanderbilt's then Stanford
White's Madison Square Garden. The Metropolitan's auxiliary building
(at the southeast corner of Madison and 24th Street) was Reverend
Parkhurst's Madison Square Presbyterian Church; it was just a few blocks
away, in Hattie Adams's brothel at 29–31 East 27th, that Parkhurst beheld, in 1892, the "dance of nature." The Flatiron's rounded wedge didn't
rise until 1903; in Parkhurst's day a squat building about ten stories high
stood there, with a blank wall that faced the square and became a favorite

site for early electric billboards. In 1898 it was from this wall that the Heinz Pickle flashed in defiance of the wooden arch that commemorated the Spanish-American War. At the time of Parkhurst's crusades, however, it wore another famous sign, which Theodore Dreiser, as a young man new to the city, saw on an evening walk. The lines lit up separately, one by one, then all went out together.

BUY HOMES ON

LONG ISLAND

SWEPT BY OCEAN BREEZES

MANHATTAN BEACH

ORIENTAL HOTEL

MANHATTAN HOTEL

GILMORE'S BAND

BROCK'S RESTAURANT

The cycle took three minutes; all the switching on and off had to be done by hand.

Though Hattie Adams and her 1890s competitors are gone, in this particular neighborhood raunch still holds its influence. On the corner of Fifth Avenue and 27th Street is the Museum of Sex; it was closed tonight and barren in a burst of heavy rain. Further east, at 17 East 27th, a battered granite building looked locked up and seemingly vacant, with its ground-level windows blocked out with plywood painted black, the traditional hallmark of New York nightlife at the edge. In fact, as its inconspicuous and unlit sign says, it's Le Trapeze, a swinging singles club in which Hattie Adams probably would have felt at home. But it was only a little after seven now and the club doesn't open until nine.

Today Madison Square is like much of downtown—an old commercial district growing increasingly residential as lower Manhattan reverts toward its early character as a city where residence and commerce cohabited block by block. Yet, despite the sedate look of Madison Square Park, with its dogs being walked in a well-planted green, and the lights on the Metropolitan Life tower turning the clouds overhead into a misty dome, it also marks the beginning of Manhattan's real nighttown. The trend back southward from Times Square began almost imperceptibly in the 1950s, continued through the turmoil and bad times of the 1960s and 70s, and is obvious now, with 23rd the first cross street to show it unmistakably.

To walk from here toward the tip of Manhattan is on the one hand to go steadily backward in time, to the Union Square Rialto of the late Gilded Age, to the theaters clustered near City Hall in the early 1800s, and finally to the harbor and 17th-century New Amsterdam. Yet the further south you are, the more you see what looks like New York's future. The crowds get younger, the restaurants more trend-conscious, the nightclubs more numerous, with the most faddish places now threatening to overwhelm the once nearly abandoned streets of old downtown neighborhoods like the tenement-packed Lower East Side and the old meatpacking center on the far western end of Greenwich Village.

At Union Square, between 17th and 14th Streets, the change is striking. Even at 7:30 the square and its surrounding streets are mobbed. Always a congregation point, it has once again become an entertainment hub, with a cluster of theaters along its eastern side. The old Amberg Theatre, just east of the square on Irving Place, has given way to Irving Plaza, tonight with a line of concertgoers stretched all the way up to 16th Street. They were mostly in their 20s and 30s, waiting to see a performance by Stellastarr, a four-piece band from Brooklyn. Just down Irving Place, Billy McGlory's infamous old Hotel Irving is gone, replaced by the Zeckendorf Towers apartment complex. The site of the old Academy of Music, home to grand opera and the chandelier-swinging orgies of the Cercle Français de l'Harmonie, now harbors a 20th-century contribution to nightlife—a New York Sports Club co-ed gym, one of dozens in Manhattan that hit their peak hours after work and serve both as dating forums and a way to pump up for a night out.

On the northeast corner of the square the staid old Guardian Life Insurance Building is now Ian Schrager's W Hotel. Just outside its street-level windows a young couple kissed, beside them a man in a dark suit barked into his cell phone. Through the lounge window I saw a table of slender young women in studied poses, chatting distractedly, their eyes scanning the room. In the next window two more young women in black sat conversing, and a third girl read a letter—until they noticed me gaping at them through the glass.

Tonight the Union Square park was empty because of the rain and the chill, but in summer or fall it's full of a college-age population that takes its cue from the square's history as a center of dissent, and draws the thousands of resident students from nearby dormitories belonging to NYU and the New School. Restaurants line the western edge of the square,

ranging from sedate and expensive places like the Union Square Café and
Blue Water Grill to the funkily stylish Coffee Shop Bar, with its diner
decor and NYU film-major clientele.

Below Union Square, the crowds grow less dense, younger still, more
diverse, and more alive, wandering alone or in small groups on quiet
streets. The stiller it gets, the cooler and the more assured the slithering
out of stereotype. Nightlife in New York has increasingly shunned the
midway crowds and lights that always characterized Broadway as its center
of gravity moved northward from City Hall to Times Square. Thus current hotspots are far south and hidden away, except for the muffled sound
of conversation and the thud of music coming from behind closed venetian blinds. These dark streets and intermittent small squares with their
hideaways and surprising, sudden crowds are more evocative of Venice or
Naples than of 1920s and 30s Manhattan.

And now, as the island begins to narrow, gradually tapering toward the
Battery, one feels the past, as if it were personified and alive, watching the
present day with a penetration that to the living seems both bracing and
ominous (another Venetian touch). Below 14th Street, the early sites and
landmarks of city history begin crowding in, rarely more than a few
blocks away from wherever one happens to be at the moment. In 1878,
the night of Madame Restell's death, Wallack's Theatre was at the corner
of Broadway and 13th Street, where Sardou's *Diplomacy* would open the
next evening.

At 8th Street, somewhere to the west, was Tommy Norris's stable, with
the gladiatorial rats and topless lady boxers that had, a few years before
Restell's death, hypnotized the seventeen-year-old Frederick Van Wyck. A
few blocks further downtown one reaches Astor Place, now home to a
Kinko's, a Starbucks, a Barnes & Noble, and Astor Wines & Spirits, but in
1849 filled with nervous militia and a stone-throwing mob. Just below it on
Lafayette Street is the Public Theatre, covering up the last location of Vauxhall Gardens, Clapp's before that, and Corneliszen's tavern before that, visited in 1679 by sour-pussed Jasper Danckaerts. (Tonight the dominant
sight in the area was a construction pit, with signs announcing a development by the Orwellian-sounding "Related Companies.")

Between Astor Place and Canal Street, Broadway is a shopping avenue.
The palatial old A. T. Stewart and Wanamaker stores in the neighborhood
have come back to life in the ranks of cast iron and loft buildings that
now house chain stores, from Crate and Barrel to Bloomingdale's. Dean

& DeLuca, the food store that began here as a neighborhood exclusive, is now a many-sited brand. The sidewalks are crowded from afternoon through early evening, but now, a little after eight o'clock, the shutters were slamming down and the pedestrian traffic vanishing. Here the axis of activity moves eastward to Lafayette Street and the Bowery, whose skid row status has been increasingly challenged by an influx both of people and fashion.

Where the Third Avenue el turned from the Bowery into Third Avenue, at the corner of 3rd Street, is Bowery Bar, once a gas station, now a scene restaurant with an outdoor garden, usually crowded but tonight closed, rain-sodden, and looking like a back yard in Queens. From here through Chinatown every third or fourth door on the Bowery, while careful not to clash with the street's venerable squalor, nevertheless houses an expensive restaurant, a club, or a double-duty business like the Bowery Tattoo Parlor, which makes bows both to the Bowery's down-and-out past and the fashionable present. At 8:15 tonight a twenty-something man could be seen through the big plate glass window, his left arm undergoing cosmetic torture next door to the Bowery Poetry Club and Café.

Here the Bowery itself was quiet, but its storefront clubs and restaurants were beginning to waken. To the west the shoppers were gone from a near-deserted Broadway, in the mid-1800s a booming theater district: Niblo's Garden was at the corner of Prince, where Walt Whitman stopped in 1861 to read the news of the just-declared Civil War. Now the corner, thanks to Dean & DeLuca, Armani, and a Victoria's Secret branch, is busy in daylight, but vacant at night. The restaurants and bars, especially the more expensive ones, inhabit the side streets surrounding the old St. Patrick's Cathedral and cemetery at the corner of Mulberry and Prince. The cemetery's high brick wall dominates the area, with just an obelisk and the branches of a large tree visible above it. The streets aren't crowded but there are constant small groups of people in black visible in the bars and tiny restaurants, some haughtily nameless.

Spring Street just east of Mott in Little Italy was where Antonio Maiori's backyard stage thundered with passionate renditions of Shakespeare. Further east, at the Bowery, was Tony Pastor's earliest theater, later a home for Yiddish drama as the Oriental. Here Broadway traverses SoHo, now largely a tourist mecca, with a few magnets like Balthazar, the calculated Paris bistro knockoff that has spawned dozens of imitators. On

Broadway at Grand Street stood the Old 444 Music Hall where Pastor first made his mark. Before that it was Mitchell's Olympic, where in 1848 Mose and Lize caused their first sensation in *A Glance at New York*. Now it's a store, Stardom.

At Canal Street the bulge of Corlaer's Hook ends and the island begins its rapid narrowing toward the Battery. Broadway remains quiet and the Bowery becomes a checkerboard, with some blocks recalling the old, desolate skid row or Little Italy, others redolent of Asia or the newly fashionable Lower East Side. Hester Street—once a teeming immigrant Jewish neighborhood and also the home, just off the Bowery, of Billy McGlory's Armory Hall—is now mainly notable for its boarded-up Chinese movie theater.

Below Canal, one enters the Bowery of the 19th century, the wide boulevard that once spread under the screeching Third Avenue el and rang with barrelhouse music, the shouts of peddlers, street performers, and milling working-class crowds in search of thrills. Now it's near the heart of Chinatown, less remarkable for noise than for its cacophony of sights and smells—the odors of fresh fish, live fish, dried fish, their flat eyes staring up from bins amid mounds of trinkets. Bolts of lurid fabric dangle or pile up on counters, eviscerated poultry hang in store windows. A frying aroma wafts from assembly-line woks in the restaurants. The Bowery is crowded again, but the people seem intense and intent; the old rowdiness is gone. At Bayard Street, where the Bowery Theatre stood through its three incarnations as a popular American, German, and finally Yiddish venue, there is now an arcade of Chinese restaurants, with a covered mall connecting the Bowery to Elizabeth Street.

They were all open tonight, though not particularly crowded, and the Bowery itself suffers from the disintegrated look it got when the vast Manhattan Bridge approach, finished in 1909, opened up a wound in its east side. The street has also been dashed apart by new apartment towers that turn their backs to it. People don't perambulate, but sit in the minimally decorated restaurants behind plate glass and under banks of merciless fluorescent lighting, or stand outside, hurling chatter into their cell phones, apparently to relatives or business associates—far different from the compulsive prattling to friends that characterizes twenty-somethings on a night out in the club-land between Union Square and Canal Street.

From here downtown the glamour venues cluster in TriBeCa, west of

Broadway. As you head south into Chatham Square you can, if you like, still pass through the doorway of the Wing Fat shopping center and go down the stairs at your left into the old branching Chinatown tunnels, now open to the public. You'll emerge a block to the northwest at 5–7 Doyers Street—the green-bricked old Chinese opera house, still standing. But in this neighborhood the crowds thin and the streets are becoming somnolent again. The Bowery ends. Broadway continues into Manhattan's government center, dull, cold, and intentionally intimidating by day, by night vacant but hostile, like an ogre in a deep sleep.

This neighborhood was the heart of early 19th- and late 18th-century nightlife, but its ghosts seem absent from the streets, desolate of either people or traffic. Worth Street leads west, from Chatham Square past Centre Street to Broadway, and this brings you through the old Five Points, now a blank intersection boxed in by barren Columbia Park, the Chatham Towers housing development, and the back of the city's Civil Courts Building (during the day it's busy with lawyers and people on jury duty, on their way to Chinatown for lunch). In 1835, when Worth was still called Anthony Street, it was where William Newman stabbed the scavenger John Van Winkle as he came home from work. It was also near here that Charles Dickens, during his stay at the Carlton House in 1842, saw the black orgy at Frank McCabe's bar. Rosina Townsend's brothel, where Helen Jewett met her death in 1836, was just to the southwest, on Thomas Street beyond Broadway.

Just above the vanished Five Points, the back of the hulking Depression-era Criminal Courts Building marks the edge of the buried Fresh Water. Its equally grim front, on Centre Street, looks down over the ragged, dug-up grass rectangle and parking lot that now covers the site of the Tombs. This was where Madame Restell, after her arrest in March 1878, spent the nights that seem to have destroyed her will and propelled her toward suicide. It was near where, before the prison went up, Caesar had been burned alive during the 1741 witch hunt of blacks, and Peggy Sorubiero strung up within sight of his rotting corpse. Somewhere nearby, in 1712, Robin the slave had been hung in chains and, protesting his innocence, slowly starved to death for having killed his master.

A block south, at Duane Street, now fenced off, was the African Burial Ground, destination of the midnight funeral processions that so unsettled the Dutch and English burghers of the early 1700s. Running along its southern border is Reade Street. In 1842, Palmo's Café des Milles Colonnes stood at the Broadway corner, with Captain Collins's Star House just down the block, the skulking sodomites that so outraged the sporting press no doubt exchanging furtive looks of appraisal as they strolled the half block between. Now the massive government high-rises and the absence of people obliterate any memory of intrigue: in the dark one could be looking at the standard-issue skyscrapers and blank sidewalks of any midwestern city.

Only the Woolworth tower, spectacularly floodlit, its pinnacle shivering out of the mist, and then shuddering back into it again like someone huddling into a coat, reasserts New-Yorkishness. As I passed the corner of Chambers and Broadway, near City Hall, a nine-man Con Ed crew was at work under a glaring bank of portable lights—resembling, in all probability, the Drummond light that in the 1840s cast its harsh beacon up Broadway from Barnum's Museum a few blocks south. In the winter of 1800 and 1801 this was also Harriet and Maria Trumbull's New York: Lady Kitty Duer's house, where they boarded, was just west of here on Chambers Street, and the Park Theatre (now the site of the J&R electronics superstore) was about a thousand feet away, across City Hall Park.

Down at Ann Street—where Barnum, adding sacrilege to noise and glare, once strung an advertising banner across Broadway from his museum of wonders and moored it on St. Paul's Chapel—the Wall Street canyons open up. The City Hotel—where Hanington's panorama of life on the moon thrilled crowds in 1835—was a few blocks down, at 111 Broadway between Cedar and Thames. It was also nearby where Officer Edward McCosker accosted and groped Thomas Carey on a winter's night in 1846. On John Street, just east of Broadway, Tyler's *The Contrast* opened in 1787. To the west, behind St. Paul's, is the Holy Ground, then the brothel quarter into which *The Contrast's* Jonathan bumbled on his way to the theater. Now it's Ground Zero; construction lights raise a tent of white mist above it, a 24-hour reminder of the disaster that still breaks the city's heart, even while we work 24 hours a day to restore it. At Liberty Street, the swirling pinnacle of the old Cities Service (now AIG) tower is visible, seeming rocklike among the more impermanent-looking glass towers that now surround it. Two blocks south, we reach the site of Jan Damen's farm, along Pine Street and just north of Trinity Church.

In 1643 the half-mile between the Wooden Horse tavern and the Damen property seemed long. It lacked landmarks like the Cities Service,

Farmers Trust, and Bank of the Manhattan Company towers to show the smallness of the triangle in which, at the island's end, the Fort and the new plantations beyond Wall Street clustered. The nearness of danger, the rough terrain, and the need for alertness surely made a midnight walk seem longer yet. Now, the towers shrink the view, and the distances appear shorter than they really are. Which is more skewed, the 17th-century eye that saw New Amsterdam as a full-fledged town, or the modern one that, deluded by height, bulk, and grandness of scale, overlooks the complexity possible in a settlement of trees, dirt lanes, and a scattering of homes, storehouses, and taverns?

Trinity Church recalls the older, smaller scale, invisible from Ann Street at night, hinted at only by a cliff of darkness in the solid rank office buildings below St. Paul's. Only at the head of Wall Street does it suddenly seem to expand, a repository of mystery, far more emotive than in the day (tonight the two pines in the south graveyard were invisible against the church in the rain).

Turning down Wall Street after dark, the old city reemerges with surprising vigor from the shadows of dormant commerce. At Broad Street, Federal Hall, built in 1842, replaced the second City Hall, to whose basement jail Peggy Sorubiero was taken in 1741. But the newer building is still on the same scale. Looking at it, one can easily imagine Washington delivering his inaugural address from the steps on the afternoon of April 30, 1789; even more vividly one can call up 1741 and Peggy Sorubiero's whisper in the basement jail: "For your life and soul of you, you son of a bitch, don't speak a word of what I have told you."

On Broad Street, heading downhill toward the East River, you're walking in the opposite direction of the 1789 fire, which roared up along the right side of the street, destroying everything in its path and clearing the land for Canvas Town, the vice-ridden slum of the post-Revolutionary era. A short walk to the corner of South William Street takes you back before the Revolution, to the site of Rebecca and Robert Hogg's shop where the opening acts of Caesar's and Peggy's drama began—and where, a few years later, Dr. Alexander Hamilton boarded on his 1744 visit. A block down was Robert Todd's tavern, where Hamilton attended a meeting of the bibulous Hungarian Club and heard the irate landlord bellow, "Dam ye bitch, wharefor winna ye bring a canle?"

Directly across Broad from South William is Stone Street, where, more than a century before the 1789 fire and the Hoggs' shop and boardinghouse, this history began. I reached it at about 10:30 in the evening—about the time when, in 1643, Jan Damen was sitting in the Wooden Horse tavern, a nervous Philip Geraerdy watching him sink into inebriation. But tonight, on first view nothing could seem more dead. Stone Street remains only one lane wide, closed off at one end by the old Custom House, and at the other by Broad Street.

There were two restaurants—the Nebraska Steak House, with a man using a pay phone in the vestibule, and A. J. Kelley's, with another lone man at the bar—both of them closing. There is still a Wooden Horse in the vicinity—but it's a block offsite, on Bridge Street. Whatever may be left of Geraerdy's premises now lies buried under the hulking office building at 2 Broadway. Between that and the massive Goldman Sachs headquarters rearing up across Broad Street, old Manhattan appears flattened and erased forever, Stone Street a chance survivor that recalls little and commemorates nothing.

And yet not quite: Stone Street reappears just behind Goldman Sachs, which conceals it from Broad Street—again one lane wide and tracing a graceful cobblestone curve to Hanover Square. In the 18th century it was called Duke Street; the buildings here today are the three- and four-story brick structures of 19th-century mercantile Manhattan (the area was heavily hit by the 1835 fire and the majority of them date from the building boom that followed). They still recall what they were when first built: shops and warehouses at the street level, living quarters and storage above. In the middle of the Stone Street arc, the Goldman Sachs building and modern lower Manhattan are, for the moment, both invisible; Mill Lane, which connects Stone to South William Street, opens off to the left, tiny, silent, and deserted.

Yet Stone Street itself, even on this damp, raw Wednesday night, was alive—a sudden, unforeseen swarm of singles released after their long Wall Street workday. The East River side of the street is a wall of pubs and restaurants—an eat-in pâtisserie, La Financière, and an Italian restaurant, Gerardi's, whose name unintentionally recalls Philip Geraerdy. There's a bistro, Cassis, and—biggest and most crowded—an Irish pub, Ulysses. The street itself is closed to traffic, and filled from sidewalk to sidewalk with outdoor tables belonging to the restaurants. On a warm night its mobbed cobblestones ring with music and talk. To anyone who comes upon it unawares, it looks like the café-crowded streets surrounding Rome's Santa Maria in Trastevere (although the faces here are unmistakably those of young and middle-aged American moneymakers).

The loud conversations, the singles maneuverings, the open-winged silver cell phones flittering around the scene like demented swallows, the Prada and Brooks Brothers and Ann Taylor and Paul Stuart clothes, are a burst of life that here nonetheless seems startlingly at one with the ghosts of New York's earliest night. All the Stone Street restaurants cut through the short block between Stone and Pearl Streets; you can walk through each bar onto Pearl, and find yourself only a few yards from the site of the Stadts Herbergh, whose foundations are outlined on the Goldman Sachs Plaza, and where glass windows in the pavement show the excavated foundations surviving from the period.

This was the place where, in 1644, John Underhill charged up the steps with his band of drunken thugs, crashed the party being given by Dr. Kierstedt, Dominie Bogardus, and their friends, and haled the Schout Fischal up from the fort to restore the shattered peace. In the 1600s, when the East River lapped Pearl Street, this was where you could buy after-hours alcohol from the city's earliest bootleggers, selling drinks from their boats in the dark to cheat the West India Company of its main source of profit. Here too, in 1658, Lodowyck Pos set out with the first formal Rattle Watch whose members would, over the following decades, exasperate homeowners with their drunkenness, laziness, and uncanny ability to be invisible wherever trouble happened and a noisy nuisance everywhere else. And it was a few hundred yards from where, in 1643, Jan Damen fumed and fought in the aftermath of the Indian massacre, and an exultant Adrienne Cuville kicked the severed heads of the slaughtered Indians across the bare ground of the Fort.

After centuries of nighttime desertion, people are living here once more, in quarters that echo the settlements of early Manhattan. Above the Stone Street bars and restaurants many windows, long vacant, are now lit, revealing all the telltale signs of ambitious Manhattan apartment living: glass-smooth paint jobs in subtle colors, expensive lighting, the tops of leather club chairs. By day the block looks like an alley full of old brick hulks unaccountably overlooked by developers, cluttered with abandoned outdoor furniture. But at night, a beneficiary of the downtown U-turn the city's nocturnal life first began to take in the 1960s, it hums as if this were the 1600s or 1700s come back to life.

Stone Street's revival may founder in a month or a year. But transience is the nature of the city night, and bars, dives, and clubs its spiritual form, opening, closing, reinventing themselves, packed one night, abandoned the next, sometimes measuring their lives in weeks. There is something frightening in this—a wanton orgy that mocks our personal impermanence, the knowledge that this hypercharged disco or bar or scene restaurant may be knocked down, folded up, and carted away in a month, to be replaced by some new attraction, by a pile of construction litter behind dirty plate glass, or by a bare lot.

But of course it's the fate of all walls to crumble, all towers to fall. Perhaps what the interrupted, deceiving, sometimes drunken voice of the urban night is telling its laced-up daytime twin is that the real source of a city's magic, and the strongest force for its survival, is the permanence of human desires and the indefatigability of human will. Skyscrapers, we've learned at great cost and pain, are not so solid as they promise. Better to look for constancy in whatever changes, from night to night and hour to hour. Night is in love with the impermanent, and its forms, faces, words, songs, bodies, battles, copulations, and meditations take shape and vanish by the hour, rendered indistinct by darkness. Yet the forms are always the same: nothing happened in 2004 that didn't echo some other comedy or tragedy, remembered or forgotten, of 1643 or 1741 or 1849 or 1948.

The movie flies out of existence the second the projector stops, and by morning last night's ecstatic debauch is a headache and remorse. Yet what was never built as an enduring monument can't, as long as one acknowledges its vanishing nature, become either a prison or a target. Dreams, the quintessential nocturnal form, are broken up to start with. They shatter, trail off, reassemble, mixing the ideal with the unspeakable, making friends of enemies and enemies of friends. They break up for good when you awake, and they can be forgotten with a speed with which we forget nothing else. The more startling their juxtapositions, the longer they're remembered; the harder they are to remember, the more meaningful they seem. In a dream even death is transient.

New York at night brings waking life to the edge of this universe of dream and nightmare, rebirth and mortality. Under night's canopy or shroud, everyone, happy or miserable, wanders for a while, emerges into a brief turmoil of crowd and light, then sinks back again into anonymity and darkness. Fame courts obscurity, beauty mates with deformity, evil dances with good, and the next morning the city awakens to live and work in the hidden atmosphere they've all conspired to spin.

By day New York turns to practicality, to the provident tasks of survival. But at night ancient Manhattan comes back as a ghost from a deeper world still living but unwisely forgotten, and reminding its children of the moment when, in Lenape legend, an island rose up from the moving water, a tree sprang up from the land, and a man and a woman stood upon it, looking out into the harbor and the future as, for the first time, the sun set within the view of human eyes.

NOTES AND SOURCES

New York Night is a work of fact, even where it ranges into obscure reaches of the city's past. Thus it necessarily relies on hundreds of sources of widely varying types. The following notes and bibliography acknowledge these specifically, but it will also be useful here to outline the general principles I've followed in screening and documenting primary and secondary material.

Where possible, I have relied on the accounts of eyewitnesses, and have attempted to note cases in which such observations may have been colored by the witness's opinions or other factors. Second-hand reports have, wherever possible, been verified by consulting alternate sources. Instances in which the truth is under dispute have been remarked as such, either in the text or in bottom notes. Otherwise, descriptions and narratives, whether of well-studied episodes, like the 1849 Astor Place riots, or of minute matters—like the look of Cornelis Van Tienhoven's face or the burglar alarm system in Madame Restell's Fifth Avenue mansion—are factual. Any speculation on my part has been identified as such.

Different kinds of sources demand differing degrees of caution. Beginning in the 1830s, for example, a proliferation of New York newspapers and magazines began offering an unprecedented wealth of detail on the doings of the urban night, but they often vary wildly in their reporting of supposed facts, particularly in the frenzy of competition generated by a sensational event. In such instances I have first tried to assess the general reliability of any given paper on any given subject at any given time, and wherever possible consulted several competing versions. Where these differ, I have used my own judgment in choosing among them, but have tried to flag all instances where the discrepancies are of moment.

New York Night's frequent method is to assemble elements from a palette of sources in order to re-create a scene or series of events that is true, realistic in the overall impression it creates, and consistent with the work, both broad and narrowly focused, of significant scholarship, both contemporary and past. This presents a challenge. New York is a vast subject, and the last twenty to thirty years can already safely be called a golden age for city history. A number of scholars, working from the base provided by 19th- and earlier 20th-century historians, have, in hundreds of books and scholarly articles, assembled richly textured and well-documented accounts of social and economic life in the city, from the slums of the Five Points to the mansions of Fifth Avenue. The city that emerges from this accumulated work requires a sharp upward revision of New York's already outsized reputation for complexity and diversity.

New York Night depends on the work of many such writers and historians. But several sources have been so continuously vital to this project, and have proved in general so useful to students of New York life, that they deserve particular mention here. Prominent among these is I. N. Phelps Stokes's six-volume masterwork, *The Iconography of Manhattan Island, 1498–1909*, published between 1915 and 1928—an indispensable resource for anyone interested in Manhattan's early history. Perhaps no other city in the world can boast such a rich or massive portrait of its founding era—intricately and voluminously detailed, uncannily accurate.

More recent general histories and works of reference on which I have relied (with some awe of the scale of achievement which each represents) include Edwin Burrows and Mike Wallace's *Gotham: A History of New York City to 1898*, James Trager's *The New York Chronology: The Ultimate Compendium of Events, People, and Anecdotes from the Dutch to the Present*, and Kenneth Jackson's *Encyclopedia of New York City*. Robert A. M. Stern's magnificent series (*New York 1880, New York 1900, New York 1930*, and *New York 1960*) offers an authoritative source of reference on architectural and technological matters. New York's tangled history of illicit sex has been remarkably chronicled in Timothy J. Gilfoyle's *City of Eros: New York City, Prostitution, and the Commercialization of Sex, 1790–1920*. For theater and many other forms of legitimate mass entertainment, George C. D. Odell's fifteen-volume *Annals of the New York Stage*, published between 1927 and 1949, is irreplaceable. And two now-classic books have also heavily influenced my overall approach toward the New York night: Luc Sante's *Low Life: Lures and Snares of Old New York* and Wolfgang

Schivelbusch's *Disenchanted Night: The Industrialization of Light in the Nineteenth Century.*

Books to which I am indebted for their portraits of particular people and events include Richard Jacoby's *Conversations with the Capeman: The Untold Story of Salvador Agron,* Donald Clarke's *Wishing on the Moon: The Life and Times of Billie Holiday,* Tim Lawrence's *Love Saves the Day: A History of American Dance Music Culture, 1970–1979,* Martin Duberman's *Stonewall,* and David Carter's *Stonewall: The Riots That Sparked the Gay Revolution.*

Archives which have granted permission to quote manuscript material include the New-York Historical Society; the Manuscripts and Archives Division of the New York Public Library, Astor, Lenox and Tilden Foundations; the Lloyd Sealy Library, Special Collections, John Jay College of Criminal Justice; and the Hampden-Booth Theatre Library.

Many other scholars and New Yorkers have proved essential in particular sections of the story, and I have tried to give them full credit in the text and in the pages that follow. For any unintentional omissions or errors of fact, I of course take full responsibility.

NOTES

Bibliographical entries listed directly beneath chapter and section headings denote sources used as a general reference for matters of fact. Notes identified by page numbers and key phrases from the text give sources for quotations, paraphrases, or distinctive interpretations. Where original texts have been reprinted in facsimile or in multiple editions, the date given is for the latest generally available version. In cases where several quotations from a single source follow each other in clear sequence, I have generally used a single note to document all the passages used. Finally, in quotations from manuscripts, newspapers, or magazines, I have silently corrected obvious typographical errors, but left spelling and grammatical anomalies intact in order to preserve the flavor of the original.

PROLOGUE

Stokes (1998); Van Laer (1924), (1974)

3   *fireworks for public display*   See Schivelbusch (1988), pp. 80–88 and 137–38.
5   *mid-1940s night photo*   Feininger (1978), p. 85.
8   *A European ship passenger*   Danckaerts (1913), p. 32ff.
8   *"as soon as you begin"*   Ibid., p. 35.
8   *"how this bay swarms"*   Ibid., p. 36.
9   *A turtle rose*   See Bierhorst (1982), pp. 28–29.
11   *standard Dutch costume*   See Singleton (1968), pp. 71–77.
11   *Sometime after dusk fell*   Van Laer (1974), vol. 2, p. 112.

CHAPTER ONE
New Amsterdam Noir: The Dark Nights of Dutch Manhattan

Bayles (1915); Burrows and Wallace (1999); Fernow (1976); Innes (1902); Jameson (1909); Kessler and Rachlis (1959); Kouwenhoven (1953); Raesly (1945); Shorto (2004); Stokes (1998); Valentine (1853) and (1860); Van Laer (1974); Wagman (1983)

12   *Monday, April 6, 1643*   Van Laer (1974), vol. 2, p. 112.

13   *moonless nights*   Burrows and Wallace (1999), p. 111.

13   *"one full fourth"*   Fernow (1976), vol. 1, pp. 6 and 48.

13n. *Clay pipes were the smoke*   Gately (2001), p. 81; Robert (1949), pp. 99–100; Penn (1902), p. 178.

14   *ride the wooden horse*   http://www.institute.blacksteel.com.

14   *imbroglio over money*   See Van Laer (1974), vol. 2, p. 172.

16   *they found it dark*   Van Laer (1974), vol. 2, p. 112.

16n. *Dutch land tenure*   van Zwieten (2001) and personal communication.

WHAT HAPPENED AT MIDNIGHT: FEBRUARY 25, 1643

17   *"draw their rations"*   Van Laer (1924), pp. 175 and 207–8.

17   *"pistolls set in Rondellos"*   Bullivant (1956), entry for June 16, 1697.

18   *"I remained that night"*   Jameson (1909), pp. 227–28.

18   *authorized a massacre*   See Shorto (2004), pp. 123–25.

18   *"when the heads"*   O'Callaghan (1969), vol. 1, p. 412.

19   *"Infants," de Vries reported*   Jameson (1909), p. 228.

19   *"the Governor . . . began"*   Ibid., p. 226.

19   *"Was not a mysterious toast"*   O'Callaghan (1969), vol. 1, p. 412.

20   *"a woman in or about the fort"*   Van Laer (1974), vol. 4, p. 122.

20   *red face and a wen*   O'Callaghan (1969), vol. 1, p. 515.

20   *"shrewd, false, deceitful"*   Jameson (1909), pp. 340–41.

20   *"to come out of the Tavern"*   O'Callaghan (1969), vol. 1, p. 513.

20   *"from lust after the prostitutes"*   Jameson (1909), p. 340.

21   *"Clear out of here"*   See Bayles (1915), pp. 9–11.

22   *"notwithstanding her husband's presence"*   Van Laer (1974), vol. 1, pp. 55–57.

23   *Griet Reyners*   See Van Rensselaer (1909), vol. 1, p. 95.

23   *In 1658, a woman*   See Fernow (1976), vol. 2, p. 407.

23   *"hoisted her petticoats"*   Ibid., vol. 3, p. 23.

24   *"drinking clubs"*   Ibid., vol. 1, p. 255.

24   *"principal citizens"*   Ibid., vol. 1, p. 92.

25   *few dining utensils*   Cantwell and Wall (2001), pp. 156–58.

FROM STADTS HUIS TO CITY HALL: THE DUTCH NIGHT ENGLISHED

26   *Deborah Careful*   See Richardson (1970), p. 9.

27   *"parcel of idle"*   Quoted in Bridenbaugh (1955), p. 109.

1679: JASPER DANCKAERTS'S NEW YORK

Danckaerts (1913)

29   *"fine, pure morning air"*   Danckaerts (1913), p. 44.

30   *still owned by his heirs*   See Stokes (1998), vol. 1, p. 238 and vol. 4, p. 335.

CHAPTER TWO
Rattle Watch Nights:
City Streets After Sundown, from Peter Stuyvesant to the Early Republic

Abbott (1974); Bridenbaugh (1955); Wilkenfield (1976)

John Crooke's Orchard and John Hughson's Tavern: Race and Violence in Pre-Revolutionary New York

Davis (1985); Harris (1993); Horsmanden (1971); Kammen (1975); Kobrin (1971); McManus (1966); Ottley and Weatherby (1967); Scott (1961); Szasz (1967)

35 *"with a slow fire"*   Quoted in Stokes (1998), vol. 4., p. 475.

36 *"He said he knew"*   Quoted in Scott (1961), p. 68.

37 *"some Negroes"*   Horsmanden (1971), p. 13.

37n. *Not the same man*   See Scott (1961), p. 57.

38 *"a person of infamous character"*   Ibid., p. 15.

38 *"motherly good advice"*   Ibid., p. 17.

38 *"If you will be true"*   Mary Burton's deposition, quoted in ibid., p. 19.

39 *"about one of the Clock"*   New-York Weekly Journal, March 23, 1741.

39 *"For your life and soul"*   Horsmanden (1971), pp. 49–50.

40 *"stood like a lifeless trunk"*   Ibid., p. 165.

41 *Caesar passed into*   See Davis (1985), p. 71.

Before the Revolution: Evenings with the Yankee Aristocracy

Altick (1978); Bayles (1915); Garrett (1978); Gottesman (1936); Hamilton (1948); Pomerantz (1938); Sussman (1999)

41 *"I was tired"*   Hamilton (1948), p. 89.

41 *"a good mowing"*   Ibid., p. 177.

41 *"Praised be God"*   Ibid., pp. 42–43.

42 *"two or three toapers"*   Ibid., p. 43.

42 *"private Hands"*   New-York Gazette, January 13, 1736.

43 *"a kind of pleasure garden"*   Bullivant (1956), p. 64.

43 *"an excellent Soupe"*   Ibid., p. 64.

45 *"standing by his tent"*   Quoted in Bayles (1915), pp. 218–19.

45 *"Six Rockets"*   Quoted in Odell (1949), vol. 1, p. 143.

45n. *A Tornant*   Personal communication, Phil Butler, Fireworks by Grucci.

46 *"a most beautiful Composition"*   Quoted in Gottesman (1936), pp. 385–86.

Into the Dark: The Great Fire of 1776 and the Urban Underworld

Stokes (1998)

47 *"the most shocking spectacle"*   Dunlap (1840), vol. 2, Appendix, pp. ccii-cciii.

48 *"men and women"*   David Grim, quoted in Stokes (1998), vol. 5, p. 1021.

49 *"a vast Pyramid"*   Quoted in ibid.

50 *"over the ruins"*   Quoted in ibid., p. 1022.

51 *"fitting up as a school"*   New-York Gazetteer, October 1, 1784, quoted in Stokes (1998), vol. 5, p. 1194.

51 *"a great half moon"*   Hamilton (1948), p. 46.

51 *"Mr. J[effrey]s told me"*   Ibid., p. 46.

52 *rarely clear how they operated*   See Greenberg (1974), p. 97.

52 *"did keep and maintain"* N-YHS, New York City Legal MSS, Box 43.
53 *the lowest conviction rate* See Greenberg (1974), pp. 89 and 93.

John Street Overture: Theater in the Later 1700s

Cronin (1950); Odell (1949)

54 *"wants the pruning knife"* Quoted in Gassner (1967), pp. xxviii-xxix.
54 *"many well dressed women"* Quoted in Stokes (1998), vol. 4, p. 862.
54 *"Mr. Morrison"* Tyler (1967), p. 15.
55 *"As I was going about"* Ibid., p. 20.
55 *"just like father's corncribs"* Ibid., p. 20.
55n. *In later New York theaters* See Johnson (1975).
56 *a dozen or so* See Dunlap (1969), vol. 1, p. 268.
56 *"First we bow round"* Tyler (1967), p. 12.
57 *"much confusion having arisen"* Quoted in Odell (1949), vol. 1, p. 426.
57 *Only by herculean efforts* Hodgkinson (1963), p. 10.
58 *in 1793 he was on Queen Street* Trow (1793).

Secrets of the Tammany Wigwam: The City Tavern, 1790–91

Horton (1867); NYPL, MS 305-C-3 (Tammany Society Records, 1791–1795)

59 *"that honest and generous"* Horton (1867), p. 18.
60 *threw a gala Wigwam* See Bayles (1915), p. 354.
60 *"huge war-clubs"* Horton (1967), p. 22.
60 *"that although the hand of death"* Ibid., p. 22.
60 *"agreeable to Law"* NYPL, MS 305-C-3, p. 1.
60 *"A Sailor and His Girl"* Ibid., p. 3.
61 *"Are we not sons of Tammany"* Ibid., pp. 4–12.

CHAPTER THREE
Hearthside and Rushlight: Old New York at Home

62 *"I found it extremely pleasant"* Kalm (1966), vol. 1, pp. 131-32.

Drawing the Shutters, Keeping the Fire: New York Houses in the 1600s and 1700s

Bingham (1975); Bushman (1988); Garrett (1990); Hayward (1962); Kalm (1966); Lockwood (1972); McCusker (1978); Morrison (1952); Plunz (1990); Singleton (1968); Thwing (1975); Waterman (1950)

63 *"all those who absent themselves"* Fernow (1976), vol. 1, p. 46.
65 *During his 1697 visit* See Bullivant (1956), p. 65.
68 *a 1688 show at Versailles* Schivelbusch (1988), p. 7.
69 *"remarkable for making a Room"* *New-York Mercury,* November 9, 1761, quoted in Gottesman (1936), p. 123.
69 *"about 8 o'clock"* Gaine (1902), entry for January 22, 1798.
69 *"luxury of Warm Bathing"* Longworth (1830–31), front advertisement.

Manhattan Season: Winter, 1800–1801

Garrett (1990); Morgan (1969)

71 *"tolerably entertained"*   Morgan (1969), p. 146.
71 *"I am sorry"*   Ibid., p. 132 and n.
72 *"I believe it is the first time"*   Ibid., p. 148.
72 *"I hardly know which is best"*   Ibid., p. 148.
73 *"wrote, read and played cards"*   Ibid., p. 108.

OLD MR. DUNLAP: GREENWICH VILLAGE IN THE 1830S

Collins (1934); Dayton (1882); Dizikes (1993); Dunlap (1969); Williams (1833) and (1834)

74n. *The first theater*   Stokes (1998), vol. 5, pp. 1616 and 1618; Collins (1934), pp. 55–57.
74n. *"the color of the light"*   New York (Evening) Post, October 1, 1821.
75 *"a ride in it"*   Quoted in Stokes (1998), vol. 3, p. 1701.
75 *"Ride down town"*   Dunlap (1969), vol. 3, p. 687.
76 *the fare was*   See Morning Courier and New-York Enquirer, September 11, 1835, advertisement.
76n. *Construction on the railroad*   See Condit (1980), p. 25; Greene (1926), p. 7; Harlow (1947), pp. 115, 121, and 126.

CHAPTER FOUR
Broadway After Dark:
Pleasures and Horrors of Federal New York

Blunt (1818); Bowers (1998); Dayton (1882); Foster (1990); Goldman (1997); Harris (1973); Jenkins (1911); Odell (1949)

79 *"Let us start fair"*   Foster (1990), p. 70.
80 *"four spacious Saloons"*   Williams (1834), p. 187.
80 *"Miss Honey"*   Morning Courier and New-York Enquirer, September 1, 1835.
80 *"livid, ghastly glare"*   Foster (1990), p. 71.
81 *"speaking, singing, toasting"*   Hone (1969), vol. 1, p. 126.
81 *"New York palais royal"*   Ibid., vol. 1, p. 121.
82 *"for the extent of glasses"*   Williams (1834), p. 187.

BROADWAY DELUXE: GLAMOUR IN THE 1840S

Buckley (1984); Harlow (1931); Williams (1833) and (1834)

82 *"This beautiful street"*   New York (Morning) Herald, September 5, 1835.
83 *"Now," Bennett remarked*   Ibid., September 5, 1835.
84 *"It captivated the eye"*   Francis (1865), p. 254.
84 *"a style of magnificence"*   Hone (1969), vol. 1, p. 104.
84 *"The Gardens will be"*   New-York Commercial Advertiser, July 5, 1836, advertisement.
85 *a half-hour refreshment period*   Morning Courier and New-York Enquirer, September 14, 1835.
85 *ferried customers*   Commercial Advertiser, July 5, 1836.
85 *"A shameful spectacle"*   Strong (1952), vol. 1, p. 7.
85 *"During the whole night"*   Herald, July 6, 1836.

86   *"the street is always crowded"*   Strong (1952), vol. 1, p. 150.
86   *"the shoe and covering"*   *Commercial Advertiser,* July 5, 1836.
86   *"One by one the late shops"*   Foster (1990), p. 75.
87   *"Go there at midnight"*   Child (1998), p. 11.

City Beat: The Moon in the Morning and the *Sun* at Night

Barth (1980); Foster (1990); Mott (1950); Moran (1973); O'Brien (1928)

88   *Cylinder presses*   See Moran (1973), p. 105.
88   *"all persons apprehended"*   Mitchill (1807), pp. 60–61.
89   *"Patrick Ludwick was sent up"*   *Sun,* July 4, 1834, quoted in Mott (1950), pp. 223–24.
90   *the steam boilers*   See Mahony (1973), p. 179.
90   *famed for its hat-sized*   Anon. (1866), pp. 74–75.
90   *"recent discoveries in Astronomy"*   *Sun,* August 25, 1835.
91   *"We were thrilled with astonishment"*   *Sun,* August 28, 1835.
91   *had actually happened*   See Eberhart (1980).
91   *"the public mind"*   Quoted in Mott (1950), p. 226.

Hanington's Virtual Moon and the Dioramas of Monsieur Daguerre

Gernsheim (1968)

92   *"The Conflagration"*   *Morning Courier and New-York Enquirer,* September 1, 1835.
93   *"The most striking effect"*   Quoted in Gernsheim (1968), p. 17.
95   *"Were those who indulge"*   *Herald,* September 17, 1835.
95   *"grand moving panorama"*   *Commercial Advertiser,* November 27, 1835.
96   *took to the wing*   *Sun,* September 21 and 28, 1835.
96   *"not to gaze at the Comet"*   Ibid., October 1, 1835.

"AWFUL CALAMITY—UNPRECEDENTED CONFLAGRATION!!" The Great Fire of 1835

Burrows and Wallace (1999); Haswell (1896); Homberger (1994)

97   *"the numerous fires"*   *Commercial Advertiser,* August 27, 1835.
97   *"It gave a somber, ominous tone"*   Haswell (1896), p. 286.
97   *"a sheet of flame"*   *Sun,* September 18, 1835.
98   *"Evening. At about nine"*   Strong (1952), vol. 1, p. 8.
99   *"During the night"*   *Commercial Advertiser,* December 17, 1835.
100   *"like oil to the appetite"*   *Sun,* December 18, 1835.

Mansion, Slum, and Boardinghouse

102   *a moderate $2 a week*   Blunt (1818), p. 42.
102   *"there are many of great respectability"*   Greene (1837), pp. 26–27.
103   *"Boarding-house existence"*   Browne (1975), p. 205.
103   *"It was just possible"*   Gunn (1857), p. 32.
103   *"Many a powdered beauty"*   Ibid., p. 33.

"DREADFUL MURDER ON ANTHONY STREET":
The Surfacing of the Criminal Underworld

Cohen (1998); *Morning Courier and New-York Enquirer*; *New-York Commercial Advertiser*; *New York (Evening) Post*; *(New York) Journal of Commerce*; *Sun*

105 *"Watch!"* *Sun*, September 23, 1835.

105 *"taken away my comfort"* *Morning Courier and New-York Enquirer*, September 8, 1835.

105 *"So cool and deliberate"* *Commercial Advertiser*, September 23, 1835.

106 *"came in from some"* *Sun*, November 25, 1835.

106 *"Rising from the floor"* Ibid., November 25, 1835.

106 *"He was," the* Sun *interviewer* Ibid., November 25, 1835.

107 *"He appeared to be"* *Journal of Commerce*, quoted in *New York (Evening) Post*, November 20, 1835.

107 *"we understand several interesting galvanic experiments"* *Morning Courier and New-York Enquirer*, November 20, 1835.

108 *"an amateur of dark colors"* *Sun*, October 3, 1835.

108 *"he has got a knife"* Ibid., September 21, 1835.

109 *"dreadful murder"* *Morning Courier and New-York Enquirer*, September 21, 1835.

109 *"a student"* *Sun*, September 11, 1835.

110 *whose clan included* See Cohen (1998), pp. 70–71 and 101–3.

110 *"It was the most remarkable sight"* Quoted in Cohen (1998), p. 15.

111 *about Helen Jewett* See Cohen (1998), pp. 350–53.

CHAPTER FIVE
"Bowery Gals Will You Come Out To-night?"
Nighttime on the Bowery Before the Civil War

Browne (1975); Buckley (1984); Harlow (1931); Levine (1988); Monaghan (1952)

113 *he saved his shipmates* See Monaghan (1952), pp. 53–54 and 74–76.

113 *highbrow and lowbrow* See Levine (1988), pp. 30ff. and 102ff.

Bowery People: B'hoys and Sporting Men

Anbinder (2001); Browne (1975); Gunn (1857); Harlow (1931); Sutton (1874)

114 *"Hot corn! Hot corn!"* Quoted in Harlow (1931), p. 175.

114 *"I'M PADDY DOYLE'S PIG"* Ibid., p. 226.

114 *"Set down"* Browne (1975), p. 134.

115 *"Lavatory arrangements"* Gunn (1857), pp. 18–19.

115 *"no good man"* Ibid., p. 50.

116 *"He was arrayed"* *The Flash*, December 25, 1841.

117 *"the fire had reached"* Strong (1952), vol. 1, p. 266.

118 *some of the engravings* See Sutton (1874), p. 102.

119 *"additional curl"* *Weekly Rake*, September 23, 1842.

A Sockdoliger in the Bellows-Mover:
The Bowery Steps Out in the 1840s

Baker (189?); Delattre (2000); Dizikes (1993); Gilfoyle (1992); Harlow (1931); Lott (1993)

120 *John Searle's 1822 drawing*   In the collection of the New-York Historical Society

120 *"sent a sockdoliger"*   The Whip and Satirist of New-York and Brooklyn, May 7, 1842.

121 *"pack'd from ceiling to pit"*   Whitman (1902), vol. 6, pp. 190–91.

121 *"no act of my public life"*   Hone (1969), vol. 1, p. 348.

121 *"[o]aths, shouts, shrieks"*   New York Sporting Whip, February 11, 1843.

122 *"gut the theatre"*   New York Times, letter from William Cauldwell, July 27, 1902.

122 *vaulted over several rows*   NYPL-PAL, clipping file for Mitchell's Olympic, unidentified clipping.

122 *"trembling like an aspen leaf"*   New York Times, letter from William Cauldwell, July 27, 1902.

122 *T. Allston Brown, a theater historian*   New York Times, August 3, 1902.

123 *one of the great feats*   Odell (1949), vol. 5, p. 374.

123 *"hit me over de gourd"*   This and quotations following from Baker (189?), pp. 10–15, 20–21, and 32.

123 *"it was the baby"*   New York Times, letter from William Cauldwell, July 27, 1902.

125 *"Blow yah nose"*   Quoted in Harlow (1931), p. 265.

125 *This is a point*   Lott (1993), p. 39ff.

126 *as Lott has remarked*   Ibid., pp. 40–49.

126 *"De Bowery gals"*   Clifton (1845).

127 *Orange Street*   See Gilfoyle (1992), p. 41.

128 *"intolerable to the inhabitants"*   Quoted in Gilfoyle (1992), pp. 40 and 338n.

128 *"the blasphemous language"*   The Whip and Satirist of New-York and Brooklyn, April 2, 1842.

129 *"the life of the imperial city"*   Delattre (2000), p. 122 (translated).

SEX AND THE ANTEBELLUM CITY: GAY, STRAIGHT, WHITE, BLACK, AND CHARLES DICKENS

Gilfoyle (1992); Henderson (1973); Katz (1976)

130 *nearly fell into a swoon*   See The Whip and Satirist of New-York and Brooklyn, March 12, 1842.

130 *"Where dogs would howl"*   Dickens (1968), p. 110.

131 *"revel in her"*   Weekly Rake, November 5, 1842.

131 *"You will probably spend"*   NYCMA, police court cases, April 17, 1849, Box 7646.

131n. *The trades of the attackers*   See Gilfoyle (1992), pp. 321–29.

132 *"During a ministry"*   Quoted in Gilfoyle (1992), p. 18.

132 *"who those young men are"*   Weekly Rake, July 30, 1842.

132 *"Is there a man"*   Ibid., September 10, 1842 [?] (front page missing).

133 *"There is not one so degraded"* All quotations on Collins from *The Whip and Satirist of New-York,* February 12, 1842.

134 *"At dark, the shutters are put up"* The Whip and Satirist of New-York, March 5, 1842.

135 *"miserable beast"* Weekly Rake, October 1, 1842.

135 *"man-monsters"* The Flash, August 14, 1842.

135 *"he made use of very gross"* Quoted in Katz (1976), pp. 29–30.

136 *"I am setting on a spar"* Quoted in ibid., p. 31.

136 *"induced me to dress"* NYCMA, District Attorney records, June 16, 1836, *People v. Peter Sewally.*

137 *"certain persons"* Ibid., August 11, 1812, *People v. Rachel Underwood.*

Showdown at Astor Place, 1849

Anbinder (2001); Berthold (1999); Buckley (1984); Burrows and Wallace (1999); Moody (1958) and (1960); Wilentz (1984)

138 *"Order, and form"* Browne (1975), p. 130.

140 *Spartacus, Othello* See portraits in Moody (1960), following pp. 50, 146, and 252.

140 *"a vulgar, arrogant loafer"* Hone (1969), vol. 2, p. 866.

141 *"WORKINGMEN"* Quoted in Moody (1960), p. 130.

142 *"You can't go in there"* Quoted in idem (1958), p. 154.

142 *"I went gaily, I may say"* Macready (1969), p. 424–26.

143 *"Workingmen, shall Americans"* Quoted in Moody (1958), p. 155.

144 *"water was running"* Macready (1969), pp. 425–26.

144 *"Some of the cavalry"* Strong (1952), vol. 1, p. 353.

145 *Gilfoyle has shown* See Gilfoyle (1992), p. 206.

145 *Sean Wilentz* See Wilentz (1984), p. 109.

146 *black and Irish squatters* See Rosenzweig and Blackmar (1992), pp. 62–73.

146 *"no organization"* Quoted in Wilentz (1984), p. 300.

147 *"Massacre Opera House"* Harlow (1931), p. 332.

CHAPTER SIX
"Under the Rain of Gaslights"
From the Civil War to the Gilded and Gruesome 1870s

Anon. (1866); Bernstein (1990); Monaghan (1952); Trager (2003); Stern, Mellins, and Fishman (1999)

148 *"WAR HAS BEGUN"* New York Times, April 13, 1861.

148 *"I heard in the distance"* Whitman (1982), p. 706.

By Owl Train to Harlem

Erenberg (1984); Gilfoyle (1992); McCabe (1882); Nevins (1982); Stern, Mellins, and Fishman (1999)

151 *"On we go"* Quoted in McCabe (1882), pp. 190–91.

153 *"Night transit"* Howells (1976), pp. 76–77.

154   *"I've been having chuck"*   Quoted in Gilfoyle (1992), p. 203.

155   *the only actor*   See Erenberg (1984), pp. 107–9.

Blazing City, Hidden City

Black (1976); Browne (1974); Gilfoyle (2003); Goldman (1997); Hawes (1993); McCabe (1970); Plunz (1990); Quinn (1998); Sutton (1973); Whitton (1897)

156   *Murderers' Alley*   See Plunz (1990), p. 6 and fig. 1.2.

156   *"a dark region"*   Crane (1969), p.7.

156   *"The work of manufacturing"*   Quoted in Plunz (1990), p. 34.

157   *"the finest apartment"*   Hawes (1993), p. 43.

157   *an Egyptian tomb*   See Sutton (1973), p. 48.

158   *Cells were dungeonlike*   See Gilfoyle (2003), p. 528.

158   *"tobacco spit, vomit and filth"*   Sutton (1970), p. 329.

158   *"You enter a wide"*   Quoted in ibid., pp. 330–31.

159n. *Poe's first job*   See Quinn (1998), p. 410.

160   *Modeled on its famed*   *New York Times,* June 20, 1866, and Browne (1974), p. 282.

160   *"The dark waters"*   McCabe (1970), pp. 841–42.

161   *a series of stereopticon photographs*   NYPL Photography Collection, NYPG91-F214:002.

161   *"Legs are staple articles"*   Whitton (1897), p. 5.

161   *"clothes-line"*   Ibid., p. 9.

161   *"Arch Fiend . . . Queen of the Golden Realm"*   Playbill, September 29, 1866.

162   *"My boy, I have a fortune"*   Whitton (1897), p. 9.

162   *"the scenery is magnificent"*   Quoted in Odell (1949), vol. 8, p. 154.

162   *"You may talk of love and sighing"*   Lyrics and tune available at http://www.pdmusic.org.

162   *"ballet, spectacle"*   Strong (1952), vol. 4, p. 183.

The Devil and Anthony Comstock: Vice and Vigilantism in the 1870s

Fabian (1990); Keller (1981)

163   *"a Negro man"*   Quoted in Fabian (1990), p. 147.

163   *"The opposite conditions"*   N-YHS John Jay Papers, Box 4.

164   *"cunningly calculated"*   All quotations from New York Society for the Suppression of Vice (1876), (1877), and (1886).

Woman in the Dark: March 31 to April 1, 1878

Biggs (1862); Browder (1988); Collins (1934); Greer (1979); Homberger (1994); Keller (1981); Lynch (1927); Mohr (1978); Nevins (1982); Stern, Mellins, and Fishman (1999)

165   *as much as $60,000*   See Mohr (1978), p. 52.

165   *"Madame Restell's experience"*   *Sun,* March 3, 1846, quoted in Mohr (1978), p. 51.

166   *Photographs show*   See Stern, Mellins, and Fishman (1999), pp. 580–81.

166   *she quickly acquired*   See Keller (1981), p. 66.

168   *"What shall I do?"*   Browder (1988), pp. 181–82.
168   *Frantic three-man crews*   See Biggs (1862), pp. 14–28.
168   *Fogs of dingy-looking*   Collins (1934), p. 136.
169   *"What shall I do?"*   Browder (1988), pp. 181–82.
171   *"such as is found"*   Herald, April 2, 1878.
173   *"the lower part"*   Commercial Advertiser, April 1, 1878.
173   *In the crowded First District court*   NYCMA (Criminal Police Courts records), April 1, 1878.
174   *"Yes, you can laugh!"*   NYPL-PAL MS, Victorien Sardou, *Diplomacy*, tr. Bolton and Savile Rowe, Act 4.
175   *"Oh, what shall I do?"*   See Lynch (1927), pp. 413–15.
175   *She lay in a Tarrytown cemetery*   See Culbertson and Randall (1987), pp. 320–21.

CHAPTER SEVEN
Electric Costumes and Brass Knuckles:
Glamour, Crime, Sports, and the Commercialization of Night in the 1890s

Hirschfield (1957); Snyder (1989); Stern, Mellins, and Fishman (1999); Valentine (1860)
176   *"he is taller and fatter"*   New York Post, March 27, 1883.
177   *"while yet in his right mind"*   New York Times, March 27, 1883.
178   *The building covered*   See New York Times, July 15, 1853; Hirschfield (1957), p. 106.

Rialto Market:
The Business of Entertainment After the Civil War

Baker (189?); Chappell (1925); Durante and Kofoed (1931); Hapgood (1967); Howard (1964); Levine (1988); Lifson (1965); Sandrow (1996); Sogliuzzo (1985); Zellers (1971)
180   *"not only . . . fair"*   Town Topics, January 9, 1890.
181   *"Harold Routledge dead!"*   Howard (1964), p. 125.
181   *"fountains, temples"*   Chappell (1925), p. 20.
182   *spectacular scene*   NYPL-PAL (Program Scrapbook), MWEZ.x.p.c.17.
182   *Antonio Maiori*   See Sogliuzzo (1985), pp. 79–80.
182   *"to many sewing machine women"*   Sandrow (1996), p. 77.
182   *"the poor and ignorant"*   Hapgood (1967), pp. 113–14.
182n.   *Part of this tunnel*   See Solis (2005), pp. 152–55.
183   *"Tailor, Actor and Playwright"*   Quoted in Sandrow (1996), p. 45.
183   *"Great enthusiasm"*   Hapgood (1967), p. 16.
183   *"For some reason"*   Quoted in Sandrow (1967), p. 109.
184   *"Leave those rotten children"*   Quoted in ibid., p. 102.
185   *"hole in Twenty-first street"*   Foster (1990), p. 81.
185   *"Grand March of the Amazons"*   See Zellers (1971), p. xvii.
186   *"de wawdeville plays"*   Baker (189?), p. 21.
186   *"The Great Family"*   Quoted in Snyder (1989), p. 17.

186 *"Romeo and Juliet"* Quoted in Zellers (1971), p. 36.
187 *"women flashily dressed"* *New York Times,* July 30, 1902.

BLOOD UNDER THE GASLIGHTS:
PRIZEFIGHTING AND THE RISE OF NIGHTTIME SPORTS

Durante and Kofoed (1931); Durso (1979); Gorn (1986); Riess (1989); Stern, Mellins, and Fishman (1999); Walling (1887)

187 *"LOVERS NOT WANTED"* Durante and Kofoed (1931), p. 14.
188 *field sports* See Riess (1989), p. 13ff.
188 *a Yankee nativist* See Gorn (1986), pp. 69 and 110.
190 *"Astley Belt"* See article, "Old Time Walk," by Kelly Collins, at http://www.lehigh.edu.
191 *Along with scalpers* See *New York Times* and *New York Herald,* January 20, 1880.
191 *"slim, . . . with dark"* Walling (1887), p. 484.
191 *"The social cake"* *New York Herald,* January 20, 1880.
192 *"Drop that mountain of loveliness"* Walling (1887), p. 495.

"DEPRAVITY OF A DEPTH UNKNOWN":
THE TURN-OF-THE-CENTURY UNDERWORLD

Barnett (1975); Chauncey (1994); Gardner (1931); Gilfoyle (1992); Gorn (1986); JJCCJ, Trial Transcripts of the County of New York (1883–1927); Parkhurst (1970); Sante (1991); Van Wyck (1932); Walling (1887)

193 *"big husky rats"* Van Wyck (1932), p. 114.
193n. *These, probably* See Barnett (1975), pp. 122–23 and 129.
194 *"the women throw their legs"* Walling (1887), p. 489.
196 *"What do you mean"* JJCCJ, Trial Transcripts of the County of New York (1883–1927), *People v. William McGlory,* p. 18.
196 *"Q. Do you ever remember"* Ibid., p. 152.
197 *"singing and dancing"* Ibid., p. 170.
197 *"I have called for liquor"* Ibid., p. 194.
197 *"And you saw McGlory"* Ibid., pp. 135–36.
198 *"If the bloody bitch"* Ibid., p. 189.
199 *"a lying, perjured"* Parkhurst (1970), p. 10.
200 *"Hey, whiskers"* Gardner (1931), pp. 13–21.
200 *"each of which"* Ibid., p. 58.
200 *"a scraggy, thin, little woman"* Ibid., p. 56.
201 *"Social vice"* Parkhurst (1970), p. 155.
201 *"to the ladies"* New York City Madison Square Presbyterian Church (1896), pp. 10–11.
202 *"Depravity of a Depth"* *Herald,* January 5, 1892; see also Chauncey (1994), pp. 37–40.

CENTURY'S END

Durso (1979); Erenberg (1984); Hood (1993); Johnson (1985); Nye (1990); Stern, Mellins, and Fishman (1999); Starr and Hayman (1998); Trager (2003)

208   'shrewdest operators'   Herald, November 13, 1889.

208   A ghost   Ibid., November 13, 1889.

208   the Reverend William Hart Dexter   Ibid., November 2, 1899.

208   Thomas Daw   Ibid., November 6, 1899.

208   A baby   Ibid., November 2, 1899.

209   "décolleté patrons"   Town Topics, December 28, 1899.

209   "57 GOOD THINGS"   See Starr and Hayman (1998), p. 80, and Nye (1990), p. 51.

210   "residents of New York"   Herald, November 6, 1899.

CHAPTER EIGHT
Mr. Dieter Vanishes, November 1923:
The Volstead Act, Jazz, and *Earl Carroll's Vanities*

Douglas (1995); Howard (1893); Mellow (1984)

212   "started the flapper movement"   Hearst's International, May 1973.

213   "Within a few months"   Quoted in Mellow (1984), p. 95.

214   "Dick was a homebody"   Brooklyn Daily Eagle, November 6, 1923.

214   A photo shows   See ibid., November 5, 1923.

214   "a very small man"   Ibid., November 8, 1923.

215   "They are crying for their daddy"   Ibid., November 6, 1923.

215   "his manner"   Daily News, November 6, 1923.

216   "My God, Lola"   Eagle, November 9, 1923.

216   "an extremely good-looking young woman"   Daily News, November 8, 1923.

216   "Jeffe said he was going to hound me"   Ibid., November 8, 1923.

216   "I was almost in nervous collapse"   Eagle, November 8, 1923.

217   a photo shows the detective   Ibid., November 8, 1923.

217   "lay in a coma"   Daily News, November 8, 1923.

217   "youthful matron"   Ibid., November 6, 1923.

217   "the insinuations"   Ibid., November 7, 1923.

218   "recently obtained a divorce"   New York Times, November 7, 1923.

218   "My darling, blue-eyed boy"   Ibid., November 18, 1923.

218   Jeffe, pointing   Eagle, November 11, 1923.

220   "there are domestic difficulties"   Ibid.

YOU CANNOT MAKE YOUR SHIMMY SHAKE ON TEA:
PROHIBITION UNLEASHED

Barr (1999); Burnham (1968); Chauncey (1994); Ellis (1966); Kahn and Hirschfeld (2003); Kyvig (2000); Lender and Martin (1982); Miron and Zwiebel (1991); Moats (1933); Pegram (1998); Rorabaugh (1979); Rose (1996); Walker (1933)

222   "There was a bar"   Walker (1933), p. 25.

222   Absolute consumption of alcohol   See Rorabaugh (1979), Table A1.1, p. 233.

223   a 1930 study   See Kyvig (2000), p. 28.

223   "A reformer"   Quoted in Walker (1933), p. 224.

223   whiskey cost about   Pegram (1998), p. 163.

223   75 percent of liquor   Barr (1999), p. 238.

223n. *National Temperance Council*   See Committee on Prohibition Studies (1923).

223n. *claims that drinking*   Miron and Zwiebel (1991), p. 246.

224   *"once a woman has felt a brass rail"*   Moats (1933), p. 172.

224   *George Chauncey*   See Chauncey (1994), pp. 306–9.

224   *"They went to a lot of speakeasies"*   O'Hara (2003), p. 110.

Supper Clubs: Benzine and White Rock at 3 a.m.

Barr (1999); Berliner (1993); Gabler (1994); Johnson (1985); Kahn and Hirschfeld (2003); Lender and Martin (1982); Merz (1969); Moats (1983)

225   *"Exclusiveness is the night club's"*   Walker (1933), p. 289.

225n. *150 unbroken bottles*   See Lender and Martin (1982), p, 143.

226   *"Hello, suckers!"*   Berliner (1993), p. 2.

226   *established that Tex's father*   See ibid., pp. 9–15.

227   *In 1922 Guinan was in New York*   Ibid., pp. 4, 96–98, and 152.

228   *hard cider and raw alcohol*   Ibid., p. 98.

228   *"She 'invented' the gossip column"*   Winchell (1975), p. 50.

229   *additives like iodine*   See Merz (1969), p. 116.

229   *the Leroi*   Kahn and Hirschfeld (2003), p. 62.

229   *"Cocktail parties have become"*   Moats (1983), p. 186.

Jazz and the Jazz Age Night

230   *"Our aim"*   NYPL-PAL (Souvenir program), *MGZB (Castle).

231   *"Dance Which Made"*   Europe and Dabney (1914).

Way Downtown, Way Uptown: Greenwich Village and Harlem

Anderson (1981); Chappell (1925); Erenberg (1993); Hood (1993); Johnson (1969); Lewis (1979); McFarland (2001); Shaw (1931); Ware (1965); Wetzsteon (2002)

234   *"selling-of-bohemia"*   McFarland (2001), p. 191.

234   *"centralizing, magnetic"*   Quoted in Trager (2003), p. 337.

234   *"Whereas, whereas"*   See Wetzsteon (2002), pp. 2–3.

235   *one woman*   See Ware (1965), pp. 252–55.

237   *the Talented Tenth were suspicious*   See Lewis (1979), pp. 144–45.

237   *"To many, especially among colored"*   Johnson (1969), p. 179–80.

238   *"rambling, subterranean"*   Shaw (1931), pp. 75–76.

238   *"Lights gleam from a huge half watermelon"*   Chappell (1925), p. 119.

239   *"The white man"*   Beaton (1938), p. 167.

Nude and Stewed: The Story of the Bathtub Girl

Gabler (1994); Joyce (1930); McIntyre (1924); Murray (1976); Rosenblum (2000); Stern, Gilmartin, and Mellins (1987); Trachtenberg (1982)

240   *"I have married Everett Archer"*   Joyce (1930), p. 25.

240   *"I lie awake sometimes"*   Ibid., p. 156.

240   *Constance Rosenblum*   See Rosenblum (2000), pp. 24ff.

240 *"When the Carroll cunning"*   Quoted in Murray (1976), p. 62.

241 *"so adorable"*   Quoted in ibid., p. 36.

241 *"Then Earl turned to me"*   Quoted in Rosenblum (2000), p. 37.

242 *Theresa Daugelas*   Details of Daugelas's life have been compiled from the sources listed for this section and from the *Daily Mirror,* the *New York Times,* and the *Daily News,* between February and July, 1926.

243 *"forever discharge"*   Quoted in Murray (1976), p. 65.

243 *didn't even clearly violate Prohibition law*   See Murchison (1994), p.8.

243 *"her bare limbs"*   *Daily Mirror,* February 26, 1926.

244 *"All right, baby"*   Quoted in *New York Times,* May 26, 1926.

244 *"NUDE AND STEWED"*   *Daily News,* May 26, 1926.

245 *Alan Trachtenberg*   See Trachtenberg (1982), pp. 101–3.

245 *"At this fair"*   Bunyan (1966), p. 211 (text slightly modernized).

246 *"she was a vision"*   *Daily News,* May 26, 1926.

246 *"MODEL TAKES BATH IN WINE"*   *Daily Mirror,* February 25, 1926.

247 *"another advertising stunt"*   *New York Times,* July 26, 1926.

CHAPTER NINE
From Poorhouse to Penthouse and Back:
At Home, Homeless, and On the Town in the Mid-1930s

Crouse (1986); Josephson (1933); Rippiger (1934); Mitchell (2001); Stern, Gilmartin, and Mellins (1987)

248 *more than 5,000*   See Rippiger (1934).

249 *"You cannot legislate"*   Quoted in ibid., September 24, 1933.

249n. *Not for long*   See *New York Times,* September 9, 1933.

250 *Pasqua gripped the armrests*   See Mitchell (2001), pp. 205–11 and *Daily Mirror,* June 8, 1934.

251 *$3 a day*   See *New York Times,* May 26, 1933.

251 *Publicity photos*   See Crouse (1986), pp. 70–74.

HOOVERVILLE LULLABY

Crouse (1986); Newhouse (1934); Rosenzweig and Blackmar (1992); Smith (2001); Starr and Hayman (1998); Stott (1973)

252 *giant trout*   *New York Times,* February 15, 1930. Other versions of this legend identify the fish as a salmon.

252 *by 1931 the original lodging house*   See *New York Times,* January 31, 1931.

252 *2,230,086 overnight stays*   See Crouse (1986), p. 70.

252n. *By 1931 about 400*   See *New York Times,* September 27, 1931.

253 *A photo in the* Mirror   *Daily Mirror,* December 17, 1930.

254 *"Radio City"*   See *New York Times,* September 22, 1932.

254 *Six hundred people*   See Crouse (1986), pp. 100–101.

254n. *Ralph Redfield*   See Rosenzweig and Blackmar (1992), p. 443.

255 *"Hobo" was supposed to be*   See Crouse (1986), p. 94.

255 *historian William Stott*   See Stott (1973), pp. 33–45 and 267ff.

255   *"I guess I must have done"*   Quoted in Smith (2001), p. 47.
255   *he spent three weeks*   See ibid., p. 75.
256   *"As darkness came on"*   Newhouse (1934), p. 75.

SKYSCRAPER NOCTURNE

Alpern (1975); Brown (1928); Crouse (1986); Hawes (1993); Stayton (1990)
257   *D line units*   See Alpern (1975), p. 114.
257   *As Elizabeth Hawes remarks*   Hawes (1993), p. 37ff.
257n. *the John Schenck house*   See Stayton (1990), p. 16.
258   *about half of middle-class New Yorkers*   Ibid., p. 146.
258   *"intended for low rental"*   Brown (1928), p. 183.
258   *assembled 75 small properties*   *Real Estate Record and Builder's Guide*, April 6, 1929.
258   *900 square feet*   Alpern (1975), p. 124, floor plan.
259   *"a hybrid forged in the hothouse"*   Brown (1928), p. 204.
259n. *A more cynical reason*   See ibid.
260   *"each provided"*   *Real Estate Record and Builder's Guide*, June 30, 1928.
260   *"The Central Park Reservoir"*   *New Yorker,* April 21, 1928.
260   *"all that is necessary"*   Ibid., April 7, 1928.
261   *"The dark was coming"*   Thurber (1935), p. 215.
261   *"Wasn't it a good thing"*   O'Hara (2003), p. 163.

DECO DEFIANCE: GOOD TIMES IN HARD TIMES

Allen (1940); Beaton (1938); Blumenthal (2000); Mitchell (2001); Shaw (1931); Starr and Hayman (1998); Stern, Gilmartin, and Mellins (1987); Sylvester (1956)
263   *He'd opened his first speakeasy*   See Blumenthal (2000), pp. 100–103.
264   *"Nobody wants anything"*   Sylvester (1956), p. 226.
264   *cheaper thrills*   See Shaw (1931), pp. 47, 51, and 57.
264   *"a low ceilinged inferno"*   Beaton (1938), p. 122.
264   *Hudson Night Line*   See Mitchell (2001), p. 201.

MRS. MURPHY'S PARLOR:
RADIO NIGHTS AND EVENINGS AT HOME IN THE DEPRESSION

Allen (1940); Balio (1995); Barnouw (1966) and (1968); Parlett (1999); Perkins (1946); Rogers, Allen, and Weyer (1934)
265   *price of a radio*   See Balio (1995), p. 14.
267   *a cluster of midtown bars*   See Barnouw (1968), p. 109.
269   *"To me the studio visit"*   *New York Times,* November 11, 1934.
269   *National Industrial Conference Board*   See Allen (1940), p. 146.
269   *Monopoly*   See Parlett (1999), pp. 350–53.

HARLEM ONCE MORE: FLOOR SHOW AT THE CLUB BARRON, 1937

Barnouw (1968); Davis (1999); Fielding (Interview, 2004); Hulick and Marshall (1998); Shaw (1931); Sylvester (1956)
271   *Ellington played there*   See Ellington (1976), p. 64.
271   *still apparently open in the late 1930s*   Fielding, interview, 2004.

272   *Siskind shied away*   Ibid.
273   *as Siskind later remembered*   Ibid.
274   *to photograph Herbert Hoover*   Newhall (1982), p. 231.
274   *Large-aperture lenses*   Hulick and Marshall (1998), p. 55.
274   A Wet Night   Reproduction in Davis (1999), p. 89.

CHAPTER TEN
When the Lights Went Out:
World War II, the 1950s, and the Suburbanization of Night

Berger (1942); Rosenwaike (1972); Starr and Hayman (1998)
277n.   *On March 31*   See *New York Times,* April 1, 1942.
278   *any lamp*   Text of Dimout Order, ibid., May 18, 1942.
278   *"People don't realize it"*   Quoted in Berger (1942).
279   *75,000 vacant apartments*   See Trager (2003), p. 537.

MINSKY AGONISTES:
TIMES SQUARE AT WAR

Allen (1991); Friedman (2000); HBTL, Callahan Collection; Kessner (1989); Minsky and Machlin (1986); Sherman (1995)
280   *"Vice Admiral"*   See Sherman (1995), p. 120.
281   *"burlesque is the Czechoslovakia"*   Quoted in Friedman (2000), p. 92.
282   *historians have disagreed*   See Allen (1991), pp. 108–9.
282   *"made the girl's skin"*   Minsky and Machlin (1986), p. 115.
282   *"Red-Hot Dancers"*   HBTL, Callahan Collection.
283   *Minsky's in a photograph*   See Minsky and Machlin (1986), p, 168.
283   *"I'm holding up a box"*   Quoted in ibid., p. 65.
285   *3.5 murders*   See Trager (2003), p. 531.

UNEASY SUMMER:
1948, DRUGS, AND THE SOURING OF POSTWAR NEW YORK

Berger (2002); Clarke (1994); Courtwright (1982) and (2001); Jonnes (1996); McCabe (1970); Mezzrow (1961); Reppetto (2004)
285   *3.8 per cent*   http://www.bls.gov/cps.
288   *trying to relieve suffering*   See Courtwright (1982), p. 46.
288   *Courtwright estimates*   Ibid., pp. 28–40.
289   *"a series of beds"*   McCabe (1970), pp. 735–37.
289   *Dope Cola*   See Jonnes (1996), p. 21.
290   *After he was murdered*   See Reppetto (2004), p. 189.
290   *"The vipers . . . come up"*   Mezzrow (1961), pp. 97 and 101.
291   *"special recordings"*   Berger (2002), pp. 417–18.
291   *A scan of news stories*   In the *New York Times* and the *Readers' Guide to Periodical Literature*
292   *the Daisy Chain*   See Clarke (1994), p. 78.
292   *"When we got off at night"*   Quoted in Clarke (1994), p. 221.
293   *"She would smoke opium"*   Quoted in ibid., p. 223.
293   *decked two sailors*   See ibid., p. 248.

Postwar Blues: Lost in Beat Manhattan, 1950–1960

Consolidated Edison (1948); Courtwright, Joseph, and Des Jarlais (1989); HBTL, Callahan Collection; Holmes (1952); Jonnes (1996); McCarthy (1948); McNally (2003); Mitchell (1992); Street (1973); Zolotow (1950)

295   *"We won't stand for more bumps"*   Quoted in Zolotow (1950).

295   *annual statistics*   from New York City Police Department Annual Reports; see also Trager (2003), p. 531.

296   *"a mixture of Puerto Ricans"*   McCarthy (1948).

296   *"I'm stabbed"*   Ibid.

297   *"More than mere weariness"*   Holmes (1952).

298   *He regarded this as a breakthrough*   See McNally (2003), pp. 139–40.

298   *"For in the wildest hipster"*   Holmes (1952).

298   *a 1948 study*   Consolidated Edison (1948).

299   *Joe Gould*   See Mitchell (1992), pp. 623–24 and 711–16.

299   *"wearing the proud mantles"*   Yates (1961), pp. 20–21.

Nightclub Requiem:
Modernity, Crime, and the Nervous Streets of the Late 1950s

Barnouw (1970); Blumenthal (2000); Claiborne (1958); Gabler (1994); Jacoby (2000); Kaiser (1997); McDarrah (1996); MTRNY; Stern, Mellins, and Fishman (1995)

300   *a cluster of bars*   See Kaiser (1997), p. 106.

301   *photographic records of Greenwich Village*   See McDarrah (1996), especially p. 53.

302   *"TONIGHT takes America"*   *New York Times,* September 7, 1954, full page advertisement.

303   *a surviving tape*   MTRNY, Program #574 (1957).

304   *"As we both grew older"*   Winchell (1975), pp. 319–20.

305   *The food was dressed up*   For recipes, see *McCall's* (October 1958), p. 42.

306   *"angels, temptresses, and caged birds"*   *Life,* July 7, 1958.

307   *"Saturday night"*   Quoted in Jacoby (2000), p. 172.

308   *a broken arm*   See Jacoby (2000), p. 139.

The Night They Busted Sophie Tucker

Field (2003); Jacobs (1961); Stern, Mellins, and Fishman (1995)

309   *"spangled sentimentality"*   Quoted in Field (2003), p. 230.

309   *"When I kiss men"*   Quoted in ibid., p. 140.

310   *"'regular' visits by some cops"*   *Variety* (New York), November 23, 1960.

CHAPTER ELEVEN
Full Moon Over the Stonewall:
The Gay Epiphany, Discomania, and the Surfacing of Hidden Night

Alden (1964); Lawrence (2003); Leo (1967); Mohr (1964); Post (1947); Stern, Mellins, and Fishman (1995); Talese (1965); Taylor (1965); Wilson (1963)

312   *Crime had begun*   New York City Police Department Annual Reports.

313   *"One attraction of the discothèque"*   Wilson (1963).

314   *"The swingiest, zingiest"*   *New York Times,* July 26, 1964, advertisement.

316   *David Mancuso*   See Lawrence (2003), pp. 10–11, 22, and 35.

REVOLUTION IN SHERIDAN SQUARE:
THE STONEWALL RIOTS, JUNE 27–28, 1969

Carter (2004); Chauncey (1994); Crane (Interview, 2004); Doty (1963); Duberman (1994); Fields (Interview, 2004); Kaiser (1997); Lawrence (2003); Newfield (1965)

316   *"the new urban class"*   Lawrence (2003), pp. 16–17.

317   *As Charles Kaiser observes*   Kaiser (1997), pp. 156–57.

317   *"The old idea"*   Doty (1963).

318   *"MacDougal Street at midnight"*   Newfield (1965).

318   *"an earnest, compassionate effort"*   *Village Voice,* April 10, 1969.

319   *The Stonewall Inn, a Christopher Street bar*   See Duberman (1994), pp. 181–90.

321   *"You could feel the electricity"*   Quoted in Duberman (1994), p. 196.

321   *"The crowd had grown"*   Quoted in Carter (2004), p. 147.

321   *"Why don't you guys"*   Quoted in ibid., p. 152.

322   *"There was never any time"*   Quoted in Duberman (1994), p. 160.

323   *"We are the Stonewall girls!"*   Quoted in Carter (2004), p. 176.

323   *"Full Moon Over the Stonewall"*   *Village Voice,* July 2, 1969.

THE RETURN OF MONSIEUR DAGUERRE:
POSTMODERN NIGHT, 1970–2004

Carter (2004); Haden-Guest (1997); Lawrence (2003)

326   *"the guys there"*   Quoted in Carter (2004), p. 199.

327   *"You would look around"*   Quoted in Haden-Guest (1997), p. xiv.

328   *Studio 54's star-mobbed opening*   Ibid., pp. 41–48.

329   *Haden-Guest estimates*   Ibid., p. xv.

EPILOGUE
Spring 2004:
Back to the Wooden Horse

342   *"BUY HOMES ON"*   Starr and Hayman (1998), pp. 56–57.

349   *"For your life"*   Horsmanden (1971), pp. 49–50.

349   *"Dam ye bitch"*   Hamilton (1948), pp. 42–43.

Archival Sources

Manuscripts and Other Archival Material

Following is a list of abbreviations of institutions on which I have relied for unique or difficult-to-locate materials. Particular collections from these archives are identified in relevant notes.

AAS: American Antiquarian Society, Worcester, MA

AKS: Archives, Artkraft Strauss Sign Corporation, New York, NY

HBTL: Hampden-Booth Theatre Library at the Players Club, New York, NY

JJCCJ: Lloyd Sealy Library, John Jay College of Criminal Justice, City University of New York, New York, NY

LOC: Library of Congress, Washington, DC

MCNY: Museum of the City of New York, New York, NY

MTRNY: Museum of Television and Radio, New York, NY

NYCMA: New York City Municipal Archives, New York, NY

N-YHS: New-York Historical Society, New York, NY

NYPL: Manuscripts and Archives Division, The New York Public Library, Astor, Lenox and Tilden Foundations, New York, NY

NYPL-PAL: Billy Rose Theatre Collection, New York Public Library for the Performing Arts, Astor, Lenox and Tilden Fundations, New York, NY

NYSocL: New York Society Library, New York, NY

NYStaL: New York State Library, Albany, NY

RMG: Robert Mann Gallery, New York, NY

Newspapers Before 1900

I am including the following list because modern readers may not be familiar with early newspapers, whose titles and mastheads often changed frequently and confusingly.

Daily Advertiser
Mercantile Advertiser
Morning Courier and New-York Enquirer
New-York Commercial Advertiser
New York (Evening) Post
New-York Gazette
New-York Gazetteer
(New York) Journal of Commerce
New York (Morning) Herald
New York Sporting Whip
New-York Mercury
New-York Weekly Journal
Sun
The Flash
The Whip and Satirist of New-York and Brooklyn
Town Topics
Tribune
Weekly Rake

BIBLIOGRAPHY

Abbott, Carl. "The Neighborhoods of New York, 1760–1775." *New York History* 55, no. 1 (1974): 35–54.

Alden, Robert. "El Morocco Discotheque Brings Jet Set Back." *New York Times,* December 15, 1964.

Allen, Frederick Lewis. *Since Yesterday: The Nineteen-Thirties in America, September 3, 1929–September 3, 1939.* New York: Harper and Brothers, 1940.

Allen, Robert C. *Horrible Prettiness: Burlesque and American Culture.* Chapel Hill: University of North Carolina Press, 1991.

Alpern, Andrew. *Apartments for the Affluent: A Historical Survey of Buildings in New York.* New York: McGraw-Hill, 1975.

Altick, Richard. *The Shows of London.* Cambridge, MA: Belknap Press, 1978.

Anbinder, Tyler. *Five Points: The 19th-Century New York Neighborhood That Invented Tap Dance, Stole Elections, and Became the World's Most Notorious Slum.* New York: Free Press, 2001.

Anderson, Jervis. *This Was Harlem: A Cultural Portrait, 1900–1950.* New York: Farrar, Straus and Giroux, 1981.

Anon. *Night Side of New York: A Picture of the Great Metropolis After Nightfall by Members of the New York Press.* New York: Excelsior Publishing House (J. C. Haney), 1866.

Axtell, James. *After Columbus. Essays in the Ethnohistory of Colonial North America.* New York: Oxford University Press, 1988.

Baker, Benjamin A. *A Glance at New York.* New York: Samuel French, 189?.

Balio, Tino. *Grand Design: Hollywood as a Modern Business Enterprise, 1930–39,* vol. 5 of *History of the American Cinema,* ed. Charles Harpole. Berkeley: University of California Press, 1995.

Barnett, S. A. *The Rat: A Study in Behavior.* Chicago: University of Chicago Press, 1975.

Barnouw, Erik. *The Golden Web: A History of Broadcasting in the United States, Volume II, 1933 to 1953.* New York: Oxford University Press, 1968.

———. *A History of Broadcasting in the United States, Volume III—from 1953: The Image Empire.* New York: Oxford University Press, 1970.

———. *A Tower in Babel: A History of Broadcasting in the United States, Volume I—to 1933.* New York: Oxford University Press, 1966.

Barr, Andrew. *Drink: A Social History of America.* New York: Carroll and Graf, 1999.

Barth, Gunther. *City People: The Rise of Modern City Culture in Nineteenth-Century America*. New York: Oxford University Press, 1980.

Batterberry, Michael, and Ariane Batterberry. *On the Town in New York, from 1776 to the Present*. New York: Scribner, 1973.

Bayles, J. H. *Old Taverns of New York*. New York: Allaben Genealogical, 1915.

Beaton, Cecil. *Cecil Beaton's New York*. Philadelphia: Lippincott, 1938.

Berger, Meyer. "The Not-So-Gay White Way." *New York Times*, May 24, 1942.

———. "Tea for a Viper," *New Yorker*, March 12, 1938, reprinted in David F. Musto, ed., *Drugs in America: A Documentary History*. New York: New York University Press, 2002.

Berliner, Louise. *Texas Guinan: Queen of the Nightclubs*. Austin: University of Texas Press, 1993.

Bernstein, Iver. *The New York City Draft Riots: Their Significance for American Society and Politics in the Age of the Civil War*. New York: Oxford University Press, 1990.

Berthold, Dennis. "Class Acts: The Astor Place Riots and Melville's 'The Two Temples,'" *American Literature* 71, no. 3 (September 1999): 429–61.

Bierhorst, John. *Mythology of the Lenape: Guide and Texts*. Tucson: University of Arizona Press, 1982.

Biggs, David. "Gas and Gasmaking." *Harper's New Monthly Magazine*, December 1862.

Bingham, R. W. "The Light of Other Days," in L. S. Cooke, ed., *Lighting in America: From Colonial Rushlight to American Chandeliers*. New York: Main Street/Universe, 1975.

Black, Mary, ed. *Old New York in Early Photographs, 1853–1901: Prints from the Collection of the New-York Historical Society*. New York: Dover, 1976.

Blumenthal, Ralph. *Stork Club: America's Most Famous Nightspot and the Lost World of Café Society*. Boston: Little, Brown, 2000.

Blunt, Edmund M. *The Stranger's Guide to New York*. London: S. Leigh, 1818.

Bowers, Brian. *Lengthening the Day: A History of Lighting Technology*. New York: Oxford University Press, 1998.

Brand, Donald R. *Corporations and the Rule of Law: A Study of the National Recovery Administration*. Ithaca, NY: Cornell University Press, 1988.

Bridenbaugh, Carl. *Cities in Revolt: Urban Life in America, 1743–1776*. New York: Knopf, 1955.

Browder, Clifford. *The Wickedest Woman in New York: Madame Restell the Abortionist*. Hamden, CT: Archon, 1988.

Brown, Frank Choteau. "Some Recent Apartment Buildings." *Architectural Record*, March 1928.

Browne, Junius Henri. *The Great Metropolis: A Mirror of New York*. 1869. Reprint, New York: Arno Press, 1974.

Buckley, Peter G. "To the Opera House: Culture and Society in New York City, 1820–1860." Ph.D. diss., SUNY Stony Brook, 1984.

Bullivant, Benjamin. "A Glance at New York in 1697: The Travel Diary of Dr. Benjamin Bullivant," ed. Wayne Andrews. *NYHSQ* 40 (1956): 55–73.

Bunyan, John. *Grace Abounding to the Chief of Sinners and The Pilgrim's Progress*, ed. Roger Sharrock. Oxford: Oxford University Press, 1966.

Burnham, John C. "New Perspectives on the Prohibition 'Experiment' of the 1920s." *Journal of Social History* 2 (1968): 51–68.

Burrows, Edwin G., and Mike Wallace. *Gotham: A History of New York City to 1898*. New York: Oxford University Press, 1999.

Bushman, R. and C. "The Early History of Cleanliness in America." *Journal of American History* 74 (1988): 1213–38.

Cantwell, Anne-Marie, and Diana diZerega Wall. *Unearthing Gotham: The Archaeology of New York City*. New Haven: Yale University Press, 2001.

Carter, David, *Stonewall: The Riots That Sparked the Gay Revolution*. New York: St. Martin's Press, 2004.

Chappell, George S. *The Restaurants of New York*. New York: Greenberg, 1925.

Chauncey, George. *Gay New York: Gender, Urban Culture, and the Making of the Gay Male World*. New York: Basic Books, 1994.

Cheape, Charles W. *Moving the Masses: Urban Public Transit in New York, Boston, and Philadelphia, 1880–1912*. Cambridge, MA: Harvard University Press, 1980.

Child, Lydia Maria. *Letters from New-York*, ed. Bruce Mills. Athens, GA: University of Georgia Press, 1998.

Claiborne, Craig. "Two Restaurants." *New York Times*, January 6, 1958.

Clarke, Donald. *Wishing on the Moon: The Life and Times of Billie Holiday*. New York: Viking, 1994.

Clifton, William. "The Bowery Gal." Sheet music, New York: Thomas Birch, 1845.

Cohen, Patricia Cline, *The Murder of Helen Jewett*. New York: Knopf, 1998.

Collins, Frederick L. *Consolidated Gas Company of New York: A History*. New York: Consolidated Gas Co., 1934.

Collins, Kelly. "Old Time Walk." http://www.lehigh.edu/dmd1/public/www-data/kelly.html.

Committee on Prohibition Studies. *New York City Under Prohibition*. New York: National Temperance Council, 1923.

Condit, Carl W. *The Port of New York: A History of the Rail and Terminal System from the Beginnings to Pennsylvania Station*. Chicago: University of Chicago Press, 1980.

Consolidated Edison, *Population of New York City, 1940–1948*. New York: Consolidated Edison, 1948.

Courtwright, David T. *Dark Paradise: Opiate Addiction in America Before 1940*. Cambridge, MA: Harvard University Press, 1982.

———. *Forces of Habit: Drugs and the Making of the Modern World*. Cambridge, MA: Harvard University Press, 2001.

Courtwright, David T., Herman Joseph, and Don Des Jarlais. *Addicts Who Survived: An Oral History of Narcotic Use in America, 1923–1965*. Knoxville: University of Tennessee Press, 1989.

Crane, Stephen. *Maggie: A Girl of the Streets*, in *The Portable Stephen Crane*, ed. Joseph Katz. New York: Viking, 1969.

Cronin, James E. "Elihu Hubbard Smith and the New York Theatre (1793–98)." *New York History* 31 (1950): 136–48.

Crouse, Joan M., *The Homeless Transient in the Great Depression*. Albany: State University of New York Press, 1986.

Culbertson, Judi, and Tom Randall. *Permanent New Yorkers: A Biographical Guide to the Cemeteries of New York*. Chelsea, VT: Chelsea Green, 1987.

Danckaerts, Jasper. *Journal of Jasper Danckaerts,* ed. B. B. James and J. F. Jameson, in *Original Narratives of Early American History.* New York: Scribner's, 1913.

Davenport, Marcia Clark. "The New Apartments." *New Yorker,* April 7 and 21, 1928.

Davis, Keith F. *An American Century of Photography from Dry-Plate to Digital.* New York: Hallmark Cards, in association with Abrams, 1999.

Davis, Thomas J. *A Rumor of Revolt: The "Great Negro Plot" in Colonial New York.* New York: Free Press, 1985.

Dayton, Abram. *Last Days of Knickerbocker Life in New York.* New York: Harlan, 1882.

Delattre, Simone. *Les Douze Heures noires: La Nuit à Paris au XIXᵉ siècle.* Paris: Albin Michel, 2000.

Dickens, Charles. *American Notes,* ed. Christopher Lasch. Gloucester, MA: Peter Smith, 1968.

Dizikes, John. *Opera in America: A Cultural History.* New Haven: Yale University Press, 1993.

Doggett, John. *Doggett's New York City Directory.* Series. New York: John Doggett, various dates.

Doty, Robert. "Growth of Overt Homosexuality in City Provokes Wide Concern." *New York Times,* December 17, 1963.

Douglas, Ann. *Terrible Honesty: Mongrel Manhattan in the 1920s.* New York: Farrar, Straus and Giroux, 1995.

Duberman, Martin. *Stonewall.* New York: Plume, 1994.

Dunlap, William. *Diary of William Dunlap, 1766–1839.* 3 vols. 1930. Reprint, New York: B. Blom, 1969.

———. *History of the American Theatre, and Anecdotes of the Principal Actors.* 1832. Reprint, New York: Burt Franklin, 1963.

———. *History of the New Netherlands.* 2 vols. New York: Carter and Thorp, 1840.

Durante, Jimmy, and Jack Kofoed. *Night Clubs.* New York: Knopf, 1931.

Durso, Joseph. *Madison Square Garden: 100 Years of History.* New York: Simon & Schuster, 1979.

Eberhart, George M. *A Geo-bibliography of Anomalies: Primary Access to Observations of UFOs, Ghosts, and Other Mysterious Phenomena.* Westport, CT: Greenwood Press, 1980.

Ellington, Edward Kennedy (Duke). *Music Is My Mistress.* New York: Da Capo Press, 1976.

Ellis, Edward Robb. *The Epic of New York City.* New York: Old Town Books, 1966.

Erenberg, Lewis A. *Steppin' Out: New York Nightlife and the Transformation of American Culture, 1890–1930.* Chicago: University of Chicago Press, 1984.

———. "Greenwich Village Nightlife," in Rick Beard and Leslie Cohen Berlowitz, eds., *Greenwich Village: Culture and Counterculture.* New Brunswick: Rutgers University Press, 1993.

Europe, James Reese, and Ford T. Dabney. "The Castle Walk: Trot and One-Step." Sheet music, New York: J. W. Stern, 1914.

Fabian, Ann. *Card Sharps, Dream Books, and Bucket Shops: Gambling in Nineteenth-Century America.* Ithaca, NY: Cornell University Press, 1990.

Feininger, Andreas, text by John von Hartz. *New York in the Forties*. New York: Dover, 1978.

Fernow, Berthold. *The Records of New Amsterdam from 1653 to 1674*. 7 vols. 1897. Reprint, Baltimore: Genealogical Publishing Company, 1976.

Field, Armond. *Sophie Tucker: First Lady of Show Business*. Jefferson, NC: McFarland, 2003.

Foster, George G. *New York by Gas-Light*. 1850, ed. Stuart M. Blumin. Berkeley: University of California Press, 1990.

Francis, John W. *Old New York: Or, Reminiscences of the Past Sixty Years*. New York: Widdleton, 1865.

Friedman, Andrea. *Prurient Interests: Gender, Democracy, and Obscenity in New York City, 1909–1945*. New York: Columbia University Press, 2000.

Gabler, Neal. *Winchell: Gossip, Power, and the Culture of Celebrity*. New York: Knopf, 1994.

Gaine, Hugh. *The Journals of Hugh Gaine, Printer*, ed. P. L. Ford. 2 vols. New York: Dodd, Mead, 1902.

Gardner, Charles W. *The Doctor and the Devil: or, Midnight Adventures of Dr. Parkhurst*. 1894. Reprint, New York: Vanguard Press, 1931.

Garrett, Elisabeth D. *At Home: The American Family, 1750–1870*. New York: Abrams, 1990.

Garrett, Thomas M. "The History of Pleasure Gardens in New York City, 1700–1865." Ph.D. diss., New York University, 1978.

Gassner, J. and M., eds. *Best Plays of the Early American Theatre*. New York: Crown, 1967.

Gateley, Iain. *La Diva Nicotina: The Story of How Tobacco Seduced the World*. New York: Simon & Schuster, 2001.

Gernsheim, Helmut, and Alison Gernsheim. *L. J. M. Daguerre: The History of the Diorama and the Daguerrotype*. New York: Dover, 1968.

———. *The History of Photography from the Camera Obscura to the Beginning of the Modern Era*. New York: McGraw Hill, 1969.

Gilfoyle, Timothy J. *City of Eros: New York City, Prostitution, and the Commercialization of Sex, 1790–1920*. New York: Norton, 1992.

———. "'America's Greatest Criminal Barracks:' The Tombs and the Experience of Criminal Justice in New York City, 1838–1897." *Journal of Urban History* 29 (2003): 525–54.

Goldman, Joanne Abel. *Building New York's Sewers: Developing Mechanisms of Urban Management*. West Lafayette, IN: Purdue University Press, 1997.

Gorn, Elliott J., *The Manly Art: Bare-Knuckle Prizefighting in America*. Ithaca, NY: Cornell University Press, 1986.

Gottesman, R. S. *The Arts and Crafts in New York, 1726–76*. New York: New-York Historical Society, 1936.

Greenberg, Douglas. *Crime and Law Enforcement in the Colony of New York, 1691–1776*. Ithaca, NY: Cornell University Press, 1974.

Greene, Asa. *A Glance at New York*. New York: Greene, 1837.

Greene, Joseph Warren. *New York City's First Railroad: The New York and Harlem (1832–1867)*. New York: New-York Historical Society, 1926. Reprint from *New-York Historical Society Quarterly*, January 1926.

Greer, William. *A History of Alarm Security*. Washington, DC: National Burglar and Fire Alarm Association, 1979.

Gunn, Thomas Butler. *The Physiology of New York Boarding-Houses*. New York: Mason Bros., 1857.

Haden-Guest, Anthony. *The Last Party: Studio 54, Disco, and the Culture of the Night*. New York: Morrow, 1997.

Hamilton, Alexander. *Gentleman's Progress: The Itinerarium of Dr. Alexander Hamilton, 1744*, ed. Carl Bridenbaugh. Chapel Hill: University of North Carolina Press, 1948.

Hapgood, Hutchins. *The Spirit of the Ghetto*, ed. Moses Rifkin. 1902. Reprint, Cambridge, MA: Belknap Press, 1967.

Harlow, Alvin F. *Old Bowery Days: The Chronicles of a Famous Street*. New York: Appleton, 1931.

———. *Old Wires and New Waves: The History of the Telegraph, Telephone, and Wireless*. New York: Appleton-Century, 1936.

———. *The Road of the Century: The Story of the New York Central*. New York: Creative Age Press, 1947.

Harris, Gale, et al. *The African Burial Ground and the Commons Historic District Designation Report*. New York: Landmarks Preservation Commission, 1993.

Harris, Neil. *Humbug: The Art of P. T. Barnum*. Boston: Little, Brown, 1973.

Haswell, Charles. *Reminiscences of an Octogenarian of the City of New York (1816 to 1860)*. New York: Harper, 1896.

Hawes, Elizabeth. *New York, New York: How the Apartment House Transformed the Life of the City (1869–1930)*. New York: Knopf, 1993.

Hayward, A. H. *Colonial Lighting*. New York: Dover, 1962.

Henderson, Mary C. *The City and the Theater: New York Playhouses from Bowling Green to Times Square*. Clifton, NJ: James T. White, 1973.

Hirschfeld, Charles. "America on Exhibition: America's Crystal Palace," *American Quarterly* 9, no. 2 (1957): 101-16.

Hodgkinson, John. *A Narrative of His Connection with the Old American Company, from the Fifth September, 1792 to the Thirty-first of March, 1797*. Reprinted in William Dunlap, *History of the American Theatre*. New York: Burt Franklin, 1963.

Holmes, [John] Clellon. "This Is the Beat Generation." *New York Times Magazine*, November 16, 1952.

Homberger, Eric. *Scenes from the Life of a City: Corruption and Conscience in Old New York*. New Haven: Yale University Press, 1994.

———. *The Historical Atlas of New York City: A Visual Celebration of Nearly 400 Years of New York City's History*. New York: Henry Holt, 1994.

Hone, Philip. *The Diary of Philip Hone*, ed. Allan Nevins. 2 vols. 1927. Reprint, New York: Kraus Reprint, 1969.

Hood, Clifton. *722 Miles: The Building of the Subways and How They Transformed New York*. Baltimore: Johns Hopkins University Press, 1993.

Horowitz, Helen. *Rereading Sex: Battles over Sexual Knowledge and Suppression in Nineteenth-Century America*. New York: Knopf, 2002.

Horsmanden, Daniel. *The New York Conspiracy*, ed. Thomas Davis. Boston: Beacon Press, 1971.

Horton, R. G. *A Brief Memorial of the Origin and Earlier History of the Tammany Society or Columbian Order.* New York: New York Printing Co., 1867.

Howard, Bronson. *The Banker's Daughter and Other Plays by Bronson Howard,* ed. A. G. Halline. Bloomington: Indiana University Press, 1964.

Howard, Henry W. B., ed. *History of the City of Brooklyn.* 2 vols. Brooklyn, NY: Brooklyn Daily Eagle, 1893.

Howells, William Dean. *A Hazard of New Fortunes,* ed. A. Hazard et al. Bloomington: Indiana University Press, 1976.

Hulick, Diana Emery, with Joseph Marshall. *Photography: 1900 to the Present.* Englewood Cliffs, NJ: Prentice Hall, 1998.

Innes, J. H. *New Amsterdam and Its People: Studies, Social and Topographical, of the Town under Dutch and Early English Rule.* New York: Scribner's, 1902.

Jackson, Kenneth T., ed. *Encyclopedia of New York City.* New Haven, CT: Yale University Press, 1995.

Jacobs, Jane. *The Death and Life of Great American Cities.* New York: Random House, 1961.

Jacoby, Richard. *Conversations with the Capeman: The Untold Story of Salvador Agron.* New York: Painted Leaf Press, 2000.

Jameson, J. Franklin, ed. *Narratives of New Netherland.* New York: Scribner's, 1909.

Jenkins, Stephen. *The Greatest Street in the World: The Story of Broadway, Old and New, from the Bowling Green to Albany.* New York: Putnam's, 1911.

Johnson, Claudia. "That Guilty Third Tier: Prostitution in Nineteenth-Century American Theaters." *American Quarterly* 27, no. 5 (1975): 575–84.

Johnson, James Weldon. *Black Manhattan.* 1930. Reprint, New York: Atheneum, 1969.

Johnson, Steven Burge. *The Roof Gardens of Broadway Theatres, 1883–1942.* Ann Arbor: UMI Research Press, 1985.

Jonnes, Jill. *Hep-Cats, Narcs, and Pipe Dreams: A History of America's Romance with Illegal Drugs.* New York: Scribner, 1996.

Josephson, Matthew. "The Other America." *New Republic,* vol. 75, May 15, 1933: 14–16.

Joyce, Peggy Hopkins. *Men, Marriage and Me.* New York: The Macaulay Company, 1930.

Kahn, Gordon, and Al Hirschfeld. *The Speakeasies of 1932.* Milwaukee, WI: Glenn Young Books, 2003.

Kaiser, Charles. *The Gay Metropolis, 1940–1996.* Boston: Houghton Mifflin, 1997.

Kalm, Peter. *Travels in North America,* ed. and trans. A. B. Benson. 2 vols. New York: Dover, 1966.

Kammen, Michael. *Colonial New York: A History.* New York: Scribner's, 1975.

Katz, Jonathan. *Gay American History: Lesbians and Gay Men in the U.S.A.* New York: Crowell, 1976.

Keller, Allan. *Scandalous Lady: The Life and Times of Madame Restell, New York's Most Notorious Abortionist.* New York: Atheneum, 1981.

Kessler, H. H. and E. Rachlis. *Peter Stuyvesant and His New York.* New York: Random House, 1959.

Kessner, Thomas. *Fiorello H. La Guardia and the Making of Modern New York.* New York: McGraw Hill, 1989.

Kobrin, David. *The Black Minority in Early New York.* Albany, NY: New York State Education Department, 1971.

Kouwenhoven, J. A. *The Columbia Historical Portrait of New York.* New York: Doubleday, 1953.

Kyvig, David E. *Repealing National Prohibition,* 2nd ed. Kent, OH: Kent State University Press, 2000.

Lawrence, Tim. *Love Saves the Day: A History of American Dance Music Culture, 1970–1979.* Durham, NC: Duke University Press, 2003.

Lender, M. E., and J. K. Martin. *Drinking in America: A History.* New York: Free Press, 1982.

Leo, John. "Swinging in the East Village Has Its Ups and Downs." *New York Times,* July 15, 1967.

Levine, Lawrence W. *Highbrow/Lowbrow: The Emergence of Cultural Hierarchy in America.* Cambridge, MA: Harvard University Press, 1988.

Lewis, David Levering. *When Harlem Was in Vogue.* New York: Oxford University Press, 1979.

Lifson, David S. *The Yiddish Theatre in America.* New York: Thomas Yoseloff, 1965.

Lockwood, Charles. *Bricks and Brownstone: The New York Row House, 1783–1929: An Architectural and Social History.* New York: McGraw Hill, 1972.

Longworth, David. *Longworth's American Almanac, New York Register, and City Directory.* Series. New York: David Longworth, various dates.

Lott, Eric. *Love and Theft: Blackface Minstrelsy and the American Working Class.* New York: Oxford University Press, 1993.

Lynch, Denis Tilden. *Boss Tweed: The Story of a Grim Generation.* New York: Boni and Liveright, 1927.

Macready, William Charles. *The Diaries of William Charles Macready, 1833–1851,* ed. William Toynbee. 2 vols. 1912. Reprint, New York: B. Blom, 1969.

Mahony, John C. Memoir in Charles Sutton, *The New York Tombs: Its Secrets and Its Mysteries,* ed. J. B. Mix and S. A. Mackeever. 1874. Reprint, Montclair, NJ: Patterson Smith, 1973.

McCabe, James D. *Lights and Shadows of New York Life: Or, the Sights and Sensations of the Great City.* 1872. Facsimile edition, New York: Farrar, Straus and Giroux, 1970.

———. *New York by Sunlight and Gaslight: A Work Descriptive of the Great American Metropolis.* Philadelphia: Hubbard Bros., 1882.

McCarthy, Joe. "A Night on the Beat." *Life,* June 21, 1948.

McCusker, J. J. *Money and Exchange in Europe and America, 1600–1775: A Handbook.* Chapel Hill: University of North Carolina Press, 1978.

McDarrah, F. W., and G. S. McDarrah. *Beat Generation: Glory Days in Greenwich Village.* New York: Schirmer Books (Simon & Schuster), 1996.

McFarland, George W. *Inside Greenwich Village: A New York City Neighborhood, 1898–1918.* Amherst: University of Massachusetts Press, 2001.

McIntyre, O. O. *White Light Nights.* New York: Cosmopolitan Book Co., 1924.

McManus, Edgar J. *History of Negro Slavery in New York.* Syracuse: Syracuse University Press, 1966.

McNally, Dennis. *Desolate Angel: Jack Kerouac, the Beat Generation, and America.* 1979. Reprint, New York: Da Capo Press, 2003.

Mellow, James R. *Invented Lives: F. Scott and Zelda Fitzgerald.* Boston: Houghton Mifflin, 1984.

Merz, Charles. *The Dry Decade.* 1930. Reprint, Seattle: University of Washington Press, 1969.

Mezzrow, Milton. *Really the Blues,* excerpted in David Ebin, ed., *The Drug Experience: First-Person Accounts of Addicts, Writers, Scientists and Others.* New York: Orion Press, 1961.

Minsky, Morton and Milt Machlin. *Minsky's Burlesque.* New York: Arbor House, 1986.

Miron, Jeffrey A., and Jeffrey Zwiebel. "Alcohol Consumption During Prohibition." *American Economic Review* 81, no. 2 (May 1991): 242–47.

Mitchell, Joseph. *My Ears Are Bent.* 1938. Reprint, New York: Pantheon, 2001.

———. *Up in the Old Hotel and Other Stories.* New York: Pantheon, 1992.

Mitchill, Samuel Latham. *The Picture of New-York; or, The Traveller's Guide through the Commercial Metropolis of the United States.* New York: Riley, 1807.

Moats, Alice-Leone. *No Nice Girl Swears.* 1933. Reprint, New York: St. Martin's/Marek, 1983.

Mohr, Charles. "World of Affluent Youth Favors 'In' Dancing at City Hideaways." *New York Times,* March 30, 1964.

Mohr, James. *Abortion in America: The Origins and Evolution of National Policy, 1800–1900.* New York: Oxford University Press, 1978.

Monaghan, Jay. *The Great Rascal: The Life and Adventures of Ned Buntline.* Boston: Little, Brown, 1952.

Moody, Richard. *Edwin Forrest: First Star of the American Stage.* New York: Knopf, 1960.

———. *The Astor Place Riot.* Bloomington: University of Indiana Press, 1958.

Moran, James. *Printing Presses: History and Development from the Fifteenth Century to Modern Times.* Berkeley: University of California Press, 1973.

Morgan, Helen M., ed. *A Season in New York, 1801: Letters of Harriet and Maria Trumbull.* Pittsburgh: University of Pittsburgh Press, 1969.

Morris, Lloyd. *Incredible New York: High Life and Low Life of the Last Hundred Years.* New York: Random House, 1951.

Morrison, Hugh. *Early American Architecture from the First Colonial Settlements to the National Period.* New York: Oxford University Press, 1952.

Mott, F. L. *American Journalism: A History of Newspapers in the United States Through 260 Years: 1690 to 1950.* New York: Macmillan, 1950.

Mumford, Lewis. "The Sky Line: Beer and Grass." *New Yorker,* October 7, 1933.

Murchison, Kenneth M. *Federal Criminal Law Doctrine: The Forgotten Influence of National Prohibition.* Durham, NC: Duke University Press, 1994.

Murray, Ken. *The Body Merchant: The Story of Earl Carroll.* Pasadena, CA: Ward Ritchie Press, 1976.

Mushabac, Jane, and Angela Wigan. *A Short and Remarkable History of New York City.* New York: Fordham University Press, 1999.

Nevins, Deborah, ed. *Grand Central Terminal: City Within the City.* New York: Municipal Art Society, 1982.

New York City Madison Square Presbyterian Church. *Yearbook.* New York: New York City Madison Square Presbyterian Church, 1896.

New York Society for the Suppression of Vice. *Second Annual Report*. New York: Society for the Suppression of Vice, 1876.

————. *Third Annual Report*. New York: Society for the Suppression of Vice, 1877.

————. *Twelfth Annual Report*. New York: Society for the Suppression of Vice, 1886.

Newfield, Jack. "MacDougal at Midnight: A Street Under Pressure." *Village Voice*, April 8, 1965.

Newhall, Beaumont. *The History of Photography: 1839 to the Present*. New York: Museum of Modern Art, 1982.

Newhouse, Edward. *You Can't Sleep Here*. New York: The Macaulay Company, 1934.

Nye, David E. *Electrifying America: Social Meanings of a New Technology, 1880–1940*. Cambridge, MA: MIT Press, 1990.

O'Brien, Frank M. *The Story of the Sun: New York: 1833–1928*. New York: Appleton, 1928.

O'Callaghan, E., ed. *Documents Relative to the Colonial History of the State of New York: Procured in Holland, England, and France, by John Romeyn Brodhead*. 10 vols. 1856. Reprint, New York: AMS Press, 1969.

O'Hara, John. *BUtterfield 8*. 1935. Reprint, New York: Modern Library, 2003.

Odell, George C. D. *Annals of the New York Stage*. 15 vols. New York: Columbia University Press, 1927–49.

Ottley, Roi and William J. Weatherby, eds. *The Negro in New York: An Informal Social History*. New York: New York Public Library, 1967.

Parkhurst, Charles. *Our Fight with Tammany*. 1895. Reprint, New York: Arno Press, 1970.

Parlett, David. *The Oxford History of Board Games*. Oxford: Oxford University Press, 1999.

Pegram, Thomas R. *Battling Demon Rum: The Struggle for a Dry America, 1800–1933*. Chicago: Ivan R. Dee, 1998.

Penn, W. A. *The Soverane Herbe: A History of Tobacco*. New York: E. P. Dutton, 1902.

Perkins, Frances, *The Roosevelt I Knew*. New York: Viking, 1946.

Plunz, Richard. *A History of Housing in New York City: Dwelling Type and Social Change in the American Metropolis*. New York: Columbia University Press, 1990.

Police Department, New York City. *Annual Reports*, 1950–1969.

Pomerantz, S. I. *New York: An American City, 1783–1803*. New York: Columbia University Press, 1938.

Post, Emily. *Etiquette: The Blue Book of Social Usage*. New York: Funk and Wagnalls, 1947.

Quinn, Arthur Hobson. *Edgar Allan Poe: A Critical Biography*. 1941. Reprint, Baltimore: Johns Hopkins University Press, 1997.

Raesly, E. L. *Portrait of New Netherland*. New York: Columbia University Press, 1945.

Reichl, Alexander J. *Reconstructing Times Square: Politics and Culture in Urban Development*. Lawrence: University Press of Kansas, 1999.

Reppetto, Thomas. *American Mafia: A History of Its Rise to Power*. New York: Henry Holt, 2004.

Richardson, James F. *The New York Police: Colonial Times to 1901*. New York: Oxford University Press, 1970.

Riess, Steven A. *City Games: The Evolution of American Urban Society and the Rise of Sports.* Urbana: University of Illinois Press, 1989.

Rippiger, Henrietta. "The Restaurant Enjoys a Revival." *New York Times,* July 29, 1934.

Robert, Joseph C. *The Story of Tobacco in America.* New York: Knopf, 1949.

Rogers, Agnes, Frederick Lewis Allen, and Edward M. Weyer. *Metropolis: An American City in Photographs.* New York: Harper and Brothers, 1934.

Rorabaugh, A. J. *The Alcoholic Republic: An American Tradition.* New York: Oxford University Press, 1979.

Rose, Kenneth D. *American Women and the Repeal of Prohibition.* New York: New York University Press, 1996.

Rosenblum, Constance. *Golddigger: The Outrageous Life and Times of Peggy Hopkins Joyce.* New York: Metropolitan Books, 2000.

Rosenwaike, Ira. *Population History of New York City.* Syracuse, NY: Syracuse University Press, 1972.

Rosenzweig, Roy, and Elizabeth Blackmar. *The Park and the People: A History of Central Park.* Ithaca, NY: Cornell University Press, 1992.

Sagalyn, Lynne B. *Times Square Roulette: Remaking the City Icon.* Cambridge, MA: MIT Press, 2001.

Sandrow, Nahma. *Vagabond Stars: A World History of Yiddish Theater.* Syracuse, NY: Syracuse University Press, 1996.

Sante, Luc. *Low Life: Lures and Snares of Old New York.* New York: Farrar, Straus and Giroux, 1991.

Schivelbusch, Wolfgang. *Disenchanted Night: The Industrialization of Light in the Nineteenth Century.* New York: Berg, 1988.

Scott, Kenneth. "The Slave Insurrection in New York in 1712." *N-YHSQ* 65 (1961): 43–74.

Shaw, Charles. *Nightlife:* Vanity Fair's *Guide to New York After Dark.* New York: John Day, 1931.

Sherman, Janann. "'The Vice Admiral': Margaret Chase Smith and the Investigation of Congested Areas in Wartime," in K. P. O'Brien and L. H. Parsons, eds., *The Home-Front War: World War II and American Society.* Westport, CT: Greenwood Press, 1995.

Shorto, Russell. *The Island at the Center of the World: The Epic Story of Dutch Manhattan and the Forgotten Colony That Shaped America.* New York: Doubleday, 2004.

Singleton, Esther. *Dutch New York.* 1909. Reprint, New York: Benjamin Blom, 1968.

Smith, Billy Ben. *The Literary Career of Proletarian Novelist and New Yorker Short Story Writer Edward Newhouse.* Lewiston, NY: The Edwin Mellen Press, 2001.

Snyder, Robert W. *Voice of the City: Vaudeville and Popular Culture in New York.* New York: Oxford University Press, 1989.

Sogliuzzo, A. Richard. "Shakespeare, Sardou, and Pulcinella: Italian American Working-Class Theatre in New York, 1880–1940," in Bruce A. McConachie and Daniel Friedman, eds., *Theatre for Working-Class Audiences in the United States, 1830–1980.* Westport, CT: Greenwood Press, 1985.

Solis, Julia. *New York Underground: The Anatomy of a City.* New York: Routledge, 2005.

Starr, Tama, and Edward Hayman. *Signs and Wonders.* New York: Doubleday, 1998.

Stayton, Kevin. *Dutch by Design: Tradition and Change in Two Historic Brooklyn Houses: The Schenck Houses at The Brooklyn Museum.* New York: Brooklyn Museum, 1990.

Stern, Robert A. M., Thomas Mellins, and David Fishman. *New York 1960: Architecture and Urbanism Between the Second World War and the Bicentennial.* New York: Monacelli Press, 1995.

———. *New York 1880: Architecture and Urbanism in the Gilded Age.* New York: Monacelli Press, 1999.

Stern, Robert A. M., Gregory Gilmartin, and Thomas Mellins. *New York 1930: Architecture and Urbanism Between the Two World Wars.* New York: Rizzoli, 1987.

Stokes, I. N. Phelps. *The Iconography of Manhattan Island, 1498–1909.* 6 vols. 1915–28. Reprint, New York: Lawbook Exchange, 1998.

Stott, William. *Documentary Expression and Thirties America.* New York: Oxford University Press, 1973.

Street, Leroy [pseud.]. *I Was A Drug Addict.* 1953. Reprint, New Rochelle, NY: Arlington House, 1973.

Strong, George Templeton. *Diary,* ed. A. Nevins and M. H. Thomas. 4 vols. New York: Macmillan, 1952.

Sussman, Mark. "Performing the Intelligent Machine: Deception and Enchantment in the Life of the Automaton Chess Player." *The Drama Review* 43, no. 3 (1999): 81–96.

Sutton, Charles. *The New York Tombs: Its Secrets and Its Mysteries,* ed. J. B. Mix and S. A. Mackeever. 1874. Reprint, Montclair, NJ: Patterson Smith, 1973.

Sylvester, Robert. *No Cover Charge: A Backward Look at the Night Clubs.* New York: Dial Press, 1956.

Szasz, F. M. "The New York Slave Revolt of 1741: A Re-Examination." *New York History* 48 (1967), pp. 215–30.

Talese, Gay. "What Do You Call Discotheque? 'In' Anglophiles Say 'Arthur.'" *New York Times,* April 30, 1965.

Taylor, Angela. "Arthur, Once a Hairdo, Is Now a Discotheque." *New York Times,* May 7, 1965.

Thurber, James. "One Is a Wanderer," in *The Middle-Aged Man on the Flying Trapeze.* New York: Harper and Brothers, 1935.

Thwing, Leroy. "A Note about Rushlamps," in L. S. Cooke, ed., *Lighting in America: From Colonial Rushlight to American Chandeliers.* New York: Main Street/Universe, 1975.

Trachtenberg, Alan. *The Incorporation of America: Culture and Society in the Gilded Age.* New York: Hill and Wang, 1982.

Trager, James. *The New York Chronology: The Ultimate Compendium of Events, People, and Anecdotes from the Dutch to the Present.* New York: Harper Collins, 2003.

Traub, James. *The Devil's Playground: A Century of Pleasure and Profit in Times Square.* New York: Random House, 2004.

Trow, J. F. *Trow's New York City Directory.* Series. New York: J. F. Trow, various dates.

Tyler, Royall. *The Contrast,* ed. J. and M. Gassner, in *Best Plays of the Early American Theatre.* New York: Crown, 1967.

Valentine, David T. *History of the City of New York.* New York: Putnam, 1853.

———. *Manual of the Corporation of the City of New-York for 1853.* New York: Common Council of the City of New York, 1853.

———. *Manual of the Corporation of the City of New-York for 1860.* New York: Common Council of the City of New York, 1860.

Van der Zee, Henri and Barbara. *A Sweet and Alien Land: The Story of Dutch New York.* New York: Viking, 1978.

Van Helden, Albert. "The Thermometer." http://cnx.rice.edu/content/m11978/latest.

Van Laer, A. J. F., ed. and trans. *Documents Relating to New Netherland, 1624–1626, in the Henry E. Huntington Library.* San Marino, CA: Huntington Library, 1924.

———., ed. and trans. *New York Historical Manuscripts: Dutch.* 5 vols. Baltimore: Genealogical Publishing Co., 1974.

Van Rensselaer, Mariana [Mrs. Schuyler Van Rensselaer]. *History of the City of New York in the Seventeenth Century.* 2 vols. New York: The Macmillan Company, 1909.

Van Wyck, Frederick. *Recollections of an Old New Yorker.* New York: Liveright, 1932.

Van Zwieten, Adriana E. "'A little land . . . to sow some seeds:' Real Property, Custom, and Law in the Community of New Amsterdam (New York)." Ph.D. diss., Temple University, 2001.

Wagman, Morton. "Liberty in New Amsterdam: A Sailor's Life in Early New York." *New York History* 64 (1983): 101–19.

Walker, Stanley. *The Night Club Era.* New York: Frederick A Stokes, 1933.

Walling, George W. *Recollections of a New York Chief of Police.* New York: Caxton, 1887.

Ware, Caroline F. *Greenwich Village, 1920–1930.* 1935. Reprint, New York: Harper and Row, 1965.

Waterman, Thomas Tileston. *The Dwellings of Colonial America.* Chapel Hill: University of North Carolina Press, 1950.

Wetzsteon, Ross. *Republic of Dreams: Greenwich Village: The American Bohemia, 1910–1960.* New York: Simon & Schuster, 2002.

White, Norval, and Elliot Willensky. *AIA Guide to New York City,* 4th edition. New York: Three Rivers Press, 2000.

Whitman, Walt. "Opening of the Secession War," in *Complete Poetry and Selected Prose.* New York: Library of America, 1982.

———. "The Old Bowery: A Reminiscence of New York Plays and Acting Fifty Years Ago," in *November Boughs, Complete Writings of Walt Whitman,* ed. R. M. Buche et al. New York: Putnam's, 1902.

Whitton, Joseph. *"The Naked Truth!" An Inside History of the Black Crook.* Philadelphia: H. W. Shaw, 1897.

Wilentz, Sean. *Chants Democratic: New York City and the Rise of the American Working Class.* New York: Oxford University Press, 1984.

Wilkenfeld, B. M. "New York City Neighborhoods, 1730." *New York History* 57, no. 2 (1976): 165–82.

Williams, Edwin, ed. *New-York As It Is.* Vols. 1 and 2. New York: Disturnell, 1833–34.

Wilson, John S. "Village Vanguard Tries New Format." *New York Times,* December 14, 1963.

Winchell, Walter. *Winchell Exclusive.* Englewood Cliffs, NJ: Prentice-Hall, 1975.

Yates, Richard. *Revolutionary Road.* New York: Vintage, 1961.

Zellers, Parker. *Tony Pastor: Dean of the Vaudeville Stage.* Ypsilanti, MI: Eastern Michigan University Press, 1971.

Zolotow, Sam. "Todd's New Show Checked by City." *New York Times,* June 30, 1950.

Acknowledgments

To my partner James O'Shea, who showed his usual mixture of critical intelligence, forbearance, and patience, I owe an incalculable debt; I've lost count entirely of the occasions on which his willingness to read, reread, sympathize, and make suggestions, helped me. Nor could *New York Night* have been completed without the extraordinarily generous, judicious, and acute help of my editor at Scribner, Colin Harrison, who read multiple versions of the manuscript with eagle-eyed attention to detail and an almost uncanny understanding of where I meant the book to go, even when the material before him made this obscure indeed. And finally I must thank Ann Rittenberg, my remarkable agent, for her unwavering support during the nearly twenty years we have worked together, through a series of projects. Her willingness to discuss and encourage an imperfectly formed manuscript through revision after revision has more than once helped me make a book out of an idea that might have gone awry or died without her sympathetic intuition and her rigorous intelligence.

Deborah Bell of Deborah Bell Photographs spent hours of valuable time instructing me in the arcana of urban night photography, directing me to galleries, collections, and people, and putting up with my novice's questions. Polly Shulman offered unfailing help as an editor and fellow writer. Sarah Knight at Scribner was a rock of patience and good sense in preparing the manuscript for the press. And I owe special thanks to Nan Graham, editorial director at Scribner, for her strong support of this project from its inception.

A number of other individuals have helped me as well. The following were generous in granting me interviews: Bill Crane, Jed Fielding, Willet Fields, and Robert Rubinksy. Others helped me solve some of the many research problems to which a book of this type is inevitably subject; these include Chap Attwell, M.D., Elaine Crane, Joanne Dobson, Tom Dolby, Jim Falconi, Maria Farland, James Gavin, Timothy Gilfoyle, Moshe Gold, Charles and Elaine Hallett, John Hart, Larry Kramer, Hilary Lewis, Eric Lott, Caroline Marshall, Nicolaus Mills, Andrew Nahema, Geoffrey O'Brien, Daniel Papernik, M.D., Roger Probert, Scott Rao, Franz Schulze, David Soyer, Daniel Smail, Marina van Zuylen, Adriana van Zwieten, and Stephan Wolohojian.

Institutions, businesses, and their staffs often went out of their way to help with the completion of this book. Among these people I owe particular thanks to Nancy Burkett, Vincent Golden, and Dennis Laurie of the American Antiquarian Society; Arthur Boehm and Tama Starr of the Artkraft Strauss Sign Corporation; Joe Schick and Mike Wilcken of Con Edison; James McCabe of the Fordham University Libraries; Joe Struble at the George Eastman House; Phil Butler of Fireworks by Grucci; Angela Mattia, Eileen Morales, and Bob Shamis of the Museum of the City of New York; Janny Venema of the New Netherland Project at the New York State Library; David Bernhauser, Margi Hofer, Ted O'Reilly, and Denny Stone of the New-York Historical Society; Raymond Wemmlinger of the Hampden-Booth Theatre Library at the Players Club; Debra Bozniak of the Robert Mann Gallery; Michael Cronin of the New York City Police Museum; and Gwynedd Cannan, historian and archivist of Trinity Church.

Other libraries and collections which have been invaluable include the Brooklyn Public Library, the Manuscripts and Archives office at Yale University Library, the New York Municipal Archives, the New York Public Library, the New York Society Library, and the Sealy Library at the John Jay College of Criminal Justice.

Finally, I owe a debt of gratitude to Fordham University for its generous support.

INDEX

ABOUT THE AUTHOR

MARK CALDWELL is the author of *The Last Crusade: The War on Consumption, 1862–1954* and *A Short History of Rudeness: Manners, Morals, and Misbehavior in Modern America*. He teaches at Fordham University.